2033

MW00442796

Compañeros

Spanish for Communication
BOOK 1

Ruth A. Moltz, M.A.
Chair, Foreign Language Department
Southfield High School
Southfield, Michigan

Thomas A. Claerr, Ph.D.
Professor of Spanish
Henry Ford Community College
Dearborn, Michigan

AMSCO SCHOOL PUBLICATIONS, INC.
315 Hudson Street/New York, N.Y. 10013

Ancillaries

A cassette program (with script) to accompany **Compañeros,** Spanish for Communication, Book 1 is available separately from the publisher (ordering code **N 634 C**). It is designed to reinforce the skills presented in the textbook and in the accompanying ancillaries. The voices are those of native speakers of Spanish.

To order other ancillaries, please specify:
Teacher's Annotated Edition **R 634 TH**
Cuaderno (Workbook) **R 634 W**
Test Package **R 634 TB**

When ordering this book, please specify:
R 634 H *or* **Compañeros,** Spanish for Communication, Book 1 (Hardbound Edition) *or*
R 634 P *or* **Compañeros,** Spanish for Communication, Book 1 (Softbound Edition)

ISBN 1-56765-451-7 (Hardbound Edition)
ISBN 1-56765-450-9 (Softbound Edition)

NYC Item 56765-451-6 (Hardbound Edition)
NYC Item 56765-450-8 (Softbound Edition)

Printed in the United States of America

1 2 3 4 5 6 7 8 9 10   04 03 02 01 00 99 98 97

Photo Credits

A. Garrido
page 67

GRT Photographic
page 87

Literary Graphics
pages 44, 61, 75, 95, 98, 158, 181, 190, 259, 265 (both), 267 (top), 269, 272, 279, 301, 355, 356, 389, 424 (three), 426, 434, 439

Ministerio de Información y Turismo
pages 381, 419

Ruth A. Moltz
page 386

Howard Petlack
page 394 (both)

Spanish National Tourist Office
page 198 (top right)

Elise B. Spiro
pages 91, 192 (top), 207, 218, 263, 319 (three), 360, 393 (bottom), 423

United Nations
United Nations/A. Jongen: pages 33, 310
UN Photo 153474/John Isaac: page 47

Visuals Unlimited
page 192 (bottom); page 240; page 247
Bruce Berg: page 113
Francis/Donna Caldwell: pages 392, 393 (top)
A.J. Copley: pages 169, 277 (bottom)
Mark E. Gibson: pages 198 (bottom right), 293 (top)
Jeff Greenberg: pages 28, 40, 50, 58, 102, 111, 143, 147, 151, 173, 183, 217, 280 (both), 302, 306 (both), 347, 398, 404, 412, 415, 435, 442
Mark J. Goebel: page 140
A. Gurmankin: page 165
Arthur R. Hill: pages 73, 153 (bottom), 198 (left)
Max and Bea Hunn: page 153 (top)
Steve McCutcheon: page 277 (top)
Charles Rushing: page 293 (bottom)
Bernd Wittich: page 364

Acknowledgments

Cover design by A GOOD THING, INC.
Text design and composition by A GOOD THING, INC.
Cover art by Luis Domínguez
Text illustrations by Susan Detrich, Luis Domínguez, Chuck Melvin

Dedication

*To my husband, Mort, and daughters, Kathleen and Cyndi,
for their encouragement, patience, and love . . .
and to my students, who challenged me to "go for it."*

R.A.M.

*To my wife, Christine, and daughter, Amelia,
without whose support and patience
this project could not have been completed.*

T.A.C.

¡Hola, estudiantes!

Learning to communicate in another language is a lot like building a house. You need materials and tools to do the job. In learning a language, the materials are the words. The tools you need in order to put your words together are the grammar points. The more words you know, the more you will be able to talk about. The better you understand grammar, the more accurately you will be able to talk.

At the beginning of each unit, you will find the *Tools* section that contains all the words *(Vocabulary)* and grammar points *(Structure)* for the entire unit. They are given to you at the beginning so that they will be available as you need them. As you go through the lessons, you will learn how to use *Vocabulary* and *Structure.* However, if you find some vocabulary or structure in the *Tools* section that you want to use before it has been formally taught in a lesson, give it a try! (The lesson in which the use of a tool is taught is indicated in parentheses, so look ahead if you need to. And there is a dictionary at the end of the book for you to look up additional words.) Don't be afraid to "make a mistake." You'll eventually learn to say it right.

This book is designed to help you talk about the past, present, and future in Spanish as early as possible. There are a lot of pictures to give you visual clues that will help you learn and remember vocabulary. There are also many dialogues and readings that show people interacting with each other in settings that will be familiar to you. In addition to learning language, you will also learn about culture—that is, the way Hispanic people live.

Spanish is one of the most important languages in the world. It is spoken by over three hundred million people; it is the official language of twenty countries, and it is one of the five languages used in the United Nations. In addition, there are millions of people in the United States who use Spanish as a part of their daily lives at home, at work, or for travel.

You will soon meet Paulina and her friends. (Their pictures are below.) They are Americans of Hispanic heritage attending high school, and their lives are much like yours. As you follow their experiences throughout this book, we hope they will become your **Compañeros** *(Friends).*

¡Bienvenidos al mundo de habla española!
(Welcome to the Spanish-speaking world!)

Ruth A. Moltz   Thomas A. Claerr

Paulina

Jaime

Rosita

Raúl

Inés

Pablo

Salvador

Eduardo

Sean

LOS COMPAÑEROS

Author Acknowledgments

The authors wish to thank Dr. Elsa Puig de Corral for her help in proofreading the manuscript. Thanks also to Cecile Pizer and Flora Ciccone de Quintanilla for piloting this material in their classrooms.

Table of Contents

⪢ Unidad I ⪡

⊰ Unidad II ⊱

⊰ Unidad III ⊱

⚛Unidad IV⚛

⟫ Unidad I ⟪

⇻Unidad I⇺
Tools

Vocabulario

Los saludos *Greetings*
(Lección 1)

Buenos días.	*Good morning.*
Buenas tardes.	*Good afternoon.*
Buenas noches.	*Good evening, Good night.*
Hola.	*Hello, Hi.*

Las despedidas *Farewells*
(Lección 1)

Adiós.	*Good-bye.*
Hasta la vista.	*See you later.*
Hasta mañana.	*See you tomorrow.*
¡Chau!	*Bye!*

Los títulos *Titles*
(Lección 2)

señor/Sr.	*Mr.*
señora/Sra.	*Mrs., Ms.*
señorita/Srta.	*Miss, Ms.*
don/doña	*[used with first names to show respect]*

Las personas *People*
(Lección 2)

un/el hombre	*a/the man*	unos/los hombres	*some/the men*
una/la mujer	*a/the woman*	unas/las mujeres	*some/the women*
un/el joven	*a/the young person [m.]*	unos/los jóvenes	*some/the young people*
una/la joven	*a/the young person [f.]*	unas/las jóvenes	*some/the young people*
un/el muchacho	*a/the boy*	unos/los muchachos	*some/the boys*
una/la muchacha	*a/the girl*	unas/las muchachas	*some/the girls*
un/el niño	*a/the small boy*	unos/los niños	*some/the children*
una/la niña	*a/the small girl*	unas/las niñas	*some/the children*

Las personas *People* (continued)
(Lección 2)

un/el bebé	*a/the baby boy*	unos/los bebés	*some/the babies*
una/la bebé	*a/the baby girl*	unas/las bebés	*some/the babies*
un/el amigo	*a/the friend [m.]*	unos/los amigos	*some/the friends*
una/la amiga	*a/the friend [f.]*	unas/las amigas	*some/the friends*
un/el novio	*a/the boyfriend*	unos/los novios	*some/the boyfriends*
una/la novia	*a/the girlfriend*	unas/las novias	*some/the girlfriends*

Las letras del alfabeto español *Letters of the Spanish alphabet*
(Lección 2)

a (a)	h (hache)	ñ (eñe)	u (u)
b (be)	i (i)	o (o)	v (uve)
c (ce)	j (jota)	p (pe)	w (doble ve)
d (de)	k (ka)	q (cu)	x (equis)
e (e)	l (ele)	r (ere)	y (i griega)
f (efe)	m (eme)	s (ese)	z (zeta)
g (ge)	n (ene)	t (te)	

La familia *The family*
(Lección 3)

un/el abuelo	*a/the grandfather*	unos/los abuelos	*some/the grandfathers*
una/la abuela	*a/the grandmother*	unas/las abuelas	*some/the grandmothers*
		los abuelos	*grandparents*
un/el padre	*a/the father*	unos/los padres	*some/the fathers*
una/la madre	*a/the mother*	unas/las madres	*some/the mothers*
		los padres	*parents*
un/el hermano	*a/the brother*	unos/los hermanos	*some/the brothers*
una/la hermana	*a/the sister*	unas/las hermanas	*some/the sisters*
		los hermanos	*siblings*
un/el hijo	*a/the son*	unos/los hijos	*some/the sons*
una/la hija	*a/the daughter*	unas/las hijas	*some/the daughters*
		los hijos	*children*
un/el nieto	*a/the grandson*	unos/los nietos	*some/the grandsons*
una/la nieta	*a/the granddaughter*	unas/las nietas	*some/the granddaughters*
		los nietos	*grandchildren*
un/el tío	*a/the uncle*	unos/los tíos	*some/the uncles*
una/la tía	*a/the aunt*	unas/las tías	*some/the aunts*
		los tíos	*aunts and uncles*
un/el primo	*a/the cousin [m.]*	unos/los primos	*some/the cousins*
una/la prima	*a/the cousin [f.]*	unas/las primas	*some/the cousins*
		los primos	*cousins*

un/el esposo	*a/the husband*	unos/los esposos	*some/the husbands*
una/la esposa	*a/the wife*	unas/las esposas	*some/the wives*
		los esposos	*married couple*
un/el padrastro	*a/the stepfather*	unos/los padrastros	*some/the stepfathers*
una/la madrastra	*a/the stepmother*	unas/las madrastras	*some/the stepmothers*
		los padrastros	*stepparents*
un/el hermanastro	*a/the stepbrother*	unos/los hermanastros	*some/the stepbrothers*
una/la hermanastra	*a/the stepsister*	unas/las hermanastras	*some/the stepsisters*
		los hermanastros	*stepsiblings*

Los números *Numbers*
(Lección 3)

0 cero				
1 uno	11 once	21 veinte y uno	31 treinta y uno	10 diez
2 dos	12 doce	22 veinte y dos	32 treinta y dos	20 veinte
3 tres	13 trece	23 veinte y tres	33 treinta y tres	30 treinta
4 cuatro	14 catorce	24 veinte y cuatro	*etc.*	40 cuarenta
5 cinco	15 quince	25 veinte y cinco		50 cincuenta
6 seis	16 diez y seis	26 veinte y seis		60 sesenta
7 siete	17 diez y siete	27 veinte y siete		70 setenta
8 ocho	18 diez y ocho	28 veinte y ocho		80 ochenta
9 nueve	19 diez y nueve	29 veinte y nueve		90 noventa
10 diez	20 veinte	30 treinta		

Las funciones aritméticas *Arithmetic functions*
(Lección 3)

+ y, más	*and, plus*
− menos	*minus*
× por	*by, times*
÷ dividido por	*divided by*
= es/son	*equals*

El cuerpo *The body*
(Lección 4)

la cabeza	*head*	la espalda	*back*
el pelo	*hair*	el corazón	*heart*
la cara	*face*	el estómago	*stomach*
el ojo	*eye*	el brazo	*arm*
la nariz	*nose*	el codo	*elbow*
la boca	*mouth*	la mano	*hand*
el diente	*tooth*	el dedo	*finger*
la oreja	*ear*	la pierna	*leg*
el cuello	*neck*	la rodilla	*knee*
la garganta	*throat*	el pie	*foot*
el cuerpo	*body*	el dedo del pie	*toe*

La ropa   *Clothing*
(Lección 5)

el suéter	*sweater*	la corbata	*tie*
el sombrero	*hat*	la camisa	*shirt*
el gorro	*cap*	la blusa	*blouse*
el abrigo	*coat*	la falda	*skirt*
el vestido	*dress*	la chaqueta	*jacket*
el traje	*suit*	las medias	*stockings*
los calcetines	*socks*	los lentes	*eyeglasses*
los pantalones	*pants*	los lentes de contacto	*contact lenses*
los zapatos	*shoes*		

El tiempo   *Weather*
(Lección 5)

¿Qué tiempo hace?	*What's the weather like?*
Hace buen tiempo.	*It's nice weather.*
Hace mal tiempo.	*It's bad weather.*
Hace sol.	*It's sunny.*
Hace mucho sol.	*It's very sunny.*
Hace mucho viento.	*It's very windy.*
Hace mucho frío.	*It's very cold.*
Hace mucho calor.	*It's very warm/hot.*
Hace fresco.	*It's cool.*
Nieva.	*It's snowing.*
Llueve.	*It's raining.*
Está húmedo.	*It's humid.*
Está nublado.	*It's cloudy.*
Está claro.	*It's clear.*

Las estaciones   *Seasons*
(Lección 5)

en el invierno	*in the winter*
en la primavera	*in the spring*
en el verano	*in the summer*
en el otoño	*in the fall, autumn*

Las comidas   *Meals*
(Lección 6)

el desayuno	*breakfast*	la cena	*supper, evening meal, dinner*
el almuerzo	*lunch*	el postre	*dessert*
la comida	*dinner, midday main meal*	una merienda	*snack*

La comida   *Food*
(Lección 6)

la leche	*milk*	el refresco	*soft drink*
la hamburguesa	*hamburger*	el té	*tea*
la papa	*potato*	el jugo	*juice*
las papas fritas	*French fries*	el rosbif	*roast beef*
la ensalada	*salad*	el huevo	*egg*
la lechuga	*lettuce*	el perro caliente	*hot dog*
la sopa	*soup*	el pollo	*chicken*
la torta	*cake*	el pescado	*fish*
el agua	*water*	el jamón	*ham*
las frutas	*fruit*	el sándwich	*sandwich*
las legumbres	*vegetables*	el helado	*ice cream*
las papitas fritas	*potato chips*	el pan	*bread*
el café	*coffee*		

Los animales   *Animals*
(Lección 6)

el perro	*dog*	el mono	*monkey*
el gato	*cat*	el elefante	*elephant*
el pájaro	*bird*	el león	*lion*
el pez	*fish*	el burro	*donkey*
los peces	*fish*	el conejo	*rabbit*
el caballo	*horse*	el tigre	*tiger*
el cerdo	*pig*	la araña	*spider*
el toro	*bull*	la vaca	*cow*
el gallo	*rooster*	la gallina	*hen*
el pato	*duck*	la oveja	*sheep*
el oso	*bear*	la ardilla	*squirrel*
el ratón	*mouse*		

La casa y el apartamento   *The house and the apartment*
(Lección 7)

el cuarto	*room*	el pasillo	*hallway*
el desván	*attic*	el comedor	*dining room*
el primer piso	*second floor, one floor up*	la cocina	*kitchen*
la planta baja	*ground floor*	la escalera	*stairs*
el sótano	*basement*	la sala	*living room*
la alcoba	*bedroom*	la sala de estar	*family room, den*
el baño	*bathroom*	el patio	*inner courtyard, yard*

Los colores   *Colors*
(Lección 7)

rojo(a)	*red*	negro(a)	*black*
amarillo(a)	*yellow*	blanco(a)	*white*
azul	*blue*	gris	*gray*
anaranjado(a)	*orange*	pardo(a)	*brown*
verde	*green*	rosado(a)	*pink*
morado(a)	*purple*		
… oscuro(a)	*dark …*		
… claro(a)	*light …*		

Las formas y los tamaños   *Shapes and sizes*
(Lección 7)

grande	*big*	alto(a)	*tall, high*
pequeño(a)	*small*	bajo(a)	*low, short (in height)*
mediano(a)	*medium*	largo(a)	*long*
ancho(a)	*wide*	corto(a)	*short (in length)*
estrecho(a)	*narrow*	plano(a)	*flat*
cuadrado(a)	*square*	redondo(a)	*round*
circular	*circular*		

Las cosas en el aula   *Things in the classroom*
(Lección 8)

la pizarra	*chalkboard*	la cartera	*briefcase*
la tiza	*chalk*	la mochila	*backpack*
el borrador	*eraser*	la papelera	*wastepaper basket*
el estante	*bookshelf*	la computadora	*computer*
el reloj	*clock*	la calculadora	*calculator*
el armario	*locker, closet*	la grabadora	*tape recorder*
la bandera	*flag*	la cinta	*tape*
el globo	*globe*	el cuaderno	*notebook*
el mapa	*map*	el papel	*paper*
el libro	*book*	el lápiz	*pencil*
el archivador	*file cabinet*	el bolígrafo	*ballpoint pen*
el escritorio	*teacher's desk*	la goma	*pencil eraser*
el pupitre	*student desk*	la silla	*chair*
el diccionario	*dictionary*	la mesa	*table*

Otras cosas   *Other things*
(Lección 8)

el estéreo	*stereo*	la escuela	*school*
el disco compacto	*CD, compact disc*	la casa	*house*
el televisor	*television set*	la tienda	*store*
el radio	*radio*	la biblioteca	*library*
la bicicleta	*bicycle*	la puerta	*door*
el auto, el coche, el carro	*the car*	la ventana	*window*
		la carta	*letter*
el autobús	*bus*	el teléfono	*telephone*
el avión	*airplane*		

El calendario   *The calendar*
(Lección 9)

EL DÍA	*DAY*	EL MES	*MONTH*
el lunes	*Monday*	enero	*January*
el martes	*Tuesday*	febrero	*February*
el miércoles	*Wednesday*	marzo	*March*
el jueves	*Thursday*	abril	*April*
el viernes	*Friday*	mayo	*May*
el sábado	*Saturday*	junio	*June*
el domingo	*Sunday*	julio	*July*
		agosto	*August*
		septiembre	*September*
		octubre	*October*
		noviembre	*November*
		diciembre	*December*

La hora   *Time*
(Lección 9)

¿Qué hora es?	*What time is it?*
Es mediodía.	*It's noon.*
Es medianoche.	*It's midnight.*
Es la una.	*It's one o'clock.*
Son las dos.	*It's two o'clock.*
… y cuarto.	*quarter after . . .*
… y media.	*half past . . . (thirty)*
… menos cuarto.	*quarter to . . .*
… y (number).	*. . . minutes after the hour.*
… menos (number).	*. . . minutes to the hour.*
… de la mañana.	*. . . in the morning, A.M.*
… de la tarde.	*. . . in the afternoon, P.M.*
… de la noche.	*. . . in the evening, P.M.*

Las clases *Classes*
(Lección 9)

el arte	*art*
el español	*Spanish*
el inglés	*English*
la clase de computadoras	*computer class*
la economía	*economics*
la educación física	*physical education*
la historia	*history*
la mecánica	*mechanics*
la música	*music*
la orquesta	*band, orchestra*
las matemáticas	*math*
las ciencias	*science*

Lo que hacemos *What we do*
(Lección 10)

Note: Verbs with asterisks (*) are irregular in some of their forms.

bailar	*to dance*
caminar	*to walk*
comprar (algo)	*to buy (something)*
cantar (canciones)	*to sing (songs)*
cocinar (la cena)	*to cook (dinner)*
cuidar de los niños	*to babysit*
dar* (regalos)	*to give (presents)*
escuchar (discos compactos)	*to listen to (CDs)*
estudiar (algo)	*to study (something)*
esquiar (en la nieve)	*to snowski*
(en el agua)	*to waterski*
ganar (un juego)	*to win (a game)*
ganar (dinero)	*to earn (money)*
gastar (dinero)	*to spend (money)*
hablar (por teléfono)	*to talk (on the phone)*
hablar (español)	*to speak (Spanish)*
llevar (la ropa)	*to wear (clothing)*
llevar (mi almuerzo)	*to bring (my lunch)*
manejar (un auto)	*to drive (a car)*
mirar (la televisión)	*to watch (television)*
nadar	*to swim*
practicar (un deporte)	*to practice (a sport)*
preparar (la comida)	*to prepare (food)*

tocar (un instrumento)	*to play (an instrument)*
(el piano, el violín	*(piano, violin*
la guitarra, etc.)	*guitar, etc.)*
tomar	*to drink, to take*
trabajar	*to work*
viajar (a un lugar)	*to travel (to a place)*
visitar (a un amigo)	*to visit (a friend)*
jugar* (ue) (al béisbol)	*to play (baseball)*
(al fútbol)	*(soccer, football)*
(al básquetbol)	*(basketball)*
(al tenis)	*(tennis)*
(a un juego)	*(a game)*
(a los naipes)	*(cards)*
aprender (español)	*to learn (Spanish)*
(a manejar)	*(to drive)*
beber (leche)	*to drink (milk)*
comer (el helado)	*to eat (ice cream)*
correr (en la pista)	*to run (track)*
leer (un libro)	*to read (a book)*
poder* (ue) hacer algo	*to be able to do something, can*
dormir* (ue)	*to sleep*
escribir (una carta)	*to write (a letter)*
ir* (al cine)	*to go (to the movies)*
(a la escuela)	*(to school)*
(a la iglesia)	*(to church)*
recibir (algo)	*to receive (something)*
vivir (en una casa)	*to live (in a house)*

Los números grandes *Big numbers*
(Lección 10)

100	cien(to)	1.000	mil
200	doscientos	2.000	dos mil
300	trescientos	1.000.000	un millón
400	cuatrocientos	2.000.000	dos millones
500	quinientos		
600	seiscientos		
700	setecientos		
800	ochocientos		
900	novecientos		

Conversación

Saying hello
(Lección 1)

Buenos días.	*Good morning.*
Buenas tardes.	*Good afternoon.*
Buenas noches.	*Good evening, Good night.*
Hola.	*Hello, Hi.*

Saying good-bye
(Lección 1)

Adiós.	*Good-bye.*
Hasta la vista.	*See you later.*
Hasta mañana.	*See you tomorrow.*
¡Chau!	*Bye!*

Talking about health
(Lección 1)

¿Cómo estás?	*How are you? [informal]*
¿Cómo está usted (Ud.)?	*How are you? [formal]*
¿Cómo está (el muchacho)?	*How is (the boy)?*
Yo estoy muy bien.	*I am very well.*
muy mal.	*very bad.*
regular.	*fair, OK.*
así, así.	*so-so.*
Lo siento.	*I'm sorry.*
Qué lástima.	*That's too bad.*
¿Y tú?	*And you? [informal]*
¿Y Ud.?	*And you? [formal]*
¿Qué tal?	*How's everything?*
¿Qué pasa?	*What's happening?*
Nada, No mucho.	*Nothing, Not much.*

Saying please and thank you
(Lección 1)

Por favor.	*Please.*
Gracias.	*Thank you.*
De nada.	*You're welcome.*

Being courteous
(Lección 1)

Con permiso.	*Excuse me. [before doing something]*
Perdón.	*Pardon me. [after doing something]*

Indicating knowledge and understanding
(Lección 1)

Yo sé.	*I know.*
No sé.	*I don't know.*
Yo comprendo.	*I understand.*
No comprendo.	*I don't understand.*

Asking for speech change
(Lección 1)

Más alto.	*Louder.*
Más despacio.	*Slower.*
Repita, por favor.	*Repeat, please.*

Asking for the word in Spanish/English
(Lección 1)

¿Cómo se dice… en español/inglés?	*How do you say . . . in Spanish/English?*
¿Qué quiere decir…?	*What does . . . mean?*

Telling who you are and finding out who someone else is
(Lección 2)

Yo soy…	*I am . . .*
¿Quién eres tú?	*Who are you? [informal]*
¿Quién es Ud.?	*Who are you? [formal]*
¿Quién es el muchacho?	*Who is the boy?*
¿Quién es la muchacha?	*Who is the girl?*
El muchacho es…	*The boy is . . .*
La muchacha es…	*The girl is . . .*

Asking what someone is
(Lección 2)

¿Qué eres tú?	*What are you?*
Yo soy un joven.	*I'm a young person.*
¿Qué es él?	*What is he?*
Él es un hombre.	*He is a man.*

Asking what someone is (continued)
(Lección 2)

¿Qué son ustedes (Uds.)?	*What are all of you?*
Nosotros somos amigos.	*We are friends.*
¿Qué son Paulina y Jaime?	*What are Paulina and Jaime?*
Ellos son novios.	*They are boyfriend and girlfriend.*

Asking about spelling
(Lección 2)

¿Qué letra es?	*What letter is it?*
¿Cómo se escribe…?	*How do you spell . . . ?*
¿Cómo se escribe tu nombre?	*How do you spell your name?*
Se escribe…	*It's spelled . . .*

Asking about names
(Lección 2)

¿Cómo te llamas?	*What's your name? [informal]*
¿Cómo se llama Ud.?	*What's your name? [formal]*
Me llamo…	*My name is . . .*
¿Cómo se llama el muchacho/la muchacha?	*What's the boy's/the girl's name?*
Se llama…	*His/Her name is . . .*
¿Cuál es tu apellido?	*What's your last name?*
Mi apellido es…	*My last name is . . .*
¿Cómo se escribe tu apellido?	*How do you spell your last name?*
Se escribe…	*It's spelled . . .*

Meeting someone for the first time
(Lección 2)

Mucho gusto, señor/señora/señorita.	*I'm pleased to meet you, sir/ma'am/miss.*
El gusto es mío.	*The pleasure is mine.*
Igualmente.	*The same here, Likewise.*

Telling where someone is
(Lección 3)

Yo estoy aquí y tú estás allí.	*I am here and you are there.*
¿Dónde está tu padre ahora?	*Where is your father now?*
Él está en su trabajo.	*He is at his work.*
¿Dónde están tus hermanas?	*Where are your sisters?*
Ellas están en casa.	*They are at home.*
¿Dónde están Uds.?	*Where are you?*
Estamos en la escuela.	*We are in school.*

Asking and telling how many there are
(Lección 3)

¿Cuántos/Cuántas… hay?	*How many . . . are there?*
Hay… *[number + noun]*	*There is/are . . . [number + noun]*
Hay más (muchachos) que (muchachas).	*There are more (boys) than (girls).*
Hay menos (muchachas) que (muchachos).	*There are fewer (girls) than (boys).*
Hay tantos (muchachos) como (muchachas).	*There are as many (boys) as (girls).*

Asking and telling about age
(Lección 3)

¿Cuántos años tienes?	*How old are you? [informal]*
¿Cuántos años tiene Ud.?	*How old are you? [formal]*
Tengo… años.	*I'm . . . years old.*
¿Cuántos años tiene tu hermano?	*How old is your brother?*
Tiene… años.	*He is . . . years old.*
¿Cuántos años tienen tus padres?	*How old are your parents?*
Ellos tienen… años.	*They are . . . years old.*

Asking and telling what something is
(Lección 4)

¿Qué es esto?	*What is this?*
Éste es el cuerpo.	*This is the body.*
Ésta es la cabeza.	*This is the head.*
¿Qué son éstos?	*What are these?*
Éstos son los dedos.	*These are the fingers.*
Éstas son las orejas.	*These are the ears.*

Talking more about health
(Lección 4)

¿Cómo estás?	*How are you? [informal]*
¿Cómo está Ud.?	*How are you? [formal]*
Tengo catarro.	*I have a cold.*
fiebre.	*a fever.*
la gripe.	*the flu.*
dolor de…	*a sore . . ./a . . . ache.*
¿Qué te duele?	*What hurts? [informal]*
¿Qué le duele?	*What hurts? [formal]*
Me duele el/la…	*My . . . hurts me. [singular noun]*
Me duelen los/las…	*My . . . hurt me. [plural noun]*
¡Salud!	*Bless you, Good health to you! [said when someone sneezes]*

Asking what something is

(Lección 5)

¿Qué es eso?	*What is that?*
Ése es un abrigo.	*That is a coat.*
Ésa es una falda.	*That is a skirt.*
¿Qué son ésos?	*What are those?*
Ésos son unos zapatos.	*Those are shoes.*
Ésas son unas medias.	*Those are stockings.*

Telling who something belongs to

(Lección 5)

¿De quién son ésos?	*Whose are those?*
Ese vestido es mío.	*That dress is mine.*
Esa camisa es mía.	*That shirt is mine.*
Esos zapatos son míos.	*Those shoes are mine.*
Esas chaquetas son mías.	*Those jackets are mine.*

Talking about what one is wearing

(Lección 5)

¿Llevas…?	*Do you wear . . . ?, Are you wearing . . . ?*
¿Qué ropa llevas?	*What clothing are you wearing?, What clothing do you wear?*
¿Qué llevas cuando…	*What do you wear when . . .*
Yo llevo…	*I wear . . . , I am wearing . . .*
Yo no llevo…	*I don't wear . . . , I'm not wearing . . .*

Talking about the weather

(Lección 5)

¿Qué tiempo hace?	*What's the weather like?*
Hace buen tiempo.	*It's nice weather.*
Llueve.	*It's raining.*
Está húmedo.	*It's humid.*

Telling when one wears something

(Lección 5)

¿Cuándo llevas una chaqueta?	*When do you wear a jacket?*
La llevo cuando hace fresco.	*I wear it when it's cool.*
¿Cuándo llevas lentes?	*When do you wear glasses?*
Los llevo en la escuela.	*I wear them in school.*

Talking about what one eats and drinks
(Lección 6)

Yo como ensalada.	*I eat salad.*
¿Cuándo la comes?	*When do you eat it?*
La como para el almuerzo.	*I eat it for lunch.*
¿Comes huevos?	*Do you eat eggs?*
No, no los como.	*No, I don't eat them.*
Qué bebes para el desayuno?	*What do you drink for breakfast?*
Yo bebo café con leche.	*I drink coffee with milk.*

Telling what one likes and dislikes
(Lección 6)

Me gusta el/la…	*I like [singular noun].*
Me gustan los/las…	*I like [plural noun].*
No me gusta(n)…	*I don't like . . .*
¿Te gusta(n)…?	*Do you like . . . ?*
¿Le gusta(n)…?	*Do you like . . . ?*
Le gusta(n)…	*He/She likes . . .*
A (Juan) le gusta(n)…	*(Juan) likes . . .*

Describing things
(Lección 7)

¿Cómo es el/la…?	*What is the . . . like?*
¿Cómo son los/las…?	*What are the . . . like?*
¿De qué (color/forma/tamaño) es el/la…?	*What (color/shape/size) is the . . . ?*
¿De qué (color/forma/tamaño) son los/las…?	*What (color/shape/size) are the . . . ?*
El/La… es…	*The . . . is . . .*
Los/Las… son…	*The . . . are . . .*

Comparing things
(Lección 7)

Éste es más (largo).	*This one is (long)er.*
Éste es más (largo) que ése.	*This one is (long)er than that one.*
Éste es menos (largo).	*This one is not as (long).*
Éste es menos (largo) que ése.	*This one is not as (long) as that one.*
Éste es tan (largo).	*This one is as (long).*
Éste es tan (largo) como ése.	*This one is as (long) as that one.*

Talking about where someone lives
(Lección 7)

¿Dónde vives?	*Where do you live?*
Vivo en una casa.	*I live in a house.*
Mi amigo vive en…	*My friend lives in . . .*
Mis amigos viven en…	*My friends live in . . .*
Nosotros vivimos en…	*We live in . . .*

Telling where things are
(Lección 7)

¿Dónde está el/la…?	*Where is the . . . ?*
¿Dónde están los/las…?	*Where are the . . . ?*
El/La… está…	*The . . . is . . .*
Los/Las… están…	*The . . . are . . .*

Telling where one is going
(Lección 8)

¿Adónde vas?	*Where are you going?*
Voy a…	*I'm going to . . .*
¿Cómo vas?	*How are you going?*
Voy en…	*I'm going by . . .*

Asking the day
(Lección 9)

¿Qué día es hoy?	*What day is today?*
mañana?	*tomorrow?*
pasado mañana?	*the day after tomorrow?*
¿Qué día fue ayer?	*What day was yesterday?*
anteayer?	*the day before yesterday?*

Asking the date
(Lección 9)

¿Cuál es la fecha de hoy?	*What is today's date?*
Es el *[date]* de *[month]* de *[year]*.	*It is . . .*
¿Cuál es la fecha de tu cumpleaños?	*What is the date of your birthday?*

Es el primero de *[month]*.   *It's the first of [month].*
Es el (dos) de *[month]*.   *It's the (second) of [month].*
¿Cuándo es...?   *When is . . . ?*

Asking the time
(Lección 9)

¿Qué hora es?   *What time is it?*
Es la una y media.   *It's one-thirty.*
Son las tres menos cuarto.   *It's a quarter to three.*
¿A qué hora es (la clase)?   *At what time is (the class)?*
A las (dos).   *At (two) o'clock.*

Asking and telling what one likes or dislikes doing
(Lección 10)

¿Qué te gusta hacer?   *What do you like to do? [informal]*
¿Qué le gusta hacer?   *What do you like to do? [formal]*
¿Qué no te/le gusta hacer?   *What don't you like to do?*
Me gusta (cantar y bailar).   *I like (to sing and dance).*
No me gusta (cocinar).   *I don't like (to cook).*

Telling what one is going to do, has to do, and knows how to do
(Lección 10)

Voy a (aprender mucho).   *I am going to (learn a lot).*
Tengo que (escribir una carta).   *I have to (write a letter).*
Sé (tocar el piano).   *I know how to (play the piano).*

Telling what one can and cannot do
(Lección 10)

Puedo (nadar bien).   *I can (swim well).*
¿Puedes (ir conmigo)?   *Can you (go with me)?*
No puedo (viajar a Europa).   *I can't (travel to Europe).*

Estructura

Articles
(Lección 2)

un/una	*a/an*
unos/unas	*some*
el/la/los/las	*the*

Comparison
(Lección 7)

más... que	*more . . . than*
menos... que	*less/fewer . . . than*
tan... como	*as . . . as*

Possessive adjectives
(Lección 3)

mi(s)	*my*
tu(s)	*your*
su(s)	*your, his, her, their*
nuestro(a)/nuestros(as)	*our*

Subject pronouns
(Lecciones 2, 3)

yo	*I*
tú	*you [informal]*
usted (Ud.)	*you [formal]*
él	*he*
ella	*she*
nosotros(as)	*we*
ustedes (Uds.)	*you [plural]*
ellos	*they [masculine/mixed]*
ellas	*they [feminine]*

Possessive pronouns
(Lección 5)

mío(a)/míos(as)	*mine*
tuyo(a)/tuyos(as)	*yours*
suyo(a)/suyos(as)	*yours, his, hers, theirs*
nuestro(a)/nuestros(as)	*ours*

Indirect object pronouns
(Lección 4)

me	*to me*
te	*to you*
le	*to you, to him, to her, to it*
nos	*to us*
les	*to you, to them*

Direct object pronouns
(Lección 5)

me	*me*
te	*you*
lo/la	*you, him, her, it*
nos	*us*
los/las	*you, them*

Demonstrative pronouns
(Lección 4)

esto	*this*		
éste	*this*	éstos	*these*
ésta	*this*	éstas	*these*

(Lección 5)

eso	*that*		
ése	*that*	ésos	*those*
ésa	*that*	ésas	*those*

PRESENT-TENSE VERBS

	estar *to be* *(Lecciones 1, 3)*	**ser** *to be* *(Lección 2)*	**llamarse** *to be called/named* *(Lección 2)*
yo	estoy	soy	me llamo
tú	estás	eres	te llamas
Ud., él, ella	está	es	se llama
nosotros(as)	estamos	somos	nos llamamos
Uds., ellos, ellas	están	son	se llaman

	tener *to have* *(Lección 3)*	**llevar** *to wear* *(Lección 5)*	**comer** *to eat* *(Lección 6)*
yo	tengo	llevo	como
tú	tienes	llevas	comes
Ud., él, ella	tiene	lleva	come
nosotros(as)	tenemos	llevamos	comemos
Uds., ellos, ellas	tienen	llevan	comen

	vivir *to live* *(Lección 7)*	**ir** *to go* *(Lección 8)*	
yo	vivo	voy	
tú	vives	vas	
Ud., él, ella	vive	va	
nosotros(as)	vivimos	vamos	
Uds., ellos, ellas	viven	van	

	saber *to know (how)* *(Lección 10)*	**poder** *can, to be able* *(Lección 10)*	
yo	sé	puedo	
tú	sabes	puedes	
Ud., él, ella	sabe	puede	
nosotros(as)	sabemos	podemos	
Uds., ellos, ellas	saben	pueden	

	-ar *endings*	**-er** *endings*	**-ir** *endings*
yo	-o	-o	-o
tú	-as	-es	-es
Ud., él, ella	-a	-e	-e
nosotros(as)	-amos	-emos	-imos
Uds., ellos, ellas	-an	-en	-en

Los saludos
Greetings

Conversación

Saying hello

Buenos días.	*Good morning.*
Buenas tardes.	*Good afternoon.*
Buenas noches.	*Good evening, Good night.*
Hola.	*Hello, Hi.*

Saying good-bye

Adiós.	*Good-bye.*
Hasta la vista.	*See you later.*
Hasta mañana.	*See you tomorrow.*
¡Chau!	*Bye!*

Talking about health

¿Cómo estás?	*How are you? [informal]*
¿Cómo está usted (Ud.)?	*How are you? [formal]*
¿Cómo está (el muchacho)?	*How is (the boy)?*
Yo estoy muy bien.	*I am very well.*
muy mal.	*very bad.*
regular.	*fair, OK.*
así, así.	*so-so.*

ESTAR		*to be*
yo	estoy	*I am*
tú	estás	*you are*
usted	está	*you are*
él	está	*he is*
ella	está	*she is*

Lo siento.	*I'm sorry.*
Qué lástima.	*That's too bad.*
¿Y tú?	*And you? [informal]*
¿Y Ud.?	*And you? [formal]*
¿Qué tal?	*How's everything?*
¿Qué pasa?	*What's happening?*
Nada, No mucho.	*Nothing, Not much.*

Note: Informal *you* (**tú**) is used with family, friends, and people you call by their first name. Formal *you* (**usted**) is used with people you call by a title and their last name. **Usted** is usually abbreviated **Ud.**

Saying please and thank you

Por favor.	*Please.*
Gracias.	*Thank you.*
De nada.	*You're welcome.*

Being courteous

Con permiso.	*Excuse me. [before doing something]*
Perdón.	*Pardon me. [after doing something]*

Indicating knowledge and understanding

Yo sé.	*I know.*
No sé.	*I don't know.*
Yo comprendo.	*I understand.*
No comprendo.	*I don't understand.*

Asking for speech change

Más alto.	*Louder.*
Más despacio.	*Slower.*
Repita, por favor.	*Repeat, please.*

Asking for the word in Spanish/English

¿Cómo se dice… en español/inglés?	*How do you say . . . in Spanish/English?*
¿Qué quiere decir…?	*What does . . . mean?*

1 Write ten different times of the day in English. Choose times from the morning, afternoon, and evening. Have your partner tell what the appropriate greeting would be for the times you have chosen.

EJEMPLOS: 10:00 A.M.   Buenos días.
                    2:00 P.M.   Buenas tardes.
                    9:15 P.M.   Buenas noches.

2 When we talk to older people we are often more formal than when we are talking to a friend. Make a list of five people you address using their last names and another list of five people you address using their first names. Practice greeting these people.

EJEMPLO: **TITLE AND LAST NAME**   **FIRST NAME**
                   the principal   *my best friend*
                   my doctor   *my little sister*
                   my teacher   *my classmate*

3 Find out from several classmates how they are feeling today.

    EJEMPLO: ¿Cómo estás?   *How are you?*

                   Estoy bien, gracias.   *I am fine, thank you.*

4 Based on what you have learned in Activity 3, tell your partner how several of your classmates are feeling today.

    EJEMPLOS: Juan está bien.   *Juan is well.*
                   Mariana no está bien.   *Mariana is not well.*

5 *Sit-Con (Situation-Conversation)*   Pretend you and your partner are in an area of the United States where Spanish is spoken. Greet each other, ask about each other's health, and say good-bye. Since you are talking to a friend, use informal expressions.

6 *Sit-Con*   Prepare a conversation for the following situation. You have gone to dinner with your parents, and you meet your Spanish teacher at the restaurant. Greet your teacher. Write the conversation between you and your teacher. Because the person is your teacher, you must use formal expressions. Work with a group of three other people t o present your situation.

7 Ask your teacher what various objects are called in Spanish.

    EJEMPLO: ¿Cómo se dice «*chair*» en español?   *How do you say "chair" in Spanish?*

                   Se dice «**silla.**»   *You say "**silla.**"*

8 Tell some situations where you would use the various expressions from this lesson.

    EJEMPLOS: *I would say "**Perdón**" if I interrupt someone.*
                   *I would say "**No sé**" if I don't know something.*

Note: Use the expressions in this lesson whenever an opportunity occurs. For example, if you don't hear someone, tell him or her, **Más alto, por favor.** If someone gives you something, say, **Gracias.** Remember, the more you use your new language, the faster you will learn it.

ENCUENTROS PERSONALES

I. Señor González and Señora Fernández are teachers at the high school. They meet at the end of the first day of classes. Here is their conversation.

II. Paulina meets her friend at the bus stop after school.

III. It's the second day of classes and Señor González is telling his students about their textbook.

¿Comprendes?

1. When do Señor González and Señora Fernández meet?
2. How is Señor González?
3. How is Señora Fernández?
4. When will they see each other again?
5. How is Rosita?

6. How is Paulina?
7. Is anything special happening to Rosita?
8. What does Señor González want Paulina to tell him?
9. Does Paulina know the answer?
10. Who knows the answer?

¡Te toca!   *Your turn!*

A. With a partner, practice reading the three conversations on pages 26 and 27.

B. Now practice the conversations with different classmates, using your own names.

¡Así es!   *That's the way it is!*

Greetings

Buenos días is used to greet people usually from sunup until noon. **Buenas tardes** is used only until sundown. **Buenas noches** can mean "Good evening" or, when saying good-bye, it may mean "Good night."

In Spanish-speaking countries, it is customary to make some kind of physical contact when you greet a person and when you say good-bye. Men and women will often shake hands or, if they know each other well, they may give each other **un abrazo** *(a hug)*. Women will often hug and give each other **un beso** *(a kiss)* on each cheek. Men may also give each other **un abrazo fuerte** *(a strong hug)*. Failure to give some type of physical greeting may give the impression that you are not really glad to see the person.

PRONUNCIACIÓN

Vowels

A has the sound of *a* as in *father*.
E has the sound of *a* as in *late*.
I has the sound of *e* as in *beet*.
O has the sound of *o* as in *boat*.
U has the sound of *oo* as in *boot*.

Practice saying the following vowel sounds.

A E I O U   A E I O U   I O E A U   O U A E I

I U O A E   U I O A E   E U A I O   A E I U O

Sometimes **y** is used as a vowel. It has the same sound as the letter **i.**

… el estudiante y el profesor
El profesor es muy popular.

Diversión

Here are some rhymes that Spanish-speaking children learn to help them remember the vowels. Practice saying them. Both can be used for choosing something just as "Eenie meenie miney moe" is used in English.

1. Do you know where Peru is located? Find it on a map.

   A - E - I - O - U   A - E - I - O - U
   Arbolito del Perú   Little tree from Peru
   ¿Cuántos años tienes tú?   How old are you?

2. The donkey is still used as a form of transportation and as a means of carrying cargo in many Spanish-speaking countries. Do you know what donkeys are like?

   A - E - I - O - U   A - E - I - O - U
   El burro sabe más que tú. The donkey knows more than you.

Los nombres, las personas y las letras
Names, people, and letters

Vocabulario

Los nombres españoles *Spanish names*

LAS MUCHACHAS	*GIRLS*	LOS MUCHACHOS	*BOYS*
Alicia	Josefina	Alberto	Javier
Alma	Juana	Alejandro	Jesús
Ana	Juanita	Alfonso	Jorge
Anita	Julia	Alonso	José
Bárbara	Linda	Álvaro	Juan
Beatriz	Lucía	Andrés	Luis
Blanca	Luisa	Antonio	Manuel
Carlota	Luz	Arturo	Marcos
Carmen	Manuela	Benjamín	Mauricio
Carolina	Margarita	Carlos	Miguel
Catalina	María	Daniel	Nicolás
Cecilia	Mariana	Diego	Pablo
Clara	Marta	Domingo	Pedro
Cristina	Mercedes	Eduardo	Ramón
Diana	Patricia	Enrique	Raúl
Dolores	Paz	Ernesto	Ricardo
Dorotea	Pilar	Esteban	Roberto
Elena	Raquel	Federico	Salvador
Emilia	Rosa	Felipe	Santiago
Estela	Susana	Fernando	Teodoro
Eva	Teresa	Francisco	Timoteo
Francisca	Verónica	Gregorio	Tomás
Gloria	Virginia	Guillermo	Vicente
Inés	Yolanda	Jaime	Víctor
Isabel			

Los títulos *Titles*

señor/Sr.	*Mr.*
señora/Sra.	*Mrs., Ms.*
señorita/Srta.	*Miss, Ms.*
don/doña	*[used with first names to show respect]*

Las personas *People*

1. un/el hombre	*a/the man*	unos/los hombres	*some/the men*
2. una/la mujer	*a/the woman*	unas/las mujeres	*some/the women*
3. un/el joven	*a/the young person [m.]*	unos/los jóvenes	*some/the young people*
4. una/la joven	*a/the young person [f.]*	unas/las jóvenes	*some/the young people*
5. un/el muchacho	*a/the boy*	unos/los muchachos	*some/the boys*
6. una/la muchacha	*a/the girl*	unas/las muchachas	*some/the girls*
7. un/el niño	*a/the small boy*	unos/los niños	*some/the children*
8. una/la niña	*a/the small girl*	unas/las niñas	*some/the children*
9. un/el bebé	*a/the baby boy*	unos/los bebés	*some/the babies*
10. una/la bebé	*a/the baby girl*	unas/las bebés	*some/the babies*
11. un/el amigo	*a/the friend [m.]*	unos/los amigos	*some/the friends*
12. una/la amiga	*a/the friend [f.]*	unas/las amigas	*some/the friends*
13. un/el novio	*a/the boyfriend*	unos/los novios	*some/the boyfriends*
14. una/la novia	*a/the girlfriend*	unas/las novias	*some/the girlfriends*

When talking about a mixed group of males and females and the words are similar, use the male form.

un muchacho y una muchacha = unos muchachos
el amigo y la amiga = los amigos

un/una	*a/an*
unos/unas	*some*
el/la/los/las	*the*

Conversación

Telling who you are and finding out who someone else is

Yo soy…	*I am . . .*
¿Quién eres tú?	*Who are you? [informal]*
¿Quién es Ud.?	*Who are you? [formal]*
¿Quién es el muchacho?	*Who is the boy?*
¿Quién es la muchacha?	*Who is the girl?*
El muchacho es…	*The boy is . . .*
La muchacha es…	*The girl is . . .*

Asking what someone is

¿Qué eres tú?	*What are you?*
Yo soy un joven.	*I'm a young person.*
¿Qué es él?	*What is he?*
Él es un hombre.	*He is a man.*
¿Qué son Uds.?	*What are all of you?*
Nosotros somos amigos.	*We are friends.*
¿Qué son Paulina y Jaime?	*What are Paulina and Jaime?*
Ellos son novios.	*They are boyfriend and girlfriend.*

SER		*to be*
yo	soy	*I am*
tú	eres	*you are*
Ud.	es	*you are*
él/ella	es	*he/she is*
nosotros(as)	somos	*we are*
Uds.	son	*you are*
ellos(as)	son	*they are*

1 Tell the people sitting near you who you are and find out who they are.

EJEMPLO: Yo soy Miguel. ¿Quién eres tú?   *I am Miguel. Who are you?*

Yo soy Anita.   *I am Anita.*

2 Ask your partner who various people are. If your partner knows, he or she should answer with the person's name. If not, he or she should tell you so.

EJEMPLOS: ¿Quién es el muchacho?   *Who is the boy?*

El muchacho es Carlos.   *The boy is Carlos.*

¿Quién es la muchacha?   *Who is the girl?*

No sé.   *I don't know.*

3 Point to each picture on page 31 and identify the different people.

EJEMPLOS: Ella es una mujer.   *She is a woman.*
Él es un joven.   *He is a young person.*

4 Point to each picture on page 31 and ask your partner questions that can be answered with **sí** or **no.**

EJEMPLOS: ¿Es un hombre?   *Is he a man?*

Sí, es un hombre.   *Yes, he's a man.*

¿Es una bebé?   *Is she a baby?*

No, no es una bebé.   *No, she's not a baby.*

5 Point to the pictures again in any order and ask your partner what person is in each picture. Your partner will answer. Notice that when you ask **¿Qué?** the answer uses **un, una, unos,** or **unas.**

EJEMPLO: *[pointing to* **el niño***]* ¿Qué es?   *What is he?*

Es un niño.   *He's a little boy.*

6 Point to the pictures in any order and ask your partner who is in the picture. Your partner will answer. Notice that when you ask **¿Quién?** the answer uses **el, la, los,** or **las.**

EJEMPLO: ¿Quién es?   *Who is he?*

Es el niño.   *He's the little boy.*

7 **Juego: *Stump your partner*** Take turns pointing to a picture. Identify the picture for your partner. Every so often give the incorrect word. Your partner has to correct you. A point is scored every time a correction is made.

EJEMPLOS: *[pointing to* **el hombre***]*

Es un hombre.   *It's a man.*

Sí, es un hombre.   *Yes, it's a man.*

[pointing to **el bebé***]*

Es una mujer.   *It's a woman.*

No, no es una mujer. Es un bebé.   *No, it isn't a woman. It's a baby.*

Vocabulario

Las letras del alfabeto español   *Letters of the Spanish alphabet*

a (a)	h (hache)	ñ (eñe)	u (u)
b (be)	i (i)	o (o)	v (uve)
c (ce) ch (che)	j (jota)	p (pe)	w (doble ve)
d (de)	k (ka)	q (cu)	x (equis)
e (e)	l (ele) ll (elle)	r (ere) rr (erre)	y (i griega)
f (efe)	m (eme)	s (ese)	z (zeta)
g (ge)	n (ene)	t (te)	

Until 1994 **ch** and **ll** were separate letters of the alphabet. Dictionaries printed before that date will have separate sections for words beginning with **ch** and **ll** and they will be alphabetized with **ch** coming after **cu** and **ll** after **lu**.

How many letters are there in Spanish? Which letter don't we have in English?

Conversación

Asking about spelling

¿Qué letra es?	*What letter is it?*
¿Cómo se escribe…?	*How do you spell . . . ?*
¿Cómo se escribe tu nombre?	*How do you spell your name?*
Se escribe…	*It's spelled . . .*

8 Take turns pointing to letters for your partner to identify.

9 Dictate ten letters for your partner to write. Then switch roles.

10 Spell your name and other people's names in Spanish. Use the list of names on page 30.

11 Ask your partner how to spell different words.

EJEMPLO: ¿Cómo se escribe «hombre»?   *How do you spell "hombre"?*

Se escribe H-O-M-B-R-E.   *It's spelled H-O-M-B-R-E.*

(hache)(o)(eme)(be)(ere)(e)

Conversación

Asking about names

LLAMARSE	*to be named*	
yo	me	llamo
tú	te	llamas
Ud./él/ella	se	llama
nosotros(as)	nos	llamamos
Uds./ellos/ellas	se	llaman

¿Cómo te llamas?	*What's your name? [infomal]*
¿Cómo se llama Ud.?	*What's your name? [formal]*
Me llamo…	*My name is . . .*
¿Cómo se llama el muchacho/la muchacha?	*What's the boy's/the girl's name?*
Se llama…	*His/Her name is . . .*
¿Cuál es tu apellido?	*What's your last name?*
Mi apellido es…	*My last name is . . .*
¿Cómo se escribe tu apellido?	*How do you spell your last name?*
Se escribe…	*It's spelled . . .*

Meeting someone for the first time

Mucho gusto, señor/señora/señorita.   *I'm pleased to meet you, sir/ma'am/miss.*
El gusto es mío.   *The pleasure is mine.*
Igualmente.   *The same here, Likewise.*

12 **Sit-Con (Situation-Conversation)** Your parents are meeting your teacher at Open House. With your partner, create the conversation between them. Use formal expressions.

13 Find a classmate whom you have not met. Use the informal expressions above and the greetings from Lesson 1 to get to know each other. Review the phrases on page 34 and then do the following:

- Greet each other.
- Ask how the other person is.
- Ask the other person's first and last name.
- Ask how to spell the last name.
- Say you are glad to meet him or her.
- Say good-bye.

14 Write out both parts of your conversation from Activity 13. Practice your conversation, and then be prepared to do it aloud for the class.

15 Point to various members of the class and ask your partner who each person is. If you don't know, say: **No sé** *(I don't know)*.

EJEMPLOS: ¿Cómo se llama el muchacho?   *What's the boy's name?*

Se llama Juan.   *His name is Juan.*

¿Cómo se llama la muchacha?   *What's the girl's name?*

No sé.   *I don't know.*

Remember that you can also ask **¿Quién es?** to find out who someone is.

16 **Encuesta** *Survey* Find out the names of several of your classmates and write a report about it. You may have to ask them how to spell their last name.

EJEMPLO: ¿Cómo te llamas?   *What's your name?*

Me llamo Steven Myers.   *My name is Steven Myers.*

¿Cómo se escribe tu apellido?   *How do you spell your last name?*

Se escribe M-Y-E-R-S.   *It's spelled M-Y-E-R-S.*

Report: Los muchachos se llaman Steven Myers y ...
        The boys' names are Steven Myers and . . .

ENCUENTRO PERSONAL

Raúl Martí and Sean McIlroy are meeting for the first time.

¿Comprendes?

1. How is Sean?
2. What does Raúl ask Sean to do?
3. What is Sean's last name?
4. Does Raúl know how to spell it?
5. Why do you suppose Sean doesn't ask Raúl to spell his name?

¡Te toca!

A. With a partner, practice reading the conversation. Remember to use the names of the letters in the Spanish alphabet.

B. Practice the conversation using your name instead of Sean's and Raúl's.

¡Así es!

Last names

Ramón Mendoza Sánchez

Juanita Báez Colón de Mendoza

Eugenio Mendoza Báez

María Mendoza Báez

María Mendoza de Romero

In Spanish-speaking countries, people use two last names. They use their father's family name first and then their mother's family name. For example, in the case of Eugenio Mendoza Báez, **Mendoza** is Eugenio's father's family name, and **Báez** is his mother's family name. He is called by his father's name in conversation. For example, one would say, **Es mi amigo Eugenio Mendoza.**

A female follows the same custom of using her father's and mother's names until she marries. Before marriage, Eugenio's sister María would be called **María Mendoza Báez.** When she gets married, she drops her mother's name and takes her husband's name preceded by **de** meaning *of*. Sometimes she is called only by her husband's name preceded by **de**. If María were to marry Paco Romero, she would be called **María Mendoza de Romero** or **María de Romero.**

17 Find out the second family names of your classmates. Practice writing their full names.

EJEMPLOS: *Paquita Smith Clark*
Juan Grant Spenser

18 Interview five classmates. Ask them their names and write them down. Then report to the class using the patterns in the following examples.

EJEMPLOS: El muchacho se llama…   *The boy's name is . . .*
La muchacha se llama…   *The girl's name is . . .*

Nosotros
María y Francisco
Confirmamos nuestros sentimientos ante Dios
ante los hombres ante nosotros
Y deseamos unirnos con amor y para siempre por medio del
Sacramento del Matrimonio en la Misa que se celebrará
el día seis de Mayo a las veinte horas
en la Iglesia de San Mateo Apóstol de la Col. San Isidro
dignándose impartir la Bendición Nupcial el Pbro. Rafael Rojas Obregón
Participan nuestros Padres

Ramón Mendoza Sánchez   *Javier Romero Herrera*
Juana Báez Colón de Mendoza   *Eva Zarzosa de Romero*

PRONUNCIACIÓN

Diphthongs

When an unaccented **u, i,** or **y** is next to another vowel, the two sounds are pronounced but count as one syllable. They are called "diphthongs." Practice saying these words with your teacher.

AI-AY	EI-EY	OI-OY	IA	IE	IO	IU
baile	veinte	oigo	gracias	pie	precio	ciudad
hay	seis	hoy	novia	fiesta	vio	viuda
Jaime	ley	doy	India	siento	odio	miura
traigo	peine	sois	hacia	siete	premio	oriundo
caigo	disteis	soy	diario	cielo	patio	diurético

AU	EU	UA	UE	UI-UY	UO
aula	Europa	cuando	bueno	ruido	cuota
causa	deuda	manual	suelo	cuidar	monstruo
pausa	reunir	aduana	pues	ruina	continuo
autor	neutro	agua	escuela	cuidado	mutuo
auto	feudal	cuatro	abuelo	muy	antiguo

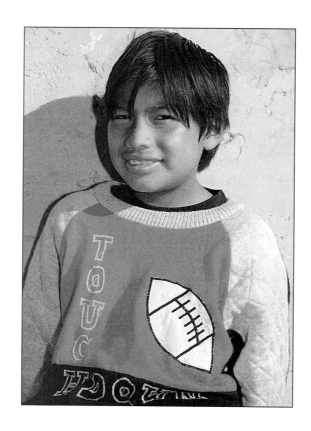

Diversión

1. Here is a popular lullaby. If you had grown up in a Spanish-speaking country, your mother or father might have sung it to you.

DUÉRMETE, NIÑITO	GO TO SLEEP, LITTLE ONE
Duérmete, niñito,	Go to sleep, little one
duérmete solito,	Go to sleep all alone
que cuando te despiertes	And when you wake up
te daré atolito.	I'll give you a drink.
Duérmete, mi vida,	Go to sleep, my life
duérmete, mi cielo,	Go to sleep, my heaven
que la noche es fría	For the night is cold
y habrá nieve y hielo.	And there will be snow and ice.
Duérmete, bien mío,	Go to sleep, my dear one
duerme sin cuidado,	Sleep without cares
que cuando te despiertes	And when you wake up
te daré un centavo.	I'll give you a penny.

2. When Spanish-speaking children are trying to choose something or determine who will be "it" in a game, they often use this rhyme, pointing to a different person with each word. What is a popular "counting-out" rhyme in English?

Tin, marín, de don Pingüé,
¡cúcara, mácara, títere fue!

(nonsense syllables like "Eenie meenie miney moe")

3. Spanish-speaking children like to play with vowels by using the same phrase but using only one vowel for all the words. Try it with the following phrases.

Una mosca parada en la pared,
en la pared, en la pared.

A fly standing on the wall,
on the wall, on the wall.

(with a)
Ana masca parada an la parad,
an la parad, an la parad.

(with o)
Ono mosco porodo on lo porod,
on lo porod, on lo porod.

(with e)
Ene mesce perede en le pered,
en le pered, en le pered.

(with u)
Unu muscu purudu un lu purud,
un lu purud, un lu purud.

(with i)
Ini misci piridi in li pirid,
in li pirid, in li pirid.

La familia, los números, la edad
The family, numbers, age

Vocabulario

La familia   *The family*

un/el abuelo	*a/the grandfather*	unos/los abuelos	*some/the grandfathers*
una/la abuela	*a/the grandmother*	unas/las abuelas	*some/the grandmothers*
		los abuelos	*grandparents*
un/el padre	*a/the father*	unos/los padres	*some/the fathers*
una/la madre	*a/the mother*	unas/las madres	*some/the mothers*
		los padres	*parents*
un/el hermano	*a/the brother*	unos/los hermanos	*some/the brothers*
una/la hermana	*a/the sister*	unas/las hermanas	*some/the sisters*
		los hermanos	*siblings*
un/el hijo	*a/the son*	unos/los hijos	*some/the sons*
una/la hija	*a/the daughter*	unas/las hijas	*some/the daughters*
		los hijos	*children*
un/el nieto	*a/the grandson*	unos/los nietos	*some/the grandsons*
una/la nieta	*a/the granddaughter*	unas/las nietas	*some/the granddaughters*
		los nietos	*grandchildren*
un/el tío	*a/the uncle*	unos/los tíos	*some/the uncles*
una/la tía	*a/the aunt*	unas/las tías	*some/the aunts*
		los tíos	*aunts and uncles*
un/el primo	*a/the cousin [m.]*	unos/los primos	*some/the cousins*
una/la prima	*a/the cousin [f.]*	unas/las primas	*some/the cousins*
		los primos	*cousins*
un/el esposo	*a/the husband*	unos/los esposos	*some/the husbands*
una/la esposa	*a/the wife*	unas/las esposas	*some/the wives*
		los esposos	*married couple*
un/el padrastro	*a/the stepfather*	unos/los padrastros	*some/the stepfathers*
una/la madrastra	*a/the stepmother*	unas/las madrastras	*some/the stepmothers*
		los padrastros	*stepparents*
un/el hermanastro	*a/the stepbrother*	unos/los hermanastros	*some/the stepbrothers*
una/la hermanastra	*a/the stepsister*	unas/las hermanastras	*some/the stepsisters*
		los hermanastros	*stepsiblings*

Conversación

Telling where someone is

Yo estoy aquí y tú estás allí.	*I am here and you are there.*
¿Dónde está tu padre ahora?	*Where is your father now?*
Él está en su trabajo.	*He is at his work.*
¿Dónde están tus hermanas?	*Where are your sisters?*
Ellas están en casa.	*They are at home.*
¿Dónde están Uds.?	*Where are you?*
Estamos en la escuela.	*We are in school.*

ESTAR	*to be*	
yo	estoy	*I am*
tú	estás	*you are*
Ud.	está	*you are*
él/ella	está	*he/she is*
nosotros(as)	estamos	*we are*
Uds.	están	*you are*
ellos/ellas	están	*they are*

1 Choose one of the people in the family tree on page 42 and tell how others are related to her or him. Choose other people and tell how they are related to each other.

EJEMPLOS: Es el padre.   *He is the father.*
Es la hermana.   *She is the sister.*

2 Find a picture of a family in a magazine. Tell who each person is.

EJEMPLOS: Aquí está el padre.   *Here is the father.*
Aquí está la madre.   *Here is the mother.*

3 Create a family. Give each member of the family a name. Tell who they are. Use names from the list on page 30.

EJEMPLOS: El padre se llama José González.
The father's name is José González.

La madre se llama Marta Rodríguez de González.
The mother's name is Marta Rodríguez de González.

4 Make a chart of your immediate family. Your partner will make a family tree also. Ask each other who each person is.

EJEMPLO: ¿Quién es tu padre?
Who is your father?

[point to a picture] Es mi padre.
He is my father.

mi(s)	*my*
tu(s)	*your*
su(s)	*his, her, your, their*
nuestro(a)/nuestros(as)	*our*

5 Find out where various members of your partner's family are now. What do you say if you don't know?

EJEMPLOS: ¿Dónde está tu tía?   *Where is your aunt?*

Ella está en su trabajo.   *She is at her work.*

¿Dónde está tu tío?   *Where is your uncle?*

No sé dónde está mi tío.   *I don't know where my uncle is.*

Vocabulario

Los números   *Numbers*

0 cero			
1 uno	11 once	21 veinte y uno	31 treinta y uno	10 diez
2 dos	12 doce	22 veinte y dos	32 treinta y dos	20 veinte
3 tres	13 trece	23 veinte y tres	33 treinta y tres	30 treinta
4 cuatro	14 catorce	24 veinte y cuatro	*etc.*	40 cuarenta
5 cinco	15 quince	25 veinte y cinco		50 cincuenta
6 seis	16 diez y seis	26 veinte y seis		60 sesenta
7 siete	17 diez y siete	27 veinte y siete		70 setenta
8 ocho	18 diez y ocho	28 veinte y ocho		80 ochenta
9 nueve	19 diez y nueve	29 veinte y nueve		90 noventa
10 diez	20 veinte	30 treinta		

6 Practice the numbers by doing the following.

- Count from 0 to 25 by ones.
- Count from 0 to 50 by even numbers.
- Count from 0 to 50 by odd numbers.
- Count from 99 to 0 by ones.

7 **Juego: ¿Cuál es el número?**   Take turns writing a numeral between 0 and 99 for your partner to say in Spanish. Score one point for each correct answer.

Vocabulario

Las funciones aritméticas   *Arithmetic functions*

+	y, más	*and, plus*
−	menos	*minus*
×	por *entre*	*by, times*
÷	~~dividido por~~	*divided by*
=	es/son	*equals*

$2 + 3 = \ ?$ ¿Cuántos son dos y tres?
$2 + 3 = 5$ Dos y tres son cinco.
$35 \times 2 = 70$ Treinta y cinco por dos son setenta.

8 Pretend that your partner is in second grade. Write ten simple arithmetic problems for your partner to do out loud in Spanish. Take turns.

Conversación

Asking and telling how many there are

¿Cuántos/Cuántas... hay?	*How many . . . are there?*
Hay... [number + noun]	*There is/are . . .[number + noun]*
Hay más (muchachos) que (muchachas).	*There are more (boys) than (girls).*
Hay menos (muchachas) que (muchachos).	*There are fewer (girls) than (boys).*
Hay tantos (muchachos) como (muchachas).	*There are as many (boys) as (girls).*

9 Point to groups of objects in the classroom and ask your partner how many there are.

EJEMPLO: ¿Cuántos hay? *[pointing to the books]   How many are there?*

Hay cinco.   *There are five.*

10 Ask your partner how many different people there are in your school.

EJEMPLO: ¿Cuántos muchachos hay en la clase?   *How many boys are there in the class?*

Hay quince muchachos.   *There are fifteen boys.*

11 **Encuesta**   Find out how many people there are in several of your classmates' families. Also find out who the family members are.

EJEMPLO: ¿Cuántas personas hay en tu familia?
How many people are there in your family?

Hay cinco personas.
There are five people.

¿Quiénes son?
Who are they?

Mi madre, mi padrastro, mi hermano, mi hermanastra y yo.
My mother, my stepfather, my brother, my stepsister and I.

12 Compare the number of male and female relations in your family with your partner.

EJEMPLO: En mi familia hay más tías que tíos. Hay tres tías y dos tíos. ¿Cuántos tíos hay en tu familia?
In my family there are more aunts than uncles. There are three aunts and two uncles. How many aunts and uncles are there in your family?

Hay tantas tías, pero más tíos.
There are as many aunts, but more uncles.

Conversación

Asking and telling about age

¿Cuántos años tienes?	How old are you? [informal]
¿Cuántos años tiene Ud.?	How old are you? [formal]
Tengo… años.	I'm . . . years old.
¿Cuántos años tiene tu hermano?	How old is your brother?
Tiene… años.	He is . . . years old.
¿Cuántos años tienen tus padres?	How old are your parents?
Ellos tienen… años.	They are . . . years old.

TENER		to have
yo	tengo	I have
tú	tienes	you have
Ud.	tiene	you have
él/ella	tiene	he/she has
nosotros(as)	tenemos	we have
Uds.	tienen	you have
ellos/ellas	tienen	they have

13 Ask your partner her or his age and the ages of other members of the family. Use the family tree on page 42 as a guide.

EJEMPLO: ¿Cuántos años tienes?   *How old are you?*

Tengo quince años.   *I am fifteen years old. [I have fifteen years.]*

¿Cuántos años tiene tu padre?   *How old is your father?*

Mi padre tiene treinta y siete años.   *My father is thirty-seven years old.*

14 Prepare a report about your family. Answer the following questions to tell who the people are in your family, their names, and their ages. Tell where they are now.

- ¿Cuántas personas hay en tu familia?
- ¿Quiénes son?
- ¿Cómo se llaman?
- ¿Cuántos años tienen?
- ¿Dónde están ahora *(now)*?

ENCUENTRO PERSONAL

Sean McIlroy has joined Paulina, Rosita, and Jaime for lunch. They're talking about their families while looking at photos from their wallets.

¿Comprendes?

1. Who is the woman in Sean's photo?
2. How old is his grandmother?
3. What is her name?
4. Who are the men in the photo?
5. How old are they?
6. Who is Uncle Albert's brother?
7. How old is Sean's mother?
8. How old are Rosita's parents?
9. How old is Paulina's mother?

¡Te toca!

A. Practice reading the conversation out loud with others.

B. If you have a photograph of your own family, use the preceding conversation as a model to talk about it with your partner.

¡Así es!

The Hispanic family

The word *family* has a broader meaning for Spanish-speaking people than just parents, brothers, and sisters. It includes grandparents, aunts, uncles, cousins, and godparents (**padrinos**). In some families, grandparents, parents, children, and/or other relatives may live together. The family is the basic social and economic unit of Hispanic life. It is good manners to inquire about how the family is when greeting a friend.

Pronunciación

The following Spanish consonants have pronunciations that differ significantly from English.

GE, GI, J are pronounced like the *h* in *house*.

gente	Argentina	agenda	ligero	general
colegio	gimnasio	gitano	agitado	escogido
jugar	dibujo	jugo	jardín	lejos

H is never pronounced. It is always silent. Exept after the letter c

hola	ahora	helado	hay	cohete

QU has the sound of *k*.

porque	queso	cheque	raqueta	querer
quiso	aquí	quién	quinto	esquina

R has no English equivalent. It is pronounced by tapping the tip of the tongue against the roof of the mouth in the same place as the *tt* in *kitty*. At the beginning of a word, it is pronounced with multiple taps. (See Lesson 4.)

pero	para	grande	verano	libro
madre	padre	por	flor	vivir

V is pronounced like the *b* in *book* but is a little softer in the middle of a word. It is pronounced the same as the Spanish **b**.

ventana	verde	vaca	veinte	violeta
favor	revista	clave	avenida	evidente

Z is pronounced like the *s* in *sister*. (In Spain **z, ce,** and **ci** are pronounced like the *th* in *thick.*)

taza	zapato	zona	azul	diez

Diversión

1. Here is a Spanish counting song.

LOS PERRITOS
Uno, dos, tres perritos,
cuatro, cinco, seis perritos,
siete, ocho, nueve perritos,
diez perritos hay.

THE LITTLE PUPPIES
One, two, three little puppies
Four, five, six little puppies
Seven, eight, nine little puppies
There are ten little puppies.

2. María del Socorro Caballero, a teacher in Mexico, collected many traditional rhymes for children. She published them in a book entitled *Jugando con las palabras*. Here are some of the traditional rhymes that children in Mexico use for learning their numbers. Because these rhymes are passed orally from one generation to the next, there are many variations found in different areas.

MULTIPLICANDO
Dos y dos son cuatro,
cuatro y dos son seis,
seis y dos son ocho,
y ocho dieciséis
y ocho veinticuatro
y ocho treinta y dos.
No sigo la cuenta,
ya se me olvidó.

MULTIPLYING
Two and two are four
Four and two are six
Six and two are eight
And eight sixteen
and eight twenty-four
and eight thirty-two.
I can't continue the count
Already I've forgotten it.   Jugando (p.79)

Start saying this rhyme very slowly and increase the speed gradually for each additional elephant. How many elephants can you add to the spider's web?

UN ELEFANTE
UN elefante se columpiaba
sobre la tela de una araña.
Como veía que resistía,
fue a buscar un camarada.
DOS elefantes se columpiaban
sobre la tela de una araña.
Como veían que resistía,
fueron a buscar un camarada.
TRES, etc.

ONE ELEPHANT
ONE elephant was swinging
on a spider's web.
As he saw that it held up,
he went to look for a friend.
TWO elephants were swinging
on a spider's web.
As they saw that it held up
they went to look for a friend.
THREE, etc.   Jugando (p.76)

El cuerpo y las enfermedades
The body and illnesses

Vocabulario

El cuerpo   *The body*

1. la cabeza — *head*
2. el pelo — *hair*
3. la cara — *face*
4. el ojo — *eye*
5. la nariz — *nose*
6. la boca — *mouth*
7. el diente — *tooth*
8. la oreja — *ear*
9. el cuello — *neck*
10. la garganta — *throat*
11. el cuerpo — *body*
12. la espalda — *back*
13. el corazón — *heart*
14. el estómago — *stomach*
15. el brazo — *arm*
16. el codo — *elbow*
17. la mano — *hand*
18. el dedo — *finger*
19. la pierna — *leg*
20. la rodilla — *knee*
21. el pie — *foot*
22. el dedo del pie — *toe*

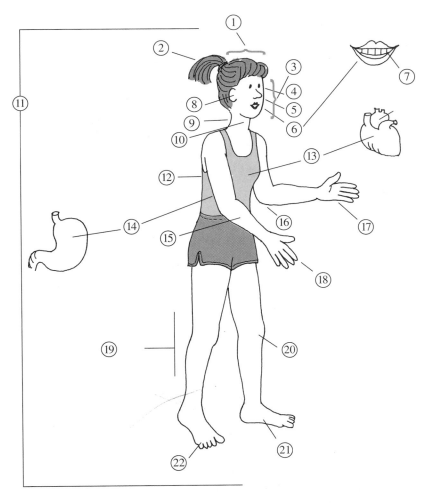

23. los dedos de los pies / el tobilla — ankle
24. el ombligos — belly button
25. el pecho — chest
26. la frente — forehead
27. los cachetes — cheeks
28. el hombro — shoulder

Note: Most nouns that end in **o** use **el**, but **mano** uses **la.** What letter do most words that use **la** end in?

29. la lengua — tongue
30. el muslo — thigh
31. la ceja — eyebrow
32. la piel — skin
33. el labio — lip

34. la uña — finger nail
35. el hueso — bone
36. la pestaña — eyelash

Conversación

Asking and telling what something is

¿Qué es esto?	*What is this?*	
Éste es el cuerpo.	*This is the body.*	
Ésta es la cabeza.	*This is the head.*	
¿Qué son éstos?	*What are these?*	
Éstos son los dedos.	*These are the fingers.*	
Éstas son las orejas.	*These are the ears.*	

N	esto	*this*
M	éste	*this*
F	ésta	*this*
M	éstos	*these*
F	éstas	*these*

1 With a partner, take turns pointing to the picture on page 53 and identifying the different parts of the body.

EJEMPLOS: Es la cabeza.   *It's the head.*
Es un dedo.   *It's a finger.*

2 Ask your partner what the different parts of the body are in the picture on page 53. Your partner will answer.

EJEMPLO: ¿Qué es esto?   *What's this?*

Ésta es una rodilla.   *This is a knee.*

3 Ask your partner where each part of the body in the list on page 53 is. Your partner will point to her or his own part of the body.

EJEMPLO: ¿Dónde está tu cabeza?   *Where is your head?*

Aquí está mi cabeza. *[pointing to her or his head] Here is my head.*

4 **Juego: ¿Cuántos tenemos?**   Form a small group of three to five people and sit in a circle. Take turns going around the circle and ask the person on your left **¿Cuántos... tenemos?** The answer is the total number of body parts for the entire group.

EJEMPLO: *[group of four people]*

¿Cuántos pies tenemos?   *How many feet do we have?*

Tenemos ocho pies.   *We have eight feet.*

5 Find a full-length picture of a person in a magazine or draw your own. Label the parts of the body.

Conversación

Talking more about health

Review the health expressions on page 12. Here are some more expressions you can use to talk about health.

¿Cómo estás?	*How are you? [informal]*
¿Cómo está Ud.?	*How are you? [formal]*
Tengo catarro.	*I have a cold.*
fiebre.	*a fever.*
la gripe.	*the flu.*
dolor de…	*a sore . . . /a . . . ache.*
¿Qué te duele?	*What hurts? [informal]*
¿Qué le duele?	*What hurts? [formal]*
Me duele el/la…	*My . . . hurts me. [singular noun]*
Me duelen los/las…	*My . . . hurt me. [plural noun]*
¡Salud!	*Bless you! Good health to you! [said when someone sneezes]*

las enfermedades

DOLER	*to hurt*
me duele(n)	*hurt(s) me*
te duele(n)	*hurt(s) you* usted
le duele(n)	*hurt(s) you/him/her*
nos duele(n)	*hurt(s) us*
les duele(n)	*hurt(s) you/them*

Estoy enfermo = I am sick

Note: Remember to use **el/la/los/las** and not **mi(s)** or **tu(s)** etc., with parts of the body in this expression: **Me duele la cabeza** (*My head hurts*).

Remember also that **tu** is used with family, friends, and people you call by their first name. **Usted (Ud.)** is used with people you call by a title and their last name.

6 Ask your partner and other people who sit near you how they are. Be sure to return the question.

EJEMPLO: ¿Cómo estás?
How are you?

Tengo dolor de cabeza y me duelen los pies. ¿Y tú?
I have a headache and my feet hurt me. And you?

7 Pretend to sneeze. **Achís** represents the Spanish sneezing sound. Your partner will respond. Remember to say **Salud** whenever someone sneezes in class. Practice using other expressions of courtesy whenever you can.

EJEMPLO: ¡Achís!   *Achoo!*

Salud.   *Bless you.*

Gracias.   *Thank you.*

De nada.   *You're welcome.*

8 *Sit-Con (Situation-Conversation)*   Your partner was absent from school today. Call her or him on the phone to find out why.

EJEMPLO: Hola… , ¿cómo estás?   *Hello . . . , how are you?*

No estoy bien. Tengo la gripe.   *I'm not well. I have the flu.*

9 *Sit-Con*   You are a nurse (**enfermero[a]**) in the emergency room of a hospital. Your classmates are the patients. There has been a bus accident, and the victims are being brought to your hospital. Ask each one what hurts. The patient must point to the part that hurts. Remember to use **duele** when it is one thing and **duelen** when it is more than one thing.

EJEMPLO: Enfermero(a):   ¿Qué le duele?   *What hurts?*
Estudiante 1:   Me duele la cabeza.   *My head hurts.*
Estudiante 2:   Me duelen las piernas.   *My legs hurt.*

ENCUENTRO PERSONAL

Sr. González, the Spanish teacher, is not feeling well and has decided to go to the clinic. Here is his conversation with the receptionist who is learning Spanish and wants to practice it with him.

¿Comprendes?

1. What is the patient's name?
2. How old is he?
3. Why did he go to the clinic?
4. Where is the doctor?
5. Why did the receptionist say **Salud**?

¡Te toca!

A. Practice reading the conversation out loud with a partner.

B. Take turns being a patient. Change the information in the conversation so you are talking about yourself.

¡Así es!

Health care

In larger cities in Latin America, modern health care of good quality is readily available. Many medications which require a prescription in the United States are sold over the counter. In many cases, pharmacists can give injections at the pharmacy. In rural areas, people often rely on **curanderos** *(curers),* who practice folk medicine and use herbs and charms to treat their patients.

PRONUNCIACIÓN

The letter **Ñ** is not found in English and has its own sound. **Ñ** has the sound of /ny/ as in *canyon* or *onion.*

año	cañón	niño	araña	señor
compañero	español	dueña	cariño	sueño

CH, LL, the initial **R,** and **RR** have sounds that are different from the letters used individually.

CH has the sound of /ch/ as in *chair* (same as English).

chico	chicle	techo	pecho	mucho
chato	muchacho	chuleta	cheque	rancho

LL has the sound of /y/ as in *yes.*

llama	medalla	allí	detalle	pasillo
cepillo	lluvia	llevar	batalla	mantequilla

R at the beginning of a word and **RR** are pronounced by making multiple taps of the tip of the tongue against the roof of the mouth just behind the teeth. Imitate the roar of a motor.

rima	rico	Ricardo	revista	ritmo
error	barril	arroz	arriba	carrusel
pizarra	burro	carreta	aburrida	guitarra

Diversión

In Mexico, a tortilla is a very thin round piece of bread made of ground corn or flour and water. It is cooked on a hot, flat pan that resembles a griddle.

1. Try this Spanish version of pat-a-cake the next time you are with a baby or small child.

TORTILLITAS *(Clapping rhyme)*
Tortillitas, tortillitas,
tortillitas para papá,
tortillitas para mamá,
tortillitas de salvado
para papá cuando está enojado.
Tortillitas de manteca
para mamá cuando está contenta.

LITTLE TORTILLAS
Little tortillas,
Little tortillas for Papa,
Little tortillas for Mama,
Little tortillas made with bran
For Papa when he's mad.
Little tortillas made with fat
For Mama when she's glad.

2. Here is a rhyme to practice the sound of **RR**!

R con R—jarro,
R con R—barril,
rápido corren los carros
allá en el ferrocarril.

R with R—pitcher
R with R—barrel
Rapidly run the train cars
There on the railroad track.

3. When something hurts, say this little poem while rubbing the hurt to make it go away.

ENCANTO PARA PORRAZOS
Sana, sana,
colita de rana,
Si no sana hoy,
sanará mañana.

CHARM FOR A "BOO-BOO"
Get better, get better
Tail of a frog.
If it's not better today,
It will be tomorrow.

4. **Juguemos**   *Let's play*

Now would be a good time to play **Simón dice**. All students stand. Your teacher will give a command: **Toquen el/la (name a part of the body).** If the command is preceded by **Simón dice…** do what you are told. Anyone who does the command without hearing **Simón dice** is out and sits down. The last one standing wins.

La ropa y el tiempo
Clothing and weather

Vocabulario

La ropa *Clothing*

1. el suéter — *sweater*
2. el sombrero — *hat*
3. el gorro — ~~cap~~ beanie
4. el abrigo — *coat*
5. el vestido — *dress*
6. el traje — *suit*
7. los calcetines — *socks*
8. los pantalones — *pants*
9. los zapatos — *shoes*
    gorra — baseball hat
10. la corbata — *tie*
11. la camisa — *shirt*
12. la blusa — *blouse*
13. la falda — *skirt*
14. la chaqueta — *jacket*
15. las medias — *stockings*
16. los lentes — *eyeglasses*
17. los lentes de contacto — *contact lenses*
18. las gafas — sunglasses

Note: Remember that to say *a* instead of *the*, you must change **el** to **un** and **la** to **una**.

Conversación

Asking what something is

¿Qué es eso?	*What is that?*
Ése es un abrigo.	*That is a coat.*
Ésa es una falda.	*That is a skirt.*
¿Qué son ésos?	*What are those?*
Ésos son unos zapatos.	*Those are shoes.*
Ésas son unas medias.	*Those are stockings.*

eso	*that*
ése	*that*
ésa	*that*
ésos	*those*
ésas	*those*

Note: **Ése, ésa, ésos, ésas** have no accent if a noun follows.

Telling who something belongs to

posessive adjectives

¿De quién son ésos?	*Whose are those?*
Ese vestido es mío.	*That dress is mine.*
Esa camisa es mía.	*That shirt is mine.*
Esos zapatos son míos.	*Those shoes are mine.*
Esas chaquetas son mías.	*Those jackets are mine.*

posesive pronouns on page 44.

mío(̃)	*mine*
tuyo(̃)	*yours*
suyo(̃)	*yours, his, hers, theirs*
nuestro(̃)	*ours*

plural

Talking about what one is wearing

¿Llevas…?	*Do you wear . . . ?, Are you wearing . . . ?*
¿Qué ropa llevas?	*What clothing are you wearing?, What clothing do you wear?*
¿Qué llevas cuando…?	*What do you wear when . . . ?*
Yo llevo…	*I wear . . . , I am wearing . . .*
Yo no llevo…	*I don't wear . . . , I'm not wearing . . .*

LLEVAR	*to wear*
yo	llevo
tú	llevas
Ud./él/ella	lleva
nosostros(as)	llevamos
Uds./ellos/ellas	llevan

ᴊABLAS DE CONVERSION DE TALLAS

EQUIVALENCIA DE DAMA

VESTIDOS

U.S.	6,8	8,10	10,12	12,14	14,16
Mexico	30,32	32,34	34,36	36,38	38,40
España	36,37,38	40	42	44	46

BLUSA/SUÉTER

U.S.	Small	Medium	Large
Mexico	Chico(a)	Medianó(a)	Grande
España	Chico(a)	Medianó(a)	Grande

ZAPATOS

U.S.	5₁/₂	6	7	8	8₁/₂	9
Mexico	2-3	3-4	4-5	5-6		6-7
España	35	36	37	38	39	40

EQUIVALENCIA DE CABALLERO

TRAJES

U.S.	36	38	40	42	44
Mexico	36	38	40	42	44
España	46	48	50	52	54

CAMISAS

U.S.	14	14₁/₂	15	15₁/₂	16₁/₂	17
Mexico	14	14₁/₂	15	15₁/₂	16₁/₂	17
España	36	37	38	40	41	42

ZAPATOS

U.S.	7	8	9	9₁/₂-10	10₁/₂-11	11₁/₂	12
Mexico	6	7	8	9	10	11	12
España	40	41	42	43	44	45	46

1 With your partner, take turns pointing to the pictures on page 60 and telling what each article of clothing is.

EJEMPLOS: [pointing to sweater] Es un suéter.   *It's a sweater.*

[pointing to shoes] Son zapatos.   *They are shoes.*

2 Point to the pictures of the clothing and take turns with your partner identifying each one. First do them in order, then mix them up. Use **esto** or **eso** in your question when there is one item, and **éstos** or **ésos** when there is more than one. Be careful to use the correct form of *that* (**ése/ésa**) or *those* (**ésos/ésas**) in your answer.

EJEMPLOS: ¿Qué es esto?   *What is this?*

Ése es un suéter.   *That is a sweater.*

¿Qué son ésos?   *What are those?*

Ésos son calcetines.   *Those are socks.*

3 Ask your partner who different clothing items belong to. Remember to use **es** when asking about one item and **son** when there is more than one.

EJEMPLOS: ¿De quién es esa blusa?   *Whose is that blouse?*

Esa blusa es suya.   *That blouse is hers.*

¿De quién son esos zapatos?   *Whose shoes are those?*

Esos zapatos son suyos.   *Those shoes are his.*

4 Ask your partner if he or she has different items of clothing. Remember to use **un** or **una** to say *a*. Leave **unos** and **unas** out of your sentences.

EJEMPLOS: ¿Tienes un sombrero?   *Do you have a hat?*

Sí, tengo un sombrero.   *Yes, I have a hat.*

¿Tienes corbatas?   *Do you have ties?*

No, no tengo corbatas.   *No, I don't have ties.*

5 **Encuesta**   Ask several people what they usually wear to a party.

EJEMPLO: ¿Qué llevas a una fiesta?
What do you wear to a party?

Yo llevo una camisa, pantalones y una corbata.
I wear a shirt, pants, and a tie.

6 Tell what several people in your class are wearing now.

EJEMPLO: Juan lleva un suéter, pantalones, zapatos y calcetines.
Juan is wearing a sweater, pants, shoes, and socks.

7 Find a magazine picture that shows several people. Tell what they are wearing.

Vocabulario

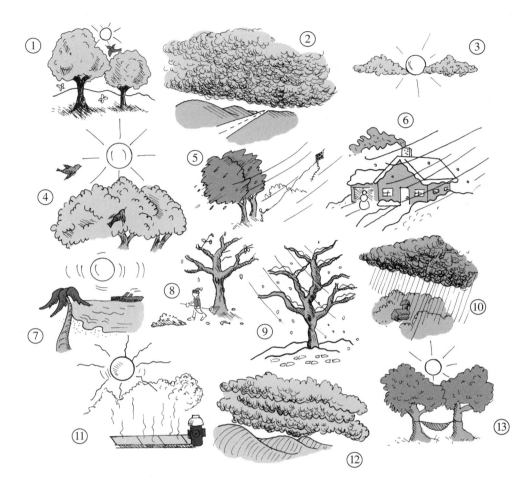

El tiempo   *Weather*

¿Qué tiempo hace?	*What's the weather like?*
1. Hace buen tiempo.	*It's nice weather.*
2. Hace mal tiempo.	*It's bad weather.*
3. Hace sol.	*It's sunny.*
4. Hace mucho sol.	*It's very sunny.*
5. Hace mucho viento.	*It's very windy.*
6. Hace mucho frío.	*It's very cold.*
7. Hace mucho calor.	*It's very warm/hot.*
8. Hace fresco.	*It's cool.*
9. Nieva. *it snows*	*It's snowing.* está nevando
10. Llueve. *it rains*	*It's raining.* está lloviendo
11. Está húmedo.	*It's humid.*
12. Está nublado.	*It's cloudy.*
13. Está claro.	*It's clear.* (bright)

14. esta oscudo   it's dark
15. lluvia   rain
16. nieve   snow
17. temperatura   temperature

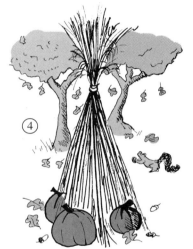

Las estaciones   *Seasons*

1. en el invierno   *in the winter*
2. en la primavera   *in the spring*
3. en el verano   *in the summer*
4. en el otoño   *in the fall, autumn*

8 Ask your partner what today's weather is like.

EJEMPLO: ¿Qué tiempo hace hoy?   *What's the weather like today?*

                  Hace buen tiempo.   *It's nice weather.*

9 Ask your partner what the weather is like where you live and in other parts of the world during different seasons.

EJEMPLO: ¿Qué tiempo hace en Los Ángeles en el verano?
               What's the weather like in Los Angeles in the summer?

                  Hace sol y hace mucho calor.
                  It's sunny and it's very hot.

10   Tell what you and your friends wear to school in each season.

EJEMPLO: Nosotros llevamos una camisa y pantalones en la primavera.
We wear a shirt and pants in the springtime.

11   Ask your partner what he or she wears in different weather conditions.

EJEMPLO: ¿Qué llevas cuando hace frío?
What do you wear when it's cold?

Cuando hace frío, llevo una chaqueta y un gorro.
When it's cold, I wear a jacket and a cap.

12   **Encuesta**   Survey several of your classmates to find out what their favorite season is.

EJEMPLO: ¿Cuál es tu estación favorita?   *Which is your favorite season?*

Mi estación favorita es el verano.   *My favorite season is summer.*

Conversación

Telling when one wears something

¿Cuándo llevas una chaqueta?	*When do you wear a jacket?*
La llevo cuando hace fresco.	*I wear it when it's cool.*
¿Cuándo llevas lentes?	*When do you wear glasses?*
Los llevo en la escuela.	*I wear them in school.*

lo	*it*
la	*it*
los	*them*
las	*them*

13   Find out from several people when they wear the following items.

EJEMPLO: un gorro

¿Cuándo llevas un gorro?   *When do you wear a cap?*

Lo llevo en el invierno.   *I wear it in the winter.*

a. un sombrero

b. un traje de jogging

c. una chaqueta

d. un traje de baño *(bathing suit)*

e. pantalones cortos *(shorts)*

f. un suéter

**Pronóstico del tiempo
para el fin de semana**

VIERNES
Alta : 65° F.
Baja : 40° F.
Parcialmente soleado, con
lluvias esporádicas, templado.

SABADO
Alta : 58° F.
Baja : 35° F.
Mañana lluviosa, viento y frío.

DOMINGO
Alta : 65° F.
Baja : 46° F.
Soleado.

ENCUENTRO PERSONAL

Paulina's cousin Eduardo is coming to the United States from Mexico to stay with her family and to attend school for the year. Listen to their telephone conversation.

¿Comprendes?

1. Whom did Eduardo call?
2. Why did he call her?
3. What is the weather like where Paulina lives?
4. What does Eduardo plan to bring for the cold weather?
5. What does Paulina tell him he needs to have for the weather?
6. What does Eduardo think Paulina's city is like in December?

¡Te toca!

A. With a partner, practice reading the conversation.

B. Personalize the conversation by telling what the weather is like where you live. Tell Eduardo what clothing he will need for a visit to your city.

¡Así es!

Seasons

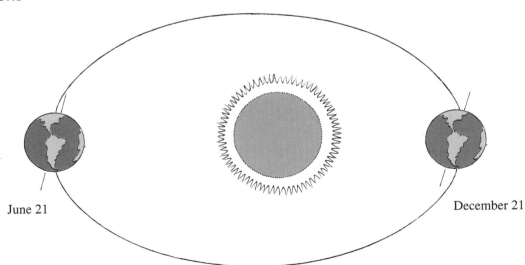

June 21

December 21

Seasons in the Northern and the Southern Hemispheres are reversed. When it's summer in the United States, it's winter south of the equator. In Peru, for example, students are in school from March to December and on summer vacation from December to February. Christmas is celebrated in the summer! Many people go to Argentina and Chile in December to escape the winter or in July to go snowskiing. Would you like to go there, too?

PRONUNCIACIÓN

Silabeo *(Syllabication—dividing words into syllables)*

Each vowel or diphthong creates a syllable. A diphthong is a combination of a vowel with an unaccented **i** or **u**. (Review page 40.)

Duérmete bien mío, duerme sin cuidado…

14 Count the number of vowels and diphthongs in the clothing vocabulary at the beginning of this lesson and tell how many syllables each word has.

15 Write the following paragraph on a separate piece of paper. Then underline each vowel or diphthong to help you determine the number of syllables. Count the number of syllables and see if you agree with the teacher.

DECLARACIÓN A LA BANDERA AMERICANA

Juro fidelidad a la bandera de los Estados Unidos de América, y a la república que representa, una nación bajo Dios, indivisible, con libertad y justicia para todos.

Do you know what the paragraph is? If you do, then you know what the words mean!

Diversión

Say this rhyme out loud.

LOS MESES DEL AÑO	THE MONTHS OF THE YEAR
En enero hace frío,	In January the weather is cold,
en febrero también.	In February also.
En marzo hace fresco,	In March it's cool,
en abril está bien.	In April it's fine.
En mayo hay flores,	In May there are flowers,
en junio—¿Qué hay, señor?	In June, "What is there, Sir?"
En julio hace viento,	In July it's windy,
en agosto el calor.	In August it's hot.
En septiembre hay neblina,	In September there is fog,
en octubre el tronar.	In October the thunder.
Noviembre trae lluvia,	November brings rain,
diciembre el nevar.	December the snow.

La comida y los animales
Food and animals

Vocabulario

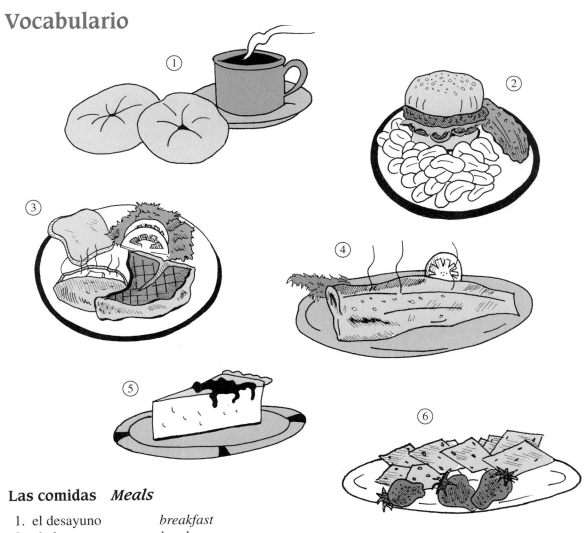

Las comidas *Meals*

1. el desayuno — *breakfast*
2. el almuerzo — *lunch*
3. la comida — *dinner, midday main meal* Food
4. la cena — *supper, evening meal, dinner*
5. el postre — *dessert*
6. una merienda — *snack*

La comida *Food*

1. la leche — *milk*
2. la hamburguesa — *hamburger*
3. la papa — *potato*
4. las papas fritas — *French fries*
5. la ensalada — *salad*
6. la lechuga — *lettuce*
7. la sopa — *soup*
8. la torta — *cake*
9. el agua* — *water*
10. las frutas — *fruit*
11. las legumbres *los vegetales* — *vegetables*
12. las papitas fritas — *potato chips*
13. el café — *coffee*

14. el refresco — *soft drink*
15. el té — *tea*
16. el jugo — *juice*
17. el rosbif — *roast beef*
18. el huevo — *egg*
19. el perro caliente — *hot dog*
20. el pollo — *chicken*
21. el pescado — *fish*
22. el jamón — *ham*
23. el sándwich — *sandwich*
24. el helado — *ice cream*
25. el pan — *bread*
26. el bistec — steak
27. el pavo — Turkey
28. la asúcar — suger

*Note: Feminine nouns that begin with a stressed **a** sound use **el**.

If you want to tell what kind of food something is, use the following pattern.

food + **de** + *kind*

ensalada de lechuga	*lettuce salad*
sándwich de pollo	*chicken sandwich*
sopa de legumbres	*vegetable soup*
torta de vainilla	*vanilla cake*
helado de chocolate	*chocolate ice cream*

If you want to make the foods plural *(more than one)*, add **s** to nouns that end in a vowel and **es** to nouns that end in a consonant. Change **el** to **los** and **la** to **las**.

el jamón	los jamones	*ham*	*hams*
la ensalada	las ensaladas	*salad*	*salads*

1 With your partner, take turns pointing to each picture and identifying the food.

2 Find pictures of foods in a magazine and ask your partner what each of the foods is. Remember to use **un** or **una** to say *a* or *an*.

EJEMPLOS: ¿Qué es esto?   *What's this?*

Es una papa.   *It's a potato.*

¿Qué es eso?   *What's that?*

Es un sándwich de pollo.   *It's a chicken sandwich.*

3 List at least three foods you like to eat for each meal.

EJEMPLO: Para el almuerzo: leche, pan, huevos

Conversación

Talking about what one eats and drinks

Yo como ensalada.	*I eat salad.*
¿Cuándo la comes?	*When do you eat it?*
La como para el almuerzo.	*I eat it for lunch.*
¿Comes huevos?	*Do you eat eggs?*
No, no los como.	*No, I don't eat them.*
¿Qué bebes para el desayuno?	*What do you drink for breakfast?*
Yo bebo café con leche.	*I drink coffee with milk.*

COMER *to eat*	
yo	como
tú	comes
Ud./él/ella	come
nosotros(as)	comemos
Uds./ellos/ellas	comen

4 Tell your partner three things you eat for each meal. Then switch roles.

EJEMPLO: Para la cena como hamburguesas, papas y legumbres.
For dinner, I eat hamburgers, potatoes, and vegetables.

5 Ask your partner if he or she eats a particular food for the different meals.

EJEMPLOS: Para el desayuno, ¿comes pescado?   *For breakfast, do you eat fish?*

No, yo no como pescado.   *No, I don't eat fish.*

Para el postre, ¿comes helado?   *For dessert, do you eat ice cream?*

Sí, como helado.   *Yes, I eat ice cream.*

6 Juan likes to eat. His twin sister, Juanita, is always watching her weight. Tell what each one eats at other times, such as lunch, dinner, dessert, snack.

EJEMPLO: Para el desayuno, Juan come huevos, jamón y pan y toma leche. Juanita come pan y toma café.
For breakfast, Juan eats eggs, ham, bread and has milk. Juanita eats bread and has coffee.

7 Find out when your partner eats various foods.

EJEMPLO: ¿Cuándo comes los sándwiches?   *When do you eat sandwiches?*

Los como para el almuerzo.   *I eat them for lunch.*

Conversación

Telling what one likes and dislikes

Gustar is not exactly the same as *like* in English. It tells what *pleases* someone. In English, we usually say *like* rather than *pleases* for **gustar**.

Me gusta el helado.   *Ice cream pleases me. I like ice cream.*
Me gustan las papas.   *Potatoes please me. I like potatoes.*

Me gusta el/la…	*I like [singular noun].*
Me gustan los/las…	*I like [plural noun].*
No me gusta(n)…	*I don't like . . .*
¿Te gusta(n)…?	*Do you like . . . ?*
¿Le gusta(n)…?	*Do you like . . . ?*
Le gusta(n)…	*He/She likes . . .*
A (Juan) le gusta(n)…	*(Juan) likes . . .*

ME gusta(n)	*I like*
TE gusta(n)	*you like*
LE gusta(n)	*you/he/she likes*
NOS gusta(n)	*we like*
LES gusta(n)	*you/they like*

8 Make a list of the foods you like and another of foods you do not like. Compare lists with your partner. How many mutual choices do you have?

EJEMPLO: Me gustan las papitas fritas. *I like potato chips.*
No me gustan las legumbres. *I don't like vegetables.*

9 Ask your partner if he or she likes each of the foods in the list on page 70.

EJEMPLOS: ¿Te gusta la sopa? *Do you like soup?*

Sí, me gusta la sopa. *Yes, I like soup.*

¿Te gusta el sándwich de jamón? *Do you like the ham sandwich?*

No, no me gusta el sándwich de jamón. *No, I don't like the ham sandwich.*

10 Ask your partner if various members of his or her family like the foods in the list on page 70. Remember to use **gustan** with plurals.

EJEMPLO: ¿A tu mamá le gustan los huevos? *Does your mother like eggs?*

Sí, a mi mamá le gustan los huevos. *Yes, my mother likes eggs.*

¿A tu hermana le gusta la torta? *Does your sister like cake?*

No, a mi hermana no le gusta la torta. *No, my sister doesn't like cake.*

Vocabulario

Los animales   *Animals*

1. el perro   *dog*
2. el gato   *cat*
3. el pájaro   *bird*
4. el pez   *fish*
   los peces*   *fish*
5. el caballo   *horse*
6. el cerdo   *pig*
7. el toro   *bull*
8. el gallo   *rooster*
9. el pato   *duck*
10. el oso   *bear*
11. el ratón   *mouse*

12. el mono   *monkey*
13. el elefante   *elephant*
14. el león   *lion*
15. el burro   *donkey*
16. el conejo   *rabbit*
17. el tigre   *tiger*
18. la araña   *spider*
19. la vaca   *cow*
20. la gallina   *hen*
21. la oveja   *sheep*
22. la ardilla   *squirrel*

*Note: Nouns ending in **z** change **z** to **c** before adding **es**.
Pescado means *fish prepared to eat;* **pez** is a live fish.

11 Ask your partner to identify where each animal is on page 74 and to tell if the animal is large or small.

EJEMPLO: ¿Dónde está el caballo?   *Where is the horse?*

Está aquí/allí.   *It is here/there.*

¿Es grande o pequeño?   *Is it big or small?*

Es grande.   *It is big.*

12   **Encuesta**   Find out if your classmates have pets. Then find out what animal they have and report your findings.

EJEMPLO: ¿Tienes un animal?   *Do you have an animal?*

Sí, tengo uno.   *Yes, I have one.*

¿Qué animal tienes?   *What animal do you have?*

Tengo un pájaro.   *I have a bird.*

13 Identify each of the animals on page 74 and say whether you like or don't like that animal.

EJEMPLOS: Éste es un perro. Me gustan los perros.   *This is a dog. I like dogs.*
Éste es un cerdo. No me gustan los cerdos.   *This is a pig. I don't like pigs.*

14 Ask your partner if he or she likes each of the animals.

EJEMPLOS: ¿Te gustan los perros?   *Do you like dogs?*

Sí, me gustan los perros.   *Yes, I like dogs.*

¿Te gustan los toros?   *Do you like bulls?*

No, no me gustan los toros.   *No, I don't like bulls.*

ENCUENTRO PERSONAL

Paulina and some of her friends are at the zoo. Paulina and Jaime want to see the animals but Rosita and Raúl can only think about eating.

¿Comprendes?

1. Which animals do the friends like to see?
2. Which animals does Paulina like?
3. Name some of the animals that Jaime likes.
4. What kind of animals does Raúl like? Why?
5. Where does Raúl want to go? Why?
6. What does he want to eat for lunch?
7. What does Rosita want for lunch?
8. Does Paulina want to go to the restaurant now?

¡Te toca!

A. With a partner, practice reading the conversation.

B. Create your own conversation to talk about animals and foods that you like.

¡Así es!

Foods

Many foods that are popular in the United States are of Hispanic origin. Some of them, such as tacos, chili con carne, corn chips, bananas, and coffee, are known to be from Spanish-speaking countries. But did you know that the following foods originated in countries that are now Spanish-speaking?

- potatoes: the Andes (Peru, Bolivia)
- tomatoes: western South America and Mexico
- corn: North America (including Mexico)
- chocolate: Mexico
- avocados: Mexico

SHAKEY'S PIZZA

		SUPREMA	ROBUSTA	CONDIMENTADA	EXOTICA			

		Chica SUFICIENTE PARA 1	Doble SUFICIENTE PARA 2	Familiar SUFICIENTE PARA 4
Natural	Tomate, Especias y Quesos Exóticos	$ 46.00	$ 69.00	$ 91.50
Salami Cocido				
Pepperoni con Especias	Chorizo Cantinpaio	53.00	80.00	108.50
Carne Molida con Cebolla Picada				
Salchicha SHAKEY'S	Carne de Cerdo con Especias			
Exótica	Pimiento Morrón y Pimiento Verde			
Tradicional de la Casa	Pepperoni y Pimiento Verde Picado			
Salami tipo Polaco		57.00	87.50	121.00
Suprema SHAKEY'S	Salami con Pimiento Verde			
Salchicha con Aceitunas				
Marinada	Pollo Cocido			
Jamón Canadiense	Lomo Canadiense			
Aceitunas Negras		62.50	99.00	137.00
Camarones del Pacífico				
Champiñones Blancos				
Sardinas	En Aceite			
De Vigilia	Camarones, Aceitunas y Champiñones	68.00	110.00	154.00
Ostiones Ahumados				
Anchoas	Recomendada a quien le gusten las Anchoas			
Especial SHAKEY'S	Combinación sin Anchoas	77.00	125.00	175.00
Gran Capitán	Combinación sin Aceitunas			

LLEVE A CASA NUESTRA DELICIOSA PIZZA Y POLLO

POLLO SHAKEY'S Y PAPAS

La pizza se come siempre con los dedos

ORDEN	PIEZAS	PRECIO
MINI	3	$ 47.50
CHICA	5	75.00
DOBLE	9	120.00
FAMILIAR	15	182.00
PAPAS		10.00

PRONUNCIACIÓN

Stress means saying a syllable stronger than the rest of the syllables in a word. Use the following rules to decide where to put the stress in a word. Remember that each vowel and diphthong counts as a syllable. (An unaccented **u** or **i** next to another vowel creates a diphthong.)

1. If a word has a written accent, stress that syllable.
   can/**ción**   te/**lé**/fo/no   te/le/vi/**sión**

2. If a word ends in a consonant other than **n** or **s**, stress the last syllable.
   ca/mi/**nar**   ac/ti/vi/**dad**   ca/pi/**tal**

3. If a word ends in a vowel or **n** or **s,** stress the next-to-last syllable in the word.
   a/ma/**ri**/llo   **tum**/bes   ca/**mi**/nan   far/**ma**/cia

15 Decide how many syllables are in each of the words on page 70, then tell where each of the words is stressed. Write out the words and circle the stressed syllable.

Diversión

1. Mexico had a great social revolution between the years 1910 and 1921. One of the leaders in this struggle was a colorful figure named Pancho Villa. There is a story that his soldiers often had to push his little black car when it broke down, so they nicknamed it **La cucaracha** (*The Cockroach*). While they were marching they made up a song about the car which has many verses and many variations, some of which appear below. Do you think the soldiers liked Pancho Villa and his car?

   Before you sing the song below, count the syllables
   and tell where the words are stressed.

   PANCHO VILLA

LA CUCARACHA	THE COCKROACH
Coro:	Chorus
La cucaracha, la cucaracha,	The cockroach, the cockroach
ya no quiere caminar,	Doesn't like to travel
porque no tiene, porque le falta	Because it doesn't have, because it needs
la patita principal.	a leg to stand on.
Una cosa me da risa,	One thing that makes me laugh
Pancho Villa sin camisa,	Pancho Villa without a shirt
ya se van los Carrancistas	Now the Carrancistas are going away
porque vienen los Villistas.	Because the Villistas are coming.
Ya murió la cucaracha,	The cockroach has already died,
ya lo llevan a enterrar,	Now they're taking it away to be buried
entre cuatro zopilotes	Between four buzzards
y un ratón de sacristán.	And a rat of a sacristan.

2. Did your parent ever bounce you on a knee and pretend that you were on a horse?
   Here is a rhyme for bouncing a little child on a knee.

EN LA RODILLA DE PAPÁ	ON FATHER'S KNEE
Caballito, caballito,	Little horse, little horse,
no me tumbes, no me tumbes.	Don't make me fall.
A galope, y a galope	Giddyap, giddyap
recio, recio, recio,	Fast, fast, fast
¡qué viva (Antonio)!	Hurrah for (Antonio)!

La casa, los colores, las formas y los tamaños
The house, colors, shapes, and sizes

Vocabulario

La casa y el apartamento   *The house and the apartment*

1. el cuarto — *room*
2. el desván — *attic*
3. el primer piso — ~~*second floor, one floor up*~~ *first floor*
4. la planta baja — *ground floor*
5. el sótano — *basement*
6. la alcoba/*dormitorio* — *bedroom*
7. el baño — *bathroom*
8. el pasillo — *hallway*
9. el comedor — *dining room*
10. la cocina — *kitchen*
11. la escalera — ~~*stairs*~~ *ladder*
12. la sala — *living room*
13. la sala de estar — *family room, den* *back*
14. el patio — *inner courtyard, yard*
15. las escaleras — stairs
16. el segundo piso — second floor
17. el portal — porch
18. el balcón — balcony

Los colores   *Colors*

rojo(a)	*red*	negro(a)	*black*
amarillo(a)	*yellow*	blanco(a)	*white*
azul	*blue*	gris	*gray*
anaranjado(a)	*orange*	pardo(a) *marrón*	*brown*
verde	*green*	rosado(a)	*pink*
morado(a)	*purple*	turqueso(a)	turquoise
platealdo (a)	silver	dorado (a)	gold
… oscuro(a)	*dark . . .*		
… claro(a)	*light . . .*		

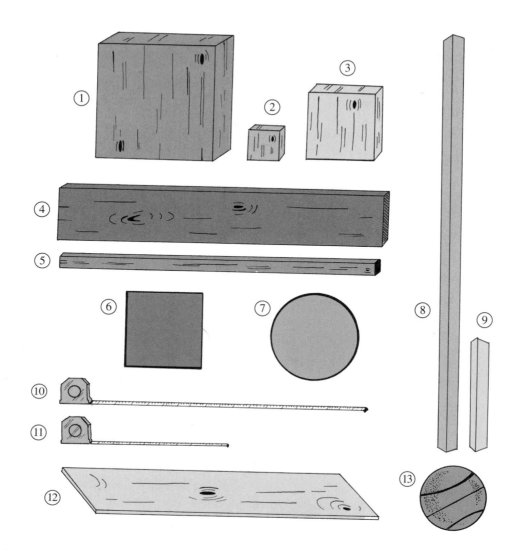

Las formas y los tamaños   *Shapes and sizes*

1. grande   *big*
2. pequeño(a)   *small*
3. mediano(a)   *medium*
4. ancho(a)   *wide*
5. estrecho(a)   *narrow*
6. cuadrado(a)   *square*
7. circular   *circular*

8. alto(a)   *tall, high*
9. bajo(a)   *low, short (in height)*
10. largo(a)   *long*
11. corto(a)   *short (in length)*
12. plano(a)   *flat*
13. redondo(a)   *round*

Note: If a noun is feminine (uses **la** for *the*), its describing word will change its ending from **o** to **a**. If a noun is plural (ends in **s**), the describing word will add an **s** after a vowel or **es** after a consonant.

La sala es pequeña.   *The living room is small.*
Las salas son pequeñas.   *The living rooms are small.*
Los patios son circulares.   *The yards are circular.*

1 Working with your partner, use the pictures on page 80 to tell the name of each room, as well as the shape and size.

2 Point out various objects in your classroom. Ask your partner about the colors, shapes, and sizes of these objects. Use the vocabulary on pages 81 and 82.

EJEMPLO: ¿Qué es verde?   *What's green?*

 [pointing to a green object] Eso es verde.   *That is green.*

3 Make your own picture book. Draw or find pictures of objects that represent the colors, shapes, and sizes presented in the lesson. Write labels for them.

Conversación

Describing things

¿Cómo es el/la…?	*What is the . . . like?*
¿Cómo son los/las…?	*What are the . . . like?*
¿De qué (color/forma/tamaño) es el/la…?	*What (color/shape/size) is the . . . ?*
¿De qué (color/forma/tamaño) son los/las…?	*What (color/shape/size) are the . . . ?*
El/La… es…	*The . . . is . . .*
Los/Las… son…	*The . . . are . . .*

4 Draw a picture of your house or apartment and label the rooms. Make a report about it.

EJEMPLO: Ésta es mi casa. En mi casa hay nueve cuartos. Hay una sala, un comedor…
This is my house. In my house there are nine rooms. There is a living room,
a dining room . . .

5 Describe your house to your partner, using at least five adjectives.

EJEMPLO: Mi casa es grande.   *My house is big.*
Hay tres alcobas.   *There are three bedrooms.*
Mi alcoba es verde claro.   *My bedroom is light green.*

6 Ask your partner questions about her or his house.

EJEMPLO: ¿Cómo es la sala?   *What's the living room like?*

Es grande y cuadrada.   *It's big and square.*

¿De qué color es?   *What color is it?*

Es rosada y gris.   *It's pink and gray.*

7 Review the vocabulary related to clothing on page 6. Then describe what you are wearing.

EJEMPLO: Mis pantalones son azules, mis zapatos son blancos y mi camisa es roja.
My pants are blue, my shoes are white, and my shirt is red.

8 **Juego**   Review the parts of the body on page 5. Then describe one of your classmates. See if your partner can guess who the person is.

EJEMPLO: La persona tiene una cara circular y ojos pardos. Él tiene pelo largo y…
The person has a round face and brown eyes. He has long hair and . . .

9 **Juego: Doce preguntas**   Describe an object from one of the previous lessons but don't tell your partner what it is you are describing. Your partner has twelve chances to guess what you are describing.

EJEMPLO: Es blanco y amarillo. Es plano y redondo. (un huevo frito)
It's white and yellow. It's flat and round. (a fried egg)

Conversación

Comparing things

Éste es más (largo).	*This one is (long)er.*
Éste es más (largo) que ése.	*This one is (long)er than that one.*
Éste es menos (largo).	*This one is not as (long).*
Éste es menos (largo) que ése.	*This one is not as (long) as that one.*
Éste es tan (largo).	*This one is as (long).*
Éste es tan (largo) como ése.	*This one is as (long) as that one.*

10 Compare various things and people with regard to size and shape.

EJEMPLOS: Un elefante es más grande que un conejo.   *An elephant is bigger than a rabbit.*
Marta es menos alta que Alicia.   *Marta is not as tall as Alicia.*

11 Compare your house or apartment with that of your best friend.

EJEMPLO: Mi casa es tan grande como la casa de mi amiga, pero las alcobas en mi casa son más grandes que las alcobas en su casa.
My house is as big as my friend's house, but the bedrooms in my house are bigger than the bedrooms in her house.

Conversación

Talking about where someone lives

¿Dónde vives?	*Where do you live?*
Vivo en una casa.	*I live in a house.*
Mi amigo vive en…	*My friend lives in . . .*
Mis amigos viven en…	*My friends live in . . .*
Nosotros vivimos en…	*We live in . . .*

VIVIR	*to live*
yo	vivo
tú	vives
Ud./él/ella	vive
nosotros(as)	vivimos
Uds./ellos/ellas	viven

12 Encuesta   Survey the class to find out if the majority of the class live in houses or in apartments. Then find out what each house or apartment is like.

EJEMPLO: ¿Vives en una casa o en un apartamento?
Do you live in a house or in an apartment?

Vivo en un apartamento.
I live in an apartment.

¿Cómo es tu apartamento?
What's your apartment like?

Es pequeño.
It's small.

DEPTOS.

AGUIRRE LAREDO Y PLU-TARCO E. CALLES, departamentos nuevos, Condominio Sahn José, 2 recámaras, gabinetes de cocina, doble estancia, boiler, alfombrada, lozeta vitreada, crédito Bancario N$5000 iniciales, tel. 13-12-48, 16-54-39. (50)

AMERICAS, muy cómodos, muy amplios y muy bonitos. 16-71-18, 16-18-99. (83)

BARRIO ALTO, enrejados, teléfono, mensualidades bajas, 16-71-18, 16-18-99. (84)

BELLA VISTA, de oportunidad, precio nuy bajo, 16-71-18, 16-18-99. (85)

13   Find out from your partner where his or her relatives live.

EJEMPLO: ¿Dónde viven tus abuelos?   *Where do your grandparents live?*

Ellos viven en Arizona.   *They live in Arizona.*

Conversación

Telling where things are

¿Dónde está el/la…?	*Where is the . . . ?*
¿Dónde están los/las…?	*Where are the . . . ?*
El/La… está…	*The . . . is . . .*
Los/Las… están…	*The . . . are . . .*

14   Find out from your partner where various rooms and items are in his or her house.

EJEMPLO: ¿Dónde están las alcobas?
Where are the bedrooms?

Las alcobas están en el primer piso.
The bedrooms are on the second floor.

¿Dónde está el teléfono?
Where is the telephone?

El teléfono está en una mesa en la cocina.
The telephone is on a table in the kitchen.

ENCUENTRO PERSONAL

Paulina and Eduardo are on the phone again. She is describing her house to him.

¿Comprendes?

1. Where does Paulina live?
2. How large is Paulina's house?
3. How many bedrooms and bathrooms are there?
4. What is the kitchen like?
5. Where are the bedrooms?
6. What color is Paulina's bedroom?
7. What color is the bedroom where Eduardo will sleep?
8. Whose room will he have?

¡Te toca!

A. Practice the conversation with a partner.

B. Personalize the conversation by telling about your own house.

¡Así es!

Spanish housing

Houses in Spanish-speaking countries often have a central patio open to the sky with all the rooms facing it. In the city, houses are built right next to each other and right up to the sidewalk with the walls touching. The windows facing the sidewalk have wrought-iron grillwork, which adds beauty to an otherwise plain exterior and provides security. In the country, the houses may be surrounded by high walls to provide security and privacy.

PRONUNCIACIÓN

Cognates—describing words (adjectives)

A *cognate* is a word that has the same meaning and the same or similar spelling in Spanish and English. The pronunciation is different because each follows the rules of its language.

Practice saying these cognates in Spanish. You may need to review the rules on stress presented on page 78. Be careful and pay attention to your vowel sounds!

ENDING IN **OSO** (English *ous*)	ENDING IN **IVO** (English *ive*)	ENDING IN **ICO** (English *ic/ical*)	DROP LAST LETTER
curioso	activo	académico	correcto/incorrecto
delicioso	colectivo	artístico	elegante
famoso	decisivo	atlético	evidente
furioso	evasivo	automático	exacto
generoso	expansivo	católico	excepto
glorioso	expresivo	democrático	expediente
industrioso	manipulativo	doméstico	extravagante
montañoso	ofensivo	económico	ignorante
nervioso	opresivo	fantástico	importante
numeroso	pasivo	hispánico	moderno
odioso	positivo	histórico	mucho
precioso	regresivo	político	rápido
religioso	represivo	público	sólido
tedioso	sucesivo	trágico	violento

15 Can you guess what the words in the pronunciation practice mean? Make a list of words that could be used to describe people.

16 Cut pictures of famous people from magazines or the newspaper. Use the adjectives above to describe them.

17 Write the names of famous people and comic strip characters. Choose four adjectives from the list to describe each of them.

18 Review pages 3, 4, and 5 for vocabulary relating to people. Describe people you know and family members using the cognates. Remember to change the **o** to **a** when describing a female person.

EJEMPLOS: Mi padre es activo.   *My father is active.*
Mi madre es activa.   *My mother is active.*

Mi hermano Carlos es atlético.   *My brother Carlos is athletic.*
Mi hermana María es atlética.   *My sister María is athletic.*

19 Use words from the cognate list to compare two people you know well.

EJEMPLO: Carmelita es más generosa que Antonia.   *Carmelita is more generous than Antonia.*

20 Choose an animal from the list on page 74 and ask your partner what it's like.

EJEMPLO: ¿Cómo es un gato?   *What is a cat like?*

Es pequeño, activo y rápido.   *It's small, active, and fast.*

Diversión

1. Here is a Spanish "finger-play." Can you guess which finger is being described?

JUEGO CON LOS DEDOS DE LA MANO
Niño chiquito y bonito,
el señor de los anillos,
el largo y flaco,
el mira lejos
y el cuadrilongo.

A GAME WITH THE FINGERS
Pretty little boy
The lord of the rings
The long and thin one
He sees far
And the oblong one.

2. Alfonsina Storni, an Argentinean poet, wrote this poem about conformity. Do you agree with her?

CUADRADOS Y ÁNGULOS
Casas enfiladas, casas enfiladas,
    casas enfiladas.
Cuadrados, cuadrados, cuadrados,
    casas enfiladas.
Las gentes ya tienen el alma
    cuadrada.
Ideas en fila
y ángulo en la espalda.
Yo misma he vertido ayer una lágrima
Dios mío, cuadrada.

SQUARES AND ANGLES
Houses in a row, houses in a row
    houses in a row.
Squares, squares, squares
    houses in a row.
The people already have a square
    soul.
Ideas in a row
Their backs at an angle.
Even I shed a tear yesterday
My goodness, it was square.

Las cosas en el aula y otras cosas
Things in the classroom and other things

Vocabulario

Las cosas en el aula*   *Things in the classroom*

1. la pizarra — *chalkboard*
2. la tiza — *chalk*
3. el borrador — *eraser*
4. el estante — *bookshelf*
5. el reloj — *clock*
6. el armario — *locker, closet*
7. la bandera — *flag*
8. el globo *del mundo* — *globe*
9. el mapa* — *map*
10. el libro — *book*
11. el archivador — *file cabinet*
12. el escritorio — *teacher's desk*
13. el pupitre — *student desk*
14. el diccionario — *dictionary*
15. la cartera — ~~*briefcase*~~/purse
16. la mochila — *backpack*
17. la papelera — *wastepaper basket*
18. la computadora — *computer*
19. la calculadora — *calculator*
20. ~~la grabadora~~ — ~~*tape recorder*~~
21. la cinta adhesiva — *tape*
22. el cuaderno — *notebook*
23. el papel — *paper*
24. el lápiz — *pencil*
25. el bolígrafo — *ballpoint pen*
26. la goma de borrar — *pencil eraser*
27. la silla — *chair*
28. la mesa — *table*
29. la marcador — marker
30. maletín — briefcase

*Note: Feminine nouns beginning with a stressed **a** sound use **el**, not **la**: **el aula**, **el agua**.
Note also that **el mapa** is masculine even though it ends in **a**.

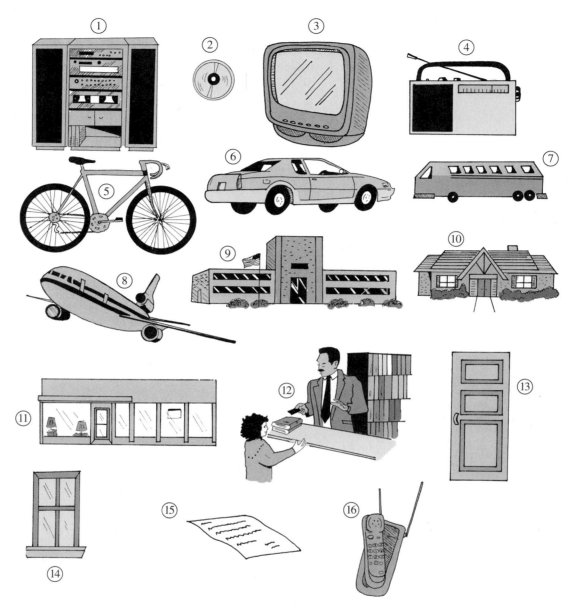

Otras cosas   *Other things*

1. el estéreo	*stereo*	9. la escuela	*school*
2. el disco compacto	*CD, compact disc*	10. la casa	*house*
3. el televisor	*television set*	11. la tienda	*store*
4. el radio	*radio*	12. la biblioteca	*library*
5. la bicicleta	*bicycle*	13. la puerta	*door*
6. el auto, el coche, el carro	*car*	14. la ventana	*window*
7. el autobús	*bus*	15. la carta	*letter*
8. el avión	*airplane*	16. el teléfono	*telephone*

1 Draw a picture of your classroom and label the various objects.

2 Using your picture from Activity 1, ask your partner to identify the objects in your drawing.

EJEMPLOS: ¿Qué es esto?   *What is this?*

Es un archivador.   *It's a file cabinet.*

¿Qué es esto?   *What is this?*

Es una computadora.   *It's a computer.*

3 **Juego**   How well do you remember where various objects in the classroom are? Take turns closing your eyes while your partner asks where different objects are. Point to them while answering. Remember to use **están** when the object is plural.

EJEMPLOS: ¿Dónde está la ventana?   *Where is the window?*

La ventana está allí.   *The window is there.*

¿Dónde están los libros?   *Where are the books?*

Los libros están aquí.   *The books are here.*

4 **Juego**   Divide a sheet of paper into sixteen squares and number them from one to sixteen. Your teacher or a classmate will tell you what to draw in each square. At the end, see if everyone has drawn the correct picture in the correct square.

EJEMPLO: Dibujen un lápiz en número cinco.   *Draw a pencil in number five.*

5 Choose three items from the lesson and describe them. Use describing words from the vocabulary on page 8.

EJEMPLO: Tengo un coche. Es grande. Es amarillo. No es cuadrado.
I have a car. It is big. It is yellow. It is not square.

6 **Juego**   Describe an object found in the classroom or in your house, but do not tell your partner what it is. See if he or she can guess from your description.

EJEMPLO: Es grande y plana. También es dura. Es negra y rectangular. (Es la pizarra.)
It is big and flat. It is hard also. It is black and rectangular. (It's the blackboard.)

7 Ask your partner if he or she has various items listed in this lesson and in previous lessons.

EJEMPLOS: ¿Tienes un bolígrafo?   *Do you have a ballpoint pen?*

Sí, tengo un bolígrafo.   *Yes, I have a ballpoint pen.*

¿Tienes cintas?   *Do you have tapes?*

No, no tengo cintas.   *No, I don't have tapes.*

8 Ask your partner how many he or she has of various items.

EJEMPLO: ¿Cuántos televisores tienes en tu casa?
How many television sets do you have in your house?

Tenemos tres televisores.
We have three television sets.

9 Ask your partner where he or she has various items. Use **lo/la/los/las** in your answer.

EJEMPLO: ¿Dónde tienes tu diccionario?   *Where is your dictionary?*

Lo tengo en mi armario.   *I have it in my locker.*

Conversación

Telling where one is going

¿Adónde vas?	*Where are you going?*
Voy a...	*I'm going to . . .*
¿Cómo vas?	*How are you going?*
Voy en...	*I'm going by . . .*

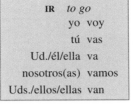

IR	*to go*
yo	voy
tú	vas
Ud./él/ella	va
nosotros(as)	vamos
Uds./ellos/ellas	van

10 Ask your partner if he or she goes to different places in your city.

EJEMPLO: ¿Vas a Discoland?
 Do you go to Discoland?

   Sí, voy a Discoland. / No, no voy a Discoland.
 Yes, I go to Discoland. / No, I don't go to Discoland.

11 Ask your partner where he or she is going after school and how he or she will get there.

EJEMPLO: ¿Adónde vas después de la escuela?   *Where are you going after school?*

   Voy a la biblioteca.   *I'm going to the library.*

   ¿Cómo vas allí?   *How are you going there?*

   Voy en autobús.   *I'm going by bus.*

12 **Encuesta**   Find out from several classmates where their family and friends are going for summer vacation. Remember to say **No sé** when you don't know.

EJEMPLO: ¿Adónde va tu familia este verano?   *Where is your family going this summer?*

   Vamos a Atlanta.   *We're going to Atlanta.*

   ¿Adónde van tus amigos?   *Where are your friends going?*

   Creo que van a Boston.   *I believe they're going to Boston.*

ENCUENTRO PERSONAL

Paulina and her friends are trying to decide what gift the class can give to their favorite teacher for his birthday.

¿Comprendes?

1. What gift does Jaime suggest?
2. Why isn't that a good idea?
3. What gift does Sean suggest?
4. What does Raúl suggest?
5. Why does Rosita say that Raúl's idea isn't a good one?
6. What idea does Rosita have for a gift?
7. What gift do they finally decide to give to Sr. González?
8. Who is going to the store?

¡Te toca!

A. Practice the conversation with a partner.

B. Change the conversation to tell about what you can give your favorite teacher as a birthday present.

¡Así es!

The guitar

When you mention Spanish music, most people think of the guitar **(la guitarra)** and rightly so, since the guitar originated in Spain in the twelfth century. The Spanish classical guitar is usually a six-stringed acoustical (not electric) instrument, although it may have four or even seven strings. Today the guitar is used for folk, popular, and classical music in all parts of the Spanish-speaking world. One of the most famous composers for guitar in modern times is Joaquín Rodrigo, whose ***Concierto de Aranjuez*** (1940) established the guitar as a serious orchestral instrument.

PRONUNCIACIÓN

Exact cognates

Many words that end in **al, el, or, ble,** or **ión** have the same or similar spelling in English and Spanish. In addition, there are many other words that are exactly the same. Practice saying the following cognates in Spanish. Be careful to pronounce the vowel sounds correctly and to put the stress on the correct syllable.

AL/EL	OR	BLE	OTHERS	ADD AN ACCENT
animal	actor	admirable	chocolate	amén
brutal	color	compatible	drama	área
capital	director	flexible	escape	cadáver
central	doctor	horrible	grave	cliché
cruel	error	indispensable	idea	fórmula
cultural	exterior	irresistible	mediocre	melón
fatal	factor	notable	mosquito	violín
final	favor	posible	piano	
general	honor	probable	plan	**IÓN**
hospital	horror	terrible	radio	decisión
hotel	inferior		excelente	diversión
ideal	inspector		video	evasión
liberal	instructor	**AR**		exclusión
mental	interior	familiar		región
natural	superior	popular		religión
normal	terror	regular		televisión
original				versión
legal				visión
real				

13 Make a list of the words listed above that are nouns *(people/things)* and a second list of adjectives *(describing words)*.

14 **Juego**   Review the letters of the alphabet on page 4 and the parts of the body on page 5. Play *Hangman* using Spanish cognates and letters. As you put each part of the man on the scaffold, tell in Spanish what part you are adding.

EJEMPLO: Le pongo la cabeza.   *I'm putting the head on him.*

15 **Juego**   Have a spelling bee using the words in this lesson.

Diversión

Trabalenguas: *Tongue Twisters*

1. Tongue twisters are popular in all languages. Try these Spanish twisters. Can you say each one rapidly?

Me han dicho un dicho que han dicho que he dicho yo. Ese dicho está mal dicho pues si lo hubiera dicho yo, estaría mejor dicho, el dicho que han dicho que he dicho yo.

They told me a saying that they said that I said. That saying is so poorly said that if I had said it it would have been better said, the saying that they have said I said.

En el juncal con don Joaquín juncos juntaba Julián. Júntase Juana a los dos y entonces juncos juntaron Juana, Joaquín y Julián.

In the reeds with don Joaquín, Julián was putting reeds together. Juana joined the pair and then Juana, Joaquín, and Julián put reeds together.

María Chucena techaba su choza y un techador que por allí pasaba le dijo: —Chucena, ¿tú techas tu choza o techas la ajena? Yo techo mi choza, no techo la ajena que techo la choza de María Chucena.

María Chucena was roofing her hut and a roofer that was passing by there said to her, "Chucena, are you roofing your hut or are you roofing someone else's?" "I'm roofing my hut, I'm not roofing another's, since I'm roofing the hut of María Chucena."

¿Cómo como? Pues, ¿cómo como si no como como como?

How do I eat? Well, how do I eat if I don't eat like I eat?

2. We have a nonsense rhyme in English that says, "See you later, alligator. After a while, crocodile." Here is a similar one that Spanish-speaking children have fun with.

¿Qué pasa, calabaza?
¡Nada, nada, limonada!

*What's happening, pumpkin?
Nothing, nothing, lemonade!*

3. Here is another tongue twister. (Remember that z and s have the same sound in Latin American Spanish.)

Un premio propuse a Rosa Riza si reza en ruso. Ahora aunque un poco confusa, reza en ruso Rosa Riza.

I proposed a prize to Rosa Riza if she prays in Russian. Now though a little confused, Rosa Riza prays in Russian.

El calendario, la hora y las clases
The calendar, time, and classes

Vocabulario

ENERO						
LUNES	MARTES	MIÉRCOLES	JUEVES	VIERNES	SÁBADO	DOMINGO
	1	2	3	4	5	6

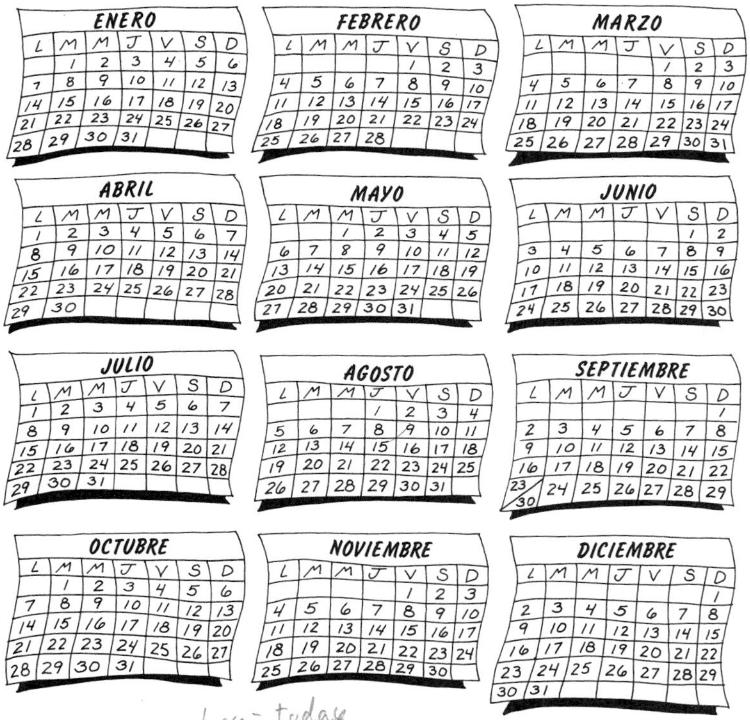

El calendario *The calendar*

EL DÍA* *DAY*

1. el lunes *Monday*
2. el martes *Tuesday*
3. el miércoles *Wednesday*
4. el jueves *Thursday*
5. el viernes *Friday*
6. el sábado *Saturday*
7. el domingo *Sunday*

EL MES *MONTH*

1. enero *January*
2. febrero *February*
3. marzo *March*
4. abril *April*
5. mayo *May*
6. junio *June*
7. julio *July*
8. agosto *August*
9. septiembre *September*
10. octubre *October*
11. noviembre *November*
12. diciembre *December*

*Note: The noun **día** ends in **a** but it uses **el**.
To say *on* with days of the week, use **el** or **los**.
el domingo *on Sunday*
los domingos *on Sundays*

hoy = today
ayer = yesterday
el año = the year
el mes = the month
la semana = the week
mañana = tomorrow

Did you notice that the days and months are NOT capitalized in Spanish and that the week begins with Monday?

Conversación

Asking the day

¿Qué día es hoy?	*What day is today?*
mañana?	*tomorrow?*
pasado mañana?	*the day after tomorrow?*
¿Qué día fue ayer?	*What day was yesterday?*
anteayer?	*the day before yesterday?*

Asking the date

¿Cuál es la fecha de hoy?	*What is today's date?*
Es el *[date]* de *[month]* de *[year]*.	*It is . . .*
¿Cuál es la fecha de tu cumpleaños?	*What is the date of your birthday?*
Es el primero de *[month]*.	*It's the first of [month].*
Es el (dos) de *[month]*.	*It's the [second] of [month].*
¿Cuándo es…?	*When is . . . ?*

Review the numbers to 99. To say the year, use **mil novecientos** (*one thousand nine hundred*) or **dos mil** (*two thousand*) before the last two numbers.

1 Practice saying the days and months until you can do so without looking at the book. If you study the months in groups of four, it will be easier to learn them.

2 Name the days of the week when you have school and those that you do not.

3 Name the months in each season.

4 Pretend that it is a different day of the week. Ask your partner what day it was yesterday and what day it is tomorrow or the day after tomorrow.

EJEMPLO: Si hoy es jueves, ¿qué día fue ayer?   *If today is Thursday, what day was it yesterday?*

Ayer fue miércoles.   *Yesterday was Wednesday.*

¿Qué día es mañana?   *What day is tomorrow?*

Mañana es viernes.   *Tomorrow is Friday.*

5 Review the weather expressions on page 6. With a partner, practice telling what the weather is usually like in each of the months.

EJEMPLO: ¿Qué tiempo hace en diciembre?
What's the weather like in December?

En diciembre hace frío y nieva mucho.
In December it's cold and it snows a lot.

6 Write today's date and the dates of the following holidays.

EJEMPLO: Hoy es el 26 de julio de 1999 (mil novecientos noventa y nueve).

Holidays

DIAS FESTIVOS EN LOS ESTADOS UNIDOS

EL PRIMERO DE ENERO	Día de año nuevo
3er LUNES DE ENERO	Aniversario de Martín Luther King
3er LUNES DE FEBRERO	Día de Presidente
ÚLTIMO LUNES DE MAYO	*Memorial Day*
EL 4 DE JULIO	Día de la Independencia
1er LUNES DE SEPTIEMBRE	Día del trabajador *(Labor Day)*
2° LUNES DE OCTUBRE	Día de Cristóbal Colón
1er MARTES DE NOVIEMBRE	Día de las elecciones
EL 11 DE NOVIEMBRE	Día de los veteranos
4° JUEVES DE NOVIEMBRE	Día de Acción de Gracias
EL 25 DE DICIEMBRE	Día de Navidad

7 Make a birthday chart of your classmates' birthdays. Begin by making a list of their names. If you have to ask their names, do it in Spanish. Review Lesson 2 if necessary. Then, in Spanish, ask the date of their birthday.

EJEMPLO: ¿Cuándo es tu cumpleaños?   *When is your birthday?*

Mi cumpleaños es el 11 de noviembre.   *My birthday is November 11.*

8 Ask your partner when the birthdays are of the people he or she asked.

EJEMPLO: ¿Cuándo es el cumpleaños de Miguel?   *When is Miguel's birthday?*

Es el 30 de octubre.   *It's October 30.*

Conversación

es mediodia

es medianoche

Es la una

Son las dos

Son las dos y cuarto

Son las dos y media

Son las dos menos cuarto

Son las dos y diez

Son las dos menos viente

Asking the time

	¿Qué hora es?	*What time is it?*
1.	Es mediodía.	*It's noon.*
2.	Es medianoche.	*It's midnight.*
3.	Es la una.	*It's one o'clock.*
4.	Son las dos.	*It's two o'clock.*
5.	… y cuarto.	*quarter after . . .*
6.	… y media.	*half past . . . (thirty)*
7.	… menos cuarto.	*quarter to . . .*
8.	… y [number].	*. . . minutes after the hour.*
9.	… menos [number].	*. . . minutes to the hour.*
	… de la mañana.	*. . . in the morning,* A.M.
	… de la tarde.	*. . . in the afternoon,* P.M.
	… de la noche.	*. . . in the evening,* P.M.
	¿A qué hora es (la clase)?	*At what time is (the class)?*
	A las (dos).	*At (two) o'clock.*

9 Look at the clocks below. Ask your partner for the time.

EJEMPLO: ¿Qué hora es?   *What time is it?*

 Son las tres.   *It's three o'clock.*

a.

b.

c.

d.

e.

f.

g.

h.

10 Practice telling time with minutes before and after the hour. Give the following times.

a. 7:10 A.M.
b. 10:15 P.M.
c. 11:30 A.M.
d. 12 noon
e. 12:35 P.M.

f. 1:05 P.M.
g. 1:45 P.M.
h. 5:50 A.M.
i. 9:27 P.M.
j. 12 midnight

11 Draw some clocks and ask your partner to tell you the time.

Vocabulario

Las clases   *Classes*

el arte	*art*
el español	*Spanish*
el inglés	*English*
la clase de computadoras	*computer class*
la economía	*economics*
la educación física	*physical education*
la historia	*history*
la mecánica	*mechanics*
la música	*music*
la orquesta	*band, orchestra*
las matemáticas	*math*
las ciencias	*science*

12 Make a schedule of your classes. Give the time each class begins. Compare your schedule with your partner's.

EJEMPLO: Mi clase de matemáticas es a las diez y media.   *My math class is at 10:30.*

Mi clase es a la una y cuarto.   *My class is at 1:15.*

13 Refer to your schedules in Activity 12 and ask another student when her or his classes are.

EJEMPLO: ¿A qué hora es tu clase de español?   *What time is your Spanish class?*

Es a las doce y media.   *It's at 12:30.*

ENCUENTRO PERSONAL

Paulina and her brother Roberto remember their mother's birthday just in time to plan a party and buy a gift.

¿Comprendes?

1. What is today's date?
2. What is happening tomorrow?
3. What are Paulina and Roberto going to do?
4. What time is it when Paulina and Roberto begin planning the party?
5. When is the party?
6. Whom are they going to invite?
7. What gift are they going to give?

¡Te toca!

A. Practice the conversation with a partner.

B. Change the conversation to tell about giving a birthday party for your friend and what you can give as a present.

¡Así es!

Twenty-four-hour time system

A twenty-four-hour time system is commonly used in Spain and Latin America, especially in transportation and entertainment schedules. In this system, the hours after 12:00 noon continue counting up to midnight, which is 24:00. If an event were to take place at 7:30 P.M., the schedule would show the time as **19:30 horas**. To convert from twenty-four-hour time to A.M./P.M. time, subtract twelve from the hour if the hour is thirteen or higher.

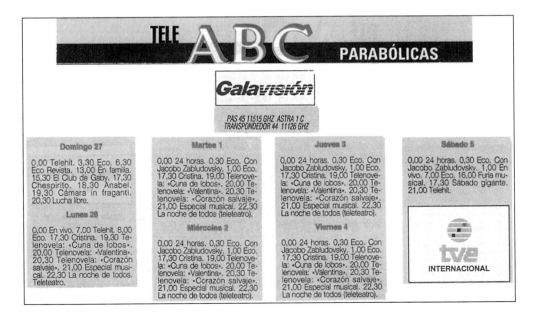

Pronunciación

———◆———

Cognates

Notice these ending patterns and practice pronouncing the words. Pay careful attention to vowel sounds and stress.

Spanish: IA/ÍA/IO English: *y*	Spanish: DAD/TAD English: *ty*	Spanish: CIÓN English: *tion*	Spanish: ENCIA English: *ence*
dormitorio	actividad	admiración	correspondencia
remedio	autoridad	atención	diferencia
fantasía	capacidad	celebración	evidencia
geografía	ciudad	civilización	experiencia
infancia	comunidad	dirección	independencia
democracia	dificultad	exclamación	influencia
farmacia	eternidad	instrucción	inteligencia
frecuencia	generosidad	invitación	
historia	libertad	nación	
	nacionalidad	producción	
	necesidad	repetición	
	posibilidad	reputación	
	realidad	revolución	
	sociedad	sección	
	unidad	situación	
	universidad		
	variedad		

All but two of these words are feminine nouns. Can you find the two that are not?

Diversión

1. Here are two birthday songs. One is similar to the American *Happy Birthday* and the other is a traditional Mexican song that is often used as a birthday serenade. Can you imagine awakening to the sound of a **mariachi** band beneath your window singing **Las mañanitas?**

FELIZ CUMPLEAÑOS

Mucha felicidad.
En el día de hoy
Le deseo a…
Mucha felicidad.

HAPPY BIRTHDAY

Much happiness.
On the day of today
I wish to . . .
Much happiness.

LAS MAÑANITAS

Éstas son las mañanitas
que cantaba el rey David.
Hoy por ser día de tu santo
te las cantamos a ti.
Despierta mi bien despierta,
mira que ya amaneció.
Ya los pajaritos cantan,
la luna ya se metió.

THE MORNING SONGS

These are the morning songs
That King David used to sing
Because it's your saint's day
We're singing them to you.
Wake up, my dear, wake up,
See that it's already dawn.
The birds are already singing
The moon has set.

2. Everyone has difficulty remembering which months have thirty-one days and which have only thirty. This rhyme should help you to remember.

EL POEMA DE LOS MESES

Hay treinta días en septiembre
abril, junio y noviembre.
Hay veintiocho en febrero,
los demás treinta y uno.

THE POEM OF THE MONTHS

There are thirty days in September,
April, June and November.
There are twenty-eight in February
The rest have thirty-one.

3. Do you remember the poem about the weather in Lesson 5? Go back to page 68 and read it again because it also tells about the months!

Lo que hacemos y los números grandes
What we do and big numbers

Vocabulario

Lo que hacemos   *What we do*

1. bailar	*to dance*
2. caminar	*to walk*
3. comprar (algo)	*to buy (something)*
4. cantar (canciones)	*to sing (songs)*
5. cocinar (la cena)	*to cook (dinner)*
6. cuidar de los niños	*to babysit*
7. dar* (regalos)	*to give (presents)*
8. escuchar (discos compactos)	*to listen to (CDs)*
9. estudiar (algo)	*to study (something)*
10. esquiar (en la nieve)	*to snowski*
(en el agua)	*to waterski*
11. ganar (un juego)	*to win (a game)*
12. ganar (dinero)	*to earn (money)*
13. gastar (dinero)	*to spend (money)*
14. hablar (por teléfono)	*to talk (on the phone)*
hablar (español)	*to speak (Spanish)*
15. llevar (la ropa)	*to wear (clothing)*
16. llevar (mi almuerzo)	*to bring (my lunch)*
17. manejar (un auto)	*to drive (a car)*
18. mirar (la televisión)	*to watch (television)*
19. nadar	*to swim*
20. practicar (un deporte)	*to practice (a sport)*
21. preparar (la comida)	*to prepare (food)*
22. tocar (un instrumento)	*to play (an instrument)*
(el piano, el violín	*(piano, violin*
la guitarra, etc.)	*guitar, etc.)*

Vocabulario *(continued)*

Lo que hacemos   *What we do* (continued)

23. tomar	*to drink, to take*
24. trabajar	*to work*
25. viajar (a un lugar)	*to travel (to a place)*
26. visitar (a un amigo)	*to visit (a friend)*
27. jugar* (ue) (al béisbol)	*to play (baseball)*
(al fútbol)	*(soccer, football)*
(al básquetbol)	*(basketball)*
(al tenis)	*(tennis)*
(a un juego)	*(a game)*
(a los naipes)	*(cards)*
28. aprender (español)	*to learn (Spanish)*
(a manejar)	*(to drive)*
29. beber (leche)	*to drink (milk)*
30. comer (el helado)	*to eat (ice cream)*
31. correr (en la pista)	*to run (track)*
32. leer (un libro)	*to read (a book)*
33. poder* (ue) hacer algo	*to be able to do something, can*
34. dormir* (ue)	*to sleep*
35. escribir (una carta)	*to write (a letter)*
36. ir* (al cine)	*to go (to the movies)*
p.95 (a la escuela)	*(to school)*
(a la iglesia)	*(to church)*
37. recibir (algo)	*to receive (something)*
38. vivir (en una casa)	*to live (in a house)*

Note: Verbs with asterisks (*) are irregular in some of their forms.

Conversación

In Lesson 6 we learned that when we say that *we like something* in English, in Spanish we say that *people and things please us.* **Me gusta** is also used with activities. When you say, **Me gusta cantar**, you are actually saying, *To sing (singing) pleases me.* Review the forms of **gustar** on page 72.

Asking and telling what one likes or dislikes doing

¿Qué te gusta hacer?	*What do you like to do? [informal]*
¿Qué le gusta hacer?	*What do you like to do? [formal]*
¿Qué no te/le gusta hacer?	*What don't you like to do?*
Me gusta cantar y bailar.	*I like to sing and dance.*
No me gusta cocinar.	*I don't like to cook.*

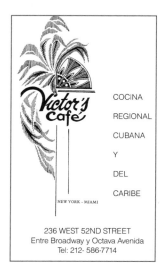

COCINA

REGIONAL

CUBANA

Y

DEL

CARIBE

NEW YORK - MIAMI

236 WEST 52ND STREET
Entre Broadway y Octava Avenida
Tel: 212- 586-7714

1 Make a list of ten things you like to do and ten things you do not like to do. Compare lists with your partner.

EJEMPLOS: Me gusta bailar.   *I like to dance.*
Me gusta hablar por teléfono.   *I like to talk on the phone.*
No me gusta esquiar.   *I don't like to ski.*
No me gusta cocinar la cena.   *I don't like to cook dinner.*

2 Ask several of your classmates what they like or do not like to do.

EJEMPLOS: ¿Qué te gusta hacer?   *What do you like to do?*

Me gusta escuchar música.   *I like to listen to music.*

¿Qué no te gusta hacer?   *What don't you like to do?*

No me gusta mirar la televisión.   *I don't like to watch TV.*

3 Tell your partner what you like to do during various seasons.

EJEMPLO: En el invierno me gusta esquiar.   *In the winter I like to ski.*

Conversación

Telling what one is going to do, has to do, and knows how to do

Voy a aprender mucho.	*I am going to learn a lot.*
Tengo que escribir una carta.	*I have to write a letter.*
Sé tocar el piano.	*I know how to play the piano.*

SABER *to know (how)*	
yo	sé
tú	sabes
Ud./él/ella	sabe
nosotros(as)	sabemos
Uds./ellos/ellas	saben

4 Review the forms of **ir** (*to go*) on page 21. (Notice that **a** comes after **ir** when an action follows.) Then tell some things that you and people you know are going to do.

EJEMPLOS: Mi madre va a cocinar la cena.   *My mother is going to cook dinner.*
Mis amigos van a correr en la pista.   *My friends are going to run track.*

5 Review the forms of **tener** (*to have*) on page 21. Notice that **que** changes the meaning from possession to obligation (*to have to*). Tell some things that you and people you know have to do.

EJEMPLOS: Mi madre tiene que comprar un vestido.   *My mother has to buy a dress.*
Nosotros tenemos que escribir la tarea.   *We have to write the homework.*

6 Find out if your partner knows how to do various activities. Use a form of **saber** in your question.

EJEMPLOS: ¿Sabes jugar al tenis?   *Do you know how to play tennis?*

No, no sé jugar.   *No, I don't know how to play.*

¿Sabes manejar un auto?   *Do you know how to drive a car?*

Sí, sé manejar.   *Yes, I know how to drive.*

Conversación

Telling what one can and cannot do

		PODER	*can, to be able*
		yo	puedo
		tú	puedes
		Ud./él/ella	puede
		nosotros(as)	podemos
		Uds./ellos/ellas	pueden

Puedo nadar bien.   *I can swim well.*
¿Puedes ir conmigo?   *Can you go with me?*
No puedo viajar a Europa.   *I can't travel to Europe.*

7 Make a list of ten things you can do and another list of things you cannot do.

8 Ask if your partner or people he or she knows can do various activities.

EJEMPLOS: ¿Puedes dormir en la clase?
Can you sleep in class?

No, no puedo dormir en la clase.
No, I can't sleep in class.

¿Tú y tus amigos pueden ir al cine el sábado?
Can you and your friends go to the movies Saturday?

Sí, podemos ir.
Yes, we can go.

VERB ENDINGS

Actions ending in **-AR** follow ending pattern for **llevar** (Lección 5).

yo	**-o**	nosotros(as)	**-amos**
tú	**-as**		
Ud./él/ella	**-a**	Uds./ellos/ellas	**-an**

Actions ending in **-ER** follow ending pattern for **comer** (Lección 6).

yo	**-o**	nosotros(as)	**-emos**
tú	**-es**		
Ud./él/ella	**-e**	Uds./ellos/ellas	**-en**

Actions ending in **-IR** follow ending pattern for **vivir** (Lección 7).

yo	**-o**	nosotros(as)	**-imos**
tú	**-es**		
Ud./él/ella	**-e**	Uds./ellos/ellas	**-en**

*Note: Verbs with asterisks are irregular in some of their forms:
> **dar: doy, das, da, damos, dan**
> **jugar: juego, juegas, juega, jugamos, juegan**
> **dormir: duermo, duermes, duerme, dormimos, duermen**

9 Make a list of ten things you do in school. Since you are talking about yourself, be sure that the action words end in **-o**. Because the **-o** ending can only be used with **yo**, it is not necessary to say **yo**. Compare your list to your partner's list. Put a check by those activities you both listed.

EJEMPLOS: Escribo papeles.   *I write papers.*
Hablo español.   *I speak Spanish.*

10 Tell your partner some things that you and your family do together. Be sure the action words end in **-mos**. Because the **-mos** ending can only be used with **nosotros**, it is not necessary to say **nosotros**.

EJEMPLOS: Comemos la cena.   *We eat dinner.*
Miramos la televisión.   *We watch TV.*

11 Ask your partner if she or he does various activities. Because the **-s** ending can only be used with **tú**, it is not necessary to say **tú**. When you answer, use the **-o** ending.

EJEMPLO: ¿Manejas un auto?
Do you drive a car?

Sí, manejo un auto. / No, no manejo un auto.
Yes, I drive a car. / No, I don't drive a car.

12 Tell some things that people you know do. Use the **-a** or **-e** ending if you are talking about one person, **-an** or **-en** if you are talking about two or more people.

EJEMPLOS: Mi hermano vende ropa.   *My brother sells clothing.*

Mis amigos estudian en la biblioteca.   *My friends study in the library.*

Quijana y asociados
ABOGADOS
LIC. RODOLFO QUIJANA GALDÓS
LIC. RICARDO QUIJANA GALDÓS
LIC. J. JOSE QUIJANA FERNÁNDEZ
LIC. JORGE G. ACALA CAMACHO
P.D. ROBERTO PRADO REYNOSA
ASUNTOS PENALES
CIVILES - MERCANTILES
LABORALES - AMPAROS
61-46-74   61-73-54
CALLE JOSÉ MARTÍ 930 NTE.

Vocabulario

Los números   *Numbers*

You have already learned the numbers from 0 to 99. Let's review them.

0	cero						
1	uno	11	once	21	veinte y uno	31 treinta y uno	10 diez
2	dos	12	doce	22	veinte y dos	32 treinta y dos	20 veinte
3	tres	13	trece	23	veinte y tres	33 treinta y tres	30 treinta
4	cuatro	14	catorce	24	veinte y cuatro	*etc.*	40 cuarenta
5	cinco	15	quince	25	veinte y cinco		50 cincuenta
6	seis	16	diez y seis	26	veinte y seis		60 sesenta
7	siete	17	diez y siete	27	veinte y siete		70 setenta
8	ocho	18	diez y ocho	28	veinte y ocho		80 ochenta
9	nueve	19	diez y nueve	29	veinte y nueve		90 noventa
10	diez	20	veinte	30	treinta		

Note: **Uno** changes to **una** before a feminine noun.

The numbers 16 through 19 may be spelled as one word: **dieciséis, dieciocho,** etc.

The numbers 21 through 29 may be spelled as one word: **veintiuno, veintiocho... ,**

The numbers 31 through 99 must be written as three words: **treinta y cuatro... ,**
cincuenta y siete... , noventa y nueve...

Los números grandes *Big numbers*

100	cien(to)	600	seiscientos	1.000	mil
200	doscientos	700	setecientos	2.000	dos mil
300	trescientos	800	ochocientos	1.000.000	un millón
400	cuatrocientos	900	novecientos	2.000.000	dos millones
500	quinientos				

Note: The numbers two hundred (**doscientos**) through nine hundred (**novecientos**) agree with the noun in gender. If the noun is feminine, change the **os** ending to **as**:

doscientos autos   **doscientas casas**

Cien is used before any noun or any larger number beginning with one hundred.

cien casas   *100 houses*
cien millones   *100 million*

Ciento is used for numbers from 101 to 199.

123   ciento veinte y tres
105   ciento cinco

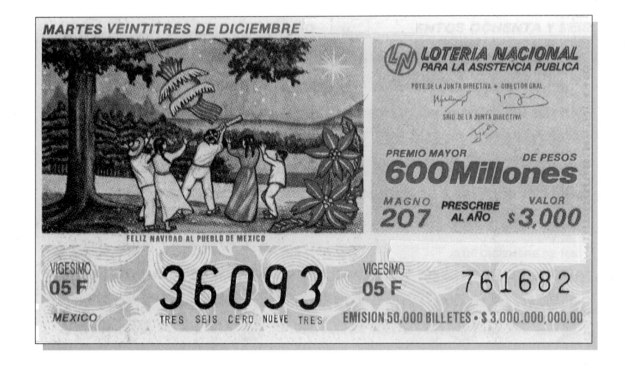

A period is often used instead of a comma to separate the millions from the thousands and the thousands from the hundreds. A comma is used instead of a decimal point.

   1.234 = mil doscientos treinta y cuatro
5.836.729 = cinco millones ochocientos treinta y seis mil setecientos veinte y nueve
   9,45 = nueve coma cuarenta y cinco

Mil never changes: **mil, dos mil, nueve mil,** etc.
Never use **un** (*one*) before **mil:**
   mil = one thousand/a thousand

Millón is preceded by **un** or a number and also adds **es** for the plural.
   un millón, dos millones
Before a noun, use **de** after **millones.**
   tres millones de personas

13 Practice counting.

   a. Count by ones from zero to 25.
   b. Count by **números pares** (even numbers) from zero to 50.
   c. Count by **números impares** (odd numbers) from zero to 50.
   d. Count by tens from zero to 100.
   e. Count by hundreds from 100 to 1,000.
   f. Create your own combinations.

14 Practice reading these numbers in Spanish.

a. 5	f. 20	k. 109	p. 764	u. 1,587,000
b. 9	g. 21	l. 115	q. 9,93	v. 3,456,321
c. 10	h. 24	m. 218	r. 1,518	w. 63,45
d. 15	i. 30	n. 500	s. 2,989	x. 92,887
e. 19	j. 38	o. 5,26	t. 5,462	

15 Dictate some big numbers to your partner, who will write them in numerical figures. Reverse roles. Practice saying them aloud.

   EJEMPLOS: mil cuatrocientos noventa y dos   1.492
               quince mil ciento veinte y cuatro   15.124

16 Write some addition and subtraction problems for your partner to solve in Spanish. Review the arithmetic functions presented on page 5.

17 Ask your partner for information that tells how many people there are in various groups.

   EJEMPLO: ¿Cuántos estudiantes hay en la escuela?
                How many students are there in the school?

                Hay mil ochocientos estudiantes en la escuela.
                There are eighteen hundred students in the school.

18 Ask your partner for information about quantities of things.

EJEMPLO: ¿Cuántas alcobas hay en tu casa?   *How many bedrooms are there in your house?*

Hay tres alcobas en mi casa.   *There are three bedrooms in my house.*

19 **Juego**   Draw or cut out newspaper or magazine pictures of some of the items of clothing presented on page 6 and things on pages 8 and 9. Write a price on the back. Other students try to guess the price. The student with the closest answer "wins" the item. Guide your class-mates by saying **caliente** *(warm)* when they're getting close and **frío** as their guesses stray from the right answer.

20 *Sit-Con*   You are a real estate agent trying to sell a house. Describe several houses and tell the price. If you have access to the houses-for-sale section of a newspaper, use it and "sell" some of the houses listed there. Don't forget the price!

EJEMPLO: tres alcobas, cocina grande. $132.599 (ciento treinta y dos
mil quinientos noventa y nueve dólares)
*three bedrooms, large kitchen. $132,599 (one hundred thirty-two thousand,
five hundred and ninety-nine dollars)*

ENCUENTRO PERSONAL

Paulina has to interview María Elena, an exchange student from Spain, for the school newspaper.

Hola, María Elena. ¿Qué tal?

Muy bien, Paulina.

¿De dónde eres *(Where are you from)*, María Elena?

Soy de Barcelona, una ciudad grande de la costa mediterránea de España. Es una ciudad industrial y es un puerto *(port)* importante y grande. Los Juegos Olímpicos de 1992 tuvieron lugar *(took place)* en mi ciudad. La lengua regional es el catalán. Se habla español también.

¿Comprendes?

1. What city is María Elena from?
2. Where is the city located?
3. Why is it an important city in Spain?
4. What languages do the people speak?
5. What things does María Elena like about the United States?
6. Why does she think Americans work so much?
7. What does she like to do for fun?

¡Te toca!

A. Practice the conversation with a partner.

B. Interview several classmates to find out where they are from and what they like to do for fun.

¡Así es!

The Spanish language

Like English, Spanish is not spoken exactly the same way wherever it is spoken. In the Spanish-speaking world, there are many regional variations in sound and vocabulary. Although the language is basically the same everywhere, there are differences. For example, in Spain, **z, ce,** and **ci** are pronounced with a *th* sound as in *thing*. Depending on the country, **ll** can sound like an English *j* or a *y*. Words can vary from one country to another also. In Spain, *potato* is **patata**, but in Latin America it is **papa**.

There are many regional languages also. **Catalán** (mentioned in the dialogue) is one of many regional languages in Spain, most of which are similar to Spanish. In the Western Hemisphere, native languages are still common, especially in Mexico, Guatemala, Peru, Bolivia, and Paraguay.

Pronunciación

More cognates

A Spanish adverb with the ending **mente** is equivalent to an English adverb ending in *ly*.

bravamente	diligentemente	inmediatamente	rápidamente
completamente	exactamente	naturalmente	raramente
cordialmente	finalmente	perfectamente	recientemente
correctamente	frecuentemente	probablemente	sinceramente

There are thousands of other cognates that have a slight spelling difference. Many of these have a predictable change from English to Spanish. For example *th* ⟶ **t**, *ph* ⟶ **f**, *ct* ⟶ **cc**, *s + consonant* ⟶ **es,** *double consonant* ⟶ *single consonant*. Here are some examples.

th ⟶ **t**	*ph* ⟶ **f**	*ct* ⟶ **cc**	*s* + consonant ⟶ **es**	double consonant ⟶ single consonant
tema	foto	acción	especial	oficial
Tomás	filosofía	ficción	estudiante	profesor
auténtico	gráfico	selección	estado	comercial

Diversión

Proverbs

1. Spanish speakers are very fond of proverbs: sayings that contain folk wisdom. Here are some that are similar to English proverbs.

   Más vale tarde que nunca.   Better late than never.
   Dónde una puerta se cierra   Where one door closes,
       otra se abre.   another opens.
   No es oro todo lo que reluce.   All that glitters is not gold.

2. Sometimes we have a saying in English that makes the same point but uses a different expression. Can you guess the English proverbs similar to these Spanish proverbs? The literal (word-for-word) translation is on the right. Answers are below.

   a. El ejercicio hace al maestro.   Exercise makes the master.
   b. Más vale un pájaro en mano que   A bird in the hand is worth a
       ciento volando.   hundred flying.
   c. Antes que te cases, mira   Before you marry, look at what
       lo que haces.   you are doing.
   d. En boca cerrada no entran moscas.   Flies don't enter a closed mouth.
   e. La gallina de la vecina siempre   The neighbor's chicken
       es más gorda que la mía.   is always fatter than mine.
   f. Más vale ser cabeza de ratón   It's better to be a mouse's head
       que cola de león.   than a lion's tail.
   g. Dime con quien andas y te diré   Tell me with whom you walk and
       quien eres.   I will tell you who you are.
   h. El que mucho abarca, poco aprieta.   He who grabs a lot, grasps little.
   i. Vísteme despacio que tengo prisa.   Dress me slowly because I'm in a hurry.

Answers

a. Practice makes perfect. b. A bird in the hand is worth two in the bush. c. Look before you leap. d. Silence is golden. e. The grass is always greener on the other side of the fence. f. It's better to be a big fish in a small pond than a small fish in a big pond. g. Birds of a feather flock together. h. Don't be greedy. i. Haste makes waste.

⟫ Unidad II ⟪

⇥Unidad II⇤
Tools

Vocabulario

La descripción física *Physical description*
(Lección 1)

fuerte	*strong*
débil	*weak*
grande	*large, big*
pequeño(a)	*small, little*
alto(a)	*tall*
bajo(a)	*short*
gordo(a)	*fat*
mediano(a)	*medium*
delgado(a)	*thin*
calvo(a)	*bald*
rubio(a)	*blond*
moreno(a)	*dark-haired, brunette*
canoso(a)	*gray-haired*
pelirrojo(a)	*redhead*
guapo(a)	*handsome, good-looking*
bonito(a)	*pretty*
feo(a)	*ugly*
viejo(a)	*old*
joven	*young*

Las expresiones de tiempo *Time expressions*
(Lección 1)

anteayer	*day before yesterday*	antes	*before*
ayer	*yesterday*	ahora	*now*
hoy	*today*	después	*after*
mañana	*tomorrow*	entonces	*then*
pasado mañana	*day after tomorrow*	luego	*then, later*
		un día	*one day*
en el pasado	*in the past*	por la mañana	*in the morning*
en el presente	*in the present*	por la tarde	*in the afternoon*
en el futuro	*in the future*	por la noche	*in the evening, at night*

Las expresiones de tiempo   *Time expressions (continued)*
(Lección 1)

siempre	*always*	una vez	*once*
frecuentemente	*often*	otra vez	*again*
mucho	*a lot, much*	(dos) veces	*(two) times*
poco	*a little, few*	de una vez	*all at once*
raramente	*rarely, seldom*	de vez en cuando	*from time to time*
nunca	*never*	algunas veces	*sometimes*
mientras	*while*		
de repente	*suddenly*	todavía	*still, yet*
de niño(a)	*as a child*	todavía no	*not yet*
de viejo(a)	*as an old person*	ya	*already*
a los… años	*at the age of . . .*	ya no	*no longer*
hace (seis meses)	*(six months) ago*		
en (seis meses)	*in (six months)*		
el año pasado	*last year*	el próximo año	*next year*
el mes pasado	*last month*	el próximo mes	*next month*
la semana pasada	*last week*	la próxima semana	*next week*
el (lunes)	*on (Monday)*	todas las semanas	*every week*
todos los (lunes)	*every (Monday)*	todos los meses	*every month*
todos los días	*every day*	todos los años	*every year*

La descripción de la personalidad   *Description of personality*
(Lección 2)

interesante	*interesting*	tímido(a)	*shy, timid*
aburrido(a)	*boring*	amistoso(a)	*friendly*
feliz	*happy*	popular	*popular*
alegre	*cheerful*	simpático(a)	*nice*
triste	*sad*	antipático(a)	*not nice*
egoísta	*selfish*	atlético(a)	*athletic*
generoso(a)	*generous*	amable	*courteous, kind*
sincero(a)	*sincere*	ambicioso(a)	*ambitious*
fantástico(a)	*great*	perezoso(a)	*lazy*
inteligente	*smart*	trabajador(a)	*hardworking*
listo(a)	*clever*	hablador(a)	*talkative*
tonto(a)	*foolish*	callado(a)	*quiet*

Las comparaciones   *Comparisons*
(Lección 2)

más… que	*more . . . than*
menos… que	*less . . . than*
tan… como	*as . . . as*

Los países y las nacionalidades   *Countries and nationalities*
(Lección 3)

PAÍS	NACIONALIDAD	PAÍS	NACIONALIDAD

Note: If no feminine form indicator appears, the same form is used for both masculine and feminine.

En Norteamérica

PAÍS	NACIONALIDAD
Canadá	canadiense
Estados Unidos (EE. UU.)	norteamericano(a), estadounidense
México	mexicano(a)

En Centroamérica

PAÍS	NACIONALIDAD	PAÍS	NACIONALIDAD
Guatemala	guatemalteco(a)	Costa Rica	costarricense
El Salvador	salvadoreño(a)	Panamá	panameño(a)
Honduras	hondureño(a)	Nicaragua	nicaragüense

En Sudamérica

PAÍS	NACIONALIDAD	PAÍS	NACIONALIDAD
Venezuela	venezolano(a)	Paraguay	paraguayo(a)
Colombia	colombiano(a)	Uruguay	uruguayo(a)
Ecuador	ecuatoriano(a)	Brasil	brasileño(a)
Perú	peruano(a)	Guayana Inglesa	guyanés(esa)
Bolivia	boliviano(a)	Guayana Francesa	guyanés(esa)
Chile	chileno(a)	Surinam	surinamita
Argentina	argentino(a)		

En el Caribe

PAÍS	NACIONALIDAD	PAÍS	NACIONALIDAD
Puerto Rico	puertorriqueño(a)	República Dominicana	dominicano(a)
Cuba	cubano(a)	Haití	haitiano(a)

En Europa

PAÍS	NACIONALIDAD	PAÍS	NACIONALIDAD
España *(Spain)*	español(a)	República Eslovaca *(Slovak Republic)*	eslovaco(a)
Portugal	portugués(esa)	Grecia *(Greece)*	griego(a)
Inglaterra *(England)*	inglés(esa)	Ucrania *(Ukraine)*	ucraniano(a)
Irlanda *(Ireland)*	irlandés(esa)	Holanda *(Holland)*	holandés(esa)
Escocia *(Scotland)*	escocés(esa)	Polonia *(Poland)*	polaco(a)
Francia *(France)*	francés(esa)	Bulgaria	búlgaro(a)
Alemania *(Germany)*	alemán(ana)	Bélgica *(Belgium)*	belga
Italia *(Italy)*	italiano(a)	Dinamarca *(Denmark)*	danés(esa)
Suiza *(Switzerland)*	suizo(a)	Suecia *(Sweden)*	sueco(a)
Austria	austríaco(a)	Noruega *(Norway)*	noruego(a)
Hungría *(Hungary)*	húngaro(a)	Rumania *(Romania)*	rumano(a)
Finlandia *(Finland)*	finlandés(esa)	Turquía *(Turkey)*	turco(a)
República Checa *(Czech Republic)*	checoslovaco(a)	Rusia *(Russia)*	ruso(a)

Los países y las nacionalidades   *Countries and nationalities* (continued)
(Lección 3)

PAÍS	NACIONALIDAD	PAÍS	NACIONALIDAD
En el Medio Oriente			
Irán	iranio(a)	Israel	israelí
Irak *(Iraq)*	iraquíes(esa)	Arabia Saudita	saudito (a)
Siria *(Syria)*	sirio(a)	*(Saudi Arabia)*	
Arabia	árabe	Jordania *(Jordan)*	jordano(a)
Líbano *(Lebanon)*	libanés(esa)		
En Asia			
China	chino(a)	Camboya *(Cambodia)*	camboyano(a)
Japón *(Japan)*	japonés(esa)	Tailandia *(Thailand)*	tailandés(esa)
Corea *(Korea)*	coreano(a)	Afganistán	afgano(a)
Vietnam	vietnamita	Pakistán	pakistaní
		India	indio(a)
En África			
África	africano(a)	Ghana	ghanés(esa)
Marruecos *(Morocco)*	marroquí	Kenya	kenyano(a)
Argelia *(Algeria)*	argelino(a)	Zaire	zaireño(a)
Túnez *(Tunisia)*	tunecino(a)	Nigeria	nigeriano(a)
Egipto *(Egypt)*	egipcio(a)	Liberia	liberiano(a)
Libia *(Libya)*	libio(a)	Etiopía *(Ethiopia)*	etíope
África del Sur	sudafricano(a)	Costa de Marfil	
(South Africa)		*(Ivory Coast)*	

Otras áreas geográficas

Indonesia	indonesio(a)
Australia	australiano(a)
Nueva Zelanda	neozelandés(esa)
Las Filipinas	filipino(a)

Las palabras interrogativas   *Question words*
(Lección 3)

¿Cómo?	*How? What?*	¿Cuándo?	*When?*
¿Dónde?	*Where?*	¿Por qué?	*Why?*
¿Adónde?	*To where?*	¿Cuánto(a)?	*How much?*
¿Quién(es)?	*Who?*	¿Cuántos(as)?	*How many?*
¿Qué?	*What?*	¿Cuál(es)?	*Which?*

Los miembros de la familia *Family members*
(Lección 4)

These words pertaining to family members were introduced in Unit I, Lesson 3.

el abuelo	*grandfather*	el tío	*uncle*
la abuela	*grandmother*	la tía	*aunt*
el padre	*father*	el primo	*cousin [m.]*
la madre	*mother*	la prima	*cousin [f.]*
el hermano	*brother*	el esposo	*husband*
la hermana	*sister*	la esposa	*wife*
el hijo	*son*	el padrastro	*stepfather*
la hija	*daughter*	la madrastra	*stepmother*
el nieto	*grandson*	el hermanastro	*stepbrother*
la nieta	*granddaughter*	la hermanastra	*stepsister*

The following is additional vocabulary pertaining to family members.

el gemelo	*twin brother*	la nuera	*daughter-in-law*
la gemela	*twin sister*	el padrino	*godfather*
el sobrino	*nephew*	la madrina	*godmother*
la sobrina	*niece*	el ahijado	*godson*
el cuñado	*brother-in-law*	la ahijada	*goddaughter*
la cuñada	*sister-in-law*	el hermano mayor	*older brother*
el suegro	*father-in-law*	la hermana mayor	*older sister*
la suegra	*mother-in-law*	el hermano menor	*younger brother*
el yerno	*son-in-law*	la hermana menor	*younger sister*

Los adjetivos posesivos *Possessive adjectives*
(Lecciones 4, 6)

mi(s)	*my*	nuestro(a)(os)(as)	*our*
tu(s)	*your*	vuestro(a)(os)(as)	*your [in Spain]*
su(s)	*your*	su(s)	*your*
su(s)	*his, her, its*	su(s)	*their*

Las profesiones *Occupations*
(Lección 5)

el/la ingeniero(a)	*engineer*	el/la contador(a)	*accountant*
el/la mecánico(a)	*mechanic*	el/la periodista	*journalist*
el/la secretario(a)	*secretary*	el/la dentista	*dentist*
el/la obrero(a)	*laborer, worker*	el/la músico(a)	*musician*
el/la estudiante	*student*	el actor	*actor*
el/la policía	*police officer*	la actriz	*actress*
el/la gerente	*manager*	el hombre de negocios	*businessman*
el/la médico(a)	*doctor*	la mujer de negocios	*businesswoman*

Las profesiones   *Occupations* (continued)
(Lección 5)

el/la mesero(a)	*waiter, waitress*	el/la banquero(a)	*banker*
el/la profesor(a)	*teacher*	el/la enfermero(a)	*nurse*
el ama de casa	*homemaker*	el/la arquitecto(a)	*architect*
el/la abogado(a)	*lawyer*	el/la farmacista	*pharmacist*
el/la agricultor(a)	*farmer*	el/la artista	*artist*
el/la dependiente(a)	*salesperson*	el/la agente	*agent*
el/la bombero(a)	*firefighter*	el/la criado(a)	*servant, housekeeper*

La existencia   *Existence*
(Lección 6)

había	*there was, there were*
hay	*there is, there are*
habrá	*there will be*

Las cosas en el aula   *Classroom objects*
(Lección 6)

These vocabulary items related to classroom objects were presented in Unit I, Lesson 8.

la pizarra	*chalkboard*	la cartera	*briefcase*
la tiza	*chalk*	la mochila	*backpack*
el borrador	*eraser*	la papelera	*wastepaper basket*
el estante	*bookshelf*	la computadora	*computer*
el reloj	*clock*	la calculadora	*calculator*
el armario	*locker, closet*	la grabadora	*tape recorder*
la bandera	*flag*	la cinta	*tape*
el globo	*globe*	el cuaderno	*notebook*
el mapa	*map*	el papel	*paper*
el libro	*book*	el lápiz	*pencil*
el archivador	*file cabinet*	el bolígrafo	*ballpoint pen*
el escritorio	*teacher's desk*	la goma	*pencil eraser*
el pupitre	*student desk*	la silla	*chair*
el diccionario	*dictionary*	la mesa	*table*

The following is additional vocabulary pertaining to classroom objects.

el calendario	*calendar*	el tablero de anuncios	*bulletin board*
el retroproyector	*overhead projector*	la videocasetera	*videocassette recorder*
el casete	*cassette*	las tijeras	*scissors*
el cuadro	*picture*	la regla	*ruler*
el sacapuntas	*pencil sharpener*		

Los colores   *Colors*
(Lección 6)

The following colors were presented in Unit I, Lesson 7.

rojo(a)	*red*	negro(a)	*black*
amarillo(a)	*yellow*	blanco(a)	*white*
azul	*blue*	gris	*gray*
anaranjado(a)	*orange*	pardo(a)	*brown*
verde	*green*	rosado(a)	*pink*
		morado(a)	*purple*
... oscuro(a)	*dark*		
... claro(a)	*light*		

Here are additional colors to add to those you have already learned.

dorado(a)	*gold*	plateado(a)	*silver*
turquesa	*turquoise*	violeta	*violet*
crema	*tan*	marrón	*brown*

Las formas y los tamaños   *Shapes and sizes*
(Lección 6)

These vocabulary items were presented in Unit I, Lesson 7.

grande	*big*	alto(a)	*high, tall*
pequeño(a)	*small*	bajo(a)	*low, short (in height)*
mediano(a)	*medium*	largo(a)	*long*
ancho(a)	*wide*	corto(a)	*short (in length)*
estrecho(a)	*narrow*	plano(a)	*flat*
cuadrado(a)	*square*	redondo(a)	*round*
circular	*circular*		

Otras cualidades de las cosas   *Other qualities of things*
(Lección 6)

duro(a)	*hard*	viejo(a)	*old*
blando(a)	*soft*	caro(a)	*expensive*
pesado(a)	*heavy*	barato(a)	*inexpensive*
ligero(a)	*lightweight*	triangular	*triangular*
nuevo(a)	*new*	rectangular	*rectangular*

Estructura

Subject pronouns
(Lección 1)

yo	*I*	nosotros/nosotras	*we*
tú	*you*	vosotros/vosotras	*you*
Ud.	*you*	Uds.	*you*
él	*he*	ellos	*they*
ella	*she*	ellas	*they*

The verb ser *(to be)*
(Lección 1)

	was/were used to be	*am/is/are*	*will be*
yo	era	soy	seré
tú	eras	eres	serás
Ud./él/ella	era	es	será
nosotros(as)	éramos	somos	seremos
vosotros(as)	erais	sois	seréis
Uds./ellos/ellas	eran	son	serán

Negative sentences
(Lección 1)

NO + verb

Yes/no questions
(Lección 2)

¿ SUBJECT + VERB ?
SUBJECT + VERB + ¿VERDAD / NO?
¿ VERB + SUBJECT ?

Information questions
(Lección 3)

¿ QUESTION WORD + VERB + SUBJECT ?

Gender of nouns
(Lección 4)

$$
\left.\begin{array}{l}
\ldots o \\
\ldots l \\
\ldots r
\end{array}\right\} = \text{masculine}
\qquad
\left.\begin{array}{l}
\ldots a \\
\ldots d \\
\ldots i\acute{o}n
\end{array}\right\} = \text{feminine}
$$

Plural of nouns
(Lección 5)

VOWEL + S
CONSONANT + ES
Z = C + ES

Articles
(Lecciones 4, 6)

	DEFINITE *the*		**INDEFINITE** *a/an/some*	
	SINGULAR	PLURAL	SINGULAR	PLURAL
MASCULINE	el	los	un	unos
FEMININE	la	las	una	unas

Descriptive adjective agreement
(Lecciones 1, 3, 5)

	SINGULAR	PLURAL	SINGULAR	PLURAL	SINGULAR	PLURAL
MASCULINE	O	OS	E	ES	(consonant)	+ ES
FEMININE	A	AS	E	ES	(consonant)	+ ES

Possessive adjectives
(Lecciones 4, 6)

mi(s)	*my*	nuestro(a)(as)(os)	*our*
tu(s)	*your*	vuestro(a)(as)(os)	*your*
su(s)	*your, his, her*	su(s)	*your, their*

Clarification of su/sus
(Lecciones 4, 6)

el/la/los/las + NOUN + de Ud./de Uds.
de él/de ellos
de ella/de ellas

Placement of adjectives
(Lección 6)

NUMBER	noun
QUANTITY	noun
POSSESSION	noun
ARTICLE	noun
	noun DESCRIPTION

Comparisons
(Lecciones 1, 2)

más… que	*more . . . than*
menos… que	*less . . . than*
tan… como	*as . . . as*

Superlatives
(Lección 6)

el/la/los/las + $\dfrac{\text{más }(most)}{\text{menos }(least)}$ + *(adjective)* + de *(of/in)*

Esqueletos

*time expression + (pro)noun + **SER** + adjective*

(Lección 1)

A los dos años yo era pequeño.   *At two years of age, I was small. [past]*
Ahora yo soy grande.   *Now I am big. [present]*
A los cincuenta años yo seré calvo.   *At the age of fifty, I will be bald. [future]*

*(pro)noun + **NO** + **SER** + adjective*

(Lección 1)

Yo no soy alta.   *I am not tall.*
Yo no era fuerte.   *I was not strong.*
Yo no seré delgada.   *I will not be thin.*

MÁS
(pro)noun + **SER** + **MENOS** + *adjective*
TAN

(Lección 1)

Yo soy más grande.   *I am taller.*
Yo soy más popular.   *I am more popular.*
Yo soy menos débil.   *I am less weak.*
Yo soy tan inteligente.   *I am as smart.*

¿ *(pro)noun* + **SER** + *adjective* **?**

(Lección 2)

¿Yo soy inteligente?   *Am I smart?*
¿Tú eres sincero?   *Are you sincere?*

(pro)noun + **SER** + *adjective*, +   **¿NO?**
                                          ¿VERDAD?

(Lección 2)

Yo soy inteligente, ¿no?   *I'm smart, right?*
Tú eres sincero, ¿verdad?   *You are sincere, aren't you?*

¿ SER + *(pro)noun* + *adjective* **?**

(Lección 2)

¿Soy yo inteligente?   *Am I smart?*
¿Eres tú sincero?   *Are you sincere?*

MÁS   **QUE**
(pro)noun + **SER** + **MENOS** + *adjective* + **QUE** + *(pro)noun*
TAN   **COMO**

(Lección 2)

Yo soy más popular que tú.   *I am more popular than you.*
Tú eres menos tímido que María.   *You are less timid than María.*
Tú eres tan alto como yo.   *You are as tall as I.*

¿ *(preposition)* + *question word* + *verb* + *(pro)noun* **?**

(Lección 3)

¿Cómo es Ud.?   *What are you like?*
¿De dónde es Ud.?   *Where are you from?*
¿Quiénes son los profesores?   *Who are the teachers?*
¿Para quién es el regalo?   *Who is the gift for?*

(pro)noun + SER + *noun*

(Lección 4)

Ella es mi hermana.   *She is my sister.*
La mujer es la abuela.   *The woman is the grandmother.*
Roberto es mi padre.   *Roberto is my father.*

(pro)noun + SER + *adjective*

(Lección 4)

Mi hermano es simpático.   *My brother is nice.*
Ella es baja.   *She is short.*
Roberto es inteligente.   *Roberto is intelligent.*

¿ DE DÓNDE + SER + (pro)noun ?

(Lección 4)

¿De dónde es tu madre?   *Where is your mother from?*
¿De dónde eres tú?   *Where are you from?*

(pro)noun + SER + DE + *place*

(Lección 4)

Mi madre es de Texas.   *My mother is from Texas.*
Él es de California.   *He is from California.*

(pro)noun + SER + *noun* + DE + *person*

(Lección 4)

Juan García es el hermano de mi padre.
Juan García is the brother of my father.
Juan García is my father's brother.

(pro)noun + SER + *occupation*

(Lección 5)

Mi abuelo es abogado.   *My grandfather is a lawyer.*
Mi tía es médica.   *My aunt is a doctor.*

(pro)noun + SER + UN / UNA + *occupation* + *adjective*

(Lección 5)

Mi abuelo es un abogado famoso.   *My grandfather is a famous lawyer.*
Mi tía es una médica buena.   *My aunt is a good doctor.*

$$\text{¿QUÉ} + \text{HAY?} \begin{array}{l}\text{HABÍA?}\\\text{HAY?}\\\text{HABRÁ?}\end{array}$$

HABÍA?
¿QUÉ + HAY?
HABRÁ?

(Lección 6)

¿Qué había en la papelera?   *What was there in the wastepaper basket?*
¿Qué hay en el aula?   *What is there in the classroom?*
¿Qué habrá en la mochila?   *What will there be in the backpack?*

¿ CUÁNTO(A)
¿ CUÁNTOS(AS)   + *noun(s)* +   HABÍA?
HAY?
HABRÁ?

(Lección 6)

¿Cuántas banderas había?   *How many flags were there?*
¿Cuánta leche hay?   *How much milk is there?*
¿Cuántos hombres habrá?   *How many men will there be?*

HABÍA
HAY   + *number* + *noun(s)*
HABRÁ

(Lección 6)

Había tres libros.   *There were three books.*
Hay una bandera.   *There is one flag.*
Habrá seis flores.   *There will be six flowers.*

(pro)noun + SER + EL/LOS + MÁS + *adjective* + DE + *noun*
LA/LAS   MENOS

(Lección 6)

La mochila de Miguel es la más cara de toda la clase.
Miguel's backpack is the most expensive in the whole class.

El libro de español es el menos aburrido de todos mis libros.
The Spanish book is the least boring of all my books.

¿Cómo soy yo?
What do I look like?

In this lesson we will focus on using the **yo** forms of the verb **ser** in order to describe ourselves—as we were, are, and will be.

SER *to be*

Here are the past, present, and future forms of the verb **ser**.

	was/were used to be	*am/is/are*	*will be*
yo	era	soy	seré
tú	eras	eres	serás
Ud./él/ella	era	es	será
nosotros(as)	éramos	somos	seremos
vosotros(as)	erais	sois	seréis
Uds./ellos/ellas	eran	son	serán

Note: **Vosotros** is used in Spain when talking to a group of friends.
Note also that the use of subject pronouns (**yo, tú, Ud.,** etc.) is optional; they are used for emphasis or clarification.

Vocabulario

La descripción física   *Physical description*

1. fuerte	*strong*	11. rubio(a)	*blond*
2. débil	*weak*	12. moreno(a)	*dark-haired, brunette*
3. grande	*large, big*	13. canoso(a)	*gray-haired*
4. pequeño(a)	*small, little*	14. pelirrojo(a)	*redhead*
5. alto(a)	*tall*	15. guapo(a)	*handsome, good-looking*
6. bajo(a)	*short*	16. bonito(a)	*pretty*
7. gordo(a)	*fat*	17. feo(a)	*ugly*
8. mediano(a)	*medium*	18. viejo(a)	*old*
9. delgado(a)	*thin*	19. joven	*young*
10. calvo(a)	*bald*	20. lindo(a)	cute

Conversación

Describing one's appearance

A los dos años yo era pequeño.	*At two years of age, I was small.*
Ahora yo soy grande.	*Now I am big,*
A los ochenta años yo seré viejo.	*At the age of eighty, I will be old.*

MASCULINE AND FEMININE FORMS OF DESCRIBING WORDS (ADJECTIVES)

Why are there two forms for many adjectives?

Did you notice that when the masculine form of the adjective ends in **o**, the feminine form ends in **a**? So, when talking about yourself, if you are a male, use the masculine forms, and if you are a female, use the feminine forms.

Vocabulario

Las expresiones de tiempo   *Time expressions*

Here are some time expressions to use in describing yourself.

anteayer	*day before yesterday*	antes	*before*
ayer	*yesterday*	ahora	*now*
hoy	*today*	después	*after*
mañana	*tomorrow*	entonces	*then*
pasado mañana	*day after tomorrow*	luego	*then, later*
		un día	*one day*

en el pasado	*in the past*	por la mañana	*in the morning*
en el presente	*in the present*	por la tarde	*in the afternoon*
en el futuro	*in the future*	por la noche	*in the evening, at night*

siempre	*always*	una vez	*once*
frecuentemente	*often*	otra vez	*again*
mucho	*a lot, much*	(dos) veces	*(two) times*
poco	*a little, few*	de una vez	*all at once*
raramente	*rarely, seldom*	de vez en cuando	*from time to time*
nunca	*never*	algunas veces	*sometimes*

mientras	*while*		
de repente	*suddenly*	todavía	*still, yet*
de niño(a)	*as a child*	todavía no	*not yet*
de viejo(a)	*as an old person*	ya	*already*
a los… años	*at the age of . . .*	ya no	*no longer*

hace (seis meses)	*(six months) ago*
en (seis meses)	*in (six months)*

el año pasado	*last year*	el próximo año	*next year*
el mes pasado	*last month*	el próximo mes	*next month*
la semana pasada	*last week*	la próxima semana	*next week*

el (lunes)	*on (Monday)*
todos los (lunes)	*every (Monday)*
todos los días	*every day*
todas las semanas	*every week*
todos los meses	*every month*
todos los años	*every year*

Esqueleto

· The **esqueletos** in this book will give you a framework that you can use over and over by substituting different words to build new sentences. Here is the first one.

time expression + (pro)noun + SER + adjective

A los dos años yo era pequeño.   *At two years of age, I was small. [past]*
Ahora yo soy grande.   *Now I am big. [present]*
A los cincuenta años yo seré calvo.   *At the age of fifty, I will be bald. [future]*

1 Make up your own sentences using the **esqueleto** on page 143. Remember to use the correct verb form to correspond to the time you're talking about.

EJEMPLOS: En el pasado yo era pequeño.   *In the past I was small.*
　　　　　　En el presente yo soy fuerte.   *In the present I am strong.*
　　　　　　En el futuro yo seré débil.   *In the future I will be weak.*

2 *Sit-Con*   Pretend that you are meeting a blind date at a restaurant. Describe yourself so your date will know who you are.

EJEMPLO: Yo soy alto(a), moreno(a) y guapo(a).   *I am tall, dark, and good-looking.*

3 *Sit-Con*   Suppose you met your third grade teacher now. He or she still looks much the same, but you have changed. To help your teacher remember you, describe yourself as you looked in third grade.

EJEMPLO: A los ocho años yo era bajo y rubio. Yo era delgado y débil.
　　　　　　At the age of eight, I was short and blond. I was thin and weak.

4 *Sit-Con*   Imagine that you travel to the future in a time machine and see yourself twenty years from now. Describe what you will be like.

EJEMPLO: En veinte años yo seré…   *In twenty years, I will be . . .*

MAKING A SENTENCE NEGATIVE

To say you are *not* something, put **no** before the verb.

Esqueleto

(pro)noun + NO + SER + adjective

Yo no soy alta.   *I am not tall.*
Yo no era fuerte.   *I was not strong.*
Yo no seré delgada.   *I will not be thin.*

5 *What I'm not* . . . Describe yourself by telling what you are not and follow up by saying what you are.

EJEMPLO: Yo no soy alta. Yo soy baja.   *I'm not tall. I'm short.*

6 Compare the way you looked at the age of ten with your present appearance.

EJEMPLO: A los diez años, no era alto; ahora soy alto.
At the age of ten, I wasn't tall; now I am tall.

A los diez años, era rubio; ahora no soy rubio.
At the age of ten, I was blond; now I'm not blond.

7 Compare the way you look now with the way you think you will look when you are seventy.

EJEMPLO: Ahora soy morena. A los setenta años, no seré morena. Seré canosa.
Now I'm dark-haired. At the age of seventy, I won't be dark-haired.
   I will be gray-haired.

Ahora no soy gorda. A los setenta años seré gorda.
Now I'm not fat. At the age of seventy, I will be fat.

COMPARING: *SO/AS*, *MORE*, OR *LESS*

To say you are *so/as*, more, or *less* something, put **tan** *(so)*, **más** *(more)*, or **menos** *(less)* in front of the adjective. Note that English sometimes uses the ending *er* to mean *more*.

más fuerte = stronger

Esqueleto

	MÁS	
	(pro)noun + SER + MENOS + *adjective*	
	TAN	

Yo soy más grande.   *I am taller.*
Yo soy más popular.   *I am more popular.*
Yo soy menos débil.   *I am less weak.*
Yo soy tan inteligente.   *I am as smart.*

8 **Juego:** *"One-up"*   Whenever your partner makes a statement about herself or himself, explain that you were the same, but more.

EJEMPLO: A los dos años, yo era pequeño.   *At the age of two, I was small.*

Yo era más pequeño.   *I was smaller.*

9 You have been given the power to change some of your characteristics. What will you be like?

EJEMPLO: Seré más alta. Seré menos gorda. Seré más fuerte.
I will be taller. I will be less fat. I will be stronger.

ENCUENTRO PERSONAL

Pablo, a student from Venezuela, is coming to Paulina's school. Since he doesn't speak English very well, the school principal has asked Paulina to call Pablo and arrange to show him around the school. Here is their telephone conversation. Since they have never met, how do you think they will recognize each other?

¿Comprendes?

1. What does Paulina look like?
2. What does Pablo look like?
3. Who is older? When are their birthdays?
4. What will Paulina be wearing when they meet?
5. What will Pablo be wearing?
6. What day of the week will they meet?

¡Te toca!

Pretend you are going to meet someone in your class for the first time. Create a telephone conversation like Pablo and Paulina's.

Leemos y contamos   *We read and we tell*

A. **¿Quién soy yo?** Read the following descriptions and match them to the pictures of Jaime, Paulina, and Rosita.

1. Yo soy rubia, baja y un poco gorda. Me gusta comer chocolate. No me gustan los deportes, pero me gusta bailar y mirar la televisión.

2. Yo soy alto, moreno y delgado. Tengo una computadora y me gusta escribir cartas en la computadora. Soy muy inteligente.

3. Yo soy morena, mediana, con los ojos negros y el pelo muy largo. Me gusta nadar. Me gustan los animales. Tengo un perro pequeño. Me gusta jugar con mi perro.

B. Write a four-sentence description of yourself similar to the descriptions above.

C. You have just received a radio communication from another planet. The extraterrestrial described himself to you. Can you picture him in your mind?

> Yo soy grande y cuadrado. Tengo un cuello muy, muy largo. Tengo una cabeza circular con cuatro ojos azules y tres orejas largas. No tengo piernas, pero tengo tres pies. Tengo cinco manos con cuatro dedos cortos. Tengo un estómago redondo como *(like)* un disco y una boca pequeña con doce dientes.

1. What shape is he?
2. What does his head look like? His neck?
3. How many arms does he have? How many legs?
4. What are his hands like?
5. What does his stomach resemble?

D. Draw a picture of what you imagine the extraterrestrial looks like based on the information you have received.

E. **Juego:** *If things could talk!* Choose an object in the classroom. Pretend to be that object and describe "yourself" without naming the object. See if your classmates can guess what you are.

EJEMPLO: Yo soy baja y circular. No soy grande. Soy gris. ¿Qué soy yo?
I am short and round. I am not big. I am gray. What am I?
[Respuesta: la papelera]   *[Answer: the wastepaper basket]*

F. **Amigos por correspondencia** *Pen pals*   Here are two letters from foreign students who want a pen pal. Read their descriptions of themselves.

¡Hola, amigo!

Me llamo Andrés Sobejano. Soy de San Juan, la capital de Puerto Rico. Soy mediano, moreno y muy atlético. Me gusta jugar al béisbol, al fútbol y al tenis. Tengo diecisiete años y mi cumpleaños es el dos de diciembre. Mi familia es muy grande. Tengo dos hermanos y tres hermanas. A los diez años yo era delgado y débil pero ahora soy menos delgado y más fuerte. A los diecinueve años yo seré muy fuerte y guapo.

Hasta la vista,
Andrés

Buenos días, amigos y amigas,

Me llamo Marisol Castro y soy de México. Me gusta estudiar, bailar y hablar por teléfono con mis amigas. Tengo los ojos verdes y el pelo corto. A los cinco años yo era baja y gorda. Ahora tengo quince años y soy alta y delgada. A los dieciocho años yo seré más alta que ahora y más bonita.

Adiós,
Tu amiga Marisol

G. Now write an answer to one of the pen pals above, telling your name, what you looked like before, what you are like now, and how you will be in the future. You may also want to mention what you like to do.

Así es

Telephones

In the larger cities of Latin America, most middle-class families have a telephone. But telephone service is very expensive, and the waiting list to receive service is often long. In the rural areas telephones are not as common. Even when there is a telephone in the home, people do not always have long-distance service. They may have to go to the drugstore, the telephone company, or some other location to place the call through an operator. Push-button telephones with their many options are practically unknown in many areas, and credit card calls are not always available. Many Hispanics are surprised to learn that households in the United States often have two or more telephones. How would you get along without a telephone in your house?

¿Cómo eres?
What are you like?

In this lesson you will learn to tell a close friend, family member, or child what you think about her or him and to ask questions using the verb **ser**.

Vocabulario

La descripción de la personalidad *Description of personality*

1. interesante	*interesting*	7. generoso(a)	*generous*
2. aburrido(a)	*boring*	8. sincero(a)	*sincere*
3. feliz	*happy*	9. fantástico(a)	*great*
4. alegre	*cheerful*	10. inteligente	*smart*
5. triste	*sad*	11. listo(a)	*clever*
6. egoísta*	*selfish*	12. tonto(a)	*foolish*

*Note: Words that end in **ista** are the same for masculine and feminine forms.
Words ending in **or** become **ora.**

13. tímido(a)	*shy, timid*	19. amable	*courteous, kind*
14. amistoso(a)	*friendly*	20. ambicioso(a)	*ambitious*
15. popular	*popular*	21. perezoso(a)	*lazy*
16. simpático(a)	*nice*	22. trabajador(a)*	*hardworking*
17. antipático(a)	*not nice*	23. hablador(a)*	*talkative*
18. atlético(a)	*athletic*	24. callado(a)	*quiet*

THE USE OF TÚ

When speakers of Spanish want to say *you* to another person in an informal situation, they use **tú**. Some examples of these situations are when talking to a friend, classmate, family member, child, or anyone else you would call by his or her first name.

As with **yo**, you may omit **tú** because the verb includes the meaning of **tú**. However, you may use **tú** to emphasize to whom you are talking.

Conversación

Describing one's personality

En el pasado tú eras interesante.	*In the past, you were interesting.*
Ahora tú eres listo.	*Now you are clever.*
En cincuenta años tú serás feliz.	*In fifty years, you will be happy.*
En el futuro, ¡tú serás fantástico!	*In the future, you will be great!*
¿Eras/eres/serás tú *[adjective]*?	*Were you/are you/will you be [adjective]?*
Sí, yo era/soy/seré *[adjective]*.	*Yes, I was/I am/I will be [adjective].*
No, yo no era/soy/seré *[adjective]*.	*No, I wasn't/I'm not/I won't be [adjective].*

1 Tell at least ten things about your classmate's personality using this **esqueleto** from Lesson 1.

    *time expression + (pro)noun + **SER** + adjective*

Use vocabulary from Lessons 1 and 2. Be careful to use the correct form of the adjective: Males use the masculine form, females use the feminine form. Help your partner by keeping track of the number of sentences he or she creates.

EJEMPLO: En el pasado tú eras pequeño.   *In the past, you were small.*
Ahora tú eres grande.   *Now you are big.*
En el futuro tú serás viejo.   *In the future, you will be old.*
En el futuro tú no serás aburrido.   *In the future, you will not be boring.*

2 Take turns telling your partner what you think he or she is like right now. Your partner will verify your opinion.

EJEMPLO: Tú eres popular.   *You are popular.*

  Sí, soy popular. / No, yo no soy popular.   *Yes I am popular. / No, I am not popular.*

FORMING *YES/NO* QUESTIONS

In Spanish there are three ways to form questions that can be answered by **sí** or **no**.

A. Raise the pitch of your voice at the end when speaking, or put questions marks before and after the sentence when writing.

    Statement: Tú eres atlético   *You are athletic.*
    Question: ¿Tú eres atlético?   *Are you athletic?*

B. Add **¿no?** or **¿verdad?** (*right?* or *aren't you?*, etc.).

    Tú eres atlético, ¿no?   *You are athletic, right?*
    Yo soy popular, ¿verdad?   *I'm popular, aren't I?*

C. Put the subject after the verb. This is very common in Spanish.

    ¿Eres tú atlético?   *Are you athletic?*

Voleibol

    (VOL) El Voleibol es un deporte de equipo consistente de seis jugadores respectivamente. El objetivo del juego es que cada equipo envíe el balón sobre la red o malla al campo de juego del equipo contrario con la intención de que el balón haga contacto en dicho campo de juego.

    Un equipo ganará un set cuando anote quince puntos con una ventaja de dos puntos sobre el equipo contrario y ganará un partido aquel equipo que gane tres de cinco sets.

Esqueletos

¿(pro)noun + SER + adjective?

¿Yo soy inteligente?   Am I smart?
¿Tú eres sincero?   *Are you sincere?*

(pro)noun + SER + adjective, +	**¿ NO ?** **¿VERDAD?**

Yo soy inteligente, ¿no?   *I'm smart, right?*
Tú eres sincero, ¿verdad?   *You are sincere, aren't you?*

¿ SER + (pro)noun + adjective?

¿Soy yo inteligente?   *Am I smart?*
¿Eres tú sincero?   *Are you sincere?*

3 Ask your partner what he or she was like as a child, is like now, and will be like when older. Your partner answers.

EJEMPLO: De niño, ¿eras atlético?   *As a child, were you athletic?*

No, no era atlético.   *No, I wasn't athletic.*

4 *Sit-Con* Your friend has set you up with a blind date for a party. You are talking on the phone to find out something about each other before the party.

EJEMPLO: ¿Eres alto o mediano?
Are you tall or average?

Soy mediano.
I'm medium.

¿Eres hablador?
Are you talkative?

No, no soy hablador. Soy callado.
No, I'm not talkative. I'm quiet.

5 **Juego: ¡No es verdad!** *That's not true.*   Make statements about yourself that are obviously untrue. Your partner makes corrections.

EJEMPLO: Soy muy bajo.
I'm very short.

   ¡No es verdad! No eres bajo. Eres muy alto.
That's not true. You are not short. You are very tall.

Now make false statements about your partner. Your partner will correct you.

EJEMPLO: Eres rubio.   *You are blond.*

   ¡No es verdad! Soy moreno.   *That's not true. I'm dark-haired.*

MAKING COMPARISONS

We can compare two people or things to show that one is more . . . than, less. . . than, or equal to *(as . . . as),* another person or thing. In Spanish, we use **mas... que** to say that something is *more . . . than,* **menos... que** to say that something is *less . . . than,* and **tan... como** to say *as . . . as.*

Esqueleto

		MÁS	+ QUE	
(pro)noun + SER +	MENOS +	*adjective* +	QUE +	*(pro)noun*
		TAN	+ COMO	

Yo soy más popular que tú.   *I am more popular than you.*
Tú eres menos tímido que María.   *You are less timid than María.*
Tú eres tan alto como yo.   *You are as tall as I.*

6 How do you compare? Tell what you are like and then make a comparison with your partner. Use the correct ending on each adjective.

EJEMPLOS: Soy inteligente, pero tú eres más inteligente que yo.
I'm intelligent, but you are more intelligent than I.

Soy ambicioso, pero tú eres menos ambicioso que yo.
I am ambitious, but you are less ambitious than I.

7 Make comparisons between your partner and other classmates.

EJEMPLOS: Eres menos alto que María.   *You're not as tall as María.*
Eres tan inteligente como Juan.   *You are as smart as Juan.*
Eres más simpático que Esteban.   *You are nicer than Esteban.*

8 **Hace diez años eras...** Tell your partner what you think he or she was like ten years ago. Your partner will tell you if you are correct.

EJEMPLO: Hace diez años eras más callado que ahora.
Ten years ago, you were quieter than now.

Tienes razón. Yo era más callado que ahora.
You're right. I was quieter than now.

No tienes razón. Yo era tan callado como ahora.
You're not right. I was as quiet as now.

ENCUENTRO PERSONAL

Pablo just found out that his friend Paulina set him up with a blind date with Inés for the homecoming football game. He asked Paulina for Inés's phone number so that he could call her and ask a few questions to see if she is his type. Do you think he will like her?

¿Comprendes?

1. How would you describe Inés? And Pablo?
2. Are they similar or different in personality?
3. Do they like the same kinds of activities?
4. Do you think they will get along well together? Why?
5. When are they getting together for their blind date?
6. Where are they planning to go next time? Do you think it's a good idea?

¡Te toca!

Tell various classmates what you think their personality traits are. If they disagree with your opinion, let them describe themselves.

Leemos y contamos

As you read the following letters, make a chart of the characteristics of each of the people. Use this as your pattern.

¿QUIÉN?	¿CUÁNDO?		
	ANTES	AHORA	EN EL FUTURO
Paulina			
Jaime	triste		
Rosita		triste, inteligente	
Raúl			enemigo
Mamá de Jaime			

A. Jaime is in love with Paulina and wrote her the following note.

Mi querida (Dear) *Paulina,*

Te quiero (I love you) *porque* (because) *eres una amiga sincera. Me gusta tu pelo negro, me gustan tus ojos negros, me gustan tu nariz pequeña y tus piernas largas. (No me gusta tu boca grande pero me gustan tus dientes bonitos.) Yo era una persona triste pero ahora soy un muchacho alegre porque te quiero. Yo era egoísta pero seré más generoso en el futuro.*

A los diez y ocho años, tú serás la muchacha más bonita del mundo (in the world) *y por eso* (for that reason) *te quiero.*

Cariñosamente   (Affectionately),
Jaime

1. Why does Jaime love Paulina?
2. What does Paulina look like?
3. What was Jaime like before he met Paulina?
4. What will Paulina be like when she is eighteen?

B. Rosita, Paulina's best friend, lost the homecoming queen contest and feels awful about it. Jaime wrote a note of encouragement to her.

Querida Rosita,

¿Cómo estás? ¿Triste? ¡Qué lástima! Tú no eres la reina (queen). Pero, en mi opinión, eres más bonita que la reina, Luisa. Tú eres tan inteligente, interesante y amable como Luisa. ¡Qué lástima que eres menos popular! Tú no eres tímida y en el futuro, serás más popular y serás la reina.

Tu amigo,
Jaime

1. Why is Rosita sad?
2. Who is the queen?
3. According to Jaime, how does Rosita compare to Luisa?
4. Why didn't Rosita win the contest?

C. Jaime is angry with Raúl because Raúl borrowed his new jacket and lost it. Jaime wrote him a note telling how he feels about him (at least for now). He didn't give Raúl the note, however. Notice that, because he is angry, he is using the more formal **Estimado** instead of **Querido** to say *Dear.*

Estimado Raúl:

¡Burro! ¡Eres más tonto que un burro! Hace frío hoy, tengo frío y no tengo mi chaqueta. ¿Dónde está mi chaqueta?

Tú eres egoísta, perezoso y antipático. Eras un amigo simpático, pero en el futuro no serás mi amigo.

Tu amigo,
Jaime

1. What is the weather like?
2. What does Jaime call Raúl to insult him?
3. Why is Jaime angry with Raúl?
4. Is the friendship between Jaime and Raúl really over?

D. Instead of buying his mother a birthday card, Jaime wrote her the following letter.

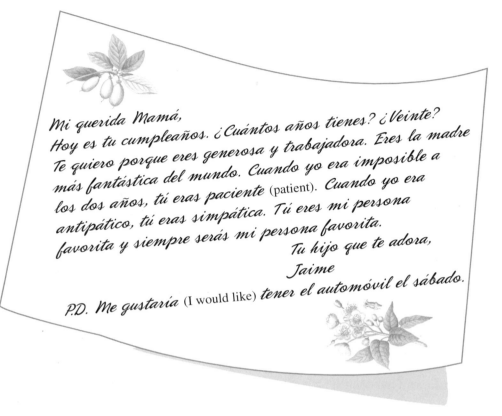

Mi querida Mamá,

Hoy es tu cumpleaños. ¿Cuántos años tienes? ¿Veinte? Te quiero porque eres generosa y trabajadora. Eres la madre más fantástica del mundo. Cuando yo era imposible a los dos años, tú eras paciente (patient). Cuando yo era antipático, tú eras simpática. Tú eres mi persona favorita y siempre serás mi persona favorita.

Tu hijo que te adora,
Jaime

P.D. Me gustaría (I would like) tener el automóvil el sábado.

Note: **P.D.** stands for **posdata** (from Latin *post datum,* "after the fact"). **P.D.** is used in Spanish for *P.S. (postscript).*

1. Why does Jaime ask if his mother is twenty years old?
2. Why does he love her?
3. What was Jaime like when he was two years old?
4. What does he want to have on Saturday?
5. What does **P.D.** stand for?

E. Choose one of the preceding situations and write your own note to someone in your class or family.

¡Así es!

Sports in the Hispanic world

As in the United States, people in Spanish-speaking countries enjoy watching and playing many different kinds of sports. Baseball is very popular, especially in countries of the Caribbean area, such as Mexico, Cuba, Puerto Rico, and the Dominican Republic. Basketball has been steadily gaining popularity; however, North American football is virtually unknown. The most popular sport by far in Hispanic countries, as well as in most of the world outside the United States, is soccer, called **fútbol** in Spanish. Countries stake their national pride on the success of their national team in the **Copa Mundial** *(World Cup)* competitions. **Jai alai** is a typical Hispanic sport that originated in the Basque area of Spain. It is mainly a spectator sport in which players hurl a small, hard ball in a three-walled court, with a wicker basket attached to their arm. It can be dangerous, as the speed of the ball approaches two hundred miles per hour!

¿De dónde es usted, señor?
Where are you from, sir?

In this lesson you will be talking about your national origin and finding out about your partner's. You will also have a chance to describe your teacher and other people!

Vocabulario

Los países y las nacionalidades *Countries and nationalities*

On pages 168 and 169 is a list of some of the countries in the world. If your country is not shown, look it up in the dictionary or ask your teacher.

TO MAKE THE FEMININE FORM OF AN ADJECTIVE OF NATIONALITY

	MASCULINE	FEMININE
If it ends in **o**, change **o** to **a**:	mexicano	mexicana
If it ends in a consonant, add **a**:	español	española
If it ends in a vowel other than **o**, use the same form:	canadiense	canadiense

Note that adjectives of nationality are never capitalized in Spanish.

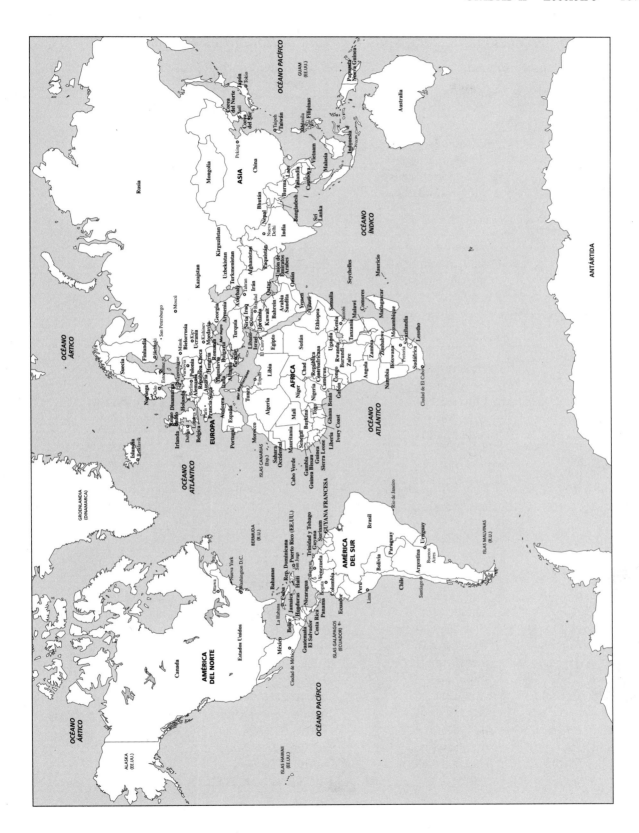

Los países y las nacionalidades *Countries and nationalities* (continued)

Note: If no feminine form indicator appears, the same form is used for both masculine and feminine.

PAÍS	NACIONALIDAD	PAÍS	NACIONALIDAD
En Norteamérica			
Canadá	canadiense		
Estados Unidos (EE. UU.)	norteamericano(a), estadounidense		
México	mexicano(a)		
En Centroamérica			
Guatemala	guatemalteco(a)	Costa Rica	costarricense
El Salvador	salvadoreño(a)	Panamá	panameño(a)
Honduras	hondureño(a)	Nicaragua	nicaragüense
En Sudamérica			
Venezuela	venezolano(a)	Paraguay	paraguayo(a)
Colombia	colombiano(a)	Uruguay	uruguayo(a)
Ecuador	ecuatoriano(a)	Brasil	brasileño(a)
Perú	peruano(a)	Guayana Inglesa	guyanés(esa)
Bolivia	boliviano(a)	Guayana Francesa	guyanés(esa)
Chile	chileno(a)	Surinam	surinamita
Argentina	argentino(a)		
En el Caribe			
Puerto Rico	puertorriqueño(a)	República Dominicana	dominicano(a)
Cuba	cubano(a)	Haití	haitiano(a)
En Europa			
España *(Spain)*	español(a)	República Eslovaca *(Slovak Republic)*	eslovaco(a)
Portugal	portugués(esa)		
Inglaterra *(England)*	inglés(esa)	Grecia *(Greece)*	griego(a)
Irlanda *(Ireland)*	irlandés(esa)	Ucrania *(Ukraine)*	ucraniano(a)
Escocia *(Scotland)*	escocés(esa)	Holanda *(Holland)*	holandés(esa)
Francia *(France)*	francés(esa)	Polonia *(Poland)*	polaco(a)
Alemania *(Germany)*	alemán(ana)	Bulgaria	búlgaro(a)
Italia *(Italy)*	italiano(a)	Bélgica *(Belgium)*	belga
Suiza *(Switzerland)*	suizo(a)	Dinamarca *(Denmark)*	danés(esa)
Austria	austríaco(a)	Suecia *(Sweden)*	sueco(a)
Hungría *(Hungary)*	húngaro(a)	Noruega *(Norway)*	noruego(a)
Finlandia *(Finland)*	finlandés(esa)	Rumania *(Romania)*	rumano(a)
República Checa *(Czech Republic)*	checoslovaco(a)	Turquía *(Turkey)*	turco(a)
		Rusia *(Russia)*	ruso(a)

PAÍS	NACIONALIDAD	PAÍS	NACIONALIDAD

En el Medio Oriente

PAÍS	NACIONALIDAD	PAÍS	NACIONALIDAD
Irán	iranio(a)	Israel	israelí
Irak *(Iraq)*	iraqués(esa)	Arabia Saudita	saudito(a)
Siria *(Syria)*	sirio(a)	*(Saudi Arabia)*	
Arabia	árabe	Jordania *(Jordan)*	jordano(a)
Líbano *(Lebanon)*	libanés(esa)		

En Asia

PAÍS	NACIONALIDAD	PAÍS	NACIONALIDAD
China	chino(a)	Camboya *(Cambodia)*	camboyano(a)
Japón *(Japan)*	japonés(esa)	Tailandia *(Thailand)*	tailandés(esa)
Corea *(Korea)*	coreano(a)	Afganistán	afgano(a)
Vietnam	vietnamita	Pakistán	pakistaní
		India	indio(a)

En África

PAÍS	NACIONALIDAD	PAÍS	NACIONALIDAD
África	africano(a)	Ghana	ghanés(esa)
Marruecos *(Morocco)*	marroquí	Kenya	kenyano(a)
Argelia *(Algeria)*	argelino(a)	Zaire	zaireño(a)
Túnez *(Tunisia)*	tunecino(a)	Nigeria	nigeriano(a)
Egipto *(Egypt)*	egipcio(a)	Liberia	liberiano(a)
Libia *(Libya)*	libio(a)	Etiopía *(Ethiopia)*	etíope
África del Sur	sudafricano(a)	Costa de Marfil	
(South Africa)		*(Ivory Coast)*	

Otras áreas geográficas

PAÍS	NACIONALIDAD
Indonesia	indonesio(a)
Australia	australiano(a)
Nueva Zelanda	neozelandés(esa)
Las Filipinas	filipino(a)

THE USE OF USTED (UD.)

In Lesson 2, you learned that speakers of Spanish use the informal **tú** to say *you* to someone they know on a first-name basis, such as friends and classmates. **Usted,** abbreviated **Ud.,** is the formal way of saying *you* and is used when addressing a person with whom you would use a title like **Doctor, Señor, Profesor,** and the like. You would use **Ud.** with a stranger, a store clerk, a police officer, and an older person, including your teacher!

USTED FORMS OF SER

Ud. era	*you were, you used to be*
Ud. es	*you are*
Ud. será	*you will be*

Usted is frequently used in conversation, both for clarity and courtesy.

Conversación

Asking and telling national origins

¿De dónde es Ud.?	*Where are you from?*
Soy de…	*I'm from . . .*
¿Es Ud. *[nationality]*?	*Are you . . . ?*
Sí, soy…	*Yes, I'm . . .*
Si Ud. es de México, entonces Ud. es mexicano, ¿verdad?	*If you are from Mexico, then you are Mexican, right?*

1 **Juego**   Pretend you are from another country. Choose different classmates and make your own conversations using the preceding expressions. Answer as though you are from the country that you have chosen.

EJEMPLO: Señor, ¿de dónde es Ud.?
Sir, where are you from?

Yo soy del Canadá.
I'm from Canada.

Si Ud. es del Canadá, entonces Ud. es canadiense, ¿verdad?
If you're from Canada, then you are Canadian, right?

Sí, soy canadiense.
Yes, I'm Canadian.

2 Use describing words (adjectives) from Lessons 1 and 2 with the **Ud.** form of **ser** to ask questions of your partner. Then have your partner respond.

EJEMPLO: ¿Es Ud. simpático?   *Are you nice?*

Sí, yo soy simpático.   *Yes, I'm nice.*

3 Using adjectives of personality from Lesson 2, tell your teacher what you think he or she is like outside of class.

EJEMPLO: Fuera de la clase, Ud. es amistoso.   *Outside of class, you are friendly.*

4 Tell your teacher what you think he or she was like at your age.

EJEMPLO: A los (catorce) años, Ud. era atlética.
At the age of (fourteen), you used to be athletic.

5 Tell your teacher what you think he or she will be like in fifteen years.

EJEMPLO: En quince años, Ud. será muy alegre.
In fifteen years, you will be very happy.

Vocabulario

Las palabras interrogativas   *Question words*

¿Cómo?	*How? What?*
¿Dónde?	*Where?*
¿Adónde?	*To where?*
¿Quién(es)?	*Who?*
¿Qué?	*What?*
¿Cuándo?	*When?*
¿Por qué?	*Why?*
¿Cuánto(a)?	*How much?*
¿Cuántos(as)?	*How many?*
¿Cuál(es)?	*Which?*

Note: **¿Quiénes?** and **¿Cuáles?** are used when a plural answer is expected.

¿Quiénes son?   *Who are they?*

¿Cuáles son de México?   *Which ones are from Mexico?*

¿Cuánto? agrees in number and gender with the noun it refers to.

¿Cuánta sopa hay?   *How much soup is there?*

¿Cuántos hombres hay?   *How many men are there?*

QUESTIONS ASKING FOR INFORMATION

When the purpose of a question is to gather information, the question word comes at the beginning of the sentence. If there is a preposition, it comes before the question word.

Esqueleto

¿ (preposition) + question word + verb + (pro)noun?

¿Cómo es Ud.?   *What are you like?*

¿De dónde es Ud.?   *Where are you from?*

¿Quiénes son los profesores?   *Who are the teachers?*

¿Para quién es el regalo?   *Who is the gift for?*

6 Make questions using the question words you have learned. Use forms of **ser**. Work with a partner and answer each other's questions.

EJEMPLO: ¿Cuándo es la fiesta? *When is the party?*

Es mañana. *It's tomorrow.*

7. *Sit-Con* You are at an embassy ball where there are representatives from all over the world. Pretend that you are from the consulate of another country. Decide on your country of origin and your nationality. Find out where the other guests (your classmates) are from.

EJEMPLO: ¿De dónde es Ud.? *Where are you from?*

Soy de México. Soy mexicano. *I'm from Mexico. I'm Mexican.*

8 *Sit-Con* You are at an international medical convention with other doctors. At lunch you are sitting with a group of doctors from Mexico. What would the conversation be like? Work with a partner. One of you is an American doctor, the other a Mexican doctor. Write the conversation between the two of you. Be sure to use the **Ud.** forms since you are strangers to each other. Use the following ideas in your conversation.

- Greet each other. [Unit I.1]
- Ask how the other person is. [Unit I.1]
- Find out each other's first and last names and how to spell them. [Unit I.2]
- Find out what city and country the other person is from. [Unit II.3]
- Find out what part of the body they specialize in. [Unit I.4]
- What does the other person like to do? [Unit I.10]
- At the end of the meal, say good-bye and that you will see each other again. [Unit I.1]

ENCUENTRO PERSONAL

When Inés took a trip to Puerto Rico to visit her cousin Andrés Sobejano, she met a middle-aged woman on the plane. Here is their conversation.

¿Comprendes?

1. Where is the woman from?
2. What kind of work does she do?
3. Where does she work?
4. What is her opinion of Puerto Rico?
5. Why does Inés like to visit the island?
6. What is their opinion of each other?

¡Te toca!

A. Think of a place you like to visit, and tell someone in your class why you like it.

B. Are your parents from a city, state, or country other than the one where you live now? Take turns asking other classmates where their parents are from.

Leemos y contamos

A. Inés went to a school counselor. This is what she was told.

Ud. es inteligente y muy atlética. Ud. es amable y popular. Es trabajadora y ambiciosa pero un poco egoísta. Ud. es una persona triste porque no es una persona generosa. En el futuro, si Ud. es más generosa, será más alegre.

1. List in English three things that the school counselor said about Inés.
2. What will Inés be like in the future?

B. This is the ad that Sean McIlroy put in the "dating column" of the school newspaper.

1. What is your opinion of Sean?
2. Do you like him or not?
3. What kind of a date does he want?
4. Do you think he will get many responses?
5. Why or why not?

> Yo soy interesante, alegre, generoso y sincero. Soy listo y amable. Soy un poco perezoso, pero soy ambicioso. Busco a *(I'm looking for)* una amiga sincera. Si Ud. es bonita, alta, (no muy alta), interesante y amistosa, llámeme *(call me)*. Si Ud. es rubia, si Ud. tiene los ojos verdes, si tiene un corazón sincero, llámeme. Si Ud. es tímida, perezosa y egoísta, por favor, ¡no me llame *(don't call me)!* Mi número de teléfono es 35-87-94. ♥

C. Have some fun with Sean. Write a letter to him pretending to be a girl who wants to meet him. Give him your phone number and ask him to call you!

D. To finance his social life, Sean needs a job and applies for a position as a bilingual travel agent. He was asked to answer the following questions. Read his responses.

PREGUNTAS PARA EMPLEO

1. ¿Cómo se llama Ud.? *Me llamo Sean McIlroy.*
2. ¿De dónde es Ud.? *Soy de los Estados Unidos de Detroit, Michigan.*
3. ¿Cuál es su origen de nacionalidad? *Soy mexicanoamericano. Mi madre es de México.*
4. ¿Es usted trabajador(a)? *Sí, soy trabajador.*
5. ¿Es usted perezoso(a)? *No, no soy perezoso.*
6. ¿Es usted ambicioso(a)? *Sí, soy ambicioso.*
7. ¿Es usted amistoso(a) o tímido(a)? *Soy amistoso, no soy tímido.*
8. ¿Es usted generoso(a)? *Sí, soy generoso.*
9. ¿Es usted sincero(a)? *Sí, soy sincero.*
10. ¿Le gusta hablar por teléfono? *Sí, me gusta hablar por teléfono.*
11. ¿Le gusta escribir cartas? *Sí, me gusta escribir cartas.*
12. ¿Le gustaría *(would you like)* viajar? *Sí, me gustaría mucho viajar a México, a España y a Sudamérica.*
13. ¿Habla Ud. español? *Sí, hablo español un poco.*

E. Now apply for the job of bilingual travel agent yourself and answer the questions above. Who do you think will get the job, you or Sean? Why do you think so?

¡Así es!

Puerto Rico

Puerto Rico is one of the largest islands in the Caribbean and one of the first areas explored by the Spaniards in the late 1400s. It became a protectorate of the United States following the Spanish-American War in 1898, and today it is a U.S. territory. Puerto Ricans have great pride in their Hispanic heritage and while many like the status quo, some dream of Puerto Rico becoming an independent country. Other Puerto Ricans would like to see their island become the fifty-first state. Since Puerto Ricans are U.S. citizens, they can easily immigrate to the U.S. mainland and there are large communities of first-, second-, and third-generation Puerto Ricans in many urban areas, such as New York and Chicago.

Mi familia
My family

In this lesson you will be talking about the members of your family.

Vocabulario

Los miembros de la familia   *Family members*

These words pertaining to family members were introduced in Unit I, Lesson 3.

el abuelo	*grandfather*	el tío	*uncle*
la abuela	*grandmother*	la tía	*aunt*
el padre	*father*	el primo	*cousin [m.]*
la madre	*mother*	la prima	*cousin [f.]*
el hermano	*brother*	el esposo	*husband*
la hermana	*sister*	la esposa	*wife*
el hijo	*son*	el padrastro	*stepfather*
la hija	*daughter*	la madrastra	*stepmother*
el nieto	*grandson*	el hermanastro	*stepbrother*
la nieta	*granddaughter*	la hermanastra	*stepsister*

The following is additional vocabulary pertaining to family members.

el gemelo	*twin brother*	la nuera	*daughter-in-law*
la gemela	*twin sister*	el padrino	*godfather*
el sobrino	*nephew*	la madrina	*godmother*
la sobrina	*niece*	el ahijado	*godson*
el cuñado	*brother-in-law*	la ahijada	*goddaughter*
la cuñada	*sister-in-law*	el hermano mayor	*older brother*
el suegro	*father-in-law*	la hermana mayor	*older sister*
la suegra	*mother-in-law*	el hermano menor	*younger brother*
el yerno	*son-in-law*	la hermana menor	*younger sister*

Note: Most family relationships change the **o** to **a** for the feminine forms.
The exceptions are: **padre/madre** (and their related forms) and **yerno/nuera.**

Last Names

Remember that Spanish-speaking people have an different system of last names. See Unit I, Lesson 2.

Men and single women use their father's family name followed by their mother's family name.

Juan Salas Romero   Julia Salas Romero
Salas is the father's family name;
Romero is the mother's family name.

Married women use their father's family name followed by **de** and their husband's family name.

Elvira Salas de Zuñiga
Salas is the father's family name;
Zuñiga is the husband's family name.

1 Using the Spanish system, tell your full name. Find out the full name (Spanish style) for at least five of your classmates.

EJEMPLO: ¿Cómo te llamas?   *What's your name?*

Me llamo Carlos García Morales.   *My name is Carlos García Morales.*

2 Find out the names (Spanish style) of other family members of your partner's family.

EJEMPLO: ¿Cómo se llama tu padre?   *What's your father's name?*

Mi padre se llama John Smith Jones.   *My father's name is John Smith Jones.*

3 Using the family tree of the Rodríguez family, identify where each person's last names came from.

EJEMPLO: Catalina Lara de Rodríguez
Lara is her father's family name.
Rodríguez is her husband's family name.

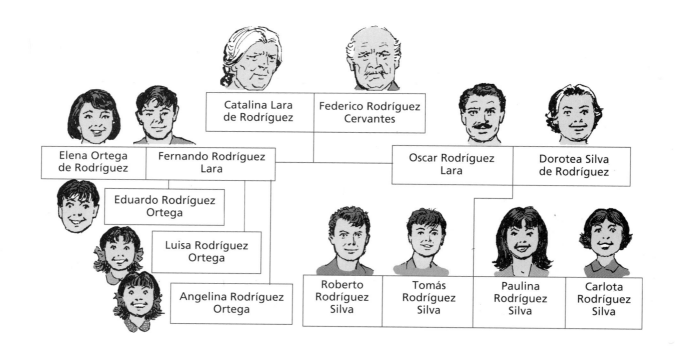

4 Answer these questions about the Rodríguez family.

a. Dorotea es la _____ de Roberto, Tomás, Paulina y Carlota; es la _____ de Eduardo, Luisa y Angelina.

b. Tomás es el _____ de Oscar y Dorotea; es el _____ de Federico y Catalina.

c. Oscar es el _____ de Dorotea; es el _____ de Federico y Catalina.

d. Dorotea es la _____ de Elena y Fernando; es la _____ de Eduardo, Luisa y Angelina.

e. Carlota es la _____ de Eduardo, Luisa y Angelina; es la _____ de Elena y Fernando.

f. Paulina es la _____ de Oscar y Dorotea; es la _____ de Fernando y Elena.

g. Luisa es la _____ de Angelina; es la _____ de Carlota.

h. Federico es el _____ de Fernando y Oscar; es el _____ de Eduardo y Roberto.

i. Catalina es la _____ de Elena y Dorotea; es la _____ de Fernando y Oscar.

IDENTIFYING AND DESCRIBING OTHER PEOPLE

HE/SHE/ NOUN WAS/IS/WILL BE

The verb form we will use with *he, she,* or a singular noun is the same as for **usted**:

él/ella/ noun **era**	*he/she/ noun was*
él/ella/ noun **es**	*he/she/ noun is*
él/ella/ noun **será**	*he/she/ noun will be*

As with **yo** and **tú**, the pronouns **él** and **ella** can be left out. They are used mainly for clarification or emphasis.

There is no word for *it* as a subject in Spanish. Use **es** to say *it is.*
    Es imposible.   *It is impossible.*

Esqueletos

(pro)noun + SER + noun

Ella es mi hermana.   *She is my sister.*
La mujer es la abuela.   *The woman is the grandmother.*
Roberto es mi padre.   *Roberto is my father.*

(pro)noun + SER + adjective

Mi hermano es simpático.   *My brother is nice.*
Ella es baja.   *She is short.*
Roberto es inteligente.   *Roberto is intelligent.*

5 Draw your family tree or make up a family using magazine pictures. Label each picture with the person's name and relationship to you. You will be using this drawing for several activities in this lesson.

6 Identify five of the people in your family. Then tell your partner three things about each person. Use the **esqueletos** on page 182.

EJEMPLO: Roberto es mi hermano.   *Roberto is my brother.*
Mi hermano es muy simpático.   *My brother is very nice.*
Él es alto y delgado.   *He is tall and thin.*
Es moreno.   *He is dark-haired.*

TELLING WHERE SOMEONE IS FROM

One way to tell where a person is from is to use a form of **ser** with the preposition **de**.

Mi padre es de Chile.   *My father is from Chile.*
¿Eres tú de España?   *Are you from Spain?*
¿De donde es tu sobrino?   *Where is your nephew from?*

Esqueletos

¿ DE DÓNDE + SER + (pro)noun ?

¿De dónde es tu madre?   *Where is your mother from?*
¿De dónde eres tú?   *Where are you from?*

(pro)noun + SER + DE + place

Mi madre es de Texas.   *My mother is from Texas.*
Él es de California.   *He is from California.*

7 Find out what city or state your partner's relatives are from using the **esqueletos** above.

EJEMPLO:  ¿De dónde es tu tío Frank?   *Where is your Uncle Frank from?*

Es de Nueva York.   *He's from New York.*

THE DEFINITE ARTICLES EL AND LA

To say *the* in Spanish, use **el** with masculine nouns and **la** with feminine nouns.

el libro	*the book*
el profesor	*the teacher*
la casa	*the house*
la madre	*the mother*

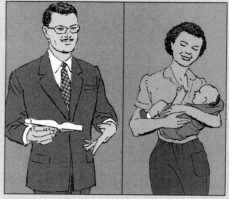

el profesor   la madre

GENDER OF NOUNS

Most nouns that end in **o, l,** or **r** and nouns referring to males are masculine.

el libro, el papel, el profesor, el padre

Most, but not all, nouns that end in **a, d,** or **ión** and nouns referring to females are feminine.

la casa, la libertad, la nación, la madre

If a noun ends in another letter or if it is an exception, you must memorize the gender.

la clase / el reloj

Exceptions: el día / la mano / el avión

8   Which word, **el** or **la**, do you use with the following nouns?

a. pared	f. mantel	k. actor
b. suelo	g. región	l. toro
c. hospital	h. fecha	m. cara
d. sección	i. techo	n. universidad
e. mesa	j. ciudad	o. escritor

SHOWING OWNERSHIP
(singular possessive adjectives)

mi = *my*
tu = *your* [informal] when talking to people you call **tú**
su = *your* [formal] when talking to people you call **Ud.**
su = *his/her/its*

Formal *your, his, her,* and *its* all use the same possessive: **su.**
Tu *(your)* does not have an accent mark but **tú** *(you* as a subject) does.

   mi hermano   *my brother*
   tu sobrina   *your niece*
   su padre   *your father/his father/her father*

9 What do you think the various members of your family will be like in twenty-five years?

EJEMPLO: Mi madre será tan simpática como ahora.   *My mother will be as nice as now.*
               Mi hermana será más bonita.   *My sister will be prettier.*

10 **Sit-Con**   You would like to invite your friend's friend to a party you are giving, but before you do, you want to know more about her or him. Ask your friend what he or she is like. Don't forget to change the adjective ending **o** to **a** when referring to a female friend.

EJEMPLO: ¿Es alta tu amiga?   *Is your friend tall?*

             Sí, mi amiga es alta.   *Yes, my friend is tall.*

             ¿Es inteligente tu amigo?   *Is your friend intelligent?*

             Sí, él es inteligente.   *Yes, he is intelligent.*

11 **Juego: Mi padre es más... que tu padre!**   Your friend tells you about the different members of his or her family. Play "One-Up" and say that your family member is more . . . !

EJEMPLO: Mi hermano es inteligente.
             My brother is intelligent.

             ¡Mi hermano es más inteligente que tu hermano!
             My brother is more intelligent than your brother!

12 Now is the time to find out something about your teacher's family. Write five questions to ask him or her.

EJEMPLO: ¿Tiene Ud. un hermano?   *Do you have a brother?*
               ¿Es su hermano amable?   *Is your brother kind?*

13 Describe your friend's family. Where are they from? Who are the family members? What are they like?

EJEMPLO: Mi amiga tiene una familia grande.   *My friend has a big family.*
Su familia es de Texas.   *Her family is from Texas.*
Su padre es muy alto.   *Her father is very tall.*
Su madre es muy simpática y generosa.   *Her mother is very nice and generous.*

DEFINING SU

Once in a while, the situation does not make it clear if **su** means *your, his,* or *her.*

El hermano de Juan es atlético. El hermano de Juanita es atlético también. Pero su hermano es más atlético.

Does **su** refer to *his* (Juan's) brother or *her* (Juanita's) brother?

When you have to clarify **su**, change **su** to:

EL/LA/LOS/LAS + *noun* + **DE** + (**UD./ÉL/ELLA**/*noun*)
El hermano <u>de Ud.</u> es atlético.   <u>*Your*</u> *brother is athletic.*
El hermano <u>de él</u> es atlético.   <u>*His*</u> *brother is athletic.*
El hermano <u>de ella</u> es más atlético.   <u>*Her*</u> *brother is more athletic.*
El hermano <u>de Juan</u> es menos atlético.   <u>*His*</u> *brother is less athletic.*

---

14 Tell about the families of your parents. Tell how they are similar and different.

EJEMPLO: Juan es el hermano de mi padre y Miguel es el hermano de mi madre. El hermano de ella es más viejo que el hermano de él.
Juan is the brother of my father, and Miguel is the brother of my mother. Her brother is older than his brother.

15 Tell about the similarities and differences of your friends' families.

EJEMPLO: María tiene una hermana y Carlota tiene una hermana también. La hermana de María es más amable y la hermana de Carlota es más ambiciosa.
María has a sister, and Carlota has a sister also. María's sister is kinder and Carlota's sister is more ambitious.

SHOWING POSSESSION USING DE + *NOUN*

Look at this Spanish sentence and its two English meanings.

Mi tío Juan es el hermano <u>de mi padre.</u>   *My uncle John is the brother of my father.*
My uncle John is <u>my father's</u> brother.

Did you notice that **de mi padre** means both *of my father* and *my father's*? Never use the apostrophe (*'s*) in Spanish to express possession. Always use **de + *noun*.**

Esqueleto

   (pro)noun + SER + *noun* + DE + *person*

Juan García es el hermano <u>de mi padre</u>.
Juan García is the brother <u>of my father</u>.
Juan García is <u>my father's</u> brother.

16 Tell how the various members of your family are related to each other.

EJEMPLO: Mi hermana es la nieta de mi abuelo.
My sister is my grandfather's granddaughter.

17 Ask whose things are in the classroom.

EJEMPLO:  ¿De quién es el libro?   *Whose book is it?*

Es el libro de Tomás.   *It's Tomás's book.*

ENCUENTRO PERSONAL

Paulina's little sister, Carlota, wants to know about her family's relatives in Mexico.

¿Comprendes?

1. What information does Carlota want to know about her relatives?
2. Who are Fernando, Elena, Eduardo, Luisa, and Angelina? Tell what they are like.
3. Why are Fernando and Elena important for Carlota?
4. Does Carlota have any other relatives in Mexico?
5. Why do you think Paulina has a headache? What clues did you find in the conversation to back up your reason?

¡Te toca!

Ask a classmate about his or her family. Ask what their names are, how they are related, and something about their personalities.

Leemos y contamos

A. Raúl is having a problem with his cousin Roberto. He is so upset with Roberto that he wrote the following letter to Anita Camacho, who writes the advice column in the daily newspaper.

> Estimada Srta. Camacho:
>
> Tengo un problema con mi primo, Roberto. Roberto también es estudiante en mi clase de matemáticas. Somos *(We are)* amigos pero somos muy diferentes. Él es muy perezoso y no le gusta trabajar ni *(nor)* estudiar. En contraste, yo soy muy ambicioso y me gusta estudiar. También soy honesto y sincero. Roberto es un estudiante malo y no recibe buenas notas *(good grades)*. Él desea copiar mis tareas. Generalmente, soy generoso pero no me gusta ser generoso con mis tareas. ¿Cuál es la solución? En el futuro, ¿será Roberto mi amigo o mi enemigo?

1. What is Roberto like?
2. What is Raúl like?
3. What is Raúl's problem?
4. What would you advise Raúl if you were Srta. Camacho?

B. Andrés, our pen pal in Lesson 1, has written us another letter. Here is what Andrés writes about his family. He has added this diagram of his family to help you.

Verónica Castro

Carlos Sobejano

Marta Ortiz de Bueno

Rafael Bueno Solís

Cristina Lara Andrés

Raúl Sobejano Ortiz

Andrés Sobejano Ortiz

Elvira Bueno Ortiz

Paco Sobejano Ortiz

Josefina Sobejano Ortiz

Juanita Sobejano Ortiz

¡Hola, amigos!

Mi familia es grande. Mis padres están divorciados. Vivo (I live) con mi madre y mi padrastro. Somos todos muy alegres. Me gusta mucho mi familia grande. Tengo dos hermanos y tres hermanas. Mi hermano mayor, Raúl, es estudiante en la Universidad de San Juan. Por la noche él es mecánico. Mi hermano Paco tiene cinco años y es muy listo. Mis hermanas son Elvira, Juanita y Josefina. Josefina es la mayor de mis hermanas y Elvira es la menor. Ella es la bebé. Ella solamente tiene seis meses (months) de edad y es muy pequeña. Tiene los ojos negros y el pelo negro.

También tengo una hermanastra, Cristina. Ella está con mi padre y mi madrastra. Cristina tiene quince años. Yo tengo diez y siete años.

¿Cómo es tu familia?

Andrés

1. ¿Cómo es la familia de Andrés?
2. ¿Cuántos hermanos tiene?
3. ¿Dónde estudia el hermano mayor?
4. ¿Qué es Raúl por la noche?
5. ¿Cuántos años tiene Paco?
6. ¿Quién es la hermana mayor?
7. ¿Cómo es la bebé?
8. ¿Quién es Cristina? ¿Con quién vive ella?
9. ¿Cuántos años tiene Cristina?
10. ¿Cuántos años tiene Andrés?

C. Using the questions above, write a brief summary of the story in English.

D. Write a letter in Spanish to Andrés telling him about your family.

¡Así es!

Saint's day celebration

Many Catholic people of Hispanic origin celebrate two days: their birthday and their saint's day. Most Spanish first names are the names of the saints of the Catholic Church. The day that the church has designated to honor individual saints is indicated on the calendar, so everyone knows when your saint's day is even if they don't know your birthday. It is customary to congratulate a person on his or her saint's day. You might say, **Felicidades en el día de tu santo**.

ENERO
1 San Justino
2 San Gregorio N.
3 Sta. Genoveva
4 San Priciliano
5 Sta. Amelia
6 Los Stos. Reyes
7 San Luciano
8 San Apolinar
9 San Julián
10 San Nicanor
11 San Higinio
12 San Alfredo
13 San Gumersindo
14 Sta. Macrina
15 San Mauro
16 San Marcelo
17 San Antonio
18 San Leobardo
19 San Mario
20 San Fabián
21 Sta. Inés
22 San Guadencio
23 San Ildefonso
24 San Francisco
25 Sta. Elvira
26 Sta Paula
27 S. J. Crisóstomo
28 San Pedro N.
29 San Aquilino
30 Sta. Martina
31 Sta. Virginia V.

FEBRERO
1 San Severo
2 Sta. Caterina
3 San Blas
4 San Gilberto
5 San Isidro
6 San Teófilo
7 San Romualdo
8 San Ciriaco
9 San Nicéforo
10 San Guillermo
11 N.S. de Lourdes
12 San Melesio
13 San Benigno
14 San Valentín
15 San Faustino
16 San Onésimo
17 San Teódulo
18 San Eladio
19 San Álvaro
20 San Eleuterio
21 San Severiano
22 San Pascasio
23 Sta. Marta
24 San Alberto
25 San Cesáreo
26 San Néstor
27 San Leandro
28 San Hilario
29 San Macario

MARZO
1 San Félix
2 San Federico
3 San Emeterio
4 San Casimiro
5 San Cristóbal
6 Sta. Felícitas
7 Sto Tomás de A.
8 San Juan de Dios
9 San Paciano
10 San Atalo
11 San Eulogio
12 San Teófanes
13 San Rodrigo
14 Sta. Matilde
15 San Raimundo
16 San Abraham
17 San Patricio
18 San Eduardo
19 San José
20 San Cutberto
21 San Roberto
22 San Octaviano
23 San Fidel
24 San Gabriel
25 San Hamberto
26 San Braulio
27 San Ruperto
28 Sta. Dorotea
29 San Eustasio
30 San Rógulo
31 San Benjamín

ABRIL
1 San Melitón
2 Sta. Ofelia
3 San Ricardo
4 San Isidoro
5 Sta. Emilia
6 San Timoteo
7 San Juan Bautista
8 San Alberto
9 San Prócoro
10 San Apolonio
11 San Estanislao
12 San Damián
13 San Hermenoglido
14 San Valeriano
15 Sta. Anastasia
16 Sta. Engracia
17 San Aniceto
18 San Perfecto
19 San Crescencio
20 San Sulpicio
21 San Anselmo
22 San Sotero
23 San Jorge
24 San Alejandro
25 San Marcos
26 San Cleto
27 Sta. Zita
28 San Prudencio
29 Sta. Catalina
30 San Jaime

MAYO
1 San Obrero José
2 San Atanasio
3 Sta. Violeta
4 Sta. Mónica
5 Sta. Floriana
6 San Evodio
7 San Flavio
8 San Bonifacio
9 San Nicolás Ob.
10 Sta. Leonor
11 Sta. Estela
12 San Aquileo
13 Sta. Imelda
14 Sta. Enedina
15 San Cecilio
16 San Ubaldo
17 San Pascual
18 San Venancio
19 Sta. Prudenciana
20 San Bernardino
21 San Valente
22 Sta. Rita de C.
23 San Epitacio
24 San Donaciano
25 San Urbano
26 San Felipe Neri
27 Sta. Carolina
28 San Germán
29 Sta. Teodosia
30 San Fernando
31 Sta. Petronila

JUNIO
1 San Pánfilo
2 San Marcelino
3 Sta. Clotilde
4 Sta. Ema
5 Sta. Zenaida
6 San Norberto
7 San Roberto
8 San Gildardo
9 San Feliciano
10 San Cirilo
11 San Bernabé
12 San Nazario
13 San Antonio de P.
14 San Eliseo
15 San Modesto
16 San Ciro
17 San Ismael
18 San Efrén
19 San Gervasio
20 San Silverio
21 San Luis Gonzaga
22 San Paulino
23 Sta. Alicia
24 San Juan Bautista
25 San Salomón
26 San Anselmo
27 N.S. de Socorro
28 San Plutarco
29 San Pedro y San Pablo
30 Sta. Lucina

JULIO
1 San Aarón
2 San Martiniano
3 San Marcial
4 Sta. Isabel
5 Sta. Filomena
6 San Isaías
7 San Fermín
8 Sta. Isabel
9 San Zenón
10 Sta. Amalia
11 San Abundio
12 San Nabor
13 San Joel
14 San Camilo
15 San Enrique
16 N.S. del Carmen
17 San Alejo
18 San Arnulfo
19 San Vicente P.
20 San Bulmaro
21 Sta. Práxedes
22 Sta. M. Magdalena
23 Sta. Brígida
24 Sta. Cristina
25 Santiago Apóstol
26 San Joaquín
27 San Celestino
28 San Víctor
29 San Próspero
30 Sta. Julieta
31. S. Ignacio de L.

AGOSTO
1 Sta. Esperanza
2 N.S. de los Ángeles
3 Sta. Lydia
4 Santo Domingo
5 San Emigdio
6 San Justo
7 San Cayetano
8 San Emiliano
9 San Román
10 Sta. Paula
11 Sta. Susana
12 Sta. Clara
13 Sta. Aurora
14 San Eusebio
15 La Asunción
16 San Roque
17 San Librado
18 Sta. Beatriz de S.
19 San Sixto
20 San Bernardo
21 San Maximino
22 San Filiberto
23 San Jacobo
24 San Bartolomé
25 San Luis Rey
26 San Ceferino
27 San Armando
28 San Agustín
29 Sta. Sabina
30 Sta. Rosa
31 San Ramón

SEPTIEMBRE
1 San Agusto
2 San Antolín
3 S. Gregorio Mag.
4 Sta. Rosalía
5 Sta. Obdulia
6 San Fausto
7 Sta. Regina
8 San Adrián
9 San Doroteo
10 San Nicolás
11 San Jacinto
12 San Leoncio
13 San Amado
14 Sta. Salustia
15 N.S. de los Dolores
16 San Cornelio
17 San Lamberto
18 Sta. Sofía
19 San Genaro
20 San Eustaquio
21 San Mateo
22 Sta. Mauricio
23 San Lino
24 San Geraldo
25 Sta. Aurelia
26 San Cipriano
27 San Cosme
28 San Wenceslao
29 San Miguel
30 San Jerónimo

OCTUBRE
1 Sta. Teresa
2 San Leodegario
3 San Gerardo
4 San Fco. de Asís
5 San Plácido
6 San Bruno
7 San Augusto
8 San Sergio
9 San Dionisio
10 San Paulino
11 San Nicasio
12 N.S. de Pilar
13 San Eduardo
14 San Calixto
15 Sta. Teresa de J.
16 Sta. Eduwiges
17 Sta. Margarita
18 San Lucas
19 Sta. Laura
20 San Artemio
21 Sta. Celia
22 Sta. Elodia
23 San Servando
24 San Rafael Arc.
25 San Gabino
26 San Evaristo
27 Sta. Florencia
28 San Simón
29 San Narciso
30 San Claudio
31 San Nemesio

NOVIEMBRE
1 Sta. Cirenia
2 San Justo
3 Sta. Silvia
4 San Carlos
5 San Zacarías
6 San Leonardo
7 San Ernesto
8 San Victorino
9 San Teodoro
10 San León Magno
11 San Martín
12 San Josafat
13 San Diego
14 San Serapio
15 San Leopoldo
16 San Fidencio
17 Sta. Salomé
18 San Teodolfo
19 San Ponciano
20 San Octavio
21 San Gelasio
22 Sta. Cecilia
23 San Clemente
24 San Crisógono
25 San Erasmo
26 San Conrado
27 San Facundo
28 San Esteban
29 San Saturnino
30 San Andrés

DICIEMBRE
1 Sta. Natalia
2 Sta. Bibiana
3 San Francisco J.
4 Sta. Bárbara
5 San Sabás
6 San Nicolás
7 San Ambrosio
8 La Inmaculada
    Concepción
9 Sta. Leocadia
10 San Melquiades
11 San Dámaso
12 N.S. de Guadalupe
13 Sta. Lucía
14 San Espiridión
15 San Arturo
16 Sta. Adelaida
17 Sta. Yolanda
18 San Ausencio
19 San Darío
20 San Filogonio
21 Santo Tomás Ap.
22 San Demetrio
23 Sta. Victoria V.
24 Sta. Irma
25 La Navidad del Sr.
26 San Marino
27 San Juan Ap.
28 Santos Inocentes
29 Santo Rey David
30 San Sabino
31 San Silvestre

¿Qué serás en el futuro?
What will you be in the future?

What do people do for a living? We will talk about occupations in this lesson, and you will learn to talk about more than one person at a time; that is, you will learn to make things plural.

Vocabulario

Las profesiones *Occupations*

1. el/la ingeniero(a)	*engineer*	9. el/la contador(a)	*accountant*
2. el/la mecánico(a)	*mechanic*	10. el/la periodista	*journalist*
3. el/la secretario(a)	*secretary*	11. el/la dentista	*dentist*
4. el/la obrero(a)	*laborer, worker*	12. el/la músico(a)	*musician*
5. el/la estudiante	*student*	13. el actor	*actor*
6. el/la policía	*police officer*	14. la actriz	*actress*
7. el/la gerente	*manager*	15. el hombre de negocios	*businessman*
8. el/la médico(a)	*doctor*	16. la mujer de negocios	*businesswoman*

el/la doctor(a)

Las profesiones   *Occupations* (continued)

17. el/la mesero(a)   *waiter, waitress*
18. el/la profesor(a)   *teacher*
19. el ama de casa   *homemaker*
20. el/la abogado(a)   *lawyer*
21. el/la agricultor(a)   *farmer*
22. el/la dependiente(a)   *salesperson*
23. el/la bombero(a)   *firefighter*

24. el/la banquero(a)   *banker*
25. el/la enfermero(a)   *nurse*
26. el/la arquitecto(a)   *architect*
27. el/la farmacista   *pharmacist*
28. el/la artista   *artist*
29. el/la agente   *agent*
30. el/la criado(a)   *servant, housekeeper*

Note: Nouns ending in **ista** and **e** are the same for masculine and feminine.
       Policía is the same for masculine and feminine. Nouns ending in **or** add **a** for feminine.

Conversación

Talking about occupations

¿Qué serás?	*What will you be?*
Creo que seré…	*I think I will be . . .*
¿Qué es *[person]*?	*What is . . . ?*
Es *[occupation]*.	*He or she is a(n) . . .?*
Es un(a) *[occupation] [adjective]*.	*He or she is a(n) [adjective] . . .*

1 Ask your partner which occupations members of her or his family have.

EJEMPLOS: ¿Qué es tu hermano?   *What is your brother?*

Mi hermano es abogado.   *My brother is a lawyer.*

¿Qué es tu prima?   *What is your cousin?*

Mi prima es estudiante.   *My cousin is a student.*

2 **Creo que seré…** *I think that I'll be . . .*   Interview five classmates about their plans for their future occupations.

EJEMPLO: ¿Qué serás en el futuro?   *What will you be in the future?*

Creo que seré bombero. ¿Y tú?   *I think I will be a firefighter. And you?*

Creo que seré arquitecto.   *I think I will be an architect.*

UN AND UNA WITH OCCUPATIONS

When telling about someone's occupation, **un** and **una** are omitted in Spanish unless the occupation is described.

Esqueletos

> ### (pro)noun + SER + occupation

Mi abuelo es abogado.   *My grandfather is a̲ lawyer.*
Mi tía es médica.o   *My aunt is a̲ doctor.*
doctora

| (pro)noun + SER + UN / UNA + occupation + adjective |

Mi abuelo es <u>un</u> abogado <u>famoso</u>.   *My grandfather is <u>a famous</u> lawyer.*
Mi tía es <u>una</u> médica <u>buena</u>.   *My aunt is <u>a good</u> doctor.*

3 *Sit-Con*   Imagine that you are at the Los Angeles airport with a friend and see several celebrities: actors, actresses, singers, and athletes. Your friend doesn't know them. Point them out to your friend and tell her or him who they are.

EJEMPLOS: Allí está Barbra Streisand.
There is Barbra Streisand.

¿Quién es?
Who is she?

Es una actriz famosa.
She's a famous actress.

Allí está Michael Jordan.
There's Michael Jordan.

¿Quién es?
Who is he?

Es un jugador de básquetbol famoso.
He's a famous basketball player.

MAKING NOUNS AND ADJECTIVES PLURAL

If the word ends in a vowel, add **s**.
  libro ⟶ libros *(books)*
  cinta ⟶ cintas *(tapes)*

If the word ends in a consonant, add **es**.
  papel ⟶ papeles *(papers)*
  televisor ⟶ televisores *(television sets)*

If the word ends in a **z**, change **z** to **c** before adding **es**.
  lápiz ⟶ lápices *(pencils)*
  pez ⟶ peces *(fish)*
  actriz ⟶ actrices *(actresses)*

PLURAL FORMS **LOS** and **LAS**

Use **los** before a masculine plural noun and **las** before a feminine plural noun to say *the*.
  <u>los</u> muchachos *(the boys)*
  <u>las</u> muchachas *(the girls)*

4 Make a list of five occupations that require university education and a second list of those that require a different type of training. Use plural forms.

EJEMPLOS: COLLEGE   OTHER TRAINING
                  los médicos   las actrices
                  las profesoras   los bomberos

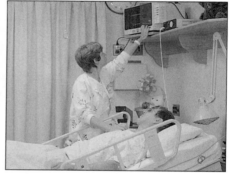

PLURAL ADJECTIVES WITH PLURAL NOUNS

When describing a noun or pronoun that is plural, be sure all the related words (articles and adjectives) are also plural.

el bombero fuerte   los bomberos fuertes
la dentista simpática   las dentistas simpáticas

5 Refer to the animals listed on page 7. List three animals that you would find as pets, three that you would find in a zoo, and three that you would find on a farm. Add a word to describe each of them. Be sure the adjectives agree in number and gender with the animals.

EJEMPLO: PETS   ZOO   FARM
               los perros pequeños   los leones fuertes   las vacas contentas

SER *to be*

Before we learn the plural forms of **ser** individually, let's see them all together.

	was/were used to be	*am/is/are*	*will be*
yo	era	soy	seré
tú	eras	eres	serás
Ud./él/ella	era	es	será
nosotros(as)	éramos	somos	seremos
vosotros(as)	erais	sois	seréis
Uds./ellos/ellas	eran	son	serán

Nosotros, vosotros, Uds., and **ellos** are used for a group that is all male or *mixed* male and female. **Nosotras, vosotras, Uds.,** and **ellas** are used for a group that is all female. **Vosotros** *(you)* is used in Spain to address a group of friends in an informal situation. In Latin America **ustedes (Uds.)** [*you* plural] is used as the plural of **usted** and **tú** to address a group in formal or informal situations.

As with other subject pronouns, **nosotros(as), vosotros(as), ustedes, ellos,** and **ellas** are usually omitted and are used mainly for clarification or emphasis.

6 *Sit-Con*   Review the description of the extraterrestrial on page 151. Send a return transmission describing humans to the extraterrestrial.

EJEMPLO: Los humanos tienen dos ojos. Sus dientes son blancos.
Humans have two eyes. Their teeth are white.

7 What are the characteristics you might associate with people in various occupations? With your partner, take turns making statements about these characteristics. Are the statements always true of these people?

EJEMPLO: Los profesores son inteligentes.
Teachers are smart.

Los bomberos son fuertes.
Firefighters are strong.

NOSOTROS FORM

Nosotros means *we* or *"anyone"* and *I*.

Tú y yo   María, Juan y yo
Ud. y yo   Mi familia y yo   } nosotros
Juan y yo   Mi madre, mi padre, mi hermano y yo

As in English, you can list everyone or just say **nosotros(as)**.

Miguel y yo éramos amigos.   *Miguel and I used to be friends.*
Nosotros éramos amigos.   *We used to be friends.*
Marta, José y yo seremos médicos.   *Marta, José, and I will be doctors.*
Nosotros seremos médicos.   *We will be doctors.*

8 What things do you have in common with your best friend? Make a list of things you both had in common in the past, what you have in common now, and what you will have in common in the future.

EJEMPLO: De niños éramos pequeños.   *As children, we used to be small.*
           Ahora somos atléticos.   *Now we are athletic.*
           En el futuro seremos ingenieros.   *In the future we will be engineers.*

9 Describe the characteristics that you and your family have in common.

EJEMPLO: Somos altos, morenos y amistosos.   *We are tall, dark, and friendly.*

10 Choose someone who is like you in some way. Tell what you both are like individually, then use **nosotros(as)** to tell what both of you have in common.

EJEMPLO: Juan es ambicioso. Yo soy ambicioso también. Nosotros somos trabajadores.
           Juan is ambitious. I am ambitious, too. We are hardworking.

USTEDES (UDS.) FORM

Ustedes (Uds.) is used to say *you* when you are talking to more than one person.

tú y él
Ud. y ellos } ustedes

As in English, you can list everyone or just say **Uds.**

Tú y Miguel son amigos.
Uds. son amigos.
Ud. y el señor García serán abogados.
Uds. serán abogados.

You and Miguel are friends.
You are friends.
You and Señor García will be lawyers.
You will be lawyers.

11 Tell your partner how he or she is like other people in class.

EJEMPLO: Tú y Juan son amables. Uds. son amables.   *You and Juan are kind. You are kind.*

12 *Sit-Con*   The Valdivia family is moving to your town and Sra. Valdivia has come to find out about your school. She wants to know what the students are like. Review the adjectives on page 128 and create the interview that she has with you. Notice that if Sra. Valdivia uses **Uds.** in her question, the student answers with **nosotros**.

EJEMPLO: Sra. Valdivia: ¿Son Uds. buenos estudiantes?   *Are you good students?*
Estudiante: Sí, somos muy trabajadores.   *Yes, we are very hardworking.*

13 *Sit-Con*   With your partner, act out the interview between Sra. Valdivia and a student at your school.

ENCUENTRO PERSONAL

Paulina's grandfather (who doesn't speak English) wants to know about her career plans and those of her brothers and sister.

¿Comprendes?

1. What was the occupation of Paulina's grandmother?
2. What does Paulina plan to be?
3. What does her sister plan to be? Why?
4. What will her brothers be? Why?
5. What will the future be like for Paulina and her brothers and sister?
   Will her life be the same as her grandparents in the past?
6. According to Paulina, what is more important than being rich?
7. Why does Paulina's grandfather thank her?

¡Te toca!

Interview classmates about the occupations of various members of their family. Be sure to ask them what they and their brothers and sisters will be.

SOLICITO:
SECRETARIA
con Conocimientos de Inglés.
4 MECANICOS DIESEL
4 AFANADORES
(personal p/limpieza)
5 CHOFERES
5 VIGILANTES
Interesados presentarse en
Aguirre Laredo #5208, Col.
Jardines de San José, con el Sr.
Simón Paredes de Rodríguez.
Tel. 13-98-77

JAVIER
SANDOVAL G.
ARQUITECTO
CED. PROF. FED. 508152
PERITO VALUADOR
Nº 1237
COMPRAVENTA
BIENES RAICES
16-15-49   13-37-99
COYOACAN 3038-1 PRONAF
C.P. 32300

Alberto Blasquez E.
INGENIERO CONSULTOR
REFRIGERACION INDUSTRIAL

Ing. Alberto Blasquez Jr.
DEPARTAMENTO TECNICO

MANZANILLO 116-1ER PISO
5-64-93-60 5-64-93-71
MEXICO 7, D. F.

Leemos y contamos

A. **¿Quiénes somos?**   Can you guess the following people's occupations based on their descriptions?

1. Estudiamos por muchos años. Somos simpáticos y generosos. Nos gusta ayudar *(help)* a las personas enfermas. Trabajamos en un hospital. ¿Qué somos?

2. Trabajamos mucho pero no trabajamos en el verano. Escribimos mucho en la pizarra. Los niños y los jóvenes son nuestros amigos. ¿Qué somos?

3. Tenemos mucho dinero. Bailamos y cantamos muy bien. Viajamos mucho también. Somos muy famosos. Aparecemos *(We appear)* en la televisión. ¿Qué somos?

4. Trabajo con las manos. Me gustan mucho los autos. Generalmente estoy en un garaje o en una estación de gasolina. ¿Qué soy yo?

5. Escribo muchas cartas. Hablo mucho por teléfono. Uso una computadora y una calculadora. Trabajo en una oficina. ¿Qué soy yo?

B. In Spanish class, Leonardo Sandoval wrote this composition about his family. Read his description and compare Leonardo's family to your family.

Mi familia

Nosotros somos una familia grande. Somos hispanos pero también somos americanos porque somos de California. Mi padre es bajo pero muy fuerte. Él es bombero en la ciudad de Los Ángeles. Mi madre no es muy bonita pero es la mejor (the best) madre del mundo (in the world) porque es amable, simpática y muy trabajadora. Ella es criada en un hotel. Mi hermano mayor, Ricardo, es policía de la ciudad. Mis hermanos menores—Esteban, José y Geraldo—y yo somos estudiantes, pero en el futuro Esteban será abogado, José será diplomático y Geraldo y yo seremos artistas. Hay muchos artistas aquí en Los Ángeles.

Mi hermana mayor, Cecilia, es contadora en la oficina de un médico. Mi hermana menor, Graciela, es muy pequeña y no sabe (know) lo que (what) será en el futuro. También tengo muchos tíos, tías y primos. Felipe es mi primo y también mi amigo. Nosotros no somos ricos, pero somos muy alegres y amables.

C. Using Leonardo's composition as a model, write a composition about the members of your own family. Include what they used to be like and what they will be like ten years from now. Refer to the vocabulary at the beginning of the unit.

D. Best friends usually have a lot in common. Read Paulinas's composition about her best friend, Rosita. (Note: Since they are both girls, Paulina uses the feminine form of adjectives.)

Mi amiga

Rosita y yo somos hispanoamericanas. Mis padres son de México y los padres de Rosita son de Cuba. Rosita y yo somos muy buenas amigas. Somos alegres y simpáticas. También somos inteligentes y estudiosas. Antes éramos un poco tímidas pero ahora somos más amistosas y populares. Ella es rubia y yo soy morena pero las dos somos muy bonitas.

Nosotras somos altas pero ella no es tan alta como yo. Somos estudiantes y en el futuro seremos profesoras de español porque deseamos (we want) ser profesoras y nos gusta hablar, leer y escribir en español.

¡Rosita y yo seremos muy buenas amigas siempre!

E. Write five questions in English about Rosita and Paulina to ask your partner.

   EJEMPLO: *Where do they live?*

F. Write a paragraph about a good friend. Tell what you have in common. This can include personal characteristics you share, what you were, are, or will be, and so on. Look through your vocabulary tools for ideas.

¡Así es!

The siesta

Some Spanish-speaking countries have the tradition of taking a break in the middle of the day. This is known as the **siesta**. Around noon, many shops and businesses as well as schools close for two or three hours when everyone comes home to enjoy the midday meal, which is the main meal of the day. After eating, the family usually sits and talks for a while, after which they retire to a quiet area of the house to relax, often by reading, listening to music, or taking a nap. When the siesta is over, everyone returns to work or school. Businesses and schools stay open later to make up the time lost. This custom probably originated because in Spain it is very hot in the middle of the day, and it is difficult to work where there is no air-conditioning. In the larger cities the siesta is giving way to a one-hour lunch period, which is more convenient for workers who commute a distance and cannot go home for the siesta. This also makes dealing with other countries easier for businesses.

En el aula
In the classroom

In this lesson, you will learn more vocabulary pertaining to objects in the classroom; you will also learn how to describe these objects.

Vocabulario

Las cosas en el aula *Classroom objects*

These vocabulary items related to classroom objects were presented in Unit I, Lesson 8.

la pizarra	*chalkboard*	la cartera/purse	*briefcase*
la tiza	*chalk*	la mochila	*backpack*
el borrador	*eraser*	la papelera	*wastepaper basket*
el estante	*bookshelf*	la computadora	*computer*
el reloj	*clock*	la calculadora	*calculator*
el armario	*locker, closet*	la grabadora	*tape recorder*
la bandera	*flag*	la cinta adhesiva	*tape*
el globo	*globe*	el cuaderno	*notebook*
el mapa	*map*	el papel	*paper*
el libro	*book*	el lápiz	*pencil*
el archivador	*file cabinet*	el bolígrafo	*ballpoint pen*
el escritorio	*teacher's desk*	la goma	*pencil eraser*
el pupitre	*student desk*	la silla	*chair*
el diccionario	*dictionary*	la mesa	*table*

Note: Feminine nouns beginning with a stressed **a** or **ha** use **el** instead of **la** because it is easier to pronounce them; nevertheless they are feminine.

el aula buena   las aulas buenas
el agua fresca   las aguas frescas

The following is additional vocabulary pertaining to classroom objects.

1. el calendario   *calendar*
2. el retroproyector   *overhead projector*
3. el casete   *cassette*
4. el cuadro   *picture*
5. el sacapuntas   *pencil sharpener*

6. el tablero de anuncios   *bulletin board*
7. ~~la videocasetera~~   ~~videocassette recorder~~
8. las tijeras   *scissors*
9. la regla   *ruler*

Los colores   *Colors*

The following colors were presented in Unit I, Lesson 7.

rojo(a)	*red*	negro(a)	*black*
amarillo(a)	*yellow*	blanco(a)	*white*
azul	*blue*	gris	*gray*
anaranjado(a)	*orange*	pardo(a)	*brown*
verde	*green*	rosado(a)	*pink*
		morado(a)	*purple*
… oscuro(a)	*dark*		
… claro(a)	*light*		

Here are additional colors to add to those you have already learned.

dorado(a)	*gold*	plateado(a)	*silver*
turquesa	*turquoise*	violeta	*violet*
crema	*tan*	marrón	*brown*

Las formas y los tamaños   *Shapes and sizes*

These vocabulary items were presented in Unit I, Lesson 7.

grande	*big*	alto(a)	*high, tall*
pequeño(a)	*small*	bajo(a)	*low, short (in height)*
mediano(a)	*medium*	largo(a)	*long*
ancho(a)	*wide*	corto(a)	*short (in length)*
estrecho(a)	*narrow*	plano(a)	*flat*
cuadrado(a)	*square*	redondo(a)	*round*
circular	*circular*		

Otras cualidades de las cosas   *Other qualities of things*

1. duro(a)   *hard*
2. blando(a)   *soft*
3. pesado(a)   *heavy*
4. ~~ligero(a)~~ liviano *lightweight*
5. nuevo(a)   *new*

6. viejo(a)   *old*
7. caro(a)   *expensive*
8. barato(a)   *inexpensive*
9. triangular   *triangular*
10. rectangular *rectangular*

INDEFINITE ARTICLES
SINGULAR AND PLURAL

	A/AN	SOME
MASCULINE	**un**	**unos**
FEMININE	**una**	**unas**

un libro   *a book*   unos libros   *some books*
una silla *a chair*   unas sillas   *some chairs*

EXISTENCE

había	*there was/were*
hay	*there is/are*
habrá	*there will be*

Note: Numbers or quantity words generally follow these expressions. In Spanish, there is only one form for both singular and plural.

No preceeds these expressions to tell what does not exist.

no había	*there wasn't/weren't*
no hay	*there isn't/aren't*
no habrá	*there won't be*

Esqueletos

¿ QUÉ + **HABÍA?**
HAY?
HABRÁ?

¿Qué había en la papelera?   *What was there in the wastepaper basket?*
¿Qué hay en el aula?   *What is there in the classroom?*
¿Qué habrá en la mochila?   *What will there be in the backpack?*

¿ CUÁNTO(A)
¿ CUÁNTOS(AS)   + *noun(s)* +   **HABÍA?**
HAY ?
HABRÁ?

¿Cuántas banderas había?   *How many flags were there?*
¿Cuánta leche hay?   *How much milk is there?*
¿Cuántos hombres habrá?   *How many men will there be?*

HABÍA	
HAY	+ *number* + *noun(s)*
HABRÁ	

Había tres libros.   *There were three books.*
Hay una bandera.   *There is one flag.*
Habrá seis flores.   *There will be six flowers.*

1 ***Sit-Con***   There is a substitute teacher in your classroom who cannot find anything. He or she asks where everything is. Your partner will be the teacher and will ask where various items are located. You reply by telling where things are.

EJEMPLO: Teacher: ¿Dónde están los lápices?   *Where are the pencils?*
Student: Hay un lápiz allí.   *There is a pencil over there.*
Teacher: ¿Dónde están las tijeras?   *Where are the scissors?*
Student: Hay unas tijeras aquí.   *There are some scissors here.*

2 **¿Qué hay en el aula?** *What is there in the classroom?*   Tell what there is in the classroom.

EJEMPLO: Hay treinta pupitres.   *There are thirty student desks.*
Hay un escritorio.   *There is one teacher's desk.*

3 **Juego**   Close your eyes and tell what things are in the classroom. No peeking! The winner is the one who remembered the most objects in the classroom.

4   List the things that were in your locker yesterday.

EJEMPLO: Había unos lápices, un libro, una calculadora…
There were some pencils, a book, calculator . . .

5   With your partner, create the classroom of the future.

EJEMPLO: Habrá computadoras en los pupitres, y no habrá profesores.
There will be computers on the desks, and there won't be any teachers.

SER FORMS WITH THINGS

Use **era/eran, es/son, será/serán** to talk about things as well as people.

La camisa era verde.	*The shirt was green.*
Los cuartos eran pequeños.	*The rooms were small.*
El libro es interesante.	*The book is interesting.*
Los lápices son baratos.	*The pencils are inexpensive.*
La película será popular.	*The film will be popular.*
Las mochilas serán caras.	*The backpacks will be expensive.*

DESCRIPTIVE ADJECTIVES

Most describing words follow the noun.

un libro <u>interesante</u>	*an interesting book*
el coche <u>viejo</u>	*the old car*

Describing words match the noun in gender and number. If the noun is feminine, the adjective is feminine. If the noun is plural, the adjective is plural.

el lib<u>ro</u> nuev<u>o</u>	*the new book*
los libr<u>os</u> nuev<u>os</u>	*the new books*
la mochil<u>a</u> nuev<u>a</u>	*the new backpack*
las mochil<u>as</u> nuev<u>as</u>	*the new backpacks*

6 Using the **esqueleto** (pro)noun + SER + *adjective,* describe things in the classroom.

EJEMPLOS: La pizarra es negra.   *The chalkboard is black.*
El globo es redondo.   *The globe is round.*
Las calculadoras son caras.   *The calculators are expensive.*

7 *Sit-Con*   Your family had a garage sale and you went through your belongings for items to sell. Make a list of the things you contributed to the sale.

EJEMPLO: Había tres suéteres pequeños.   *There were three small sweaters.*
Había cinco cintas baratas.   *There were five inexpensive tapes.*

COMPARING OBJECTS

To compare things, use the same pattern you learned in Lesson 2 to compare people.

	MÁS			QUE	
noun + SER	MENOS	+ adjective +	QUE	+ noun
	TAN			COMO	

Mi casa es <u>más</u> pequeña <u>que</u> la Casa Blanca.
My house is smaller than the White House.

Un cuaderno es <u>menos</u> caro <u>que</u> un libro.
A notebook is less expensive than a book.

Un elefante es <u>tan</u> grande <u>como</u> un coche.
An elephant is as big as a car.

Note: When saying *more* or *less (fewer) than* with a number, use: **más/menos... de...**

Tengo <u>más de</u> cinco dólares.   *I have more than five dollars.*
Tengo <u>menos de</u> veinte libros.   *I have fewer than twenty books.*

más grande   tan grande

menos grande

---

8 **¿Qué te gusta más?** *What do you like better?*   Give your partner some choices.

EJEMPLOS: ¿Te gusta más el fútbol americano o el béisbol?
Do you like football or baseball better?

Me gusta más el béisbol.
I like baseball better.

¿Qué te gusta más, la torta de chocolate o la torta de vainilla?
What do you like better, chocolate cake or vanilla cake?

Me gusta más la torta de chocolate.
I like chocolate cake better.

9 Take turns with your partner and compare different objects.

EJEMPLO: Un diccionario es más pesado que un lápiz.   *A dictionary is heavier than a pencil.*

Las mesas son más grandes que las sillas.   *The tables are bigger than the chairs.*

THE MOST. . ./THE LEAST. . .
SUPERLATIVES

To say something is *the most. . .* or *the least . . .* with an adjective, use the same pattern for comparing that you learned in Lesson 1 on page 147, but add **el/la/los/las** before **más** or **menos**.

Este cuadro es más grande.	*This picture is bigger.*
Este cuadro es <u>el</u> más grande.	*This picture is the biggest.*
Este cartera es menos cara.	*This briefcase is less expensive.*
Este cartera es <u>la</u> menos cara.	*That briefcase is the least expensive.*

If you want to say that something is *the most* or *least of* or *in* a group, use **de**.

José es el más guapo <u>de</u> la clase.   *José is the most handsome <u>in</u> the class.*

Esqueleto

(pro)noun + SER +	EL/ LOS LA/LAS	+	MÁS MENOS	+ adjective + DE + *noun*

La mochila de Miguel es <u>la</u> más cara <u>de</u> toda la clase.
Miguel's backpack is <u>the</u> most expensive <u>in</u> the whole class.

El libro de español es <u>el</u> menos aburrido <u>de</u> todos mis libros.
The Spanish book is <u>the</u> least boring <u>of</u> all my books.

10 Using the **esqueleto** above, tell about some of *the most/least [adjective]* people and things in class. Use adjectives from Unit II, Lessons 1, 2, and 6. Remember to make the adjectives agree in number and gender with the nouns they describe.

EJEMPLO: Juanita es la más simpática de la clase.   *Juanita is the nicest in the class.*
Mi cuadro es el más bonito de la clase.   *My picture is the prettiest in the class.*

11 **Chismes** *Gossip*   Choose three things or people. First make a comparison between two of them, then tell which is *the most . . .* or *the least . . .* of all. Take turns passing the gossip.

EJEMPLO: El auto de Miguel es más rápido que el auto de Juan.
Miguel's car is faster than Juan's car.

El auto de Roberto es el más rápido de todos.
Roberto's car is the fastest of all.

SHOWING OWNERSHIP
POSSESSIVE ADJECTIVES

mi(s)	*my*	nuestro(a)(os)(as)	*our*
tu(s)	*your [informal]*	vuestro(a)(os)(as)	*your [in Spain]*
su(s)	*your[formal]]/his/her/its*	su(s)	*your/their*

Nuestro and **vuestro** change **o** to **a** before a feminine noun.
   nuestr<u>o</u> herman<u>o</u>   *our brother*
   nuestr<u>a</u> herman<u>a</u>   *our sister*

Like any adjective in Spanish, possessive adjectives must add **s** before a plural noun.

SINGULAR	PLURAL	
mi amigo	mi<u>s</u> amigo<u>s</u>	*my friends*
su amigo	su<u>s</u> amigo<u>s</u>	*your/his/her/their friends*

---

12   Ask your partner if he or she has various classroom objects. Use an adjective to describe each one.

EJEMPLO: ¿Tienes tu libro nuevo?   *Do you have your new book?*

Sí, tengo mi libro nuevo.   *Yes, I have my new book.*

13   Describe some things or people that you and your partner have in common.

EJEMPLOS: Nuestra clase es muy grande.   *Our class is very big.*
Nuestro libro es interesante.   *Our book is interesting.*

14   Describe some things your family has.

EJEMPLOS: Nuestro coche es grande, viejo y rápido.   *Our car is big, old, and fast.*
Nuestra casa es bonita y moderna.   *Our house is pretty and modern.*

15   **Juego**   Play "One-up" again with your partner. Take turns telling about something you have. Then the other says that all of his or her things are . . . (Remember to make all the adjectives plural.)

EJEMPLO: Mi cuaderno es nuevo.   *My notebook is new.*

Todos mis cuadernos son nuevos.   *All my notebooks are new.*

16 Describe some of your relatives for your partner. Use singular and plural forms. Pay careful attention to the endings of **nuestro**.

EJEMPLO: Nuestros abuelos son viejos.   *Our grandparents are old.*
            Nuestra madre es bonita.   *Our mother is pretty.*

17 **Juego: ¡No, no son... ! ¡Sí son! *They're not . . . ! They are!*** Review the adjectives in Lessons 1 and 2. Tell what various people are like. Your partner will disagree and say they are the opposite. A third person will support either you or your partner.

EJEMPLO: Mis amigos son simpáticos.   *My friends are nice.*

            Tus amigos no son simpáticos.   *Your friends are not nice.*

            Sí, sus amigos son simpáticos.   *Yes, his friends are nice.*

CLARIFICATION OF SU

Because **su** or **sus** can mean *his, her, its, your,* or *their,* a clarifying expression sometimes needs to be used to tell whose things one is talking about. To clarify, instead of **su** or **sus** before the noun, use **de** + *the person following the noun.*

EL/LA/LOS/LAS + *noun* + DE + UD./ÉL/ELLA/UDS./ELLOS/ELLAS

el libro de Ud.	*your book*	el libro de Uds.	*your book*
el libro de él	*his book*	el libro de ellos	*their [masculine] book*
el libro de ella	*her book*	el libro de ellas	*their [feminine] book*

---

18 **Sit-Con** Yesterday the teacher found a book, a pencil, a calculator, a hat, a tape, and a radio left behind by María, Catalina, Ramón, and Esteban. Another student helps identify these things so they can be returned. With your partner, create the conversation between the student and the teacher.

EJEMPLO: ¿Es el lápiz de María o de Ramón?
            Is the ~~book~~ pencil María's or Ramón's?

            Es el lápiz de ella. No es el lápiz de él.
            It's her ~~book~~ pencil. It isn't his book.

PLACEMENT OF ADJECTIVES: SUMMARY

Many adjectives go before the noun just as they do in English. <u>Describing</u> adjectives usually come <u>after</u> the noun.

NUMBER	noun	dos libros	two books
QUANTITY	noun	muchos libros	many books
POSSESSION	noun	mis libros	my books
ARTICLE	noun	los libros	the books
	noun DESCRIPTION	libros interesantes	interesting books

19 You've just met a blind person who wants to know what you look like, including your clothing. Combine some descriptive adjectives *(after the noun)* with quantity and possessive adjectives *(before the noun)* to describe yourself.

EJEMPLO: Yo llevo unos zapatos grises nuevos.
I'm wearing new gray shoes.

Yo tengo muchos libros grandes.
I have a lot of big books.

Mi suéter rojo es nuevo.
My red sweater is new.

ENCUENTRO PERSONAL

Paulina decided to call her cousin Luisa in Mexico to find out about her school. Here is part of their conversation where they are comparing their classrooms.

Nuestra aula es pequeña, pero hay muchas cosas. Hay pupitres, tres archivadores y también un retroproyector y una computadora. Luisa, ¿cómo es el aula de Uds., grande o pequeña?

No hay muchos estudiantes en mi escuela, Paulina, y todos los estudiantes del mismo grado están en una aula grande.

¿Hay muchas ventanas en el aula?

Sí, hay unas ventanas altas y la puerta también tiene una ventana pequeña.

¿Comprendes?

1. Is Paulina's classroom big or small? And Luisa's?
2. What are some things in Paulina's classroom?
3. What are the windows like in Luisa's classroom?
4. Does Paulina's room have windows? Why or why not?
5. What interesting things are in Luisa's classroom?
6. What does the Mexican flag look like?
7. Why does Paulina think the Mexican flag is more interesting than the American flag?

¡Te toca!

A. Describe some of the things in your room at home to another student and ask if he or she has some of the same things in his or her room.

B. Describe other classrooms in your school.

Leemos y contamos

A. Marisol wrote a description of her classroom in her last letter to you. Draw what you think her classroom looks like.

> En el aula hay treinta estudiantes y una profesora. Hay treinta pupitres para los estudiantes y un escritorio para el profesor. También hay un mapa grande y banderas de México, España y los Estados Unidos. En la pizarra hay muchas palabras (words) en español. Hay un archivador grande de metal gris y encima (on top) del archivador hay un globo y unos papeles. Hay un estante con unos diccionarios, lápices, bolígrafos y una computadora. En la pared (wall) hay un reloj blanco y negro. También hay una mesa nueva con unas sillas rojas de plástico. Hay muchas cosas en nuestra aula, ¿no? ¿Cómo es tu aula?

B. Draw a picture of your classroom (including the teacher) and label it to send with your next letter to your pen pal.

C. Read this ambassador's description of his South American country. Do you think he is bragging? What words influenced your decision? Of course, a good ambassador would be much more diplomatic!

> Nosotros somos los más inteligentes del mundo. También somos generosos y simpáticos. Tenemos menos dinero pero más amigos que Uds., los norteamericanos. Nuestros hombres y mujeres de negocios son los más inteligentes del mundo y nuestras casas son las más bonitas. Nuestros obreros son los más trabajadores, nuestros estudiantes son los más estudiosos y nuestros autos son más rápidos que sus coches. En suma, yo creo (believe) que ¡somos los mejores del mundo!

D. **El embajador dice que...**   Write a report to your president, relaying in English what the ambassador said.

E. Because of your ability to speak Spanish, among other factors, you have just been named ambassador to a Spanish-speaking country. You must write a letter in Spanish to your counterpart. You want to make a good impression. Tell the South American ambassador about the United States. Be honest and diplomatic, but you may exaggerate a little!

F. The extraterrestrial in Lesson 1 comes from a planet where the shapes, sizes, and colors of objects are different from our world. Here is his description of what a classroom looks like on his planet.

> Nuestras pizarras son rojas y muy pequeñas.
> Nuestros armarios son cuadrados y amarillos.
> Nuestros libros son redondos y los cuadernos son triangulares.
> Nuestros lápices son muy largos.
> Nuestras banderas son de metal y son muy pesadas y duras.
> Nuestros tableros son muy altos y estrechos.
> Nuestras mesas son muy bajas y anchas.
> Nuestros archivadores son redondos, morados y verdes.
> ¡Yo creo que nuestro mundo es un mundo perfecto!

You find it hard to believe that:

a. the _____ are red and _____ .
b. the _____ are _____ and yellow.
c. the _____ are round.
d. the _____ are triangular.
e. the _____ are very long.
f. the _____ are _____ and very heavy.
g. the _____ are high and _____ .
h. the _____ are _____ and wide.
i. the _____ are _____ , purple, and _____ .

G. Draw the extraterrestrial's classroom and label the objects.

¡Así es!

The Mexican flag

The Mexican flag reflects the pride of the Mexican people in their pre-Columbian heritage. The majority of Mexicans are **mestizo,** which means "mixed," because they are of both European and Native American ancestry. After Mexico won its independence from Spain in 1821, the Mexicans chose a design for their flag that reflected their heritage: broad stripes of red, white, and green with a picture of an eagle perched on a cactus with a snake in its claws. This picture refers to an ancient Aztec legend that says the gods told them to settle at the place where they saw an eagle on a cactus eating a snake. According to the legend, that place is the site of the Mexican capital, Mexico City.

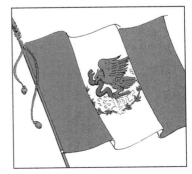

⋙ Unidad III ⋘

Unidad III
Tools

Vocabulario

El cuerpo *The body*
(Lección 1)

These words pertaining to parts of the body were presented in Unit I, Lesson 4.

la cabeza	*head*	la espalda	*back*
el pelo	*hair*	el corazón	*heart*
la cara	*face*	el estómago	*stomach*
el ojo	*eye*	el brazo	*arm*
la nariz	*nose*	el codo	*elbow*
la boca	*mouth*	la mano	*hand*
el diente	*tooth*	el dedo	*finger*
la oreja	*ear*	la pierna	*leg*
el cuello	*neck*	la rodilla	*knee*
la garganta	*throat*	el pie	*foot*
el cuerpo	*body*	el dedo del pie	*toe*

The following is additional vocabulary pertaining to parts of the body.

el cerebro	*brain*	los pulmones	*lungs*
la frente	*forehead*	el hígado	*liver*
la mejilla	*cheek*	el pulgar	*thumb*
el mentón	*chin*	la uña	*nail*
el bigote	*mustache*	la muñeca	*wrist*
la barba	*beard*	las nalgas	*buttocks*
el hombro	*shoulder*	el tobillo	*ankle*
el pecho	*chest*	el talón	*heel*

Las enfermedades *Illnesses*
(Lección 1)

¿Cómo estás?	*How are you (feeling)?*
Estoy muy bien.	*I'm very well.*
enfermo(a).	*sick, ill.*
un poco mejor.	*a little better.*
así, así.	*so-so.*

Las enfermedades   *Illnesses (continued)*
(Lección 1)

Tengo catarro.	I have a cold.	¡Qué lástima!	That's too bad.
fiebre.	a fever.	Lo siento.	I'm sorry.
tos.	a cough.	¿Y tú?	And you? [informal]
la gripe.	the flu.	¿Y Ud.?	And you? [formal]
dolor de…	a sore . . . /a . . . ache.	¡Salud!	Bless you! [said when
Tenía infección de…	I had an infected . . .		someone sneezes]
Me duele(n)…	My . . . is/are hurting me.		
Me dolía(n)…	My . . . was/were hurting me.		

Estados emocionales y físicos con «estar»
Emotional and physical states with estar
(Lección 1)

aburrido(a)	*bored*	enojado(a)	*angry*
agitado(a)	*upset*	loco(a)	*crazy*
cansado(a)	*tired*	nervioso(a)	*nervous*
celoso(a)	*jealous*	ocupado(a)	*busy*
contento(a)	*happy, content*	preocupado(a)	*worried*
enamorado(a)	*in love*	tranquilo(a)	*calm*
enfermo(a)	*sick*	triste	*sad*

Preposiciones de ubicación   *Prepositions of location*
(Lección 2)

a	*to, at*	a la derecha de	*to the right of*
de	*from*	a la izquierda de	*to the left of*
encima de	*on top of, above*	entre	*between*
en	*in, on, at*	alrededor de	*around, surrounding*
con	*with*	delante de	*in front of*
sin	*without*	detrás de	*behind*
fuera de	*outside of*	al lado de	*next to, beside*
dentro de	*inside of*	al otro lado de	*on the other side of*
sobre	*over, on*	cerca de	*near*
debajo de	*under*	lejos de	*far from*

Las partes del aula   *Parts of the classroom*
(Lección 2)

el suelo	*floor*	la pared	*wall*
el techo	*ceiling*	la puerta	*door*
el lado	*side*	la ventana	*window*
la parte de atrás	*back*	la luz	*light*
el frente	*front*	la fila	*row*

Lugares en la ciudad   *Places in the city*
(Lección 2)

el edificio	building	el teatro	theater
la casa	house	el restaurante	restaurant
la tienda	store	el cine	movie theater
el rascacielos	skyscraper	el supermercado	supermarket
el correo	post office	el almacén	department store
el banco	bank	el consultorio	medical office
el parque	park	la farmacia	pharmacy, drugstore
la playa	beach	el hospital	hospital
la escuela	school	la iglesia	church
la biblioteca	library	la sinagoga	synagogue
el museo	museum	la mezquita	mosque
el hotel	hotel	el templo	temple
la estación de gasolina	gas station		

la librería	bookstore	la heladería	ice cream parlor
la florería	flower shop	la panadería	bakery
la papelería	stationery store	la carnicería	butcher shop
la pastelería	pastry shop	la joyería	jewelry store
la zapatería	shoe store	la relojería	clock store
la ropería	clothing store	la dulcería	candy store
la lechería	dairy	la juguetería	toy store

La geografía   *Geography*
(Lección 3)

el país	country	el desierto	desert
la capital	capital	el río	river
el estado	state	el lago	lake
la ciudad	city	la costa	coast
el centro	center, downtown	la isla	island
el pueblo	town	el Océano Atlántico	Atlantic Ocean
las afueras	suburbs	el Océano Pacífico	Pacific Ocean
el campo	countryside	el Mar Caribe	Caribbean Sea
el habitante	inhabitant	el Mar Mediterráneo	Mediterranean Sea
la frontera	border	el norte	north
las montañas	mountains	el sur	south
la selva	forest, jungle	el este	east
los llanos	plains	el oeste	west

Expresiones de tiempo　*Time expressions*
(Lección 4)

The following time expressions were first presented in Unit II, Lesson 1.

anteayer	*day before yesterday*	antes	*before*
ayer	*yesterday*	ahora	*now*
hoy	*today*	después	*after*
mañana	*tomorrow*	entonces	*then*
pasado mañana	*day after tomorrow*	luego	*then, later*
		un día	*one day*
en el pasado	*in the past*	por la mañana	*in the morning*
en el presente	*in the present*	por la tarde	*in the afternoon*
en el futuro	*in the future*	por la noche	*in the evening, at night*
siempre	*always*	una vez	*once*
frecuentemente	*often*	otra vez	*again*
mucho	*a lot, much*	(dos) veces	*(two) times*
poco	*a little, few*	de una vez	*all at once*
raramente	*rarely, seldom*	de vez en cuando	*from time to time*
nunca	*never*	algunas veces	*sometimes*
mientras	*while*		
de repente	*suddenly*		
de niño(a)	*as a child*		
de viejo(a)	*as an old person*	todavía	*still, yet*
a los… años	*at the age of . . .*	todavía no	*not yet*
hace (seis meses)	*(six months) ago*	ya	*already*
en (seis meses)	*in (six months)*	ya no	*no longer*
el año pasado	*last year*	el próximo año	*next year*
el mes pasado	*last month*	el próximo mes	*next month*
la semana pasada	*last week*	la próxima semana	*next week*
el (lunes)	*on (Monday)*	todas las semanas	*every week*
todos los (lunes)	*every (Monday)*	todos los meses	*every month*
todos los días	*every day*	todos los años	*every year*

Los medios de transporte　*Means of transportation*
(Lección 4)

en auto	*by car*	por tren	*by train*
por avión	*by plane*	en bicicleta	*by bike*
en taxi	*by taxi*	por moto	*by motorcycle*
por barco	*by boat*	a pie	*on foot*
en autobús	*by bus*		

Los juguetes *Toys*
(Lección 5)

el juego de damas	*checkers game*	la carreta	*wagon*
el rompecabezas	*puzzle*	la cometa	*kite*
el tren eléctrico	*electric train*	la pelota	*ball*
el yoyo	*yo-yo*	el bate	*baseball bat*
el silbato	*whistle*	los patines de rueda	*roller skates*
el tambor	*drum*	los patines de hielo	*ice skates*
los bloques	*blocks*	el monopatín	*skateboard*
el soldado de juguete	*toy soldier*	el triciclo	*tricycle*
la muñeca	*doll*	la bicicleta	*bicycle*
el títere	*puppet*	las canicas	*marbles*
el osito de peluche	*teddy bear*	el globo	*balloon*
la casa de muñecas	*dollhouse*	el columpio	*swing*
el caballo balancín	*rocking horse*	el cajón de arena	*sandbox*

Condiciones físicas y emocionales con «tener»
Physical and emotional conditions with tener
(Lección 5)

tener (mucha) hambre	*to be (very) hungry*
tener (mucha) sed	*to be (very) thirsty*
tener (mucho) calor	*to be (very) warm/hot*
tener (mucho) frío	*to be (very) cold*
tener (mucha) prisa	*to be in a (big) hurry*
tener (mucho) sueño	*to be (very) sleepy*
tener (mucha) suerte	*to be (very) lucky*
tener (mucho) miedo	*to be (very) afraid*
tener (mucha) razón	*to be (very) right*
no tener razón	*to be wrong*
tener… años	*to be . . . years old*

Los animales *Animals*
(Lección 6)

Los animales domésticos *Domestic animals*
This vocabulary pertaining to domestic animals was presented in Unit I, Lesson 6.

el perro	*dog*	el gato	*cat*
el caballo	*horse*	la vaca	*cow*
el toro	*bull*	el cerdo	*pig*
la gallina	*hen*	el burro	*donkey*
el gallo	*rooster*	la oveja	*sheep*
el pato	*duck*		

Los animales   *Animals (continued)*
(Lección 6)

The following is additional vocabulary pertaining to domestic animals.

la cabra	*goat*	el pavo	*turkey*

Los animales salvajes   *Wild animals*

This vocabulary pertaining to wild animals was presented in Unit I, Lesson 6.

el pez	*fish*	el pájaro	*bird*
el conejo	*rabbit*	el mono	*monkey*
el elefante	*elephant*	el león	*lion*
el tigre	*tiger*	el oso	*bear*
la ardilla	*squirrel*	el ratón	*mouse*

The following is additional vocabulary pertaining to wild animals.

el periquito	*parakeet*	el perico	*parrot*
el ciervo	*deer*	el murciélago	*bat*
el gorila	*gorilla*	la rata	*rat*
la serpiente	*snake*	el leopardo	*leopard*
el rinoceronte	*rhinoceros*	el hipopótamo	*hippopotamus*
el búfalo	*buffalo*	la cebra	*zebra*
el camello	*camel*	la jirafa	*giraffe*
el canguro	*kangaroo*	el zorro	*fox*

Los animales acuáticos   *Aquatic animals*

el tiburón	*shark*	el pulpo	*octopus*
la ballena	*whale*	la tortuga	*turtle*
la rana	*frog*	el sapo	*toad*
el cangrejo	*crab*	la almeja	*clam*

Los insectos   *Insects*

la mosca	*fly*	el mosquito	*mosquito*
la hormiga	*ant*	la mariposa	*butterfly*
la abeja	*bee*	la cucaracha	*cockroach*
la araña	*spider*		

Estructura

VERBS

Estar *to be* (condition/location)
(Lecciones 1, 5)

	IMPERFECT *was/were* *used to be*	PRETERITE *was/were*	PRESENT *am/is/are*	FUTURE *will be*
yo	estaba	estuve	estoy	estaré
tú	estabas	estuviste	estás	estarás
Ud./él/ella	estaba	estuvo	está	estará
nosotros(as)	estábamos	estuvimos	estamos	estaremos
vosotros(as)	estabais	estuvisteis	estáis	estaréis
Uds./ellos/ellas	estaban	estuvieron	están	estarán

Ser *to be* (identification/characteristic/origin)
(Review II.6)
(Lección 4)

	IMPERFECT *was/were* *used to be*	PRETERITE *was/were*	PRESENT *am/is/are*	FUTURE *will be*
yo	era	fui	soy	seré
tú	eras	fuiste	eres	serás
Ud./él/ella	era	fue	es	será
nosotros(as)	éramos	fuimos	somos	seremos
vosotros(as)	erais	fuisteis	sois	seréis
Uds./ellos/ellas	eran	fueron	son	serán

The differences between ser *and* estar
(Lección 1)

SER

1. to identify a person or thing
   (noun or pronoun)
2. to tell basic characteristics/normal state
   (adjective)
3. to tell when
   (time, date, etc.)
4. to tell origin, owner, or material
   (**de** + noun))
5. to tell where an <u>event</u> takes place

ESTAR

1. to tell location
   (adverb or preposition of place)
2. to tell condition/not normal state
   (adjective)

Ser *vs.* estar *with adjectives*
(Lección 1)

SER	ESTAR
Characteristics:	Condition:
What something is normally like	How something is physically or emotionally changed
How we expect to find it	from its characteristic state

Ir   *to go*
(Lección 4)

	IMPERFECT	PRETERITE	PRESENT	FUTURE
	went	*went*	*go/goes*	*will go*
	was/were going	*did go*	*am/is/are going*	
	used to go		*do/does go*	
yo	iba	fui	voy	iré
tú	ibas	fuiste	vas	irás
Ud./él/ella	iba	fue	va	irá
nosotros(as)	íbamos	fuimos	vamos	iremos
vosotros(as)	ibais	fuisteis	vais	iréis
Uds./ellos/ellas	iban	fueron	van	irán

ir + a + *infinitive* = *to be going to . . .*

Tener   *to have*
(Lección 5)

	IMPERFECT	PRETERITE	PRESENT	FUTURE
	had	*had*	*am/is/are having*	*will have*
	was/were having	*did have*	*have/has*	
	used to have			
yo	tenía	tuve	tengo	tendré
tú	tenías	tuviste	tienes	tendrás
Ud./él/ella	tenía	tuvo	tiene	tendrá
nosotros(as)	teníamos	tuvimos	tenemos	tendremos
vosotros(as)	teníais	tuvisteis	tenéis	tendréis
Uds./ellos/ellas	tenían	tuvieron	tienen	tendrán

tener que + *infinitive* = *to have to . . .*

tener ganas de + *infinitive* = *to feel like . . . ing*

Indefinite articles after tener
(Lección 5)

Tengo un lápiz. *[affirmative sentence]*

No tengo lápiz. *[unmodified noun]*
No tengo un lápiz nuevo. *[modified noun]*

Unos and **unas** are generally omitted.

Gustar   *to be pleasing, to like*
(Lección 6)

IMPERFECT	PRETERITE	PRESENT	FUTURE	CONDITIONAL
used to please	*pleased*	*please(s)*	*will please*	*would please*
used to like	*liked*	*like(s)*	*will like*	*would like*
(me) gustaba	gustó	gusta	gustará	gustaría
(me) gustaban	gustaron	gustan	gustarán	gustarían

Preterite and imperfect
(Lección 4)

PRETERITE	IMPERFECT
Countable times	Uncountable times
(once or a stated number)	(indefinite number or unfinished)
reports:	describes:
action completed at	a. repeated (habitual) action
one point in time	b. ongoing (background) action

OTHER STRUCTURES

Contraction of de + el
(Lección 2)

>   **de + el = del**
>   Do not contract: **de la/de los/de las.**

Contraction of a + el
(Lección 4)

>   **a + el = al**
>   Do not contract: **a la/a los/a las.**

Two nouns together
(**Lección 2**)

> *noun* + **de** + *noun*

Pronouns following prepositions
(**Lección 2**)

	SINGULAR	PLURAL
Preposition +	mí	nosotros(as)
	ti	vosotros(as)
	Ud.	Uds.
	él	ellos
	ella	ellas

Mí and **ti** with **con** become **conmigo** and **contigo**.

Direct object pronouns
(**Lección 5**)

The direct object receives the action of the verb.

IT	THEM
lo	los
la	las

Direct object pronouns are placed <u>before</u> the verb with conjugated endings.

Direct object pronouns may be attached to the infinitive (**-ar, -er, -ir** endings).

Indirect object pronouns (to/for someone)
(**Lección 6**)

> **me** = *to/for me*
> **te** = *to/for you*
> **le** = *to/for you [formal]/him/her/it*
> **nos** = *to/for us*
> **os** = *to/for all of you [for that group of friends in Spain]*
> **les** = *to/for all of you/them*

Clarification of indirect object le/les
(**Lección 6**)

$$ a + \begin{cases} \text{Ud.} \\ \text{él} \\ \text{ella} \\ \text{(Juan, etc.)} \end{cases} + le \qquad\qquad a + \begin{cases} \text{Uds.} \\ \text{ellos} \\ \text{ellas} \\ \text{(Juan y María, etc.)} \end{cases} + les $$

For emphasis we can also use **a + mí/ti/nosotros/vosotros.**

Use of article with titles
(Lección 1)

> When talking <u>about</u> a person, add the article **(el/la/los/las)** before the title.
> When talking <u>to</u> a person, do not add the article before the title.

Demonstrative adjectives and pronouns
(Lección 3)

THIS	THESE	THAT	THOSE	THAT . . .	THOSE . . .	OVER THERE
este	estos	ese	esos	aquel	aquellos	[+ noun]
esta	estas	esa	esas	aquella	aquellas	

If no noun follows, put an accent mark on the first **e**.

Esqueletos

(pro)noun + **ESTAR** + *health condition*
(Lección 1)

> Yo estoy bien. *I am fine.*

(pro)noun + **TENER** + *health condition*
(Lección 1)

> Él tiene tos. *He has a cough.*
> Yo tenía fiebre. *I had a fever.*

(A + *person*) + ME/TE/LE NOS/OS/LES + DOLER + *body part*

(Lección 1)

Me duele el diente.   *My tooth hurts.*
A Juan le duelen los pies.   *Juan's feet hurt.*

(pro)noun* + ESTAR + *preposition of location* + *place

(Lección 2)

La profesora está delante de la pizarra.
The teacher is in front of the chalkboard.

Ellos estaban detrás del escritorio.
They were behind the desk.

(time expression)* + *(pro)noun* + IR + A + *place

(Lección 4)

Anoche yo fui al parque.   *Last night I went to the park.*

(pro)noun* + IR + A + *infinitive

(Lección 4)

Voy a estudiar esta noche.   *I am going to study tonight.*
Vamos a jugar al tenis mañana.   *We are going to play tennis tomorrow.*
Juan va a cantar en el coro.   *Juan is going to sing in the chorus.*

(pro)noun* + TENER + *(article)* + *noun* + *(adjective)

(Lección 5)

Miguel tiene coche.   *Miguel has a car.*
Miguel tiene un coche nuevo.   *Miguel has a new car.*
Ellos no tienen teléfono.   *They don't have a telephone.*

(pro)noun* + *object pronoun* + *verb

(Lección 5)

Yo lo tengo.   *I have it.*
Juan los tenía.   *Juan had them.*
Sara y Miguel la tendrán.   *Sara and Miguel will have it.*

(pro)noun + verb + infinitive + object pronoun

(Lección 5)

Ellos iban a escribirla.   *They were going to write it.*
Voy a comprarlos.   *I am going to buy them.*

OR

(pro)noun + object pronoun + verb + infinitive

(Lección 5)

Ellos la iban a escribir.   *They were going to write it.*
Los voy a comprar.   *I am going to buy them.*

(pro)noun + **TENER + **QUE** + infinitive**

(Lección 5)

Tengo que estudiar   *I have to study.*
Tendremos que visitar España.   *We will have to visit Spain.*
Mi tío tenía que trabajar mucho.   *My uncle had to work a lot.*

(pro)noun + **TENER + **GANAS DE** + infinitive**

(Lección 5)

Tenía ganas de descansar.   *I felt like resting.*
Tengo ganas de comer.   *I feel like eating.*
Ellos tendrán ganas de bailar.   *They will feel like dancing.*

(A + _person_) + ME/TE/LE NOS/OS/LES + GUSTAR + _noun(s)_

(Lección 6)

Me gusta el helado.   *I like ice cream.*
A Juan le gustan los tigres.   *Juan likes tigers.*
Nos gustaban las mariposas.   *We used to like butterflies.*

(A + _person_) + ME/TE/LE NOS/OS/LES + GUSTAR + _infinitive_

(Lección 6)

Me gusta bailar.   *I like to dance.*
A Raúl le gusta comer.   *Raúl likes to eat.*
Nos gustaba ir al cine.   *We used to like to go to the movies.*

Lo normal y lo anormal
¿Cómo estás?
Normal and not normal
How are you?

In this lesson, we will be reviewing the parts of the body presented on page 53 and the use of **ser** with nouns and description. Then we will learn a new verb so we can talk about health and emotional states. We will also learn to tell about what we think is not the normal state of things.

Vocabulario

El cuerpo *The body*

These words pertaining to parts of the body were presented in Unit I, Lesson 4.

la cabeza	*head*	la espalda	*back*
el pelo	*hair*	el corazón	*heart*
la cara	*face*	el estómago	*stomach*
el ojo	*eye*	el brazo	*arm*
la nariz	*nose*	el codo	*elbow*
la boca	*mouth*	la mano	*hand*
el diente	*tooth*	el dedo	*finger*
la oreja	*ear*	la pierna	*leg*
el cuello	*neck*	la rodilla	*knee*
la garganta	*throat*	el pie	*foot*
el cuerpo	*body*	el dedo del pie	*toe*

The following is additional vocabulary pertaining to parts of the body.

1.	el cerebro	*brain*	9. los pulmones	*lungs*
2.	la frente	*forehead*	10. el hígado	*liver*
3.	la mejilla	*cheek*	11. el pulgar	*thumb*
4.	el mentón	*chin*	12. la uña	*nail*
5.	el bigote	*mustache*	13. la muñeca	*wrist*
6.	la barba	*beard*	14. las nalgas	*buttocks*
7.	el hombro	*shoulder*	15. el tobillo	*ankle*
8.	el pecho	*chest*	16. el talón	*heel*

Note: When talking about the body, use **el/la/los/las,** *not* the possessive adjectives as in English, unless needed for clarification or emphasis.

Me duelen <u>los</u> pies. *<u>My</u> feet hurt me.*
Tengo infección de <u>la</u> garganta. *I have an infection in <u>my</u> throat.*

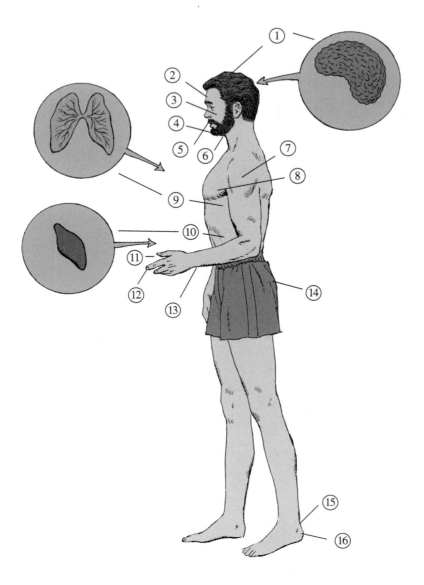

1 Take turns with a partner identifying the parts of the body. You might want to find additional pictures of people in magazines for extra practice.

EJEMPLO: ¿Qué es esto?   *What is this?*

Es la cabeza.   *It's the head.*

2 Do you remember the extraterrestrial who sent us the message describing itself on page 151? It has landed on Earth!! Review page 133 for the words relating to color, shape, and size. Describe the extraterrestrial. (How well did you draw it?)

EJEMPLO: La cabeza es redonda.   *Its head is round.*

ESTAR   *to be*

Now that we've reviewed the verb **ser** with description, we are ready to learn about the other verb used to express *to be:* **estar**. This verb is used to talk about conditions like health and emotional states as well as location. Here are the forms.

	IMPERFECT *was/were used to be*	PRESENT *am/is/are*	FUTURE *will be*
yo	estaba	estoy	estaré
tú	estabas	estás	estarás
Ud./él/ella	estaba	está	estará
nosotros(as)	estábamos	estamos	estaremos
vosotros(as)	estabais	estáis	estaréis
Uds./ellos/ellas	estaban	están	estarán

PERSON-TIME ENDINGS

The verb endings in Spanish indicate *who* is doing the action and *when*. *Who* corresponds to the subject (**yo, tú, él**, etc.) and *when* corresponds to past, present, and future. For example, the ending **-mos** on all verbs indicates the subject is *we*. And the **-aba** ending indicates that the action happened in the past. Therefore the *person–time ending* **-ábamos** indicates *we* were doing the action (or *being* in the case of **estar**) in the *past*.

Note: Remember that **vosotros** is used in Spain when talking to a group of friends.

Vocabulario

Las enfermedades   *Illnesses*

Estar is used in many health expressions referring to the condition of someone at the moment. (We already learned some in Unit I, Lesson 1.)

¿Cómo estás?	*How are you (feeling)?*
Estoy muy bien.	*I'm very well.*
enfermo(a).	*sick, ill.*
un poco mejor.	*a little better.*
así, así.	*so-so.*

peor   worse

Some health expressions use a form of the verb **tener** *(to have)*.

Tengo catarro.	*I have a cold.*
fiebre.	*a fever.*
tos.	*a cough.*
la gripe.	*the flu.*
dolor de…	*a sore . . ./a . . . ache.*
Tenía infección de…	*I had an infected . . .*

infection

Some health expressions use a form of the verb **doler** *(to hurt)*.

Me duele(n)*..	*My . . . is/are hurting me.*
Me dolía(n)…	*My . . . was/were hurting me.*

*Note: The **o** in **doler** changes to *ue* in this form.

Use the plural form **duelen** or **dolían** when there is more than one of something that hurts:

Me duele la cabeza.	*My head hurts. [one thing hurts]*
Me duelen los pies.	*My feet hurt. [two feet hurt]*

Here are some responses to health comments.

¡Qué lástima!	*That's too bad.*
Lo siento.	*I'm sorry.*
¿Y tú?	*And you? [informal]*
¿Y Ud.?	*And you? [formal]*
¡Salud!	*Bless you! [said when someone sneezes]*

Esqueletos

> **(pro)noun + ESTAR + *health condition***

Yo estoy bien.   *I am fine.*

> **(pro)noun + TENER + *health condition***

Él tiene tos.   *He has a cough.*
Yo tenía fiebre.   *I had a fever.*

> **(A + *person*) + ME/TE/LE NOS/OS/LES + DOLER + *body part***

Me duele el diente.   *My tooth hurts.*
A Juan le duelen los pies.   *Juan's feet hurt.*

3 *I'm sorry I asked!*   Ask your partner about all her or his ills—real and imagined.

EJEMPLO: ¿Cómo estás?
             How are you?

             No estoy bien. Me duelen (las piernas).
             I'm not well. My (legs) hurt me.

             Lo siento.
             I'm sorry.

4 *Sit-Con*   Tell your partner about the last time you stayed home from school because of illness.

EJEMPLO: ¿Por qué no estabas en clase?
Why weren't you in class?

Yo no estaba en clase la semana pasada porque tenía catarro y
  me dolía la garganta.
I wasn't in class last week because I had a cold and my throat hurt.

5 *Let's pretend.*   Ramón skipped school last week. When asked where he was, he said he was sick, but he couldn't keep his story straight and didn't tell the same story twice. Pretend to be Ramón and tell what he said to the following people.

a. a su profesor de matemáticas
b. a su profesor de español
c. a su consejero *(his counselor)*
d. a su pareja del laboratorio *(his lab partner)*
e. al conductor del autobús *(the bus driver)*
f. al entrenador de fútbol *(the soccer coach)*

(P.S. Ramón was caught and his parents punished him for skipping school.)

6 *Sit-Con*   It's career day and you're spending the day with Dr. García at her office. Here is her schedule:

HORA *(TIME)*	PACIENTE *(PATIENT)*	SÍNTOMAS *(SYMPTOMS)*
11:00	Sra. Catalina de Mendoza	dolor de estómago
1:00	Sr. Roberto Calderón	catarro
2:00	Sr. Pepe González	fiebre, tos, dolor de garganta
3:00	Srta. Josefa Chávez	examinación general
4:00	Sr. Javier Zamora	«no está bien» (hipocondriaco)

With your partner, recreate the initial conversation between Dr. García and each of her patients.

EJEMPLO: Médica: Buenos días, Sra. Mendoza. ¿Cómo está Ud.?
Good morning, Mrs. Mendoza. How are you?

Sra. Mendoza: No estoy bien. Tengo dolor de estómago.
I'm not well. I have a stomachache.

Médica: ¡Qué lástima!
That's too bad.

USE OF ARTICLE WITH TITLES

Some titles that may be used with a person's last name are:

señor (Sr.), señora (Sra.), señorita (Srta.), profesor(a), and **doctor(a).**

When talking <u>about</u> a person, add the article before the title. Do not add the article if you are talking <u>to</u> the person.

TALKING ABOUT	*TALKING TO*
¿Cómo está <u>el</u> señor Alcalá?	¿Cómo está Ud., señor Alcalá?
How is Mr. Alcalá?	*How are you, Mr. Alcalá?*
<u>La</u> doctora García es importante.	Buenos días, doctora García.
Dr. García is important.	*Good day, Dr. García.*

7 *Sit-Con*   Create a dialogue between Dr. García and her nurse, Srta. López, and one of the patients in Activity 6. Srta. López tells Dr. García who the next patient is, and then Dr. García finds out from the patient what the symptoms are.

EJEMPLO: Enfermera: Doctora García, aquí está el señor Calderón.
                               Dr. García, here is Mr. Calderón.
             Doctora García: Buenos días, señor Calderón. ¿Cómo está Ud. hoy?
                               Good morning, Mr. Calderón. How are you today?
             Señor Calderón: Buenos días, doctora García. Tengo catarro.
                               Good morning, Dr. García. I have a cold.

8 Back in class the next day, tell what was troubling each of Dr. García's patients in Activity 6.

EJEMPLO: La señora Mendoza no estaba bien.
                Tenía dolor de estómago.
             Mrs. Mendoza was not well.
                She had a stomachache.

Enfermedad

Fumar cigarrillos puede causar cáncer del pulmón en hombres y mujeres. Doctores del mundo entero están de acuerdo con esto. Pero, además de morir de cáncer del pulmón, los que fuman cigarrillos pueden tener toses insalubres; algunos respiran con dificultad o tienen dolores en el pecho y mareos. Otros tienen malestares del estómago y la mayoría tiene mal aliento. Los que fuman mucho pueden morir más pronto que los que no fuman, a menudo cuando están en la cumbre de ganar más dinero para el sustento de la familia.

Vocabulario

Estados emocionales y físicos con «estar»
Emotional and physical states with estar

1. aburrido(a)	*bored*	8. enojado(a)	*angry*
2. agitado(a)	*upset*	9. loco(a)	*crazy*
3. cansado(a)	*tired*	10. nervioso(a)	*nervous*
4. celoso(a)	*jealous*	11. ocupado(a)	*busy*
5. contento(a)	*happy, content*	12. preocupado(a)	*worried*
6. enamorado(a)	*in love*	13. tranquilo(a)	*calm*
7. enfermo(a)	*sick*	14. triste	*sad*

9 **¿Cómo estás?** Tell your partner how you feel when each of these things happens.

EJEMPLO: No estoy tranquilo. Estoy preocupado.   *I'm not calm. I'm worried.*

a. you have to go to the dentist
b. your brother or sister uses your stereo
c. you stay up too late
d. you have nothing to do
e. you have to take a test, and
   you are not prepared
f. you have eaten too much
g. your pet runs away
h. your pet comes back

i. your best friend is moving away
j. you meet a famous person
k. you have a headache
l. you see your girlfriend or boyfriend
m. you get an *A* in Spanish
n. you have a lot to do
o. your boyfriend or girlfriend
   goes out with someone else

THE DIFFERENCES BETWEEN SER AND ESTAR

SER

1. to identify a person or thing
   (noun or pronoun)
       Es una mesa.   *It's a table.*
       Somos estudiantes.   *We are students.*
       ¿Quién es? Soy yo.   *Who is it? It is I.*

2. to tell basic characteristics/normal state
   (adjective)
       Juan es alto.   *Juan is tall.*
       Juan es feliz.   *Juan is happy.*

3. to tell when
   (time, date, etc.)
       ¿Qué hora es?   *What time is it?*
       Es el dos de febrero.   *It's February 2.*

4. to tell origin, owner, or material
   (**de** + noun)
       Mi padre es de Chile.   *My father is from Chile.*
       El libro es de Juanita.   *The book is Juanita's.*
       La mesa es de plástico.   *The table is plastic.*

5. to tell where an <u>event</u> takes place
       El concierto será en el parque.
       The concert will be in the park.

ESTAR

1. to tell location
   (adverb or preposition of place)
       La mesa está allí.   *The table is there.*
       Estamos en la escuela.   *We are in school.*

2. to tell condition/not normal state
   (adjective)
       Juan está enfermo.   *Juan is ill.*
       Hoy Juan está triste.   *Today Juan is sad.*

Es una mesa.
Es grande.

Es mi amigo.
Es alto.
Es de Texas.

El concierto es en el parque el
lunes. Es a las 8 de la noche.

Mi amigo de
Texas está aquí.
Está enfermo.

SER VS. ESTAR WITH ADJECTIVES

SER	ESTAR
Characteristics:	Condition:
What something is normally like	How something is physically or emotionally
How we expect to find it	changed from its characteristic state

La sopa de pollo <u>es</u> caliente.   *Chicken soup is hot.*
[characteristic/the way it was expected to be]

La sopa de pollo <u>está</u> fría.   *The chicken soup is cold.*
[condition/not the way it was expected to be]

If we heat it again, then we've changed its condition.
   Ahora la sopa de pollo <u>está</u> caliente.   *Now the chicken soup is hot. [change of condition]*

When does a condition become a characteristic?
   Answer: When we expect the person or thing to be that way!

Use **ser** with these characteristics that can change.

rico *rich*	nuevo *new*	joven *young*
pobre *poor*	viejo *old*	feliz *happy*

Use **estar** with these conditions:

solo *alone*	casado *married*	roto *broken*
juntos *together*	muerto *dead*	

The meaning of some adjectives changes when used with **ser** or **estar**.

Juan es aburrido. *Juan is <u>boring</u>.*	Juan está aburrido. *Juan is <u>bored</u>.*
Yo soy lista. *I am <u>clever</u>.*	Yo estoy lista. *I am <u>ready</u>.*
Somos seguros. *We are <u>safe</u>.*	Estamos seguros. *We are <u>sure/certain</u>.*

10 Choose several people in your class and tell some of their characteristics and also the physical or emotional condition they're in.

EJEMPLO: Ricardo es alto y muy simpático.
   Ricardo is tall and very nice. [characteristics]

   Hoy Ricardo está preocupado.
   Today Ricardo is worried. [condition]

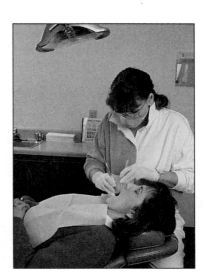

11 Rip Van Winkle slept for twenty years. When he awoke, everything had changed. The people did not look as he expected them to. Pretend that you wake up after a twenty-year sleep. Tell your partner about the condition of some things and people you know today when you wake up in twenty years. Use your imagination!

EJEMPLO: La señora Valdez era joven pero ahora está vieja.
Señora Valdez used to be young, but now she is (looks) old.

Mi amigo Juan era moreno pero ahora está canoso.
My friend Juan was dark-haired, but now he is white-haired.

ENCUENTRO PERSONAL

Paulina isn't feeling well and telephones her doctor, Dr. Calvo. Read their conversation to find out what is wrong with Paulina. (Note that they use the **Ud.** form of address since it is a formal situation.)

¿Comprendes?

1. How is Paulina today?
2. What is hurting her?
3. What symptoms doesn't she have?
4. Why does Dr. Calvo think she is not sick?
5. What does the doctor recommend?
6. What will she do if she isn't feeling better tomorrow?
7. How does Paulina feel at the end of the call?

¡Te toca!

Write your own conversation in which one person is the doctor and the other is the patient.

Leemos y contamos

A. Here is an article from a medical advice column that Rosita read in the newspaper.

Querido Dr. Sábelotodo,

   Tengo un terrible dolor de ojo cuando bebo *(I drink)* mi café. También me duelen la garganta y el estómago. Y después de comer estoy muy enfermo. En su opinión, ¿cuál es mi problema?

Enfermo en Chicago

Estimado enfermo,

   Creo que *(I think that)* su problema de la garganta y del estómago es el beber café muy caliente y el problema del dolor de ojo es el no sacar la cuchara de la taza *(take the spoon out of the cup)*. Debe *(You ought to)* beber leche fría, sin cuchara.

Dr. Sábelotodo

1. What were the symptoms that the reader reported?
2. When did they occur?
3. What was Dr. Sábelotodo's diagnosis?
4. What did he advise the reader to do?
5. Can you figure out what Dr. Sábelotodo's name means?

B. Sean missed class one Friday and the following Monday he brought this note to his teacher to explain his absence. See how many reasons you can find.

Querida maestra,

Favor de perdonar la ausencia (absence) de Sean el viernes pasado. Él estaba muy enfermo. Él es muy listo y es un buen estudiante. Siempre está en la clase pero el viernes tenía una tos terrible y una fiebre alta. También le dolía mucho la garganta y tenía un dolor de cabeza intolerable. Creo que (I believe) tenía una infección de los pulmones. Era un catarro muy serio o la gripe, pero él es un muchacho muy fuerte y ahora está perfectamente bien. Sean es un muchacho admirable, ¿no?

Gracias por su atención,
Mi abuela

1. How many things were wrong with Sean? What were they?
2. What descriptions of Sean's characteristics were given? How many were favorable and how many were not?
3. Which verb, **ser** or **estar**, was used for some of the answers to the first question? And the second question? Why was one or the other used in each instance?
4. Would you believe Sean's excuse if you were his teacher? Why or why not?

¡Así es!

The disease called Turista

Foreigners traveling in Latin America often fall victim to an intestinal disease called **turista** because it mostly affects tourists. **Turista** in its most common form is not serious and usually goes away in a couple of days. Doctors might recommend bed rest and a diet of easily digestible foods, such as bananas, rice, apples, and toast. Many pharmacies carry over-the-counter medications that will help as well. In its more serious form, **turista** is called amebic dysentery and requires medication. The problem is that the traveler has not developed the immunities needed for the local environment. It is usually caused by drinking impure water or eating unwashed, uncooked food. Some precautions to take are: drink mineral water and use ice cubes made from purified water, peel or cook fruits and vegetables, and keep your hands clean. It may surprise you to know that Latin Americans traveling in North America sometimes get **turista** too!

Gran Plan Especial		
Vuelo en Clase Turista		
Hotel Cinco Estrellas		
2 noches	**noche adicional**	
ACAPULCO		
México, D.F.	N$ 587	N$ 127
Guadalajara	N$ 661	N$ 127
Monterrey	N$ 1,057	N$ 127
CANCUN Y PLAYACAR		
México, D.F.	N$ 1,149	N$ 156
Guadalajara	N$ 1,276	N$ 156
Monterrey	N$ 1,648	N$ 156
PUERTO VALLARTA		
México, D.F.	N$ 653	N$ 116
Guadalajara	N$ 448	N$ 116
Monterrey	N$ 893	N$ 116

(Saliendo de)

- Precios por persona en base a ocupación doble.
- Gran Plan Especial, incluye transportación aérea y 2 noches de hospedaje.

¿Dónde está...?
Where is . . .?

In this lesson, we will use the verb **estar** to tell where people and things are. We'll learn the words that tell location so we can tell where things are in the classroom and in our city.

PREPOSITIONS

Prepositions are words that tell the relationship between two nouns.

estudiantes <u>con</u> libros	*students <u>with</u> books*
un lápiz <u>en</u> la mesa	*a pencil <u>on</u> the table*

Vocabulario

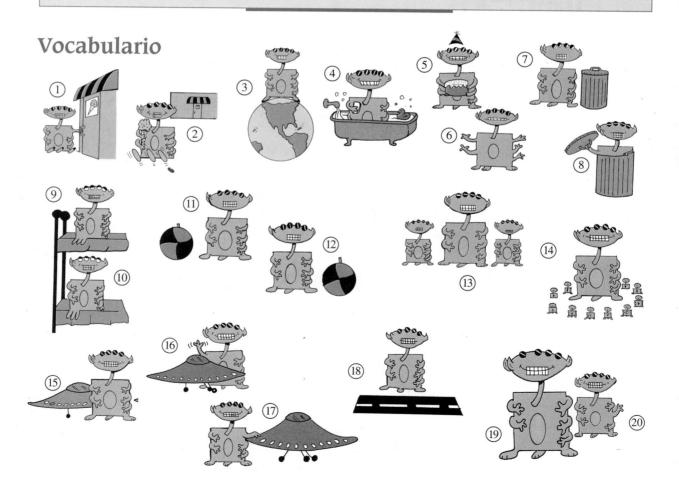

Preposiciones de ubicación   *Prepositions of location*

1. a*	*to, at*	11. a la derecha de	*to the right of*
2. de	*from*	12. a la izquierda de	*to the left of*
3. encima de**	*on top of, above*	13. entre	*between*
4. en	*in, on, at*	14. alrededor de	*around, surrounding*
5. con	*with*	15. delante de	*in front of*
6. sin	*without*	16. detrás de	*behind*
7. fuera de	*outside of*	17. al lado de	*next to, beside*
8. dentro de	*inside of*	18. al otro lado de	*on the other side of*
9. sobre	*over, on*	19. cerca de	*near*
10. debajo de	*under*	20. lejos de	*far from*

*The preposition **a** is used with verbs of motion. With **estar** and other verbs that are not motion, use **en**.

Me gusta <u>ir a</u> una fiesta.   *I like <u>to go to</u> a party.*

Me gusta <u>estar en</u> una fiesta.   *I like <u>to be at</u> a party.*

Me gusta <u>cantar en</u> una fiesta.   *I like <u>to sing at</u> a party.*

Note: **De is used with certain prepositions when a noun follows.

Vivo cerca de la escuela.   *I live near the school.*

Vivo cerca.   *I live nearby.*

Vocabulario

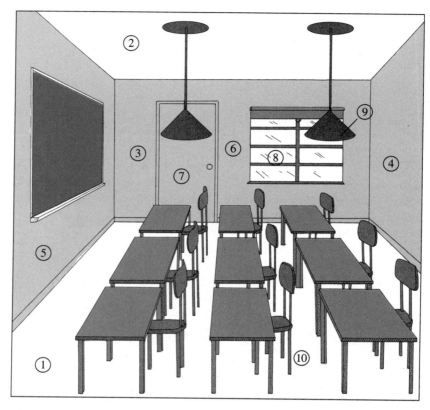

Las partes del aula   *Parts of the classroom*

1. el suelo	*floor*		6. la pared	*wall*
2. el techo	*ceiling*		7. la puerta	*door*
3. el lado	*side*		8. la ventana	*window*
4. la parte de atrás	*back*		9. la luz	*light*
5. el frente	*front*		10. la fila	*row*

CONTRACTION OF DE + EL

de + el = del

When **de** *(of, from)* is followed by **el** *(the)*, the two words become one word: **del**.

Mi pupitre está lejos <u>del</u> frente.	*My desk is far from the front.*
El profesor está delante <u>del</u> escritorio.	*The teacher is in front of the desk.*

But do <u>not</u> change **de la/de los/de las**.

El escritorio está a la izquierda <u>de las</u> sillas.	*The desk is to the left of the chairs.*

Esqueleto

(pro)noun + **ESTAR** + *preposition of location* + *place*

La profesora está delante de la pizarra.   *The teacher is in front of the chalkboard.*
Ellos estaban detrás del escritorio.   *They were behind the desk.*

Before doing the following activities, review the vocabulary pertaining to classroom objects on page 132.

1 Where are things located in your classroom? Follow the examples below to describe your classroom.

EJEMPLOS: La bandera está en el frente del aula.   *The flag is in the front of the classroom.*
El archivador está cerca del escritorio.   *The filing cabinet is near the desk.*

2 Tell where you are in the classroom in relation to others.

EJEMPLO: ¿Dónde estás en el aula?   *Where are you in the classroom?*

Estoy delante de Carlos, a la izquierda de María y detrás de Enrique.
   Estoy cerca de la puerta.
I am in front of Carlos, to the left of María, and behind Enrique.
   I am near the door.

3 Tell where you used to sit last year.

EJEMPLO: ¿Dónde estabas en el aula el año pasado?
Where were you in the classroom last year?

Yo estaba detrás de mi amigo Juan.
I was behind my friend Juan.

4 Suppose you have the opportunity to choose your own seat. Tell where you will be seated.

EJEMPLO: ¿Dónde estarás en el aula?   *Where will you be in the classroom?*

Yo estaré cerca de la pizarra.   *I will be near the chalkboard.*

5 Pretend that you are the teacher and you have to make a seating chart. Tell where various members of your class will be seated.

EJEMPLO: Paulina estará lejos de su amiga Rosita.
Paulina will be far from her friend Rosita.

Miguel y Felipe estarán cerca de la pizarra.
Miguel and Felipe will be near the chalkboard.

PRONOUNS FOLLOWING PREPOSITIONS

Preposition +	mí	nosotros(as)
	ti	vosotros(as)
	Ud.	Uds.
	él	ellos
	ella	ellas

Note: All prepositional pronouns except **mí** and **ti** are the same as the subject pronouns. The word for *my* is also **mi** but without the accent.

Juan está lejos de ti.   *Juan is far from you.*
Elsa está cerca de nosotros.   *Elsa is near us.*
Ellos estaban allí sin mí.   *They were there without me.*

When **con** immediately precedes **mí** and **ti**, the forms become **conmigo** and **contigo**.
Susana está <u>conmigo</u>.   *Susana is with me.*

Use **tú** and **yo** with the preposition **entre**.
El pupitre de Miguel está entre tú y yo.   *Miguel's desk is between you and me.*

---

6 Tell where different people sit in relation to you.

EJEMPLO: Juan está al lado de mí.   *Juan is next to me.*
           Susanita está detrás de mí.   *Susanita is behind me.*

7 Point out other people and tell where they sit, using pronouns instead of names.

EJEMPLO: Victoria está al lado de ella.   *Victoria is next to her.*
           Victoria está lejos de ti.   *Victoria is far from you.*

8 **Juego**   Describe the location of an object without telling what the object is. Your partner will try to guess what you are describing. Indicate whether your partner's guess is correct or not.

EJEMPLO: Está en la pared. Está cerca de la puerta. Está sobre la pizarra. ¿Qué es?
           It's on the wall. It's near the door. It's over the chalkboard. What is it?

           Es la bandera americana.
           It's the American flag.

           Sí, tienes razón.
           Yes, you are right.

9 Juego   Choose an object in the room. Your partner will ask questions to try to guess what you have chosen. The person who guesses with the fewest questions wins.

EJEMPLO: ¿Está en el suelo?   *Is it on the floor?*

Sí, está en el suelo.   *Yes, it's on the floor.*

¿Está cerca de la pizarra?   *Is it near the chalkboard?*

No, no está cerca de la pizarra.   *No, it's not near the chalkboard.*

TWO NOUNS TOGETHER
NOUN + DE + *NOUN*

When a noun is used to describe another noun, the word order is changed and **de** (*of*) is used between the two nouns.

la tienda <u>de</u> ropa	*the clothing store*
el libro <u>de</u> español	*the Spanish book*

There is no apostrophe s (*'s*) to show possession in Spanish. Use the two nouns separated by **de** (*of*) instead.

la silla <u>del</u> profesor	*the teacher's chair*
la casa <u>de</u> María	*María's house*

---

10 Juego   Divide the class into groups of four people. Person #1 chooses an item in the classroom. Person #2 tells who it belongs to. Person #3 tells what it is made of. Person #4 describes it. Then another person becomes #1.

EJEMPLO: #1 la silla   *the chair*
#2 Es la silla del profesor.   *It's the teacher's chair.*
#3 Es una silla de madera.   *It's a chair made of wood.*
#4 Es muy vieja.   *It's very old.*

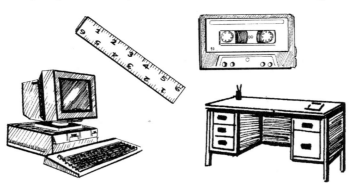

Vocabulario

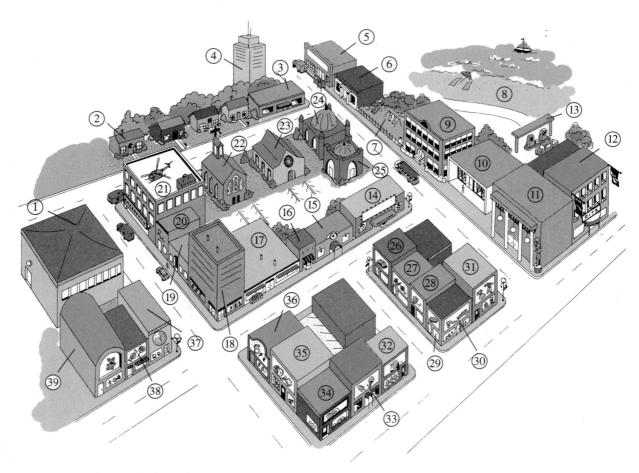

Lugares en la ciudad *Places in the city*

1.	el edificio	*building*	14.	el teatro	*theater*
2.	la casa	*house*	15.	el restaurante	*restaurant*
3.	la tienda	*store*	16.	el cine	*movie theater*
4.	el rascacielos	*skyscraper*	17.	el supermercado	*supermarket*
5.	el correo	*post office*	18.	el almacén	*department store*
6.	el banco	*bank*	19.	el consultorio	*medical office*
7.	el parque	*park*	20.	la farmacia	*pharmacy, drugstore*
8.	la playa	*beach*	21.	el hospital	*hospital*
9.	la escuela	*school*	22.	la iglesia	*church*
10.	la biblioteca	*library*	23.	la sinagoga	*synagogue*
11.	el museo	*museum*	24.	la mezquita	*mosque*
12.	el hotel	*hotel*	25.	el templo	*temple*
13.	la estación de gasolina	*gas station*			

Note: A noun that ends in **ería** means a *place to buy.*

26. libro + ería = librería	*a place to buy books / bookstore*
27. flor + ería = florería	*a place to buy flowers / flower shop*
28. la papelería	*stationery store*
29. la pastelería	*pastry shop*
30. la zapatería	*shoe store*
31. la ropería	*clothing store*
32. la lechería	*dairy*

33. la heladería	*ice cream parlor*
34. la panadería	*bakery*
35. la carnicería	*butcher shop*
36. la joyería	*jewelry store*
37. la relojería	*clock store*
38. la dulcería	*candy store*
39. la juguetería	*toy store*

11 **¿Dónde está...?**   Tell where five different places are located in relation to your school. (If you can, use a map of your city or town.)

EJEMPLO: ¿Dónde está el supermercado?   *Where is the supermarket?*

Está al oeste de la escuela.   *It's west of the school.*

12 Make a diagram of an intersection in your city or town. Work with your partner to locate the buildings. Write a brief description of your diagram for your teacher.

EJEMPLO: El restaurante está al lado del banco.   *The restaurant is next to the bank.*
La pizzería está delante del banco.   *The pizzeria is in front of the bank.*

13 Take turns with your partner. Using the map of Pueblochico, tell each other where several places are. Review the prepositions of location on page 253.

EJEMPLO: La escuela primaria está cerca de la juguetería.
The elementary school is near the toy store.

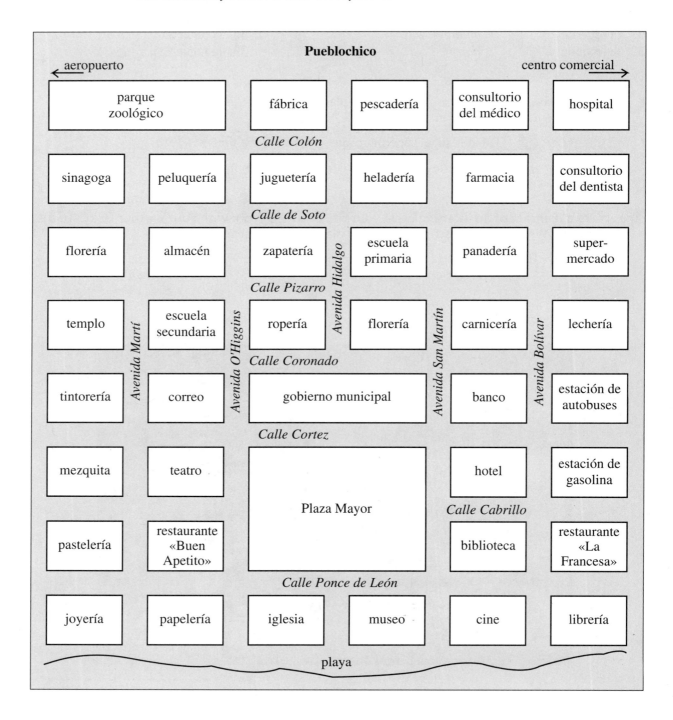

Before doing Activities 14 and 15, review the days of the week and telling time presented on page 9.

14 *Sit-Con* **¿Dónde estabas?**   Pretend that your friend is never at home when you telephone. Find out from your partner where he or she was the last five times you telephoned during the past week.

EJEMPLO: ¿Dónde estabas el sábado a las diez de la mañana?
Where were you on Saturday at ten in the morning?

Yo estaba en el supermercado.
I was at the supermarket.

15 *Sit-Con*   You want to return the book you borrowed from a friend, but she is not home when you go there. Find out where your friend will be at various times next week, and then choose the most convenient time to meet each other.

EJEMPLO: ¿Dónde estarás el miércoles a las cuatro y media?
Where will you be on Wednesday at four-thirty?

Estaré en…
I will be at/in . . .

16 **Encuesta**   Find out from several of your classmates where they think they will be living in ten years. What do they think their jobs will be?

EJEMPLO: ¿Dónde estarás en diez años?
Where will you be in ten years?

Estaré en California.
I will be in California.

¿Qué serás?
What will you be?

Seré vendedor de autos.
I'll be a car salesperson.

EMPLEOS   EMPLEOS

SE SOLICITA: SECRETARIA
CON CONOCIMIENTOS DE INGLES.
COMUNICARSE: LIC. SALAS. 574-79-76 Y
574-59-16 N$2,000 MAS PRESTACIONES.

SOLICITAMOS
PROMOTORES PARA
INSTITUTOS QUE LA-
BORAN LOS DOMIN-
GOS CON CARRERAS
QUE CAPACITAN PARA
TRABAJO. 525-29-73

SE SOLICITAN
EDECANES EXCELENTE
PRESENTACION. COMU-
NICARSE AL 594-90-54
GACY PROFESIONAL EN
EDECANES.

ESTAS GANANDO
LO QUE VALES?
NO? HAS TU PRO-
PIO NEGOCIO.
LLAMA: 554-82-
97, 658-80-06

EMPRESA AMERICANA
SOLICITA PERSONAS
QUIERAN GANAR
N$3,000 TIEMPO LIBRE.
AREA SALUD. OLIVIA
GARCIA. TEL. 538-56-50

OFREZCO MIS SERVICIOS
PARA CUIDAR CASA O TERRENO. FAMILIA: ESPOSA
2 NIÑOS. SR. RODRIGUEZ. 522-20-38 RECADO.
9:00-12:00 Y 4:00-7:00

ENCUENTRO PERSONAL

Salvador recently moved to town from the Dominican Republic, and Paulina is telling him where various places are so he will feel at home.

¿Comprendes?

1. What does Paulina tell Salvador there is near the school? Why?
2. What does Salvador ask her about next?
3. Why does Salvador ask about a restaurant?
4. Is there a restaurant near school? If not, what is there?
5. What does Salvador ask Paulina at the end of the conversation?
6. Do you think she gave it to him?

¡Te toca!

Tell someone in the class where various places are in your town or in other cities that you are familiar with.

Leemos y contamos

A. Inés is describing where various things are in her classroom. Read what she says, then draw a picture of her classroom with all of the objects she mentions in their appropriate place and label them.

El aula de mi clase de español es pequeña. Sólo hay diez y seis pupitres en cuatro filas. Mi pupitre está en el frente a la izquierda, cerca de las ventanas. El escritorio del profesor está en el frente de la clase pero un poco a la derecha, cerca de la puerta. Hay una pizarra en la pared del frente y también en la pared a la derecha. Hay una papelera en el rincón (corner) *cerca de la puerta y en el rincón a la izquierda hay una computadora. El reloj está sobre la puerta. En la parte de atrás hay un archivador gris y una mesa con dos sillas. Debajo de la mesa hay una papelera también. Mi pupitre está en la primera fila. A la derecha está mi amigo Sean. Detrás de mí está Rosita y a la derecha de ella está Paulina. ¡Yo estoy en la primera fila porque me gusta la profesora!*

B. Write a description of your classroom.

C. Imagine that your teacher has given you permission to move things around in the classroom. Describe where various objects were (**estaba[n]**) and where they will be (**estará[n]**). Draw a diagram and label the objects in their new locations.

> Una papelera estaba cerca de la puerta pero ahora estará al lado de la ventana.
> *A wastepaper basket was near the door but now it will be next to the window.*

D. Read this description of Andrés's hometown. Then answer the questions and draw a map of the town.

> *Mi casa está en las afueras* (suburbs) *al sur de la ciudad, en la calle* (street) *principal que se llama Avenida* (avenue) *Las Palmas. Más al sur hay un lago con un parque. En la costa oeste del lago hay una playa bonita. El centro de la ciudad está al norte de mi casa. En el centro hay una plaza y al norte de la plaza están el correo y la biblioteca. Al este de la plaza hay una iglesia y unos edificios del gobierno* (government).
>
> *Cerca de mi casa en la Avenida Las Palmas hay unas tiendas: una farmacia, un supermercado y una librería. Dentro del supermercado hay una panadería y una carnicería.*

Cierto o falso   *True or false*

1. La casa de Andrés está en el centro de la ciudad.
2. Su casa está en la calle principal.
3. La casa está al sur de la biblioteca.
4. La iglesia está al norte de la plaza.
5. El supermercado está lejos de la casa de Andrés.
6. La farmacia está dentro del supermercado.

E. Write a description of your city or town.

F. Our extraterrestrial has returned with a description of his city. As you read his description, draw a diagram showing where everything is. Compare your drawing with those of your classmates and decide whose is most accurate.

> Soy de una ciudad grande en una isla grande donde hay unos rascacielos rectangulares muy altos en el centro. Alrededor de la ciudad hay un lago grande. Todas las casas son triangulares y están en el lago. En la orilla *(shore)* del lago hay muchos edificios redondos donde están las tiendas. Están entre el lago y las montañas.
>
> Dentro de los rascacielos, hay muchas tiendas muy pequeñas. Por ejemplo, hay una carnicería, una panadería, unas roperías, una farmacia y una librería. Antes había también una zapatería pero ahora no llevamos zapatos. Muchos estudiantes trabajan *(work)* en las tiendas. Sobre los techos de los edificios están las escuelas y al lado de las escuelas hay una biblioteca y un museo. (Están cerca de la escuela porque los estudiantes los visitan frecuentemente.)
>
> En otro edificio lejos de las escuelas hay muchos pequeños consultorios de dentistas y de médicos. También hay un hospital y una farmacia. Detrás de este edificio está el cementerio.
>
> Al otro lado de la ciudad hay unas iglesias, mezquitas, templos y sinagogas. Al lado derecho hay un parque grande. No hay almacenes porque hay muchas tiendas pequeñas debajo del mismo *(same)* techo. No hay muchos supermercados porque hay muchas tiendas especializadas... y todas están bajo el mismo techo.
>
> Es una ciudad muy bonita y bien organizada, ¿no?

¡Así es!

The plaza

Most Spanish and Latin American towns have a central plaza that is usually paved, with trees and benches and perhaps a fountain. The church and government buildings usually face the plaza. Since in most areas of the Spanish-speaking world the weather is rather warm, the plaza is a pleasant place to spend free time and to meet people. On Sundays it is customary for the unmarried girls to walk in one direction around the plaza and the boys to walk in the other direction. The boys often make flattering remarks called **piropos,** which the girls usually pretend not to hear. Other family members come and sit on benches in the plaza to enjoy the afternoon together. Band concerts and other social events often take place there.

Una lección de geografía
A geography lesson

In Unit II, Lesson 3, we learned how to say the nationalities of people around the world. In this lesson we will learn to describe the geography of the countries where Spanish is spoken, as well as the names of their capital cities. We will also learn to point things out by saying *this, that, these, those*.

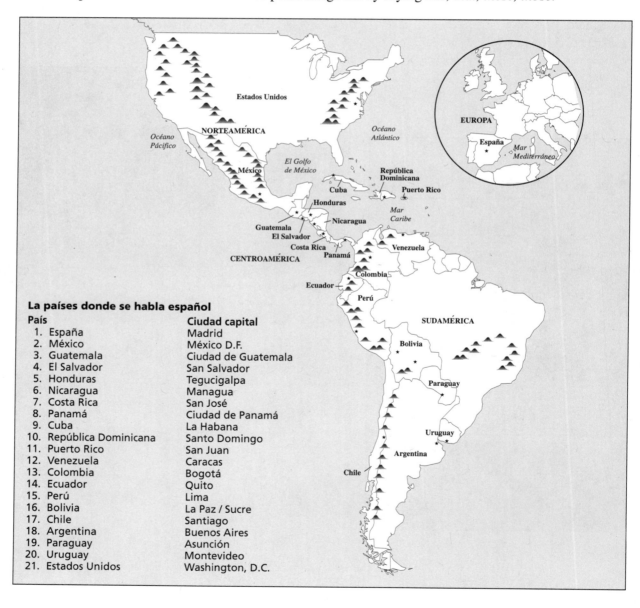

La países donde se habla español

País	Ciudad capital
1. España	Madrid
2. México	México D.F.
3. Guatemala	Ciudad de Guatemala
4. El Salvador	San Salvador
5. Honduras	Tegucigalpa
6. Nicaragua	Managua
7. Costa Rica	San José
8. Panamá	Ciudad de Panamá
9. Cuba	La Habana
10. República Dominicana	Santo Domingo
11. Puerto Rico	San Juan
12. Venezuela	Caracas
13. Colombia	Bogotá
14. Ecuador	Quito
15. Perú	Lima
16. Bolivia	La Paz / Sucre
17. Chile	Santiago
18. Argentina	Buenos Aires
19. Paraguay	Asunción
20. Uruguay	Montevideo
21. Estados Unidos	Washington, D.C.

Los países donde se habla español   *Countries where Spanish is spoken*

PAÍS	CAPITAL
En Europa	
España	Madrid
En Norteamérica	
México	México D.F. (Distrito Federal)
los Estados Unidos (EE. UU.)	Washington, D.C
En Centroamérica	
Guatemala	Ciudad de Guatemala
Honduras	Tegucigalpa
El Salvador	San Salvador
Nicaragua	Managua
Costa Rica	San José
Panamá	Ciudad de Panamá
En Sudamérica	
Colombia	Bogotá
Perú	Lima
Chile	Santiago
Argentina	Buenos Aires
Uruguay	Montevideo
Paraguay	Asunción
Bolivia	La Paz / Sucre
Venezuela	Caracas
Ecuador	Quito
En el Caribe	
Cuba	La Habana
la República Dominicana	Santo Domingo
Puerto Rico	San Juan

Vocabulario

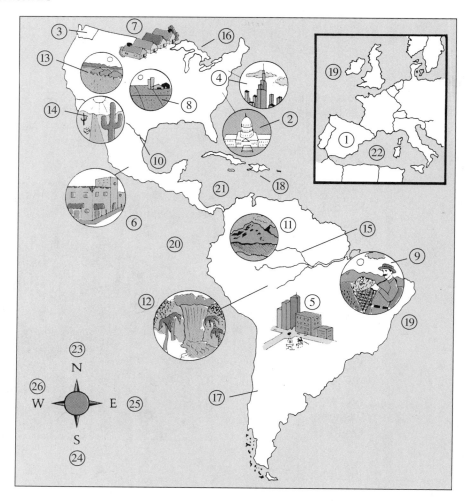

La geografía   *Geography*

1. el país	*country*	14. el desierto	*desert*
2. la capital	*capital*	15. el río	*river*
3. el estado	*state*	16. el lago	*lake*
4. la ciudad	*city*	17. la costa	*coast*
5. el centro	*center, downtown*	18. la isla	*island*
6. el pueblo	*town*	19. el Océano Atlántico	*Atlantic Ocean*
7. las afueras	*suburbs*	20. el Océano Pacífico	*Pacific Ocean*
8. el campo	*countryside*	21. el Mar Caribe	*Caribbean Sea*
9. el habitante	*inhabitant*	22. el Mar Mediterráneo	*Mediterranean Sea*
10. la frontera	*border*	23. el norte	*north*
11. las montañas	*mountains*	24. el sur	*south*
12. la selva	*forest, jungle*	25. el este	*east*
13. los llanos	*plains*	26. el oeste	*west*

1 Ask your partner where various countries are located.

EJEMPLO: ¿Donde está el Perú?   *Where is Peru?*

El Perú está en Sudamérica.   *Peru is in South America.*

2 **Los países donde se habla español** *Countries where Spanish is spoken*   On a map, point to the countries where Spanish is spoken. Tell the name of the country, its capital, and the nationality of its people. Tell on which continent it is located. Refer to pages 129–130 for the list of nationalities.

EJEMPLO: Aquí está España. La capital es Madrid. Los habitantes son los españoles.
    España está en Europa.
  Here is Spain. The capital is Madrid. The inhabitants are Spaniards.
    Spain is in Europe.

3 Tell where various cities are located.

EJEMPLO: Detroit está en Michigan.
  Detroit is in Michigan.

  Nueva York está en la costa del Océano Atlántico.
  New York is on the coast of the Atlantic Ocean.

  Miami está en el sur de Florida.
  Miami is in the south of Florida.

4 **Juego: ¡Nombre el país!** *Name the country!*   Cut a sheet of paper into twenty pieces. Write the name of a country on one side of each piece and its capital on the other side. (Leave out the United States!) Mix up the pieces of paper so that they are not in order. Looking at the capital, tell the name of the country. Take turns with a partner or play by yourself. How quickly can you tell the name of the country?

EJEMPLO: La capital es…
  The capital is . . .

  El país es…
  The country is . . .

  Tienes razón. / No tienes razón. Es…
  You are correct. / You are not correct. It's . . .

5 **Juego: ¡Nombre la capital!** *Name the capital!*   Use the same flashcards you did for Activity 4 but reverse the order. Look at the country and tell the name of the capital.

6 Answer these questions. The map on page 266 may help you.

a. ¿Cuántos países hay donde la lengua oficial es el español?
b. ¿Cuántos países hay en Norteamérica?
c. ¿Cuántos países hay en Centroamérica?
d. ¿Cuántos hay en el Mar Caribe?
e. ¿Cuántos hay en Sudamérica?
f. ¿Qué países tienen una costa en el Océano Atlántico?
g. ¿Qué países tienen una costa en el Mar Caribe?
h. ¿Qué países tienen una costa en el Océano Pacífico?
i. ¿Cuántos países hay en el hemisferio oeste donde la lengua oficial no es el español?
j. ¿Cuál es la lengua oficial de los Estados Unidos?
k. ¿Cuáles son las lenguas oficiales del Canadá?
l. ¿Cuál es la lengua oficial del Brasil?
m. ¿Cuál es la lengua oficial de Haití?
n. Hay dos países que no tienen costas. ¿Cuáles son?

THIS **AND** *THESE*

	THIS	THESE
MASCULINE	este	estos
FEMININE	esta	estas

este país	*this country*	estos países	*these countries*
esta ciudad	*this city*	estas ciudades	*these cities*

If no noun follows, use an accent mark on the first **e**.

éste	*this (one)*	éstos	*those*
ésta	*this (one)*	éstas	*those*

<u>Éste</u> es mi hermano y <u>éstas</u> son mis hermanas.
This (one) is my brother and those are my sisters.

Note: Do not confuse **ésta** *(this one [feminine])* with **está** *(he/she/it is)*. The difference is where the accent mark is placed.

7 **Juego: ¿Cómo se llama este país?**   Describe the location of a country in three sentences. Your partner will try to guess the country you have described. Keep score.

EJEMPLO: Este país está al norte de Chile. Está al sur de Colombia. Está al oeste de Bolivia. ¿Cómo se llama el país?
This country is to the north of Chile. It's to the south of Colombia. It's to the west of Bolivia. What's the name of this country?

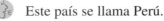 Este país se llama Perú.
The name of this country is Peru.

8 **Juego: ¿Cómo se llama esta ciudad?**   Play the same game as with the countries in Activity 7, but use cities instead.

EJEMPLO: Esta ciudad está en el oeste del país. Está en la costa. Está al norte de Chile.
         ¿Cómo se llama esta ciudad?
         This city is in the west of the country. It's on the coast. It's north of Chile.
         What's the name of this city?

    Esta ciudad se llama Lima.
    The name of this city is Lima.

9 Hold up various objects and tell that they belong to you.

EJEMPLO: Éste es mi libro.   *This is my book.*
         Ésta es mi calculadora.   *This is my calculator.*

THAT/THOSE **AND**
THAT/THOSE . . . OVER THERE

Spanish has two different ways of saying *that* and *those*. **Ese** refers to something relatively nearby. **Aquel** refers to something far away *(over there)*.

	THAT	THOSE	THAT OVER THERE	THOSE OVER THERE
MASCULINE	ese	esos	aquel	aquellos
FEMININE	esa	esas	aquella	aquellas

Don't forget to put an accent mark on the first **e** if no noun follows!

Ése es mi hermano y aquéllas son mis hermanas.
That one is my brother and those over there are my sisters.

este libro/
esta mesa

ese libro/
esa mesa

aquel libro/
aquella mesa

---

10 Compare the physical characteristics of several people in class. Review comparisons on pages 146–147.

EJEMPLO: Este muchacho es alto, ese muchacho es más alto y aquél es menos alto.
         This boy is tall, that boy is taller, and that one over there is not as tall.

    Esta muchacha es rubia, ésa es pelirroja y aquélla es morena.
    This girl is blond, that one is a redhead, and that one over there is brunette.

11 Point out different people using forms of **este, ese,** or **aquel** and tell something about each person.

EJEMPLO: Aquella muchacha es muy simpática.   *That girl is very nice.*
             Ese muchacho no está en su silla.   *That boy is not in his chair.*

12 **Juego**   Take something from someone's desk and ask the class: **¿De quién es este(a)... ?** The person who owns it says **¡Ése(a) es mi... !** Another person says **Aquel/Aquella... es de** *[person's name].*

EJEMPLO: *[A takes B's pencil. C is a witness.]*

        ¿De quién es este lápiz?   *Whose pencil is this?*

        Ése es mi lápiz.   *That's my pencil.*

        Aquel lápiz es de B.   *That's B's pencil.*

13 **Juego**   All students in a group contribute something of their own to the pile, then someone asks whose it is and the others guess. The first person who guesses correctly gets to ask the next question. Remember to make **este** and **ese** agree with the thing you're talking about.

EJEMPLO: ¿De quién es este libro?   *Who does this book belong to?*

        Ése es el libro de Juan.   *That's Juan's book.*

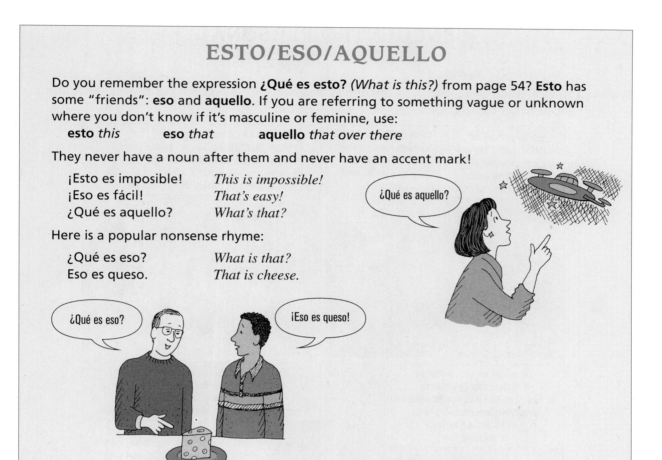

ESTO/ESO/AQUELLO

Do you remember the expression **¿Qué es esto?** *(What is this?)* from page 54? **Esto** has some "friends": **eso** and **aquello**. If you are referring to something vague or unknown where you don't know if it's masculine or feminine, use:

esto *this*   **eso** *that*   **aquello** *that over there*

They never have a noun after them and never have an accent mark!

¡Esto es imposible!	*This is impossible!*
¡Eso es fácil!	*That's easy!*
¿Qué es aquello?	*What's that?*

Here is a popular nonsense rhyme:

¿Qué es eso?	*What is that?*
Eso es queso.	*That is cheese.*

¿Qué es aquello?

¿Qué es eso?

¡Eso es queso!

14 **Juego:** *Mystery packages*   This will take some advance preparation. Make a mystery package using an object in the classroom that appears on page 132. Be sure that it cannot be identified after it is wrapped. The object of the game is for someone to guess what is in your package. Showing your package to the class, you ask, **¿Qué es esto?** Other students will guess saying **Eso es...** If they cannot guess, tell them what it is.

EJEMPLO: ¿Qué es esto?   *What is this?*

¿Es eso un lápiz?   *Is that a pencil?*

No, ésta es una regla.   *No, this is a ruler.*

15 **Juego:** *Dictionary hunt*   With your partner, take turns pointing to various objects in the classroom that you do not know the Spanish word for. Your partner will look it up in the dictionary and tell you.

EJEMPLO: *[pointing to the light switch]* ¿Qué es aquello?
                                              What is that?

[after looking it up in the dictionary] Aquél es un interruptor.
                                              That is a light switch.

ENCUENTRO PERSONAL

Profesora Blanco, a substitute teacher, is discussing the geography of North America with the students. She will replace Señor González when he retires next month.

¿Comprendes?

1. What countries does Paulina think are in the North American continent?
2. Is she correct? What is the correct answer?
3. What is the official name of Mexico and what does it mean in English?
4. How can Americans call themselves in Spanish?
5. What are Mexican-Americans called in Spanish?

¡Te toca!

Create a conversation with a classmate where one of you pretends to be traveling in Mexico and the other pretends to be a Mexican. Use the information in Professor Blanco's lesson to ask each other about your national origin.

Leemos y contamos

A. Profesora Blanco wants her students to know something about the major groups of Hispanics in the United States. Look at the questions at the end before you begin, and skim the text for the answers. The information given is based on the 1990 census.

LOS HISPANOS EN LOS ESTADOS UNIDOS

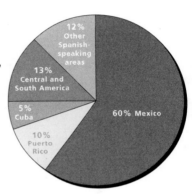

En el siglo *(century)* dieciséis ya había españoles en el área que ahora es el suroeste de los Estados Unidos porque era parte de México hasta 1848. Los hispanos de origen mexicano que tenían familia en los Estados Unidos antes de 1848 forman 20 por ciento de los mexicoamericanos nacidos *(born)* en los EE. UU. En general, los mexicoamericanos están en los estados del suroeste: California, Arizona, Nuevo México y Tejas. También hay grandes concentraciones en muchos estados, por ejemplo *(for example)*, en Illinois y Michigan. Sesenta por ciento de los hispanos en los Estados Unidos son de origen mexicano. También hay otros grupos importantes de hispanos de otros países: Puerto Rico (10 por ciento), Cuba (5 por ciento) y Centro y Sudamérica (13 por ciento).

Los puertorriqueños son un caso especial porque Puerto Rico es un territorio oficial de los EE. UU., así *(so)* todos los puertorriqueños son automáticamente ciudadanos *(citizens)* de los EE. UU. Hay concentraciones de puertorriqueños en el noreste y en las ciudades grandes, por ejemplo, Nueva York y Chicago.

Ya *(Already)* había cubanos en los Estados Unidos antes de 1960, pero después de este año llegaron *(arrived)* muchos a causa de la revolución comunista. Hoy hay millones de cubanos en la Florida, especialmente en la ciudad de Miami. También hay concentraciones importantes en Nueva York, Nueva Jersey y Chicago.

La inmigración a los Estados Unidos de Centro y Sudamérica era importante en las últimas décadas *(last decades)* y ahora los centroamericanos forman el núcleo de la población hispana en ciudades como Washington, D.C. y Philadelphia.

How well did you understand what you have just read? Answer these questions in English.

1. How long have Spanish people lived in the United States?
2. Who are the Mexican-Americans and where do they live?
3. Why are Puerto Ricans a special case of immigrants?
4. When did most of the Cubans come to the United States and why?
5. When did the immigration from Central and South America become a significant factor?
6. What percentage of Hispanics are from Mexico, Puerto Rico, Cuba, and Central and South America? Where are they concentrated in the United States?
7. Do you think it is important for Americans to study Spanish? Why?

B. The following is Profesora Blanco's lesson on the geography of Mexico. Read it and then help Paulina fill in her notes.

LA GEOGRAFÍA DE MÉXICO

México es un país en el hemisferio norte. Está en el continente norteamericano. Al este están el Mar Caribe y el Golfo de México y al oeste el Océano Pacífico. Al norte están los Estados Unidos y al sur, el país de Guatemala. Hay treinta y un estados en México, por ejemplo Chihuahua en el norte y Chiapas en el sur. La capital, la Ciudad de México, está en el Distrito Federal.

El Distrito Federal de México no es un estado. Entonces, México D.F. es como Washington D.C. No hay grandes ríos navegables en México. El Río Grande forma la frontera con el estado de Tejas en el norte. Hay dos sierras *(ranges)* de montañas que son extensiones de las Montañas Rocosas de los Estados Unidos. En el oeste del país está la Sierra Madre Occidental y en el este la Sierra Madre Oriental. Entre estas sierras hay un valle *(valley)* grande. La Ciudad de México está en este valle entre las montañas y es una de las capitales más altas del mundo, a 7.500 pies de altura *(altitude)*. En el norte de México hay un desierto grande y en el sur hay una selva *(jungle)*.

Help Paulina study for her test by filling in the missing parts of her notes.

1. Mexico is in the _____ Hemisphere.
2. It is bordered by _____ on the north, _____ on the south, _____ on the east, and _____ on the west.
3. There are _____ states in Mexico.
4. The capital is _____ .
5. There are _____ large navegable rivers in Mexico.
6. The principal mountain ranges are _____ and _____ .
7. In the north of Mexico, there is a _____ and in the south there is a _____ .

C. Here is Profesora Blanco's lesson on the geography of Spain. Follow the description on the map as you read.

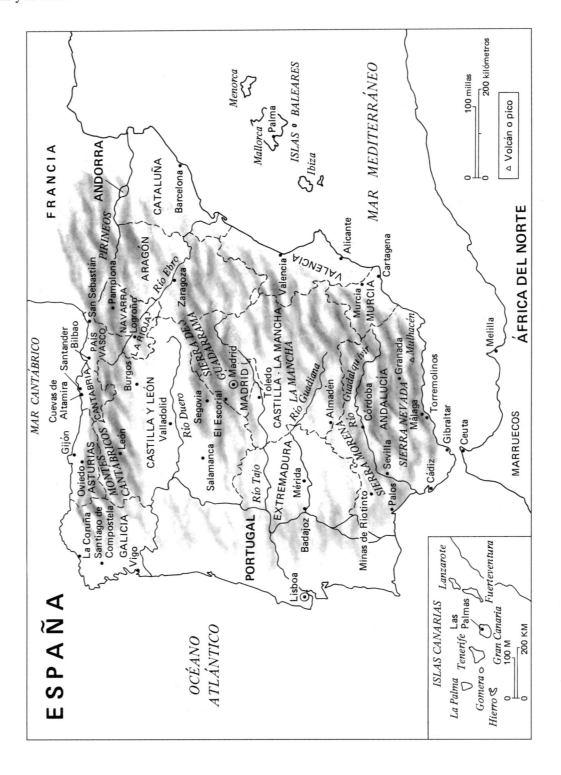

LA GEOGRAFÍA DE ESPAÑA

España es un país en la Península Ibérica, en el suroeste de Europa. Portugal está en el oeste de la misma *(same)* península.

Al norte está el Mar Cantábrico y al oeste está el Océano Atlántico, y al este está el Mar Mediterráneo. En el norte están los Pirineos y a través de *(across)* las montañas está Francia. Al sur hay una península que se llama «Gibraltar». Es un territorio de la Inglaterra. A través del mar al sur están los países de Marruecos *(Morocco)* y Argelia *(Algeria)* en el continente de África.

España es el segundo país más montañoso de Europa después de *(after)* Suiza *(Switzerland)*.

Hay cinco ríos importantes en España. El Duero está en el norte. El Ebro es el único que termina *(ends)* en el Mediterráneo. El Tajo pasa *(passes)* cerca de dos ciudades importantes: Madrid, que es ahora la capital, y Toledo, una ciudad muy antigua y que antes *(before)* era la capital. El Guadalquivir y el Guadiana están al suroeste del país.

Answer the following questions.

1. ¿Dónde está España?
2. ¿Cómo se llama el otro *(other)* país en la Península Ibérica?
3. ¿Dónde está el Océano Atlántico?
4. ¿Dónde está el Mar Mediterráneo?
5. ¿Qué país está al norte a través de los Pirineos?
6. ¿Qué países están al sur?
7. ¿Qué país tiene más montañas que España?
8. ¿Cuántos ríos importantes hay en España? ¿Cómo se llaman? ¿Dónde están?
9. ¿Cómo se llama la ciudad capital de España?

D. Using the map on page 278, write a geographical description of a Spanish-speaking country.

¡Así es!

The Hispanic minority in the United States

Were you surprised to find the United States listed at the beginning of the lesson as one of the Spanish-speaking countries? There are about twenty-five million persons of Hispanic origin in the United States, about one person out of ten. In fact, although English is the dominant language, the United States ranks fifth in the world in Hispanic population after Mexico, Spain, Colombia, and Argentina!

Unlike some other minority groups that are distinguished by racial differences, Hispanics come from countries where people of African, European, and Native American origins have been mixing for five centuries. Thus, the Hispanic minority is identified by origin, language, and cultural heritage. Hispanics are one of the fastest growing minorities in the United States because of both a high birth rate and a large number of immigrants. It is projected that by the year 2010, Hispanics will be the largest minority in the country.

¿Adónde vamos ahora?
Where are we going now?

In this lesson we begin to move in time and space! We will review the time expressions and learn the verb to go and we're on our way! We will also be learning another past form of verbs called the "preterite."

Vocabulario

Expresiones de tiempo   *Time expressions*

These time expressions were first presented in Unit II, Lesson 1.

anteayer	*day before yesterday*	antes	*before*	Anoche - last night
ayer	*yesterday*	ahora	*now*	
hoy	*today*	después	*after*	
mañana	*tomorrow*	entonces	*then*	
pasado mañana	*day after tomorrow*	luego	*then, later*	
		un día	*one day*	

en el pasado	*in the past*	por la mañana	*in the morning*
en el presente	*in the present*	por la tarde	*in the afternoon*
en el futuro	*in the future*	por la noche	*in the evening, at night*

En el presente

En el pasado

En el futuro

Expresiones de tiempo   *Time expressions (continued)*

siempre	*always*	una vez	*once*
frecuentemente	*often*	otra vez	*again*
mucho	*a lot, much*	(dos) veces	*(two) times*
poco	*a little, few*	de una vez	*all at once*
raramente	*rarely, seldom*	de vez en cuando	*from time to time*
nunca	*never*	algunas veces	*sometimes*
~~mientras~~	*while*		
de repente	*suddenly*		
de niño(a)	*as a child*		
de viejo(a)	*as an old person*	todavía	*still, yet*
a los… años	*at the age of . . .*	~~todavía no~~	*not yet*
hace (seis meses)	*(six months) ago*	ya	*already*
en (seis meses)	*in (six months)*	~~ya no~~	*~~no longer~~*
el año pasado	*last year*	el próximo año	*next year*
el mes pasado	*last month*	el próximo mes	*next month*
la semana pasada	*last week*	la próxima semana	*next week*
el (lunes)	*on (Monday)*	todas las semanas	*every week*
todos los (lunes)	*every (Monday)*	todos los meses	*every month*
todos los días	*every day*	todos los años	*every year*

1 Make separate lists of the time expressions that refer to the past, the present, and the future. Some words may be on more than one list.

THE VERB IR *to go*

Compare the person–time endings of **ir** and **estar**. How are they similar? How are they different?

	IMPERFECT *went* *was/were going* *used to go*	PRETERITE *went* *did go*	PRESENT *go/goes* *am/is/are going* *do/does go*	FUTURE *will go*
yo	iba	fui	voy	iré
tú	ibas	fuiste	vas	irás
Ud./él/ella	iba	fue	va	irá
nosotros(as)	íbamos	fuimos	vamos	iremos
vosotros(as)	ibais	fuisteis	vais	iréis
Uds./ellos/ellas	iban	fueron	van	irán

PRETERITE AND IMPERFECT
(two ways of talking about the past)

There are two forms of the past tense in Spanish: the imperfect and the preterite.

PRETERITE	IMPERFECT
Countable times (once or a stated number)	Uncountable times (indefinite number or unfinished)
reports:	describes:
action completed at one point in time	a. repeated (habitual) action
	b. ongoing (background) action

The *preterite* tells what was done once or a certain number of times at a specific time.

- El año pasado, fui <u>tres veces</u> al cine.
  Last year, I went to the movies <u>three times</u>. [specified number]
  (I tell the number of times I went.)

- Fui al cine <u>ayer</u>.
  I went to the movies <u>yesterday</u>.
  (The action was completed at a specific time. Once is implied.)

The *imperfect* is used for repeated, habitual, or ongoing action or to describe the background for the main action.

- Cuando yo era niña, <u>iba</u> al cine.
  When I was a child, <u>I used to go (went)</u> to the movies. [repeated action]
  (I went more than once but the number of times is not important.)

- Siempre <u>iba</u> al cine con mis amigos.
  I always <u>used to go</u> to the movies with my friends. [habitual action]
  (When I went to the movies, it was my habit to go with my friends.)

- Ayer, yo <u>iba</u> al cine cuando…
  Yesterday, <u>I was going</u> to the movies when . . . [ongoing action]
  (I was on my way to the movies but hadn't arrived yet when something else happened.)

- Era un buen día. Hacía sol y los pájaros cantaban.
  It was a nice day. It was sunny and the birds were singing. [background information]
  (The action was ongoing and provided the background setting for the main action.)

2 Use your list from Activity 1 and tell which past expressions would usually be used with the preterite form of the verb and which would usually be used with the imperfect form of a verb.

EJEMPLO: PRETERITE   IMPERFECT
           ayer   siempre

CONTRACTION OF A + EL

Do you remember that **de** combines with **el** to form **del**? There is one other contraction in Spanish:

A *(at/to)* before **el** *(the)* becomes **al**.

   a + el = al

   Ayer fui <u>al</u> museo.   *Yesterday, I went <u>to the</u> museum.*

Do not contract: **a la/a los/a las.**

   Fui <u>a la</u> tienda.   *I went <u>to the</u> store.*
   Ayer fui <u>a los</u> museos.   *Yesterday I went <u>to the</u> museums.*

Esqueleto

(time expression) + (pro)noun + IR + A + place

   Anoche yo fui al parque.   *Last night I went to the park.*

Before doing the following activities, review places in the city presented on page 227.

3 Find out from your partner about her or his activities in the past, present, or future. Ask the following questions. (Be careful of the verb tense.)

EJEMPLO: ¿Adónde ibas cuando estabas en la escuela primaria?
            Where did you use to go when you were in elementary school?

            Yo iba al parque.
            I used to go to the park.

            ¿Adónde fuiste la semana pasada?
            Where did you go last week?

            ¿Adónde vas todos los días?
            Where do you go every day?

            ¿Adónde irás el próximo verano?
            Where will you go next summer?

4 Repeat the questions from Activity 3, but change the person–time endings of the verb to find out about one of your partner's family members.

EJEMPLO: ¿Adónde iba tu mamá cuando ella estaba en la escuela primaria?
Where did your mother use to go when she was in elementary school?

Mi mamá iba al cine.
My mother used to go to the movies.

5 Repeat the questions but change the person–time endings of the verb to find out about your partner and her or his family.

EJEMPLO: ¿Adónde iban Uds. de vacaciones?   *Where did you (all) use to go on vacation?*

Íbamos a San Francisco.   *We used to go to San Francisco.*

Vocabulario

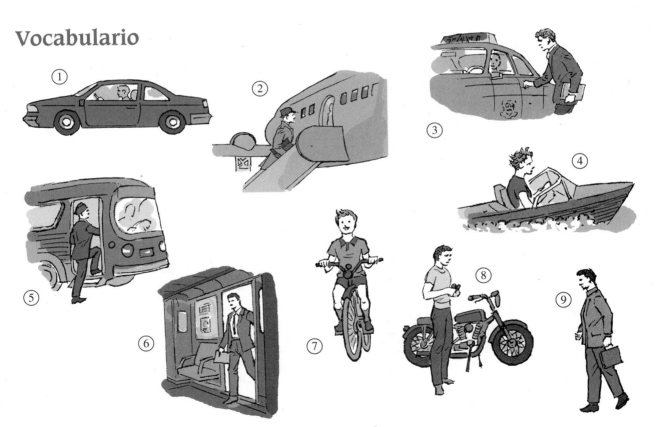

Los medios de transporte   *Means of transportation*

1. en auto	*by car*		6. por tren	*by train*
2. por avión	*by plane*		7. en bicicleta	*by bike*
3. en taxi	*by taxi*		8. por moto	*by motorcycle*
4. por barco	*by boat*		9. a pie	*on foot*
5. en autobús	*by bus*			

6 Ask several classmates where they used to go *(imperfect)* and how they got there.

EJEMPLO: ¿Adónde ibas?
              Where did you use to go?

              Yo iba a la playa con mis padres los sábados.
              I used to go to the beach with my parents on Saturday.

              Y, ¿cómo iban Uds. a la playa?
              And, how did you (all) use to go to the beach?

              Íbamos en autobús.
              We used to go by bus.

7 **Encuesta: Mis vacaciones** *My vacation*   Ask several classmates where they went for summer vacation. Ask how they went. Use the preterite.

EJEMPLO: ¿Adónde fuiste de vacaciones?
              Where did you go for vacation?

              Fui a Kansas City.
              I went to Kansas City.

              ¿Cómo fuiste?
              How did you go?

              Fui por avión.
              I went by plane.

8 Tell your partner about different places you went to, go to, and will go to, and tell the means of transportation used to get there.

EJEMPLO: El año pasado fui a la casa de mi abuela por avión.
           Last year I went to my grandmother's house by plane.

           Este fin de semana voy a Chicago en autobús.
           This weekend I'm going to Chicago by bus.

           El verano que viene iré a las montañas en auto.
           Next summer I'm going to the mountains by car.

Temas de reflexión

9 **Sit-Con**   You have a year to travel around the world and unlimited money. Arrange with your travel agent where you will go, how you will get there, and how long you will stay. Remember you have only a year. You may wish to review the countries on pages 129–130.

EJEMPLO:

¿Adónde irás?
Where will you go?

Iré a Francia.
I will go to France.

¿Cómo irás allí?
How will you go there?

Iré en avión.
I will go by plane.

¿Cuánto tiempo estarás allí?
How long will you be there?

Estaré allí por tres semanas.
I will be there for three weeks.

Entonces, ¿adónde irás?
Then, where will you go?

IR + A + *INFINITIVE*

You already know how to talk about the future by using the future endings to say you *will* do something. You can also use a present tense form of **ir** with **a** *(to)* and an infinitive **(-ar, -er, -ir)** ending to tell what someone is *going to do* now or in the near future.

Esqueleto

(pro)noun + **IR** + **A** + *infinitive*

<u>Voy a</u> estudiar esta noche.   *I <u>am going</u> to study tonight.*
<u>Vamos a</u> jugar al tenis mañana.   *We <u>are going</u> to play tennis tomorrow.*
Juan <u>va a</u> cantar en el coro.   *Juan <u>is going</u> to sing in the chorus.*

Before doing the following activites, review the verbs on pages 10–11.

10 Tell what you or you and your friends are going to do this weekend.

EJEMPLOS: Voy a mirar la televisión este fin de semana.
I am going to watch TV this weekend.

Vamos a caminar en la playa.
We're going to walk on the beach.

Mi amiga María va a trabajar en la biblioteca.
My friend María is going to work in the library.

11 Tell several things that you are going to do after school today.

EJEMPLO: Voy a hablar por teléfono con mis amigos.
I am going to talk on the phone with my friends.

PRETERITE OF SER

When **ser** describes things in the *past* it is usually used in the *imperfect* (**era**) as we have been doing so far. **Ser** also has a *preterite* form that is used to talk about what something was like at a specific point in time. Its forms are the same as the preterite of **ir** *(to go)*. The context will tell you if the meaning is *was/were* or *went*.

	was/were
yo	fui
tú	fuiste
Ud./él/ella	fue
nosotros(as)	fuimos
vosotros(as)	fuisteis
Uds./ellos/ellas	fueron

¿Cómo fue la película ayer?
How was the movie yesterday?

El año pasado mi padre fue mecánico, pero ahora es el gerente.
Last year my father was a mechanic, but now he is the manager.

---

12 Do you know anyone who has changed professions? (See pages 131–132.) Tell what he or she was at a certain time in the past and what that person is now.

EJEMPLO: El año pasado él fue estudiante y ahora es profesor.
Last year he was a student, and now he is a teacher.

ENCUENTRO PERSONAL

Paulina and her boyfriend, Jaime, are talking about their weekend. Listen and see if they are still friends at the end of the conversation.

¿Comprendes?

1. Did Jaime have a good weekend?
2. Where did he go?
3. What was Paulina's reaction to where he went?
4. Where did Paulina go and what did she do?
5. What was Jaime's reaction to what she did?
6. Do you think they will still be friends like before?

¡Te toca!

Ask one of your friends where he or she went last weekend and let your friend ask you the same question. Then ask each other what you are going to do next weekend.

Leemos y contamos

A. Paulina's teacher asked her to keep a diary of her activities for the year as a Spanish class assignment. Here are some sample entries.

15 de octubre

Hoy fue un día muy especial porque Jaime y yo fuimos al cine juntos. Él estaba muy amable y yo estaba contenta porque ya somos novios. Siempre seremos novios y en el futuro seremos esposos.

6 de noviembre

Fui a la escuela en autobús a las siete de la mañana. Fue un día interesante porque mi mamá fue conmigo de visita. Hoy era el día en que los padres visitan mi escuela. Muchos padres fueron a la escuela con sus hijos. Fuimos primero a visitar al director y después fuimos a todas mis clases. Fue muy interesante porque mi mamá fue estudiante por un día. Ella dice (says) que nunca (never) irá otra vez porque ella estaba muy cansada. Es difícil ser estudiante. Ella no será estudiante otra vez.

9 de enero

Fuimos a la escuela en autobús como siempre, pero hoy fue interesante porque había mucha nieve y a las doce fuimos a casa otra vez. Fue un día muy diferente. ¡Me gustó mucho no tener que estar en la escuela todo el día!

19 de febrero

¡Hoy fue un día terrible! Yo estaba en el autobús con Jaime. Íbamos a la escuela. Me dijo (told) que ya no (no longer) iba a ser mi novio. Ahora estoy muy triste. ¿Por qué no desea (wants) ser mi novio?

22 de febrero

¡Qué día más fantástico! Hoy en el autobús estaba el muchacho nuevo que conocí (I met) en enero. Se llama Salvador. Es muy alto, moreno y guapo. Es más guapo que Jaime. También es muy simpático y listo. Me invitó (He invited me) a ir al cine el sábado.

Cierto o falso   Based on Paulina's diary, indicate whether the following statements are **cierto** *(true)* or **falso** *(false)*.

1. Jaime y Paulina fueron juntos a una fiesta.
2. Jaime y Paulina siempre serán novios.
3. Generalmente Paulina iba a la escuela en autobús.
4. Iba siempre con su mamá.
5. Todos los días eran terribles.
6. Su mamá era estudiante durante todo el año.
7. Las dos iban juntas a la escuela todos los días.
8. Su madre no desea ser estudiante.
9. El 9 de enero no había clases todo el día.
10. Paulina está muy contenta porque Jaime no desea ser su novio.
11. Salvador es el novio nuevo de Paulina.
12. Salvador invitó a Paulina a ir al museo el sábado.

CINE

Parque de la Bombilla (junto Iglesia de San Antonio de la Florida). Del 29 de junio al 3 de septiembre. Precio: 450 ptas. Tercera edad: 250 ptas. Niños menores de 6 años, entrada libre. Horario: a partir de las 22.15 h.

■ **VIERNES 21**

P. G. *Prêt-à-porter.* Dir.: Robert Altman. *Vidas cruzadas.* Dir.: Robert Altman.

P. P. *El circo.* Dir.: Chaplin. *Siete ocasiones.* Dir.: Buster Keaton. *Casablanca.* Dir.: Michael Curtiz (V.O.)

■ **SÁBADO 22**

P. G. *Los Picapiedra.* Dir.: Brian Levant. *Lloviendo piedras.* Dir.: Ken Loach.

P. P. *Recuerda* (V.O.) Dir.: Alfred Hitchcock.

■ **DOMINGO 23**

P. G. *Entrevista con el vampiro.* Dir.: Neil Jordan. *Miami.* Dir.: Davis Frankel.

P. P. *Las aventuras de Tom Sawyer.* Dir.: Norman Taurog. *To be or not to be.* Dir.: Lubitsch.

B. Paulina's mother wrote this letter to her sister after her visit to Paulina's school.

Querida Rosario,

Hoy fue un día muy interesante. En la escuela de Paulina era el día de los padres. Fui a la escuela con ella en autobús y fui a todas sus clases. Primero fuimos a visitar al director. Es un hombre inteligente y muy serio. Entonces (Then) fuimos a la primera clase de Paulina, la clase de geometría. Era una clase difícil y yo no comprendí (I understood) nada (nothing). La segunda clase era la clase de español. El profesor es el señor González. Es un hombre viejo y canoso. A todos los estudiantes les gusta el señor González. Él es muy popular con los estudiantes. La tercera clase era historia mundial (of the world). Siempre me gustaba la historia, pero no me gustó la profesora. ¡Es una mujer muy cruel!

Paulina tiene siete clases cada (each) día. Las otras clases son biología, arte, inglés y educación física. También tiene treinta minutos para el almuerzo.

Yo estaba muy cansada al fin (at the end) del día. Le dije (I told) a Paulina que no me gustaría ser estudiante ahora. ¡Es más difícil que ser ingeniera! Pues (Well), voy a preparar la cena ahora. Toda la familia tiene hambre.

Tu hermana que te quiere,
Dorotea

1. To whom did Paulina's mother write the letter?
2. What was her opinion of the principal?
3. What was the first class they went to? Did she like it?
4. Who is the Spanish teacher and what is he like?
5. Did she like the history class?
6. Why didn't she like the history teacher?
7. How many classes does Paulina have each day? What are they?
8. How much time does she have for lunch?
9. How did Paulina's mother feel at the end of the day?
10. Would she rather be a student or an engineer? Why?

C. **Mi día en la escuela**   Write a letter to Paulina telling her about your school day. Tell what classes you have and what you do. Tell about your teachers and your classmates. Make a schedule showing times and days for each of your classes to enclose with your letter.

¡Así es!

El Cinco de Mayo *celebration*

The Fifth of May, **el Cinco de Mayo,** is a day of patriotic celebration for Mexicans. It is similar to our Fourth of July. It is a holiday in Mexico, so there is no school and most businesses are closed. The people celebrate with parades, fireworks, and public gatherings, such as concerts and picnics. The day is commemorated because on May 5, 1862 (during our Civil War), the Mexicans defeated the French near Mexico City. The French did succeed in creating a puppet empire under Emperor Maximilian for a few years, but the Mexicans finally drove them out in 1867. Another day of patriotic celebration for Mexicans is September 16. On that date in 1810, in the city of Dolores, the priest Padre Hidalgo began the struggle for independence from Spain with the **Grito** *(shout)* **de Dolores.**

¿Qué tenemos?
What do we have?

In this lesson we are going to talk about the things we possess, using the verb **tener**. Let's talk about some of the toys we used to have when we were younger, as well as the things we have now.

Vocabulario

Los juguetes *Toys*

1. el juego de damas	*checkers game*	14. la carreta	*wagon*
2. el rompecabezas	*puzzle*	15. la cometa	*kite*
3. el tren eléctrico	*electric train*	16. la pelota	*ball*
4. el yoyo	*yo-yo*	17. el bate	*baseball bat*
5. el silbato	*whistle*	18. los patines de rueda	*roller skates*
6. el tambor	*drum*	19. los patines de hielo	*ice skates*
7. los bloques	*blocks*	20. el monopatín	*skateboard*
8. el soldado de juguete	*toy soldier*	21. el triciclo	*tricycle*
9. la muñeca	*doll*	22. la bicicleta	*bicycle*
10. el títere	*puppet*	23. las canicas	*marbles*
11. el osito de peluche	*teddy bear*	24. el globo	*balloon*
12. la casa de muñecas	*dollhouse*	25. el columpio	*swing*
13. el caballo balancín	*rocking horse*	26. el cajón de arena	*sandbox*

TENER *to have*
TELLING WHAT YOU POSSESS

You have already used the verb **tener** when talking about health (for example: **Yo tenía un catarro**) and in other expressions such as **¿Cuántos años tienes?** Tener is the verb we use in Spanish to talk about what we have or possess. It cannot be used to say we have done something. Let's look at the forms and then we can talk about our possessions.

	IMPERFECT	PRETERITE	PRESENT	FUTURE
	had	*had*	*am/is/are*	*will have*
	was/were	*did have*	*having*	
	having		*have/has*	
	used to have			
yo	tenía	tuve	tengo	tendré
tú	tenías	tuviste	tienes	tendrás
Ud./él/ella	tenía	tuvo	tiene	tendrá
nosotros(as)	teníamos	tuvimos	tenemos	tendremos
vosotros(as)	teníais	tuvisteis	tenéis	tendréis
Uds./ellos/ellas	tenían	tuvieron	tienen	tendrán

Note: Many of the person–time endings are different from the verbs you have studied so far (**ser, estar,** and **ir**). What similarities and differences do you notice?

INDEFINITE ARTICLES (UN/UNA/UNOS/UNAS) WITH TENER

The indefinite articles are generally omitted with the noun following **tener,** unless the object is described or if the emphasis is on the object rather than the fact that someone possesses it.

Esqueleto

(pro)noun + TENER + (article) + noun + (adjective)

Miguel tiene coche.   *Miguel has a car.*
Miguel tiene un coche nuevo.   *Miguel has a new car.*
Ellos no tienen teléfono.   *They don't have a telephone.*

1 Tell your partner some of the toys you had as a child and find out what he or she had.

EJEMPLO: Yo tenía bicicleta. ¿Tenías bicicleta?
I had a bicycle. Did you have a bicycle?

Sí, tenía bicicleta roja. / No, no tenía bicicleta.
Yes, I had a red bicycle. / No, I did not have a bicycle.

2 Children today do not play with the same toys that the children of past generations did. What toys did your parents have that children today do not have?

EJEMPLO: Mi padre tenía carreta, pero los niños hoy no tienen carretas.
My father had a wagon, but children today do not have wagons.

3 *Sit-Con*   It's almost your birthday and your friend wants some suggestions for a present for you. Tell her or him some things that you already have and some things that you don't have but would like to receive for your birthday.

EJEMPLO: Ya tengo radio pero no tengo televisor.
I already have a radio but I don't have a television.

4 You are making a list of things to buy for your friends' birthdays. Before you decide what to buy them, make a list of things they don't have. Use vocabulary from pages 6, 8, 9, and 132 for ideas.

EJEMPLO: María no tiene discos compactos.
María doesn't have CDs.

Anita y Susita no tienen chaquetas nuevas.
Anita and Susita don't have new jackets.

5 Tell your partner about some of the things you and your friends will have when you finish school. Compare your expectations.

EJEMPLO: Yo tendré un coche nuevo.   *I will have a new car.*
Mi amiga María tendrá una casa bonita.   *My friend María will have a pretty house.*

DIRECT OBJECT PRONOUNS

The direct object receives the action of the verb. In English the direct object pronouns follow the verb, but in Spanish they come before the verb when it has the person–time endings. Here are the direct object pronouns to say *it* or *them*.

	IT	THEM
	lo	los
	la	las

Tengo <u>el libro</u>.	<u>Lo</u> tengo.	*I have it.*
Tengo <u>la chaqueta</u>.	<u>La</u> tengo.	*I have it.*
Tengo <u>los cuadernos</u>.	<u>Los</u> tengo.	*I have them.*
Tengo <u>las flores</u>.	<u>Las</u> tengo.	*I have them.*

What is the difference between **lo** and **la**?
Did you notice the similarity between the definite article *the* and the direct object pronouns? Nouns that use **la** are replaced with the pronoun **la**. Nouns that use **los** are replaced with the pronoun **los**. Nouns that use **las** are replaced with the pronoun **las**. But the nouns that use **el** are replaced with the pronoun **lo**.

Esqueleto

> ### (pro)noun + object pronoun + verb

Yo <u>lo</u> tengo.   *I have it.*
Juan <u>los</u> tenía.   *Juan had them.*
Sara y Miguel <u>la</u> tendrán.   *Sara and Miguel will have it.*

6 Tell your partner about six things you had when you were a child. Your partner will ask if you still have it/them now. Tell whether or not you do.

EJEMPLO: Cuando yo era niño(a), tenía una muñeca.
When I was a child, I had a doll.

¿La tienes ahora?
Do you have it now?

Sí, la tengo todavía. / No, ya no la tengo.
Yes, I still have it. / No, I don't have it any more.

7 Tell your partner about the things you have that people did not have when your grandparents were teenagers.

EJEMPLO: Ahora tenemos computadoras, pero no las tenían cuando mis abuelos eran jóvenes.
Now we have computers, but they did not have them when my grandparents were teenagers.

LOCATION OF OBJECT PRONOUNS

The object pronouns **lo/la/los/las** are placed before the verb when the verb has a person–time ending.

When the verb with a person–time ending is followed by an infinitive form of the verb **(-ar,-er,-ir)**, the object pronouns can be attached to the end of the infinitive form.

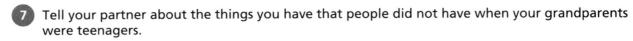

Esqueletos

(pro)noun + verb + infinitive + object pronoun

Ellos iban a escribir<u>la</u>.   *They were going to write it.*
Voy a comprar<u>los</u>.   *I am going to buy them.*

OR

(pro)noun + object pronoun + verb + infinitive

Ellos <u>la</u> iban a escribir.   *They were going to write it.*
<u>Los</u> voy a comprar.   *I am going to buy them.*

8 Tell about some things that you will have when you are working.

EJEMPLO: ¿Un auto grande? Voy a tenerlo.   *A big car? I'm going to have it.*
¿Una computadora? Voy a tenerla.   *A computer? I'm going to have it.*

Vocabulario

Estados físicos y emocionales con «tener»   *Physical and emotional states with* tener

In English, the following expressions use the verb *to be* with an adjective. But in Spanish,
they use **tener** *(to have)* with a noun.

1.	tener (mucha) hambre	*to be (very) hungry*
2.	tener (mucha) sed	*to be (very) thirsty*
3.	tener (mucho) calor	*to be (very) warm/hot*
4.	tener (mucho) frío	*to be (very) cold*
5.	tener (mucha) prisa	*to be in a (big) hurry*
6.	tener (mucho) sueño	*to be (very) sleepy*
7.	tener (mucha) suerte	*to be (very) lucky*
8.	tener (mucho) miedo	*to be (very) afraid*
9.	tener (mucha) razón	*to be (very) right*
10.	no tener razón	*to be wrong*
11.	tener… años	*to be . . . years old*

9 Tell how you are when the following events occur. Use **tener** expressions.

EJEMPLO: You forgot a jacket and you're outside in the winter.
Tengo frío.   *I'm cold.*

a. You have the winning ticket in the lottery.
b. The air conditioner isn't working and it's 95 degrees.
c. You're confronted by an escaped lion at the zoo.
d. You say that 2 + 2 = 5.
e. You say that 2 + 2 = 4.
f. You're late and your plane to Hawaii is about to leave.
g. It's 3 degrees below zero and you're walking to school.
h. You've just celebrated your birthday.
i. You haven't eaten in forty-eight hours.
j. You want to get a drink of water.
k. It's way past your bedtime.

TENER QUE + *INFINITIVE*

Tener que + *infinitive* tells what someone <u>has</u> to do.

Esqueleto

(pro)noun + TENER + QUE + *infinitive*

Tengo que estudiar.   *I have to study.*
Tendremos que visitar España.   *We will have to visit Spain.*
Mi tío tenía que trabajar mucho.   *My uncle had to work a lot.*

10 Your neighbor is planning to learn Spanish. Tell what he or she has to do to get a good grade in Spanish class.

EJEMPLO: Tienes que aprender la estructura.   *You have to learn the structure.*

11 **Encuesta**   Ask several of your classmates what they have to do this weekend. (Use verbs from pages 10–11.)

EJEMPLO:  ¿Qué tienes que hacer este fin de semana?   *What do you have to do this weekend?*

Tengo que limpiar mi alcoba.   *I have to clean my bedroom.*

TENER GANAS DE + *INFINITIVE*

Tener ganas de + *infinitive* tells what someone <u>feels like</u> doing.

Esqueleto

   (pro)noun + **TENER** + **GANAS DE** + *infinitive*

Tenía ganas de descansar.   *I felt like resting.*
Tengo ganas de comer.   *I feel like eating.*
Ellos tendrán ganas de bailar.   *They will feel like dancing.*

12 We all have things we feel like doing but can't because we have to do something else. How about you? Tell five things you feel like doing and what you have to do instead.

EJEMPLO: Tengo ganas de ir a casa, pero tengo que tomar un examen.
I feel like going home, but I have to take a test.

13 Tell about your last vacation. What did you feel like doing and what did you have to do?

EJEMPLO: Tenía ganas de nadar en la playa, pero tenía que escribir un papel para la clase de historia.
I felt like swimming at the beach, but I had to write a paper for history class.

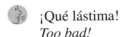 ¡Qué lástima!
Too bad!

ESTAR IN THE PRETERITE

The forms of **estar** in the preterite follow the same pattern as **tener**.

	TENER *to have*		ESTAR *to be*	
yo	tuve	*I had*	estuve	*I was*
tú	tuviste	*you had*	estuviste	*you were*
Ud./él/ella	tuvo	*you had/ he/she/it had*	estuvo	*you were/ he/she/it was*
nosotros(as)	tuvimos	*we had*	estuvimos	*we were*
vosotros(as)	tuvisteis	*you had*	estuvisteis	*you were*
Uds./ellos/ellas	tuvieron	*you/they had*	estuvieron	*you/they were*

Estar and **tener**, like **ser**, are often used in the imperfect because they usually describe what was happening over a period of time; however, the preterite is used if a specific point in time is emphasized.

Ayer <u>fue</u> un día especial porque <u>tuvimos</u> una fiesta grande y todos mis amigos <u>estuvieron</u> allí.

Yesterday <u>was</u> a special day because we <u>had</u> a big party and all my friends <u>were</u> there.

14 *Sit-Con*   Sra. Garza's favorite vase was broken yesterday morning. Each of her six children had an alibi for the time when the accident happened. Tell where they were and why.

EJEMPLO: Manuel: Ayer, a las 10:00 de la mañana estuve en la biblioteca porque tuve que estudiar.
Yesterday, at 10:00 A.M. I was in the library because I had to study.

a. Esteban:
b. Felipe:
c. Anabel:
d. Hortensia:
e. Estela:

ENCUENTRO PERSONAL

Paulina, her little sister, Carlota, and their parents are trying to plan their spring vacation. Naturally they would like to have fun, but they also have some things they have to do. Listen to their conversation, and see what solution they come up with.

¿Comprendes?

1. What does each of the family members have to do during vacation?
2. What does each of them feel like doing?
3. What does Paulina's father propose they do?
4. What is Carlota's reaction?

¡Te toca!

Now it's your turn to plan your vacation. Make a list of things you have to do and things you feel like doing during your vacation. Then have a conversation about your ideas with another member of the class.

Leemos y contamos

A. Marisol tells us what she used to be like in elementary school. In what ways were you like Marisol? How were you different? Read Marisol's description of herself.

Cuando yo estaba en la escuela primaria, siempre tenía prisa por la mañana y no comía bien. Por eso tenía mucha hambre y sed en la escuela hasta el almuerzo. Después yo tenía sueño y tenía ganas de dormir una siesta.

Yo tenía mucho miedo de los exámenes y si no tenía buenas notas *(grades),* mis padres me decían *(told)* que tenía que estudiar los sábados y los domingos. Yo no tenía ganas de hacerlo, pero yo sabía *(knew)* que ellos tenían razón. Yo tenía mucha suerte porque tenía unos padres tan inteligentes.

1. How did Marisol feel in the morning? Why?
2. How did she feel after eating lunch?
3. How did she feel about exams?
4. What did her parents say if she didn't get good grades?
5. How did Marisol feel about her parents' reaction?

B. What were you like in elementary school? Write a description of yourself at that age. Tell what you did and what you had to do.

C. Salvador expects to be very busy for the rest of the school year. He made a list of things he will have to do. See how many of these you have to do also.

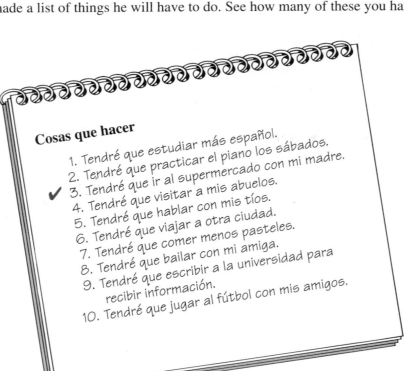

Cosas que hacer

1. Tendré que estudiar más español.
2. Tendré que practicar el piano los sábados.
   ✓ 3. Tendré que ir al supermercado con mi madre.
4. Tendré que visitar a mis abuelos.
5. Tendré que hablar con mis tíos.
6. Tendré que viajar a otra ciudad.
7. Tendré que comer menos pasteles.
8. Tendré que bailar con mi amiga.
9. Tendré que escribir a la universidad para recibir información.
10. Tendré que jugar al fútbol con mis amigos.

D. **¿Y tú?**   Now it's your turn to list what *you* will have to do this year. Can you think of at least ten things you have to do before the end of the school year?

E. **Recuerdos de mi niñez** *Memories of my childhood*   Rosita's grandmother often talks about her life as a child. Do you know someone who does that?

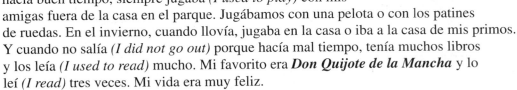

Cuando yo era niña mi vida *(life)* era muy diferente de la vida de hoy. No teníamos televisor porque no había televisión. Sí, teníamos un radio y los programas eran buenos, pero la radio no era tan importante como la televisión es hoy día. ¿Cómo era ser niña en esos días? ¿Que hacíamos *(did we do)*?

Yo tenía muchos juguetes. Tenía una muñeca muy bonita con muchos vestidos. También yo tenía una casa de muñecas. Yo era la madre y mi muñeca era mi bebé. En el verano cuando hacía buen tiempo, siempre jugaba *(I used to play)* con mis amigas fuera de la casa en el parque. Jugábamos con una pelota o con los patines de ruedas. En el invierno, cuando llovía, jugaba en la casa o iba a la casa de mis primos. Y cuando no salía *(I did not go out)* porque hacía mal tiempo, tenía muchos libros y los leía *(I used to read)* mucho. Mi favorito era ***Don Quijote de la Mancha*** y lo leí *(I read)* tres veces. Mi vida era muy feliz.

F.   When Rosita's grandmother talks about her childhood, Grandfather joins in and tells about his.

Cuando yo era niño mi vida era feliz también. Jugaba mucho con mis hermanos menores y con mi perro. No teníamos muchos juguetes pero no era importante porque teníamos mucha imaginación. Jugábamos mucho a los toros y toreros *(bullfighters)* y teníamos muchos juegos de pelota. Claro, jugábamos al fútbol y hacíamos *(we made)* cometas. Para mi décimo *(tenth)* cumpleaños mis padres me dieron *(gave me)* una bicicleta. ¡Era mi juguete favorito!

Make a list of the various childhood activities of Rosita's grandmother and grandfather. Put a check mark by each activity that you have also done.

G.   What do you remember about your childhood? Write a description of your toys and activities to tell your grandchildren some day. (Review pages 10–11 for some activities.)

¡Así es!

Leisure activities

Spanish speakers in other countries enjoy many of the same leisure activities that North Americans do, such as watching and participating in sports, playing board games like Bingo (usually called **Lotería**), Scrabble with the Spanish alphabet, Monopoly with the streets of Mexico City, and other games like Dominoes and marbles.

Of course watching TV and going to the movies are very popular. It may surprise you that many of the TV programs and movies are American like *Star Trek* (**Viaje a las estrellas**), but of course they are dubbed into Spanish. Listening to music and watching music videos are very popular, and the teenagers often sing the lyrics in English even if they don't know what the words mean.

One game children often play is "bullfight." One person pretends to be a bull (**toro**) using his or her fingers as horns and another pretends to be a bullfighter (**torero**) using a piece of red cloth as a cape. Many Hispanic children like playing bullfight as much as American children like playing cops and robbers!

LUNES 13 *Diciembre*

TVE 1 tve1	TVE 2
07.30 Pinnic	**07.00 24 horas**
09.20 La primera respuesta	**09.30 La aventura del saber**
10.10 Estrellita mía	**11.00 Los chicos**
Angelina sufre mucho por su marido ya que, antes del accidente, quería separarse de ella.	1960. 80m. ★★ Carlos, Andrés, "El chispa" y "El negro", no sobrepasan los dieciocho años. Uno es botones de un gran hotel, otro vende periódicos, otro estudia y el último es mecánico de automóviles. Todos se verán obligados a afrontar la vida que tienen por delante.
11.00 Pasa la vida	*Intérpretes: Joaquín Zarzo, osé Luis García, José Sierra. Director: Marco Ferreri.*
13.30 El menú de Karlos Arguiñano	
14.00 Informativos territoriales	
14.30 No te rías que es peor	

¡Claro que me gustan los animales!
Of course I like animals!

In this lesson, we will be learning the names of more animals and reviewing how to tell which ones we like and which we don't like.

Vocabulario

Los animales *Animals*

As you look at the following list of animals, think of which animals you like and which you don't like.

Los animales domésticos *Domestic animals*
This vocabulary pertaining to domestic animals was presented in Unit I, Lesson 6.

el perro	*dog*		el gato	*cat*
el caballo	*horse*		la vaca	*cow*
el toro	*bull*		el cerdo	*pig*
la gallina	*hen*		el burro	*donkey*
el gallo	*rooster*		la oveja	*sheep*
el pato	*duck*			

The following is additional vocabulary pertaining to domestic animals.

1. la cabra   *goat*   2. el pavo   *turkey*

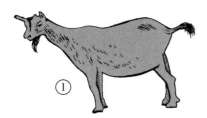

Los animales salvajes   *Wild animals*

This vocabulary pertaining to wild animals was presented in Unit I, Lesson 6.

el pez	*fish*	el pájaro	*bird*
el conejo	*rabbit*	el mono	*monkey*
el elefante	*elephant*	el león	*lion*
el tigre	*tiger*	el oso	*bear*
la ardilla	*squirrel*	el ratón	*mouse*

The following is additional vocabulary pertaining to wild animals.

3.	el periquito	*parakeet*	11. el perico/cotorra	*parrot*
4.	el ciervo	*deer*	12. el murciélago	*bat*
5.	el gorila	*gorilla*	13. la rata	*rat*
6.	la serpiente	*snake*	14. el leopardo	*leopard*
7.	el rinoceronte	*rhinoceros*	15. el hipopótamo	*hippopotamus*
8.	el búfalo	*buffalo*	16. la cebra	*zebra*
9.	el camello	*camel*	17. la jirafa	*giraffe*
10.	el canguro	*kangaroo*	18. el zorro	*fox*

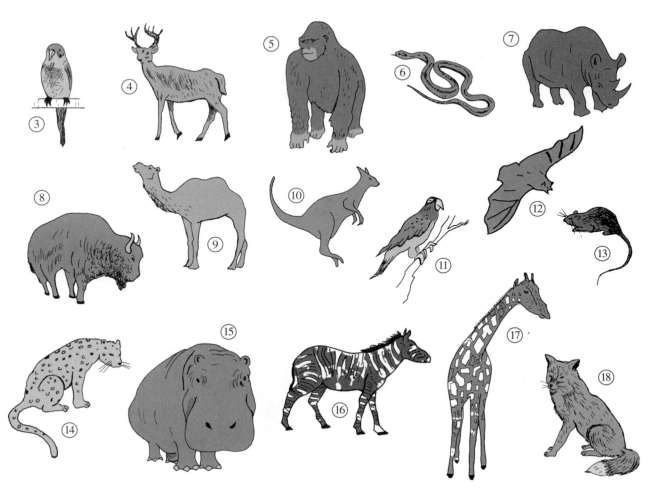

Los animales acuáticos   *Aquatic animals*

19. el tiburón   *shark*
20. la ballena   *whale*
21. la rana   *frog*
22. el cangrejo   *crab*

23. el pulpo   *octopus*
24. la tortuga   *turtle*
25. el sapo   *toad*
26. la almeja   *clam*

dolphin delfín

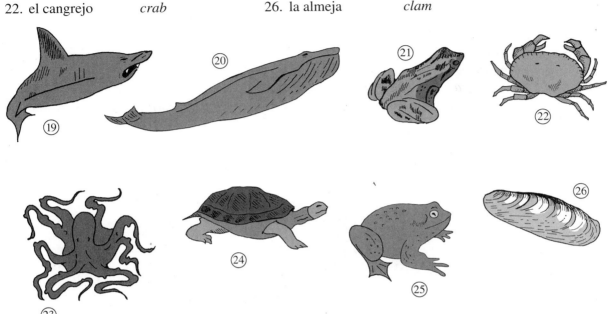

Los insectos   *Insects*

27. la mosca   *fly*
28. la hormiga   *ant*
29. la abeja   *bee*
30. la araña   *spider*

31. el mosquito   *mosquito*
32. la mariposa   *butterfly*
33. la cucaracha   *cockroach*

1 List the animals that you would find in the following places.

a. en la casa *in the house*   i. en el arboles *in the trees*
b. en la selva *in the jungle*   j. cueva *cave*
c. en la granja *in the farm*
d. en un campo *in the country*
e. en el agua *in the water*
f. en el parque zoológico *in the zoo*
g. en el bosque *(forest)* *in the woods (forest)*
h. en el oceano *in the ocean*

EJEMPLO: en el agua: los peces, las tortugas, las ballenas, etc.   *in the water: fish, turtles, whales*

2 Find out where various animals are found.

EJEMPLO:  ¿Dónde están las cucarachas?   *Where are cockroaches?*

Las cucarachas están en la casa.   *Cockroaches are in the house.*

GUSTAR   *to be pleasing, to like*

In Spanish, we talk about what pleases us, not about what we like. Can you see the difference in the point of view?

English: *I like chocolate.*

Spanish: Me gusta el chocolate.

I ———➤ *chocolate.*

To me ◄——— *chocolate.*

Chocolate is pleasing to me.

You already learned in Unit I, Lessons 6 and 10 that *I like* is **me gusta** for one thing, and **me gustan** for more than one thing. Here are all the forms of **gustar** that you will need for now.

IMPERFECT	PRETERITE	PRESENT	FUTURE	CONDITIONAL*
used to please	*pleased*	*please(s)*	*will please*	*would please*
used to like	*liked*	*like(s)*	*will like*	*would like*
(me) gustaba	gustó	gusta	gustará	gustaría
(me) gustaban	gustaron	gustan	gustarán	gustarían

Remember, after **gustar**, use **el/la/los/las** when using the noun in a general sense.

Me gusta <u>el</u> chocolate.   *I like chocolate.*

Me gustan <u>los</u> burros.   *I like donkeys.*

*Note: The *conditional* is a new form that is the equivalent of the English *would*. It is often used with **gustar** to make it more polite when asking for something.

<u>Me gustaría</u> una hamburguesa, por favor.   *<u>I would like</u> a hamburger, please.*

3 Tell which animals you like, which ones you like more, and which ones you don't like at all.

EJEMPLO: Me gustan los perros; me gustan más los gatos, pero no me gustan nada las arañas.
I like dogs; I like cats more, but I don't like spiders at all.

4 Ask your partner if he or she used to like different animals.

EJEMPLO: ¿Te gustaban los perros?
Did you use to like dogs?

Sí, me gustaban mucho los perros. / No, no me gustaban los perros.
Yes, I used to like dogs a lot. / No, I did not use to like dogs.

INDIRECT OBJECT PRONOUNS

To tell who likes something or to whom something is pleasing, use the following pronouns. These pronouns are called *indirect object pronouns* and tell *to* or *for whom* something is done.

me = *to/for me*
te = *to/for you*
le = *to/for you/him/her/it*
nos = *to/for us*
os = *to/for all of you [for a group of friends in Spain]*
les = *to/for all of you/them*

Nos gusta<u>n</u> las hamburguesas. | *Hamburgers are pleasing <u>to us</u>.*
or   *We like hamburgers.*

<u>Les</u> gusta el helado. | *Ice cream is pleasing <u>to them</u>.*
or   *They like ice cream.*

---

5 Tell several things that you and your family like.

EJEMPLO: Nos gustan los animales.
Animals are pleasing to us. (We like animals.)

Nos gustan los restaurantes mexicanos.
Mexican restaurants are pleasing to us. (We like Mexican restaurants.)

6 Tell several things your friends like.

EJEMPLO: Les gustan los animales salvajes.
Wild animals are pleasing to them. (They like wild animals.)

CLARIFICATION OR EMPHASIS WITH INDIRECT OBJECT PRONOUNS

A + *the person* can be used before the indirect object pronoun in order to clarify or emphasize to whom it refers.

a mí	+ me		a nosotros(as)	+ nos
a ti	+ te		a vosotros(as)	+ os
a Ud.			a Uds.	
a él			a ellos	
a ella	} + le		a ellas	} + les
a (Juan)			a (Juan y a María)	

¿A usted le gusta el invierno?	*Do you like winter?*
A ellos les gustó el libro.	*They liked the book.*
¿A ti te gustan las granjas?	*Do you like farms?*
A mí me gustan las granjas.	*I like farms.*

Esqueleto

(A + *person*) + ME/TE/LE NOS/OS/LES + GUSTAR + *noun(s)*

Me gusta el helado.	*I like ice cream.*
A Juan le gustan los tigres.	*Juan likes tigers.*
Nos gustaban las mariposas.	*We used to like butterflies.*

7 **Sit-Con**   You are a clerk in a clothing store. Your partner is your customer. Read this dialogue and then create a similar one. (Use the formal forms **Ud.** and **le**.)

EJEMPLO:

Me gusta esa corbata azul. ¿Cuánto cuesta?
I like that blue tie. How much is it?

Treinta dólares.
Thirty dollars.

Es muy cara.
It's very expensive.

Pues, ¿le gusta esta corbata gris?
Well, do you like this gray tie?

No, no me gusta. Voy a comprar la corbata azul.
No, I don't like it. I'm going to buy the blue tie.

GUSTAR WITH VERBS

As you learned in Unit I, Lesson 10, **gustar** forms can also be followed by the infinitive **(-ar, -er, -ir)** form of verbs to tell what actions please you (what you like to do).

¿Te gusta nadar?   *Do you like to swim?*
Sí, me gusta nadar.   *Yes, I like to swim.*

Esqueleto

(A + *person*) +   **ME/TE/LE
NOS/OS/LES**   + **GUSTAR** + *infinitive*

Me gusta bailar.   *I like to dance.*
A Raúl le gusta comer.   *Raúl likes to eat.*
Nos gustaba ir al cine.   *We used to like to go to the movies.*

8 Work with a partner. Tell what you like to do and what you do not like to do. See how many activities you both like and how many you both dislike.

EJEMPLO: Me gusta escuchar la radio.   *I like to listen to the radio.*

A mí me gusta también. / A mí no me gusta.   *I like to also. / I don't like to.*

No me gusta jugar a los naipes.   *I don't like to play cards.*

No me gusta tampoco. / A mí me gusta.   *I don't like to either. / I like to.*

9 **Encuesta**   Find out from several of your classmates what they like to do after school.

EJEMPLO: ¿Qué te gusta hacer después de la escuela?   *What do you like to do after school?*

Me gusta escuchar discos compactos.   *I like to listen to CDs.*

10 Ask your partner what he or she liked to do when he or she was younger.

EJEMPLO: Cuando eras más joven, ¿te gustaba bailar?
When you were younger, did you like to dance?

Sí, me gustaba bailar. / No, no me gustaba bailar.
Yes, I liked to dance. / No, I didn't like to dance.

11 Ask several of your classmates if they would like to do certain activities with you after school.

EJEMPLO: ¿Te gustaría escuchar discos compactos conmigo después de la escuela?
Would you like to listen to CDs with me after school?

Sí, me gustaría.
Yes, I would like to.

12 What did you have to eat yesterday? (Review the foods on page 7.) Tell what you liked or didn't like.

EJEMPLO: Me gustaron las papas fritas.   *I liked the French fries.*
No me gustó la hamburguesa.   *I didn't like the hamburger.*

13 What foods did you use to like to eat when you were younger?

EJEMPLO: Me gustaba el pollo.   *I used to like chicken.*
No me gustaban las legumbres.   *I didn't like vegetables.*

14 **Encuesta**   Find out from several classmates what they like to wear to parties and write a report about it. You will have to specify the person. (Review the clothing on page 6.)

EJEMPLO: ¿Qué te gusta llevar a las fiestas?
What do you like to wear to parties?

Me gusta llevar pantalones y un suéter.
I like to wear pants and a sweater.

Report: A Miguel le gusta llevar pantalones y un suéter.
Miguel likes to wear pants and a sweater.

15 Ask your parents what they used to like to do when they were teenagers and then report on it.

EJEMPLO: A mi mamá le gustaba bailar.   *My mother used to like to dance.*
A mi papá le gustaba ir al cine.   *My father used to like to go to the movies.*

16 What we do is not always what we would like to do. Tell your partner what four people you know would like to do during spring vacation and what they are actually going to do and why. (Review the forms of **ir a** on page 284 and **tener que** on page 300.)

EJEMPLO: A mi hermano le gustaría ir a las montañas para esquiar, pero va a trabajar en
un restaurante porque tiene que comprar un auto.
*My brother would like to go to the mountains to ski, but he is going to work in
a restaurant because he has to buy a car.*

ENCUENTRO PERSONAL

Paulina is telling her cousin Eduardo about a visit to a farm. Since she lives in the city, it was a memorable experience for her. Have you had a similar experience?

¿Comprendes?

1. Whose farm did Paulina visit?
2. What were Paulina's favorite animals? Why?
3. What kinds of animals does Eduardo like?
4. What kinds of animals did Eduardo like as a boy?
5. What kinds of animals does Paulina not like?
6. Would she like to go to a farm again? And how about you?

¡Te toca!

Talk to a friend about your visit to a farm or a zoo or about animals you have seen where you live. Then compare your likes and dislikes for various animals.

Leemos y contamos

Do you remember your pen pals Andrés and Marisol in Unit II? Well, now they want to tell you about their likes and dislikes.

A. **La carta de Andrés**

Querido amigo,

¿Qué te gusta? A mí me gustan muchas cosas pero especialmente me gusta todo tipo de (all kinds of) juegos y deportes. Me gusta jugar al Monopolio, a los naipes y a las damas. De los deportes me gustan el tenis y el básquetbol pero más que nada (more than anything) me gusta el béisbol. El béisbol es un deporte muy popular en los países del Caribe. Aquí en Puerto Rico, a muchas personas les gusta mirar y jugar al béisbol. A mis hermanos y a mí nos gusta jugar después de (after) la escuela con nuestros amigos. Cuando tenía ocho años no me gustaban mucho los deportes porque yo era pequeño y un poco débil. Pero ahora que soy más grande y más fuerte me gustan mucho los deportes. De adulto seré un famoso jugador de béisbol. ¿Qué juegos y deportes les gustan a ti y a tus amigos?

Tu amigo sincero,
Andrés

1. What types of games does Andrés like?
2. What is his favorite sport?
3. What does he do with his brothers?
4. Why didn't Andrés use to like sports?
5. Why does he like them now?
6. What does he hope to be in the future?

B. **La carta de Marisol**

Queridos amigos,
¿Qué les gusta a Uds.? ¿Les gustan los animales? Pues (Well),
¡a mí me gustan muchísimo (a lot)*! A mi familia y a mí*
nos gusta ir al parque zoológico para mirar todos los animales que
hay allí. Particularmente me gustan los animales exóticos como los
tigres, los monos y los elefantes. Antes yo tenía miedo de los leones
pero ahora me gustan los leones también.

Cuando yo era niña siempre teníamos animales domésticos en
nuestra casa. Teníamos gatos y perros, pero especialmente me gustaba
el perico grande. A él le gustaba hablar y cantar y era muy bonito y
de muchos colores. Y ahora, ¿qué animales les gustan a Uds.? Favor de
(Please) *escribirme pronto.*

Tu amiga,
Marisol

1. What kinds of animals does Marisol like?
2. How did she feel about lions?
3. How does she feel about them now?
4. What pets did her family have?
5. What pet did she like most? Why?

C. **¡Te toca!** *Now it's your turn.*   Choose one of the preceding letters to answer and tell either Andrés or Marisol what you like. Remember, you can refer to the Unit I and II vocabularies to find things and actions you may want to talk about.

D. **No soy como era.** *I'm not like I used to be.*   Have your tastes changed since you have grown older? Make a list of at least ten things you didn't use to like but like now.

   EJEMPLO: De niño, no me gustaban los gatos, pero ahora sí me gustan.
   As a child, I didn't use to like cats, but now I do like them.

E. A visitor from Spain is going to visit your classroom. Prepare a list of questions to ask him about his likes and dislikes. (Note: Since you don't know the person, use the **Ud.** form.)

   EJEMPLO: ¿A Ud. le gustan las hamburguesas?   *Do you like hamburgers?*
   ¿A Ud. le gusta la música rock?   *Do you like rock music?*
   ¿A Ud. le gusta bailar el flamenco?   *Do you like to dance flamenco?*

¡Así es!

Pets

In general Hispanics have a different attitude toward animals than North Americans do. They tend not to attribute human characteristics or feelings to them. For example, many visitors from Spanish-speaking countries are surprised to see people buying gourmet pet food, doggie sweaters, and decorative cat collars and to hear people talk about their pet as if it were a part of the family. Most Hispanics are used to having animals around, since a large percentage of Hispanics come from a rural farm setting, but the animals are regarded as being inferior to humans and exist only to serve them. In fact, there is not even an exact translation for *pet* in Spanish. They may be called **animales domésticos, animales de casa,** or **mascotas.**

❧ Unidad IV ❧

⇥Unidad IV⇤
Tools

Vocabulario

Una fiesta   *A party*
(Lección 1)

Preparar para una fiesta	***To prepare for a party***
ayudar con las preparaciones	*to help with preparations*
buscar a los amigos	*to look for friends*
cocinar la comida	*to cook the food*
comprar los refrescos	*to buy the refreshments*
hallar un lugar	*to find a place*
invitar a los amigos	*to invite friends*
llamar a los vecinos	*to call the neighbors*
lavar los platos	*to wash the dishes*
limpiar la casa	*to clean the house*
mandar las invitaciones	*to send the invitations*
planear las actividades	*to plan the activities*

Para ir a una fiesta	***To go to a party***
aceptar la invitación	*to accept the invitation*
caminar a la casa	*to walk to the house*
desear ir	*to want/wish/desire to go*
llegar tarde	*to arrive late*
temprano	*early*
llevar a los amigos	*to bring/take friends*
llevar la ropa buena	*to wear nice clothes*
manejar a la fiesta	*to drive to the party*

En una fiesta	***At a party***
comenzar la fiesta	*to begin/start/commence the party*
bailar	*to dance*
cantar	*to sing*
celebrar un cumpleaños	*to celebrate a birthday*
charlar con los invitados	*to chat/talk with the guests*
descansar un poco	*to rest a little*
escuchar la música	*to listen to music*
mirar la televisión	*to watch television*

Una fiesta *A party (continued)*
(Lección 1)

saludar a los invitados	*to greet the guests*
prestar discos compactos	*to lend CDs*
sacar fotos	*to take pictures*
tocar la guitarra	*to play the guitar*
discos compactos	*CDs*
tomar refrescos	*to drink/have refreshments*
visitar con los amigos	*to visit with friends*
dar una fiesta	*to give a party*
un regalo	*to give a present*
las gracias	*to thank*

La comida *Food*
(Lección 2)

These words pertaining to food were presented in Unit I, Lesson 6.

Las comidas	*Meals*
el desayuno	*breakfast*
la comida	*dinner, midday main meal*
el almuerzo	*lunch*
la merienda	*snack*
la cena	*supper, evening meal, dinner*

la leche	*milk*	el café	*coffee*
la hamburguesa	*hamburger*	el refresco	*soft drink*
la papa	*potato*	el té	*tea*
las papas fritas	*French fries*	el rosbif	*roast beef*
la ensalada	*salad*	el huevo	*egg*
la lechuga	*lettuce*	el perro caliente	*hot dog*
la sopa	*soup*	el pollo	*chicken*
la torta	*cake*	el pescado	*fish*
el agua	*water*	el jamón	*ham*
las frutas	*fruit*	el sándwich	*sandwich*
las legumbres	*vegetables*	el helado	*ice cream*
las papitas fritas	*potato chips*	el pan	*bread*

Here are additional words pertaining to food.

desayunar	*to eat/have breakfast*
almorzar (ue)	*to eat/have lunch*
cenar	*to eat/have dinner*
tomar	*to drink, to take*
beber	*to drink*
comer	*to eat*

Las legumbres   *Vegetables*

el tomate	*tomato*	el ajo	*garlic*
el apio	*celery*	el maíz	*corn*
el rábano	*radish*	las judías	*string beans*
la remolacha	*beet*	la batata	*sweet potato*
la coliflor	*cauliflower*	la zanahoria	*carrot*
la cebolla	*onion*	los guisantes	*peas*
los frijoles	*beans*	el pimiento	*pepper*
el pepino	*cucumber*		

Las frutas   *Fruits*

la manzana	*apple*	el plátano	*banana*
la pera	*pear*	las cerezas	*cherries*
las uvas	*grapes*	las frambuesas	*raspberries*
la toronja	*grapefruit*	los arándanos	*blueberries*
las fresas	*strawberries*	la sandía	*watermelon*
la naranja	*orange*	el limón	*lemon*
la piña	*pineapple*		

La carne   *Meat*

la ternera	*veal*	la carne de res	*beef*
la carne de cerdo	*pork*	el tocino	*bacon*
la chuleta de cerdo	*pork chop*	la carne molida	*ground meat*
la carne de cordero	*lamb*	la salchicha	*sausage*

Los mariscos   *Seafood*

la langosta	*lobster*	las almejas	*clams*
los camarones	*shrimp*	las ostras	*oysters*

El pan   *Bread*

el pan tostado	*toast*
el panecillo	*roll*
la galleta	*cracker*
el sándwich de…	*. . . sandwich*
la mantequilla de cacahuete	*peanut butter*
la jalea	*jelly*

Los cereales   *Cereals*

la avena	*oats*
el trigo	*wheat*
el arroz	*rice*

Los productos lácteos   *Dairy products*

el queso	*cheese*
la leche	*milk*
la mantequilla	*butter*
la crema	*cream*
el yogur	*yogurt*

La comida   *Food (continued)*
(Lección 2)

Las bebidas   *Beverages*

el té	*tea*	el cafe con crema	*coffee with cream*
el jugo (de)	*juice*	sin azúcar	*without sugar*

Los condimentos   *Seasonings*

la sal	*salt*	el azúcar	*sugar*
la pimienta	*pepper*	la salsa picante	*hot sauce*

El postre y los bocaditos   *Dessert and snacks*

el pastel de…	*. . . pie*	la rosquilla	*doughnut*
vainilla	*vanilla*	el flan	*custard*
chocolate	*chocolate*	los dulces	*candy*
la nuez	*nut, walnut*	la galletita dulce	*cookie*
la tableta de chocolate	*candy bar*	las palomitas de maíz	*popcorn*

Verbos que terminan en -er   *Verbs that end in* -er
(Lección 2)

aprender (a)	*to learn (to)*	deber	*to owe, ought to, should*
comprender	*to understand*	leer	*to read*
correr	*to run*	romper	*to break*
coser	*to sew*	vender	*to sell*
creer	*to believe*		

Verbos que combinan con el infinitivo
Verbs that combine with the infinitive
(Lección 2)

desear + *infinitive*	*to want to . . .*
necesitar + *infinitive*	*to need to . . .*
esperar + *infinitive*	*to hope to . . .*
odiar + *infinitive*	*to hate to . . .*
deber + *infinitive*	*ought to . . .*
aprender a + *infinitive*	*to learn to . . .*
ayudar a + *infinitive*	*to help (to) . . .*
ir a + *infinitive*	*to be going to . . .*
invitar a + *infinitive*	*to invite to . . .*
tratar de + *infinitive*	*to try to . . .*
acabar de + *infinitive*	*to have just . . .*
insistir en + *infinitive*	*to insist on . . .*
tener que + *infinitive*	*to have to . . .*
tener ganas de + *infinitive*	*to feel like . . .*

¿Dónde vives?   *Where do you live?*
(Lección 3)

¿Dónde vives?	*Where do you live?*
Vivo en la ciudad	*I live in the city*
en el campo	*in the country*
en el centro	*downtown*
en las afueras	*in the outskirts, suburbs*
en una granja	*on a farm*
en una casa	*in a house*
en un apartamento	*in an apartment*
en un condominio	*in a condominium*
de un piso	*one story*
de dos pisos	*two stories*
en un barrio…	*in a . . . neighborhood*
tranquilo	*quiet, tranquil*
ruidoso	*noisy*
moderno	*modern*
antiguo	*old*
seguro	*safe*
peligroso	*dangerous*
limpio	*clean*
sucio	*dirty*
a dos cuadras de…	*two blocks from . . .*
a dos millas de…	*two miles from . . .*
a dos kilómetros de…	*two kilometers from . . .*
¿Cuál es tu dirección?	*What is your address?*
Mi dirección es Calle… (número)	*My address is (number) . . . Street.*
Paseo…	*. . . Drive.*
Avenida…	*. . . Avenue.*
Camino…	*. . . Road.*

Un rascacielos   *A skyscraper*
(Lección 3)

el sótano	*the basement*
la planta baja	*the ground floor*
el primer piso	*the first floor (up)*
el segundo piso	*the second floor*
el tercer piso	*the third floor*
cuarto	*fourth*
quinto	*fifth*
sexto	*sixth*
séptimo	*seventh*
octavo	*eighth*
noveno	*ninth*
décimo	*tenth*
el piso once	*the eleventh floor*

Verbos que terminan en -ir   *Verbs that end in* -ir
(Lección 3)

abrir	*to open*	insistir (en)	*to insist (on)*
asistir a	*to attend*	recibir	*to receive*
discutir	*to discuss, to argue*	subir	*to go up, to get on*
escribir	*to write*	sufrir	*to suffer*

En la escuela   *In school*
(Lección 4)

tomar una clase de...   *to take a . . . class*

Las artes   *Arts*
el arte   *art*
el drama   *drama, acting*
la música   *music*

Las ciencias   *Sciences*
la biología   *biology*
la física   *physics*
la química   *chemistry*

Las ciencias sociales   *Social Sciences*
la geografía   *geography*
la historia   *history*
la sicología   *psychology*

El comercio   *Business*
la informática   *computer science*
la clase de tecleo   *keyboarding*
la taquigrafía   *shorthand*

Las lenguas extranjeras   *Foreign Languages*
el alemán   *German*
el chino   *Chinese*
el español   *Spanish*
el francés   *French*
el italiano   *Italian*
el japonés   *Japanese*
el latín   *Latin*
el ruso   *Russian*

Las matemáticas   *Math*
el álgebra   *algebra*
el cálculo   *calculus*
la geometría   *geometry*
la trigonometría   *trigonometry*

Otras materias
la educación física

Other subjects
physical education

Las escuelas y los niveles (Lección 4)

Schools and levels

la escuela primaria	*elementary school, grade school*
la escuela secundaria	*secondary school, high school*
la universidad	*college, university*
el colegio	*private high school*
el primer año de secundaria	*freshman*
el segundo año	*sophomore*
el tercer año	*junior*
el cuarto año	*senior*
el primer año de primaria	*first grade*

Lo que hacemos en la escuela (Lección 4)

What we do in school

asistir a las clases	*to attend classes*
tomar apuntes	*to take notes*
aprender	*to learn*
estudiar	*to study*
hacer la tarea	*to do homework*
escribir un tema	*to write a paper*
teclear	*to input*
leer novelas	*to read novels*
lecturas	*readings*
cuentos cortos	*short stories*
poesía	*poetry*
escuchar conferencias	*to listen to lectures*
memorizar fechas	*to memorize dates*
hechos	*facts*
hacer investigaciones	*to do research*
calcular	*to do arithmetic*
sumar	*to add*
restar	*to subtract*
multiplicar	*to multiply*
dividir	*to divide*
tomar un examen	*to take an exam*
una prueba	*a test/quiz*
sacar una A, etc.	*to get an A, etc.*
aprobar (ue) un examen	*to pass an exam*
suspender un examen	*to fail an exam*

Verbos que tienen cambios radicales *Verbs that have stem changes*
(Lección 4)

E ⟶ IE

cerrar	*to close*
pensar	*to think*
comenzar	*to begin*
perder	*to lose*
preferir	*to prefer*
querer	*to want, to love*

O ⟶ UE

volver	*to return*
almorzar	*to eat lunch*
recordar	*to remember*
costar	*to cost*
dormir	*to sleep*
morir	*to die*
poder	*to be able, can*

E ⟶ I

servir	*to serve*
pedir	*to ask for, to request, to order*
repetir	*to repeat*
seguir	*to follow, to continue*

U ⟶ UE

jugar	*to play games or sports*

Palabras neutrales y negativas *Neutral and negative words*
(Lección 4)

alguien	*someone, anyone*	nadie	*no one, nobody*
algo	*something, anything*	nada	*nothing, not anything*
alguno(a,os,as)	*some*	ninguno(a,os,as)	*none, not any, no*
siempre	*always*	nunca	*never, not ever*
también	*also*	tampoco	*neither, not either*
o... o	*either . . . or*	ni... ni	*neither . . . nor . . .*

La rutina diaria *Daily routine*
(Lección 5)

despertarse (ie)	*to wake up*
levantarse	*to get up*
lavarse	*to wash*
bañarse	*to take a bath*
ducharse	*to take a shower*
afeitarse	*to shave*
cepillarse	*to brush*
vestirse (i, i)	*to get dressed*
ponerse	*to put on (clothing)*
peinarse	*to comb one's hair*
maquillarse	*to put on makeup*
sentarse (ie)	*to sit down*
despedirse (i, i)	*to say good-bye*
irse	*to go away*
quedarse	*to stay, to remain*

divertirse (ie, i)	*to have fun, to have a good time, to enjoy oneself*
quitarse	*to take off (clothing)*
acostarse (ue)	*to go to bed, to lie down*
dormirse (ue)	*to go to sleep, to fall asleep*

De vacaciones   *On vacation*
(Lección 6)

Para hacer un viaje debemos…   ***To make a trip we should . . .***

   decidir en la destinación   *decide on the destination*
          ir a una ciudad   *to go to a city*
          ir al campo   *to go to the country*
          ir a la playa   *to go to the beach*
          ir a otro país   *to go to another country*
   comprar billetes para el avión   *buy tickets for the airplane*
                      el autobús   *the bus*
                      el tren   *the train*
   hacer la maleta   *pack the suitcase*
   llevar una bolsa   *take along a purse*
          una mochila   *a backpack, book bag*
          una cartera   *a wallet*
          un paraguas   *an umbrella*
   traer dinero   *bring money*
   decir lo que necesitamos   *tell what we need*
   decir adiós a los amigos   *say good-bye to friends*

En un viaje a la ciudad podemos…   ***On a trip to the city we can . . .***

   conocer la ciudad   *become acquainted with the city*
   conocer a la gente   *meet people*
   saber llegar a un lugar   *know how to get to a place*
   comer en restaurantes   *eat in restaurants*
   visitar museos   *visit museums*
   ir de compras   *go shopping*
   ir al teatro y a los conciertos   *go to the theater and concerts*
   ver los monumentos   *see the monuments*

En un viaje al campo podemos…   ***On a trip to the country we can . . .***

   mirar los animales   *look at the animals*
   alimentar los animales   *feed the animals*
   pasar tiempo al aire fresco   *spend time in the fresh air*
   ir a pescar   *go fishing*
   dar un paseo   *go for a walk*

En un viaje a la playa podemos…   ***On a trip to the beach we can . . .***

   oír las olas en la playa   *hear the waves on the beach*
   nadar   *swim*
   recoger conchas   *collect shells*
   broncearnos   *get a suntan*

De vacaciones *On vacation (continued)*
(Lección 6)

En un viaje a otro país podemos...   ***On a trip to another country we can . . .***

viajar por el país   *travel through the country*

aprender la lengua   *learn the language*

comprar recuerdos   *buy souvenirs*

sacar fotos   *take pictures*

enviar tarjetas postales   *send postcards*

Cuando regresamos a casa debemos...   ***When we return home we should . . .***

deshacer las maletas   *unpack the suitcases*

contar (ue) nuestras aventuras   *tell about our adventures*

descansar   *rest*

La ropa *Clothing*
(Lección 6)

These words pertaining to clothing were presented in Unit I, Lesson 5.

el suéter	*sweater*	los lentes	*eyeglasses*
el sombrero	*hat*	los lentes de contacto	*contact lenses*
el gorro	*cap*	la corbata	*tie*
el abrigo	*coat*	la camisa	*shirt*
el vestido	*dress*	la blusa	*blouse*
el traje	*suit*	la falda	*skirt*
los calcetines	*socks*	la chaqueta	*jacket*
los pantalones	*pants*	las medias	*stockings*
los zapatos	*shoes*	la bfanda	scarf
los guantes	gloves	los lentes de sol/ espejuelos	sunglasses

Here are additional words pertaining to clothing.

la camisa...		las sandalias	*sandals*
de manga larga	*long-sleeved shirt*	el cinturón	*belt*
de manga corta	*short-sleeved shirt*	el traje de baño	*swimsuit*
deportiva	*sport shirt*	el saco	*sport coat*
la camiseta	*T-shirt*	el impermeable	*raincoat*
la ropa interior	*underwear*	los zapatos tenis	*tennis shoes*
la pijama / payamas	*pajamas*	los tacones altos	*high heels*
las zapatillas	*slippers*	los pantalones vaqueros	~~blue jeans~~ cowboy pants
las botas	*boots*	los pantalones cortos	*shorts*

las guantes   gloves

la bufanda   scarf

la camisa sin mangas   sleeveless shirt

Estructura

Summary of personal pronouns and adjectives

SUBJECT	DIRECT OBJECT	INDIRECT OBJECT	REFLEXIVE	AFTER PREPOSITION	POSSESSIVE ADJECTIVE
yo	me	me	me	mí	mi
tú	te	te	te	ti	tu
Ud.	lo/la	le	se	Ud.	su
él	lo	le	se	él	su
ella	la	le	se	ella	su
nosotros(as)	nos	nos	nos	nosotros(as)	nuestro(a)
vosotros(as)	os	os	os	vosotros(as)	vuestro(a)
Uds.	los/las	les	se	Uds.	su
ellos	los	les	se	ellos	su
ellas	las	les	se	ellas	su

Object pronouns

INDIRECT OBJECT PRONOUNS
(Reviewed in Lesson 1)

me	*to/for me*	nos	*to/for us*
te	*to/for you*	os	*to/for you*
le	*to/for you/him/her/it*	les	*to/for you/them*

DIRECT OBJECT PRONOUNS
(Lesson 2)

me	*me*	nos	*us*
te	*you*	os	*you*
lo	*you/him/it*	los	*you/them*
la	*you/her/it*	las	*you/them*

Reflexive pronouns
(Lección 5)

me	*myself*	nos	*ourselves*
te	*yourself*	os	*yourselves*
se	*yourself, himself, herself, itself*	se	*yourselves, themselves*

Position of object pronouns
(Lección 1)

Before the verb with the person–time ending
Attached to the end of the **-ar/-er/-ir** form of the verb

Double object pronouns
(Lección 2)

INDIRECT OBJECT AND DIRECT OBJECT
If both begin with **l,** change the indirect object to **se**.

COMMON DOUBLE-OBJECT PATTERNS

me lo	me la	me los	me las
te lo	te la	te los	te las
nos lo	nos la	nos los	nos las
se lo	se la	se los	se las

Double-verb construction
(Lección 2)

first verb: conjugated   +   second verb: infinitive
(person–time endings)   (**-ar, -er, -ir** ending)

Using adjectives without a noun
(Lección 4)

When a noun has not been used:
    LO + *adjective = the + adjective + (thing/part)*

When the noun has already been used:
    EL/LA
    LOS/LAS   + *adjective = the + adjective + ones*

Making descriptive adverbs from adjectives
(Lección 5)

feminine singular adjective + **mente**

Comparison of adverbs
(Lección 5)

(same as comparison of adjectives)

más + *adverb* + **que**
menos + *adverb* + **que**
tan + *adverb* + **como**

Person–time endings for regular verbs
(Lecciones 1, 2 y 3)

SUBJECT	IMPERFECT *was/were -ing* *used to*		PRETERITE *did*		PRESENT *am/is/are -ing* *do/does*		FUTURE *will*
	← remove ending →						keep ending
	-AR	-ER/-IR	-AR	-ER/-IR	-AR	-ER/-IR	ALL VERBS
yo	-aba	-ía	-é	-í	-o	-o	-é
tú	-abas	-ías	-aste	-iste	-as	-es	-ás
Ud./él/ella	-aba	-ía	-ó	-ió	-a	-e	-á
nosotros(as)	-ábamos	-íamos	-amos	-imos	-amos	-emos/-imos	-emos
vosotros(as)	-abais	-íais	-asteis	-isteis	-áis	-éis/-ís	-éis
Uds./ellos/ellas	-aban	-ían	-aron	-ieron	-an	-en	-án

Spelling variations to keep the sound
(Lección 1)

$$\left.\begin{matrix} C \\ G \\ Z \end{matrix}\right\} \text{ before } \left\{\begin{matrix} A \\ O \\ U \end{matrix}\right. \text{ changes to } \left.\begin{matrix} QU \\ J \\ C \end{matrix}\right\} \text{ before } \left\{\begin{matrix} E \\ \\ I \end{matrix}\right.$$

(Lección 2)

vowel + **i** + vowel ⟶ vowel + **y** + vowel

Stem-changing verbs
(Lección 4)

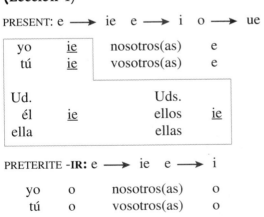

PRESENT: e ⟶ ie   e ⟶ i   o ⟶ ue

yo	ie	nosotros(as)	e
tú	ie	vosotros(as)	e

Ud.		Uds.	
él	ie	ellos	ie
ella		ellas	

PRETERITE -**IR:** e ⟶ ie   e ⟶ i

yo	o	nosotros(as)	o
tú	o	vosotros(as)	o

Ud.		Uds.	
él	u	ellos	u
ella		ellas	

Summary of irregular verbs
(Lección 6)

Following is a summary of the patterns of irregular verbs you have learned in this book. You will need to add the person endings.

IMPERFECT

ir ⟶ IBA

ser ⟶ ERA

ver ⟶ VEÍA

PRETERITE: "COMBO" VERBS

IRREGULAR STEM	"COMBO" ENDINGS
tener ⟶ TUV-	-E
estar ⟶ ESTUV-	-ISTE
poder ⟶ PUD-	-O
poner ⟶ PUS-	-IMOS
saber ⟶ SUP-	-ISTEIS
venir ⟶ VIN-	-IERON*
hacer ⟶ HIC-	
querer ⟶ QUIS-	*Note: No **i** after **j**
decir ⟶ DIJ-	
traer ⟶ TRAJ-	

PRESENT: Irregular YO forms

-GO		**-OY**		**OTHER**	
tener ⟶ TENGO		ser ⟶ SOY		ver ⟶ VEO	
venir ⟶ VENGO		estar ⟶ ESTOY		saber ⟶ SÉ	
hacer ⟶ HAGO		dar ⟶ DOY		conocer ⟶ CONOZCO	
poner ⟶ PONGO		ir ⟶ VOY			
decir ⟶ DIGO					
traer ⟶ TRAIGO					
salir ⟶ SALGO					
oír ⟶ OIGO					

FUTURE: Irregular stems

hacer $\longrightarrow$ HAR-
poder $\longrightarrow$ PODR-
decir $\longrightarrow$ DIR-
querer $\longrightarrow$ QUERR-
tener $\longrightarrow$ TENDR-
venir $\longrightarrow$ VENDR-
poner $\longrightarrow$ PONDR-
salir $\longrightarrow$ SALDR-

Ser and **ir** are irregular in all tenses except the future. (See charts.)

	IMPERFECT	PRETERITE	PRESENT	FUTURE
SER	ERA	FUI	SOY	SERÉ
IR	IBA	FUI	VOY	IRÉ

IRREGULAR VERB CHARTS
(irregularities indicated in **bold**)

CONOCER *to know, to be acquainted with*

PRESENT
know

yo   **conozco**
(only one irregular form)

DAR *to give*

	IMPERFECT *gave* *was/were giving* *used to give*	PRETERITE *gave* *did give*	PRESENT *give(s)* *am/is/are giving* *do/does give*	FUTURE *will give*
yo	daba	**di**	**doy**	daré
tú	dabas	**diste**	das	darás
Ud./él/ella	daba	**dio**	da	dará
nosotros(as)	dábamos	**dimos**	damos	daremos
vosotros(as)	dabais	**disteis**	dais	daréis
Uds./ellos/ellas	daban	**dieron**	dan	darán

DECIR *to say, to tell*

	IMPERFECT *said/told* *was/were saying/telling* *used to say/tell*	PRETERITE *said/told* *did say/tell*	PRESENT *say(s)/tell(s)* *am/is/are saying/telling* *do/does say/tell*	FUTURE *will say/tell*
yo	decía	**dije**	digo	diré
tú	decías	**dijiste**	dices	dirás
Ud./él/ella	decía	**dijo**	dice	dirá
nosotros(as)	decíamos	**dijimos**	decimos	diremos
vosotros(as)	decíais	**dijisteis**	decís	diréis
Uds./ellos/ellas	decían	**dijeron**	dicen	dirán

ESTAR *to be*

	IMPERFECT *was/were* *used to be*	PRETERITE *was/were*	PRESENT *am/is/are*	FUTURE *will be*
yo	estaba	**estuve**	**estoy**	estaré
tú	estabas	**estuviste**	estás	estarás
Ud./él/ella	estaba	**estuvo**	está	estará
nosotros(as)	estábamos	**estuvimos**	estamos	estaremos
vosotros(as)	estabais	**estuvisteis**	estáis	estaréis
Uds./ellos/ellas	estaban	**estuvieron**	están	estarán

HACER *to do, to make*

	IMPERFECT *did/made* *was/were doing/making* *used to do/make*	PRETERITE *did/made* *did do/make*	PRESENT *do/does/make(s)* *am/is/are doing/making* *do/does do/make*	FUTURE *will do/make*
yo	hacía	**hice**	**hago**	**haré**
tú	hacías	**hiciste**	haces	**harás**
Ud./él/ella	hacía	**hizo**	hace	**hará**
nosotros(as)	hacíamos	**hicimos**	hacemos	**haremos**
vosotros(as)	hacíais	**hicisteis**	hacéis	**haréis**
Uds./ellos/ellas	hacían	**hicieron**	hacen	**harán**

IR *to go*

	IMPERFECT *went* *was/were going* *used to go*	PRETERITE *went* *did go*	PRESENT *go/goes* *am/is/are going* *do/does go*	FUTURE *will go*
yo	**iba**	**fui**	**voy**	iré
tú	**ibas**	**fuiste**	**vas**	irás
Ud./él/ella	**iba**	**fue**	**va**	irá
nosotros(as)	**íbamos**	**fuimos**	**vamos**	iremos
vosotros(as)	**ibais**	**fuisteis**	**vais**	iréis
Uds./ellos/ellas	**iban**	**fueron**	**van**	irán

OÍR *to hear*

	IMPERFECT *heard* *was/were hearing* *used to hear*	PRETERITE *heard* *did hear*	PRESENT *hear(s)* *am/is/are hearing* *do/does hear*	FUTURE *will hear*
yo	oía	oí	**oigo**	oiré
tú	oías	oíste	**oyes**	oirás
Ud./él/ella	oía	**oyó**	**oye**	oirá
nosotros(as)	oíamos	oímos	oímos	oiremos
vosotros(as)	oíais	oísteis	oís	oiréis
Uds./ellos/ellas	oían	**oyeron**	**oyen**	oirán

PODER (ue) *to be able, can*
[preterite: *succeeded*]

	IMPERFECT *could* *was/were able* *used to be able*	PRETERITE *succeeded* *did succeed*	PRESENT *can* *am/is/are able*	FUTURE *will be able*
yo	podía	**pude**	puedo	**podré**
tú	podías	**pudiste**	puedes	**podrás**
Ud./él/ella	podía	**pudo**	puede	**podrá**
nosotros(as)	podíamos	**pudimos**	podemos	**podremos**
vosotros(as)	podíais	**pudisteis**	podéis	**podréis**
Uds./ellos/ellas	podían	**pudieron**	pueden	**podrán**

PONER *to put*

	IMPERFECT *put* *was/were putting* *used to put*	PRETERITE *put* *did put*	PRESENT *put(s)* *am/is/are putting* *do/does put*	FUTURE *will put*
yo	ponía	**puse**	**pongo**	**pondré**
tú	ponías	**pusiste**	pones	**pondrás**
Ud./él/ella	ponía	**puso**	pone	**pondrá**
nosotros(as)	poníamos	**pusimos**	ponemos	**pondremos**
vosotros(as)	poníais	**pusisteis**	ponéis	**pondréis**
Uds./ellos/ellas	ponían	**pusieron**	ponen	**pondrán**

QUERER (ie) *to want, to love*
[preterite: *tried* /preterite negative: *refused*]

	IMPERFECT *wanted* *was/were wanting* *used to want*	PRETERITE *tried* *did try*	PRESENT *want(s)* *am/is/are wanting* *do/does want*	FUTURE *will want*
yo	quería	**quise**	quiero	**querré**
tú	querías	**quisiste**	quieres	**querrás**
Ud./él/ella	quería	**quiso**	quiere	**querrá**
nosotros(as)	queríamos	**quisimos**	queremos	**querremos**
vosotros(as)	queríais	**quisisteis**	queréis	**querréis**
Uds./ellos/ellas	querían	**quisieron**	quieren	**querrán**

SABER *to know (how)*
[preterite: *found out*]

	IMPERFECT *knew* *used to know*	PRETERITE *found out* *did find out*	PRESENT *know(s)* *am/is/are knowing* *do/does know*	FUTURE *will know*
yo	sabía	**supe**	**sé**	**sabré**
tú	sabías	**supiste**	sabes	**sabrás**
Ud./él/ella	sabía	**supo**	sabe	**sabrá**
nosotros(as)	sabíamos	**supimos**	sabemos	**sabremos**
vosotros(as)	sabíais	**supisteis**	sabéis	**sabréis**
Uds./ellos/ellas	sabían	**supieron**	saben	**sabrán**

SALIR *to go out, to leave*

	IMPERFECT *left* *was/were leaving* *used to leave*	PRETERITE *left* *did leave*	PRESENT *leave(s)* *am/is/are leaving* *do/does leave*	FUTURE *will leave*
yo	salía	salí	**salgo**	**saldré**
tú	salías	saliste	sales	**saldrás**
Ud./él/ella	salía	salió	sale	**saldrá**
nosotros(as)	salíamos	salimos	salimos	**saldremos**
vosotros(as)	salíais	salisteis	salís	**saldréis**
Uds./ellos/ellas	salían	salieron	salen	**saldrán**

SER *to be*

	IMPERFECT *was/were* *used to be*	PRETERITE *was/were*	PRESENT *am/is/are*	FUTURE *will be*
yo	**era**	**fui**	**soy**	seré
tú	**eras**	**fuiste**	**eres**	serás
Ud./él/ella	**era**	**fue**	**es**	será
nosotros(as)	**éramos**	**fuimos**	**somos**	seremos
vosotros(as)	**erais**	**fuisteis**	**sois**	seréis
Uds./ellos/ellas	**eran**	**fueron**	**son**	serán

TENER *to have*

	IMPERFECT *had* *was/were having* *used to have*	PRETERITE *had* *did have*	PRESENT *have/has* *am/is/are having* *do/does have*	FUTURE *will have*
yo	tenía	**tuve**	**tengo**	**tendré**
tú	tenías	**tuviste**	tienes	**tendrás**
Ud./él/ella	tenía	**tuvo**	tiene	**tendrá**
nosotros(as)	teníamos	**tuvimos**	tenemos	**tendremos**
vosotros(as)	teníais	**tuvisteis**	tenéis	**tendréis**
Uds./ellos/ellas	tenían	**tuvieron**	tienen	**tendrán**

TRAER *to bring*

	IMPERFECT *brought* *was/were bringing* *used to bring*	PRETERITE *brought* *did bring*	PRESENT *bring(s)* *am/is/are bringing* *do/does bring*	FUTURE *will bring*
yo	traía	**traje**	**traigo**	traeré
tú	traías	**trajiste**	traes	traerás
Ud./él/ella	traía	**trajo**	trae	traerá
nosotros(as)	traíamos	**trajimos**	traemos	traeremos
vosotros(as)	traíais	**trajisteis**	traéis	traeréis
Uds./ellos/ellas	traían	**trajeron**	traen	traerán

VENIR *to come*

	IMPERFECT *came* *was/were coming* *used to come*	PRETERITE *came* *did come*	PRESENT *come(s)* *am/is/are coming* *do/does come*	FUTURE *will come*
yo	venía	**vine**	**vengo**	**vendré**
tú	venías	**viniste**	vienes	**vendrás**
Ud./él/ella	venía	**vino**	viene	**vendrá**
nosotros(as)	veníamos	**vinimos**	venimos	**vendremos**
vosotros(as)	veníais	**vinisteis**	venís	**vendréis**
Uds./ellos/ellas	venían	**vinieron**	vienen	**vendrán**

VER *to see*

	IMPERFECT *saw* *was/were seeing* *used to see*	PRETERITE *saw* *did see*	PRESENT *see(s)* *am/is/are seeing* *do/does see*	FUTURE *will see*
yo	**veía**	vi	**veo**	veré
tú	**veías**	viste	ves	verás
Ud./él/ella	**veía**	vio	ve	verá
nosotros(as)	**veíamos**	vimos	vemos	veremos
vosotros(as)	**veíais**	visteis	veis	veréis
Uds./ellos/ellas	**veían**	vieron	ven	verán

Esqueletos

(pro)noun + verb + thing

(Lección 1)

El niño mira la televisión.   *The child watches television.*
Yo celebré mi cumpleaños.   *I celebrated my birthday.*

(pro)noun + verb + A + person

(Lección 1)

Yo invito a mi hermano.   *I'm inviting my brother.*
Yo llamo a María.   *I'm calling María.*

(pro)noun + object pronoun + main verb

(Lección 1)

María lo invitará.   *María will invite him.*
Ellos le hablaban a Juan.   *They used to talk to Juan.*

(pro)noun + verb + (preposition) + infinitive + object pronoun

(Lección 1)

María va a invitarlo.   *María is going to invite him.*
Ellos deseaban hablarle.   *They wanted to talk to him.*

OR

(pro)noun + object pronoun + verb + (preposition) + infinitive

(Lección 1)

María lo va a invitar.   *María is going to invite him.*
Ellos le deseaban hablar.   *They wanted to talk to him.*

(pro)noun + verb + (preposition) + infinitive

(Lección 2)

Yo voy a visitar a mi abuela mañana.
I am going to visit my grandmother tomorrow.

Ella desea comprar un auto nuevo.
She wants to buy a new car.

negative word + *verb*

(Lección 4)

Yo nunca voy.   *I never go. / I don't ever go.*
Nadie habla.   *Nobody is talking.*

NO + *verb* + *negative word*

(Lección 4)

Yo no voy nunca.   *I never go. / I don't ever go.*
No habla nadie.   *Nobody is talking.*

Vamos a dar una fiesta
Let's give a party

We have already learned the importance of the verb endings in telling *who* is doing the action and *when*. By learning a few basic patterns now, we will be able to work with lots of verbs and talk about all kinds of activities. Let's begin by giving a party.

Vocabulario

Una fiesta   *A party*

Preparar para una fiesta	***To prepare for a party***
ayudar con las preparaciones	*to help with preparations*
buscar a los amigos	*to look for friends*
cocinar la comida	*to cook the food*
comprar los refrescos	*to buy the refreshments*
hallar un lugar	*to find a place*
invitar a los amigos	*to invite friends*
llamar a los vecinos	*to call the neighbors*
lavar los platos	*to wash the dishes*
limpiar la casa	*to clean the house*
mandar las invitaciones	*to send the invitations*
planear las actividades	*to plan the activities*
Para ir a una fiesta	***To go to a party***
aceptar la invitación	*to accept the invitation*
caminar a la casa	*to walk to the house*
desear ir	*to want/wish/desire to go*
llegar tarde	*to arrive late*
temprano	* early*
llevar a los amigos	*to bring/take friends*
llevar la ropa buena	*to wear nice clothes*
manejar a la fiesta	*to drive to the party*

En una fiesta

		At a party
1.	comenzar la fiesta	*to begin/start/commence the party*
2.	bailar	*to dance*
3.	cantar	*to sing*
4.	celebrar un cumpleaños	*to celebrate a birthday*
5.	charlar con los invitados	*to chat/talk with the guests*
6.	descansar un poco	*to rest a little*
7.	escuchar la música	*to listen to music*
8.	mirar la televisión	*to watch television*
9.	saludar a los invitados	*to greet the guests*
10.	prestar discos compactos	*to lend CDs*
11.	sacar fotos	*to take pictures*
12.	tocar la guitarra	*to play the guitar*
13.	discos compactos	*CDs*
14.	tomar refrescos	*to drink/have refreshments*
15.	visitar con los amigos	*to visit with friends*
16.	dar* una fiesta	*to give a party*
17.	un regalo	*to give a present*
18.	las gracias	*to thank*

*Note: **Dar** is an irregular verb. See the chart on page 352.

1 What do you have to do to prepare for a party? Make a list and then tell your partner what you have to do.

EJEMPLO: ¿Qué tienes que hacer para preparar para una fiesta?
What do you have to do to prepare for a party?

Yo tengo que limpiar la casa y llamar a mis amigos.
I have to clean the house and call my friends.

2 What things do you like or not like to do at a party? Make a list from the vocabulary on page 346, then take turns with your partner asking and answering.

EJEMPLO: ¿Qué te gusta hacer en una fiesta?
What do you like to do at a party?

Me gusta charlar pero no me gusta bailar.
I like to chat, but I do not like to dance.

Note: Remember to use **en** to say *at* when referring to a location where something happens; use **a** for a destination.

Me gusta descansar <u>en</u> la fiesta.   *I like to rest <u>at</u> the party.*
Voy a estudiar <u>en</u> casa.   *I'm going to study <u>at</u> home.*
Voy <u>a</u> la fiesta con Miguel.   *I'm going <u>to</u> the party with Miguel.*

THE INFINITIVE AND PERSON–TIME ENDINGS FOR -AR VERBS

The infinitive form of a verb (action word) in Spanish is made of two parts: a <u>stem</u> which tells what the action is and an <u>ending</u> which is the equivalent of *to*.

INVITAR   *to invite*

STEM	ENDING
invit	**ar**

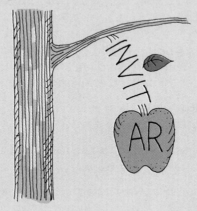

The infinitive ending of the verb (**-ar, -er,** or **-ir**) does not tell us who is doing the action or when. To tell <u>who</u> and <u>when,</u> in the past or present, we must add a <u>person–time</u> <u>ending</u> to the stem of the verb. In the future, add the <u>person–time</u> <u>ending</u> to the infinitive.

For the past and present, remove **-ar,** then add the person–time ending indicated in bold. Do <u>not</u> remove **-ar** for the future!

	IMPERFECT *-ed* *was/were -ing* *used to*	PRETERITE *-ed* *did*	PRESENT *-(s)* *am/is/are -ing* *do/does*	FUTURE *will*
yo	**-aba**	**-é**	**-o**	**-é**
tú	**-abas**	**-aste**	**-as**	**-ás**
Ud./él/ella	**-aba**	**-ó**	**-a**	**-á**
nosotros(as)	**-ábamos**	**-amos**	**-amos**	**-emos**
vosotros(as)	**-abais**	**-asteis**	**-áis**	**-éis**
Uds./ellos/ellas	**-aban**	**-aron**	**-an**	**-án**

Most verbs in Spanish are "regular," meaning that once we learn one set of endings, we can use these for many other verbs that follow the same pattern.

Let's see how it works when we invite our guests to the party.

INVITAR   *to invite*

	IMPERFECT *invited* *was/were* *inviting* *used to invite*	PRETERITE *invited* *am/is/are* *inviting* *did invite*	PRESENT *invite(s)* *do/does invite*	FUTURE *will invite*
yo	invit**aba**	invit**é**	invit**o**	invit**aré**
tú	invit**abas**	invit**aste**	invit**as**	invit**arás**
Ud./él/ella	invit**aba**	invit**ó**	invit**a**	invit**ará**
nosotros(as)	invit**ábamos**	invit**amos**	invit**amos**	invit**aremos**
vosotros(as)	invit**abais**	invit**asteis**	invit**áis**	invit**aréis**
Uds./ellos/ellas	invit**aban**	invit**aron**	invit**an**	invit**arán**

If you want to say *I will invite,* start at the line with **yo** and follow across to the column labeled FUTURE: *will invite.* The word where the column and the line meet is **invitaré** which means *I will invite.*

Invitar is a regular **-ar** verb, so you can use the same endings (in bold print above) on any regular **-ar** verb.

3 How would you say the following in Spanish?

a. He invited
b. We were inviting
c. They are inviting
d. Do you invite
e. You [plural] used to invite
f. We invite
g. Will they invite?
h. They invited

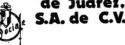
PERSONAL A

When a person who is not the one doing the action follows a verb, put **a** before the person except after **ser** and **tener**.

Juan invita <u>a</u> sus amigos.   *Juan invites his friends.*

Esqueletos

(pro)noun + verb + thing

El niño mira la televisión.   *The child watches television.*
Yo celebré mi cumpleaños.   *I celebrated my birthday.*

(pro)noun + verb + A + person

Yo invito a mi hermano.   *I'm inviting my brother.*
Yo llamo a María.   *I'm calling María.*

4 Think of a party you hosted at some time in the past. Tell whom you invited. (Use the preterite tense since it happened at a specific point in time.)

EJEMPLO: Yo invité a mi amigo Tomás.   *I invited my friend Tomás.*

5 Pretend you're planning to have a party. Mention ten people you will invite to the party. Use the future tense.

EJEMPLO: Invitaré a Juan.   *I will invite Juan.*
Invitaré a mi abuela.   *I will invite my grandmother.*

SPELLING VARIATIONS

Since Spanish spells words the way they sound, we may have to make a "spelling variation" in some verb forms. For **-ar** verbs this variation will happen before the **-é** ending of the preterite **yo** form of verbs that end in **-car**, **-gar**, or **-zar** because **c** and **g** are "hard" before an **a**, **o**, or **u** and "soft" before an **e** or **i**, and **z** is never found before an **e** or **i**.

If the verb ends in **-car**, change the **c** to **qu** in the **yo** form of the preterite.
 buscar   *to look for*   yo bus<u>qu</u>é   *I looked for*

If the verb ends in **-gar**, change the **g** to **gu** in the **yo** form of the preterite.
 llegar   *to arrive*   yo lle<u>gu</u>é   *I arrived*

If the verb ends in **-zar**, change the **z** to **c** in the **yo** form of the preterite.
 comenzar   *to begin*   yo comen<u>c</u>é   *I began*

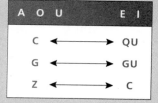

A O U		E I
C	⟷	QU
G	⟷	GU
Z	⟷	C

6 Tell who accepted the invitations to your party mentioned in Activity 5. Use the preterite tense since they only accepted once.

EJEMPLO: Juan aceptó mi invitación.   *Juan accepted my invitation.*
Mi abuela no aceptó mi invitación.   *My grandmother did not accept my invitation.*

Use other verbs from the party vocabulary on pages 345 and 346 to do Activities 7 through 13.

7 Tell what you did to prepare for the party.

EJEMPLOS: Limpié la casa.   *I cleaned the house.*
Compré refrescos.   *I bought soft drinks.*

8 Tell what your guests did at the party.

EJEMPLOS: Cantaron muchas canciones.   *They sang a lot of songs.*
Hablaron con sus amigos.   *They talked with their friends.*

9 **Encuesta**   Ask people three things they do at parties. Use the present tense.

EJEMPLO: ¿Qué son tres cosas que Uds. hacen en las fiestas?
What are three things that you do at parties?

Bailamos, charlamos con amigos y tomamos refrescos.
We dance, chat with friends, and have refreshments.

10 Tell what you used to do as a child. Use the imperfect tense.

EJEMPLOS: De niño(a) caminaba a la escuela.   *As a child, I used to walk to school.*
Miraba «Sesame Street».   *I used to watch "Sesame Street."*

11 Tell what you did yesterday. Use the preterite tense.

EJEMPLOS: Ayer lavé los platos.   *Yesterday I washed the dishes.*
Preparé la comida.   *I prepared the food.*

12 Tell what you do regularly. Use the present tense.

EJEMPLOS: Todos los días estudio.   *Every day I study.*
Trabajo en un restaurante.   *I work in a restaurant.*

13 Tell what you will do next summer. Use the future tense.

EJEMPLOS: El próximo verano esquiaré en el agua.   *Next summer I will water ski.*
Practicaré el español.   *I will practice Spanish.*

DAR   *to give*

Dar has the regular **-ar** endings except for the **yo** form of the present tense (**doy**) and all forms of the preterite tense (**di**, etc.).

	IMPERFECT *gave* *was/were giving* *used to give*	PRETERITE *gave* *am/is/are giving* *did give*	PRESENT *give(s)* *do/does give*	FUTURE *will give*
yo	daba	**di**	**doy**	daré
tú	dabas	**diste**	das	darás
Ud./él/ella	daba	**dio**	da	dará
nosotros(as)	dábamos	**dimos**	damos	daremos
vosotros(as)	dabais	**disteis**	dais	daréis
Uds./ellos/ellas	daban	**dieron**	dan	darán

14 What did you receive for your last birthday? Tell what you received and who gave it to you. Use the preterite tense.

EJEMPLOS: Mi mamá me dio un suéter.   *My mother gave me a sweater.*
Carmen me dio un libro.   *Carmen gave me a book.*

Remember: When you want to say *to/for whom,* you must use an indirect object pronoun in the sentence (**me, te, le, nos, les**). (See page 312.)

15 It's not too early to plan next year's holiday gifts. Tell what you will give to your friends and family.

EJEMPLOS: Le daré un disco compacto a mi hermano.
I'll give a CD to my brother.

A mi novia le daré una caja de chocolate.
I will give a box of chocolates to my girlfriend.

16 **Un informe** *A report*   Tell about a party you went to. Use as many **-ar** verbs as you can. Be sure to tell *who, where, when,* and *why* and any other information you can about the party.

EJEMPLO: Miguel dio una fiesta el sábado pasado.   *Miguel gave a party last Saturday.*
La fiesta fue en su casa…   *The party was at his house . . .*

17 Do your teachers give you a lot of homework? Tell what assignments they gave you for tonight.

EJEMPLOS: Mi profesor de inglés nos dio a leer cinco páginas.
My English teacher gave us five pages to read.

Mi profesor de ciencias nos dio un informe.
My science teacher gave us a report.

18 **Sit-Con**   It's your best friend's birthday next week. You are going to give him or her a surprise party. Tell what you will have to do. Be sure to tell whom you will invite, where it will be, etc.

EJEMPLO: La próxima semana mi amigo celebrará su cumpleaños.
My friend will celebrate his birthday next week.

Yo daré una fiesta en mi casa en su honor.
I will give a party at my house in his honor.

VEGA SEÑORIAL
SALON DE RECEPCIONES
Con Pista y Cupo para 280
Personas Cómodamente
Servicio de Banquetes con
Buffetes o Desayunos

IDEAL PARA:
• GRADUACIONES   • BAUTIZOS
• SEMINARIOS   • SHOWERS
• CONFERENCIAS   • BODAS, ETC.
• AMPLIO ESTACIONAMIENTO
PLUTARCO ELIAS CALLES 2138 SUR

TELS.: 17-22-29   16-41-17

REVIEW OF DIRECT OBJECT PRONOUNS
LO, LA, LOS, LAS

(Review Unit III, Lesson 5.)
The direct object tells *who* or *what* received the action of the verb. To find the direct object, look for the verb and ask *who* or *what* it affected. The noun that answers the question is the direct object.

> *Robert cooked the food.*
>   *What* did Robert cook? The food.
>   *Food* is the direct object.

If we don't want to repeat the name of the person or thing that is the direct object, we can replace it with an object pronoun.

Roberto cocinó <u>la comida</u>.	*Roberto cooked <u>the food</u>.*
Roberto <u>la</u> cocinó.	*Roberto cooked <u>it</u>.*
Juanita compró <u>las invitaciones</u>.	*Juanita bought <u>the invitations</u>.*
Juanita <u>las</u> compró.	*Juanita bought <u>them</u>.*
Marisa invitó a <u>Paco</u>.	*Marisa invited <u>Paco</u>.*
(Why is **a** before Paco?)	
Marisa <u>lo</u> invitó.	*Marisa invited <u>him</u>.*

Lo replaces a masculine singular noun.   *(him, it [masculine])*
La replaces a feminine singular noun.   *(her, it [feminine])*
Los replaces a masculine plural noun.   *(them [masculine])*
Las replaces a feminine plural noun.   *(them [feminine])*

Note: If you want to say *you* as a direct object in the **Ud.** form, use **lo** or **la** and for **Uds.** use **los** or **las**.

<u>Lo</u> visitaré, profesor.	*I will visit <u>you</u>, professor.*
Yo <u>las</u> invito, mis amigas.	*I'm inviting <u>you</u>, my friends.*

POSITION OF DIRECT OBJECT PRONOUNS

As with indirect object pronouns, direct object pronouns go *before* the verb with the person–time ending or are attached to the *end* of the infinitive (verb with **-ar**, **-er**, or **-ir**).

Invito a mis amigos. <u>Los</u> invito.	*I invite my friends. I invite <u>them</u>.*
Voy a invitar a mis amigos.	*I'm going to invite my friends.*
Voy a invitar<u>los</u>.	*I'm going to invite <u>them</u>.*

Remember that when you have an infinitive ending, there is also the option of placing the object pronoun in its usual place: before the verb with the person–time ending:

Voy a invitar a mis amigos. <u>Los</u> voy a invitar.

Esqueletos

(pro)noun + object pronoun + main verb

María <u>lo</u> invitará.   *María will invite him.*
Ellos <u>le</u> hablaban a Juan.   *They used to talk to Juan.*

(pro)noun + verb + (preposition) + infinitive + object pronoun

María va a invitar<u>lo</u>.   *María is going to invite him.*
Ellos deseaban hablar<u>le</u>.   *They wanted to talk to him.*

OR

(pro)noun + object pronoun + verb + (preposition) + infinitive

María <u>lo</u> va a invitar.   *María is going to invite him.*
Ellos <u>le</u> deseaban hablar.   *They wanted to talk to him.*

19 Tell about some people or places you visit and when you visit them. Don't forget to use the personal **a** with people.

EJEMPLO: Visito a mi hermana en Madrid.   *I visit my sister in Madrid.*
Visito a mi hermana en Madrid.
La visito en el verano.   *I visit her in the summer.*

20 Tell about some things you listen to and when you listen to them.

EJEMPLO: Escucho la música popular.   *I listen to popular music.*
            La escucho durante la tarde.   *I listen to it in the afternoon.*

21 Ask your partner whom he or she is going to visit when he or she goes on vacation.
Answer using the direct object pronoun.

EJEMPLO: 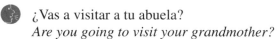   ¿Vas a visitar a tu abuela?
            Are you going to visit your grandmother?

            Sí, voy a visitarla. / No, no voy a visitarla.
            Yes, I will visit her. / No, I will not visit her.

OTHER DIRECT OBJECT PRONOUNS: ME, TE, NOS

These pronouns are used the same way as **lo, la, los,** and **las.**

me	*me*	**nos**	*us*
te	*you*	**os**	*all of you* [Spain]

¿Quién <u>te</u> invitó?   *Who invited <u>you</u>?*
Marisa <u>me</u> invitó.   *Marisa invited <u>me</u>.*

Ella va a invitar<u>nos</u> también.   *She is going to invite <u>us</u> also.*

As with **lo, la, los,** and **las,** the pronouns **me, te, nos,** and **os** go before the verb when it has the person–time ending or may be attached to the infinitive when there is one.

El Club Peruano de Michigan
Celebrará el 175 Aniversario
de su Independencia
con una comida bailable
en el Club San Marino,
con la música de la
Orquesta Latina de
Pablo Ramírez de Chicago.
Para información llamar al
(810) 777-8105

22 Talk about some people who visit you. Be careful of the word order.

EJEMPLOS: Juan me visita.   *Juan visits me.*
Mi abuela me visita.   *My grandmother visits me.*

23 Ask your partner if different people visit her or him.

EJEMPLO: ¿Te visita tu primo?
Does your cousin visit you?

Sí, mi primo me visita. / No, mi primo no me visita.
Yes, my cousin visits me. / No, my cousin doesn't visit me.

24 Talk about different people who have visited you and your family.

EJEMPLO: Mi tío nos visitó el verano pasado.   *My uncle visited us last summer.*

ENCUENTRO PERSONAL

Paulina is planning a party with her friend Rosita. Listen to their conversation regarding the plans.

¿Comprendes?

1. What kind of party does Paulina want to give?
2. What preparations does Rosita say need to be done?
3. What does Paulina want to do at the party? And Rosita?
4. What idea does Paulina have for dividing the chores?
5. What will Tomás do?

¡Te toca!

Plan a party (imaginary or real) with some of your classmates. Be sure to include what preparations have to be done and what each one of you wants to do at the party.

Leemos y contamos

A. **Yo hacía mucho. *I used to do a lot.*** Your pen pal Andrés wants to tell you what he used to do when he was younger. Did you use to do any of these things? (Notice that he uses the imperfect form of the verb because these are things he used to do.)

*Cuando yo era más joven, yo hacía muchas cosas con mis amigos.
Por la mañana, iba a la casa de mi amigo, Carlitos. La casa
de Carlitos estaba muy cerca de mi casa. Después, caminábamos con
Geraldo y Felipe a la escuela. La casa de Geraldo estaba al lado de la
casa de Carlitos y la casa de Felipe estaba al otro lado de la calle.
La escuela no estaba muy lejos de nuestras casas.*

*Teníamos casi todas las clases juntos y almorzábamos en el patio
de la escuela todos los días a las doce. Carlitos comía frijoles con
arroz o plátano con cerdo, y Felipe siempre comía fruta con
un sándwich.*

*Después de las clases íbamos todos a la farmacia, donde comprábamos
unos refrescos y hablábamos de nuestros planes para la tarde y la
noche. En el verano nadábamos en el río o caminábamos por
el parque. Después de comer, generalmente estudiábamos juntos,
escuchábamos la radio o mirábamos la televisión.*

*Los sábados jugábamos al fútbol en el parque con otros amigos.
(El fútbol en los países de habla española es lo que se llama «soccer»
en los Estados Unidos.) De vez en cuando había una fiesta e* (and) *
íbamos a las fiestas juntos. No íbamos con las muchachas pero
había muchachas en las fiestas. En las fiestas hablábamos con los
otros amigos pero no bailábamos. ¡No me gustaban las muchachas!*

*Algunas veces yo iba a la iglesia con
mi familia los domingos. Otras
veces iba a visitar a mis abuelos
o a mis tíos y primos. Me gustaba
mucho jugar con ellos. Cuando
yo era joven, mi vida era muy
feliz y todavía* (still) *es feliz.*

Make a list of at least ten things that Andrés used to do when he was younger.

B. When you were younger, was your life similar to Andrés's? Write a paragraph telling what you used to do when you were younger.

C. **Un día especial** *A special day*   Marisol wants to tell us about a special day she had two weeks ago. Notice that she uses the preterite form because these things happened once, and we are talking about a specific point in time.

Hace dos semanas yo tuve un día muy especial. La fecha fue el ocho de marzo y fue el día de mi cumpleaños. Afortunadamente (Luckily) fue un sábado y mis amigos y yo no tuvimos que ir a la escuela. Por la mañana fuimos al jardín zoológico donde miramos todos los animales, hablamos, comimos helados y caminamos por el parque. Me gustaron mucho los pingüinos y compré un pingüino de plástico en la tienda de recuerdos (souvenirs).

Después mis amigos y yo fuimos a la casa de Elena y jugamos unos juegos de vídeo. La mamá de Elena preparó una comida especial en honor de mi cumpleaños. Cocinó una torta de chocolate (mi favorito) que tenía quince velas porque yo cumplí quince años ese día. Todos celebramos y hablamos todo el día. Por la tarde mi papá y mi mamá me dieron un reloj de pulsera (wristwatch) muy bonito. Fue un día magnífico.

D. **¿Tuviste un día especial?**   Write about a special day that you had.

E. **El día de mis sueños** *The day of my dreams*   Paulina tells what she will do on a special day she dreams about. Can you guess what the occasion is before she lets on what it is?

Un día yo aceptaré una invitación de mi novio. Mis padres nos ayudarán a invitar a toda la familia y también a todos nuestros amigos. Mi mamá no tendrá que preparar la comida porque comeremos todos en un restaurante muy elegante.

Yo llevaré un vestido blanco muy bonito y mi novio me dará un ramillete (bouquet) de flores frescas. Yo le daré un beso (kiss) romántico.

Antes de la cena iremos a la iglesia donde celebraremos mi día especial. El coro (chorus) cantará mi canción favorita, «Sólo acabamos de comenzar» (We've Only Just Begun). Después de recitar nuestras promesas en frente de todo el mundo (everyone), iremos al restaurante donde todo ya estará preparado. Los invitados nos darán regalos para la casa, como platos, relojes de pared y algunos nos darán dinero (money). Un fotógrafo sacará muchas fotos para recordar (remember) mi día especial.

Cuando la banda toque nuestra canción favorita, mi novio y yo bailaremos solos mientras todos nos mirarán. Yo bailaré con mi papá y mi novio bailará con su mamá. Entonces todo el mundo bailará. Después de la fiesta, ¡iremos a nuestra casa!

¿Qué día es mi día especial? Sí, ¡el día de mi matrimonio!

F. Is there a special day in your future? Write a description of what you think it will be like.

¡Así es!

The quinceañera

On her fifteenth birthday, a young Hispanic woman is called a **quinceañera**. It is a very special day because she is considered to be passing from childhood to womanhood. In more traditional families where her activities were somewhat restricted, she is now permitted to have steady boyfriends (**novios**) and to date. At this age she can use makeup and wear adult clothing, such as high heels and jewelry.

It is a day to celebrate! The form of celebration varies according to the social and financial standing of the family, but it may range from a simple family gathering to something resembling a formal wedding. Many **quinceañeras** have a celebration that begins with a religious ceremony at the church and is followed by a formal dinner dance in the evening attended by family and friends. In some of the bigger celebrations, she may have fifteen young women and fifteen young men in her court!

...¡Tan excelente y divertido como tú! Feliz Quinceañero

Deseándote un Quinceañero

¿Qué comes?
What do you eat?

Are you hungry? Let's learn some words for food and the verb **comer** (*to eat*). Then we can talk about what we like to eat.

Vocabulario

La comida *Food*

These words pertaining to food were presented in Unit I, Lesson 6.

Las comidas	*Meals*
el desayuno	*breakfast*
la comida	*dinner, midday main meal*
el almuerzo	*lunch*
la merienda	*snack*
la cena	*supper, evening meal, dinner*

la leche	*milk*	el café	*coffee*
la hamburguesa	*hamburger*	el refresco	*soft drink*
la papa	*potato*	el té	*tea*
las papas fritas	*French fries*	el rosbif	*roast beef*
la ensalada	*salad*	el huevo	*egg*
la lechuga	*lettuce*	el perro caliente	*hot dog*
la sopa	*soup*	el pollo	*chicken*
la torta	*cake*	el pescado	*fish*
el agua*	*water*	el jamón	*ham*
las frutas	*fruit*	el sándwich	*sandwich*
las legumbres	*vegetables*	el helado	*ice cream*
las papitas fritas	*potato chips*	el pan	*bread*

*Feminine nouns that begin with a stressed **a** sound use **el**.

Here are additional words pertaining to food.

desayunar	*to eat/have breakfast*
almorzar (ue)*	*to eat/have lunch*
cenar	*to eat/have dinner*
tomar	*to drink, to take*
beber	*to drink*
comer	*to eat*

*Note: The **o** changes to **ue** in all forms of the present except in the **nosotros** and **vosotros** forms. Other verbs like this are presented in Lesson 4.

yo alm<u>ue</u>rzo (*I eat lunch*)   nosotros alm<u>o</u>rzamos (*we eat lunch*)

Las legumbres   *Vegetables*

1. el tomate   *tomato*
2. el apio   *celery*
3. el rábano   *radish*
4. la remolacha   *beet*
5. la coliflor   *cauliflower*
6. la cebolla   *onion*
7. los frijoles   *beans*
8. el pepino   *cucumber*

9. el ajo   *garlic*
10. el maíz   *corn*
11. las judías   *string beans*
12. la batata   *sweet potato*
13. la zanahoria   *carrot*
14. los guisantes   *peas*
15. el pimiento   *pepper*

Las frutas   *Fruits*

1. la manzana — *apple*
2. la pera — *pear*
3. las uvas — *grapes*
4. la toronja — *grapefruit*
5. las fresas — *strawberries*
6. la naranja — *orange*
7. la piña — *pineapple*

8. el plátano — *banana*
9. las cerezas — *cherries*
10. las frambuesas — *raspberries*
11. los arándanos — *blueberries*
12. ~~la sandía~~ el melón — *watermelon*
13. el limón — *lemon*

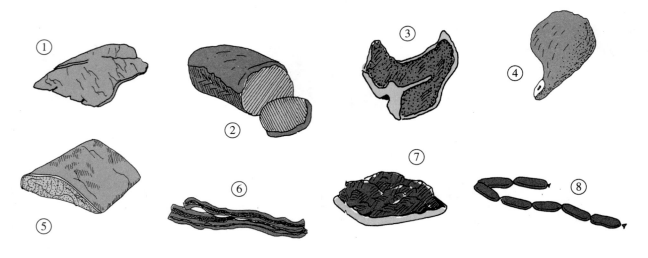

La carne   *Meat*

1. la ternera — *veal*
2. la carne de cerdo — *pork*
3. la chuleta de cerdo — *pork chop*
4. la carne de cordero — *lamb*

5. la carne de res — *beef*
6. el tocino — *bacon*
7. la carne molida — *ground meat*
8. la salchicha — *sausage*
9. el bistec — steak
10. el pollo — chicken
11. el pavo — turkey

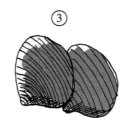
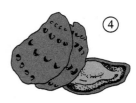

Los mariscos   *Seafood*

1. la langosta   *lobster*
2. los camarones   *shrimp*
3. las almejas   *clams*
4. las ostras   *oysters*
5. el pescado   fish
6. el cangrejo   crab

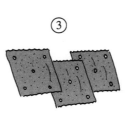

El pan   *Bread*

1. el pan tostado   *toast*
2. el panecillo   *roll*
3. la galleta   *cracker*
4. el sándwich de…   maní   *. . . sandwich*
5. la mantequilla de cacahuete   *peanut butter*
6. la jalea   *jelly*
7. la galletita   cookie

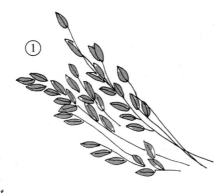

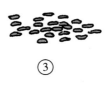

Los cereales   *Cereals*

1. la avena   *oats*
2. el trigo   *wheat*
3. el arroz   *rice*

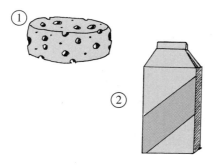
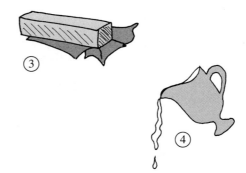

Los productos lácteos *Dairy products*

1. el queso — *cheese*
2. la leche — *milk*
3. la mantequilla — *butter*
4. la crema — *cream*
5. el yogur — *yogurt*

Las bebidas *Beverages*

1. el té — *tea*
2. el jugo (de) — *juice*
3. el cafe con crema — *coffee with cream*
4. … sin azúcar — *… without sugar*

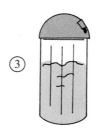
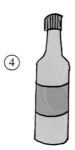

Los condimentos *Seasonings*

1. la sal — *salt*
2. la pimienta — *pepper*
3. el azúcar — *sugar*
4. la salsa picante — *hot sauce*

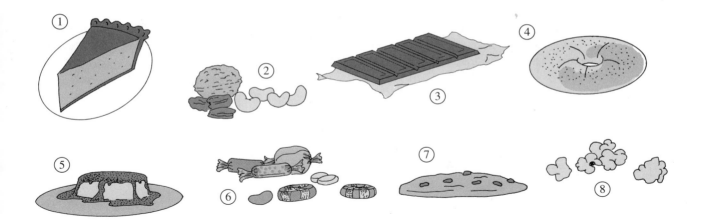

El postre y los bocaditos   *Dessert and snacks*

1. el pastel de…   . . . *pie*
       vainilla   *vanilla*
       chocolate   *chocolate*
2. la nuez   *nut, walnut*
3. la ~~tableta~~ de chocolate   *candy bar*
       barra

4. la rosquilla   *doughnut*
5. el flan   *custard*
6. los dulces   *candy*
7. la galletita dulce   *cookie*
8. las palomitas de maíz *popcorn*

1 **Encuesta** *Survey*   Find out what your classmates like to eat and drink for each meal. Make an entry for each person so you can report to the class.

EJEMPLO: ¿Qué te gusta comer o beber para el desayuno?
                What do you like to eat or drink for breakfast?

                Para el desayuno me gusta comer pan tostado con jalea y café
                   con crema, sin azúcar.
                For breakfast, I like to eat toast with jelly and coffee with cream,
                   without sugar.

PERSON–TIME ENDINGS FOR -ER VERBS

There are three main groups of verbs in Spanish: **-ar, -er, -ir**. You have already learned the endings for the verbs that end in **-ar**. In this lesson you will learn the endings for the second group of verbs: those that end in **-er**.

REVIEW OF THE -AR PATTERN

For the past and present tenses, remove **-ar**, then add the person–time ending. Do *not* remove **-ar** for the future.

	IMPERFECT -ed was/were -ing used to	PRETERITE -ed did	PRESENT -(s) am/is/are -ing do/does	FUTURE will
yo	-aba	-é	-o	-é
tú	-abas	-aste	-as	-ás
Ud./él/ella	-aba	-ó	-a	-á
nosotros(as)	-ábamos	-amos	-amos	-emos
vosotros(as)	-abais	-asteis	-áis	-éis
Uds./ellos/ellas	-aban	-aron	-an	-án

Compare the **-ar** pattern to the **-er** pattern.

-ER VERB PATTERN

For the past and present tenses, remove **-er**, then add the person–time ending. Do *not* remove **-er** for the future.

	IMPERFECT -ed was/were -ing used to	PRETERITE -ed did	PRESENT (s) am/is/are -ing do/does	FUTURE will
yo	-ía	-í	-o	-é
tú	-ías	-iste	-es	-ás
Ud./él/ella	-ía	-ió	-e	-á
nosotros(as)	-íamos	-imos	-emos	-emos
vosotros(as)	-íais	-isteis	-éis	-éis
Uds./ellos/ellas	-ían	-ieron	-en	-án

Note: Spelling variation: If the verb ends in **-ger** or **-gir** change the **g** to **j** before **o**.

escoger ⟶ escojo

recoger ⟶ recojo

Now, let's eat!! Here is the verb **comer** with the person–time endings for -er verbs in bold print.

COMER *to eat*

	IMPERFECT *ate* *was/were* *eating* *used to eat*	PRETERITE *ate* *did eat*	PRESENT *eat(s)* *am/is/are* *eating* *do/does eat*	FUTURE *will eat*
yo	comía	comí	como	comeré
tú	comías	comiste	comes	comerás
Ud./él/ella	comía	comió	come	comerá
nosotros(as)	comíamos	comimos	comemos	comeremos
vosotros(as)	comíais	comisteis	coméis	comeréis
Uds./ellos/ellas	comían	comieron	comen	comerán

Antes yo comía mucho.

Ahora como legumbres. Estoy a dieta.

En el futuro, comeré poco.

2 **¿Qué comiste ayer?** *What did you eat yesterday?* Find out what your partner ate yesterday.

EJEMPLO: ¿Qué comiste para el desayuno? *What did you eat for breakfast?*

Comí cereal con leche y fresas. *I ate cereal with milk and strawberries.*

3 **¿Qué comes cuando estás en...?** *What do you eat when you are at . . . ?* Ask your partner what he or she eats when he or she goes to the following places.

a. la playa *(beach)*
b. el circo *(circus)*
c. un restaurante caro *(expensive)*
d. la casa de un amigo
e. la cafetería de la escuela
f. un picnic
g. el cine *(movies)*
h. un restaurante de comida rápida *(fast food)*

4 ***Sit-Con:* ¿Comes tú zanahorias? *Do you eat carrots?*** Your mother has invited your partner to dinner next week and wants you to find out what foods he or she doesn't like. Ask your partner about different foods your family eats to find out if he or she eats them. Use **lo, la, los,** or **las** in the answer.

EJEMPLO: ¿Comes zanahorias?   *Do you eat carrots?*

Sí, las como. / No, no las como.   *Yes, I eat them. / No, I don't eat them.*

5 Tell your mother what your partner eats so she can plan the menu.

EJEMPLO: Mi amigo(a) come zanahorias pero no come guisantes.
My friend eats carrots, but does not eat peas.

Vocabulario

Verbos que terminan en -er   *Verbs that end in* -er

1. aprender (a)	*to learn (to)*	
2. comprender	*to understand*	
3. correr	*to run*	
4. coser	*to sew*	
5. creer	*to believe*	

6. deber	*to owe, ought to, should*	
7. leer	*to read*	
8. romper	*to break*	
9. vender	*to sell*	

Note: Spelling variation: If a vowel comes before **-ió** or **-ieron,** change **i** to **y.** An unaccented **i** between two vowels becomes **y**.

leer:	él le<u>y</u>ó	ellos le<u>y</u>eron
creer:	él cre<u>y</u>ó	ellos cre<u>y</u>eron

6 Using verbs that end in **-er,** make a list of things you and the people you know do and tell where and when you do them. Use this pattern: *who / verb / what / where / when.*

EJEMPLO: Yo leo mi libro en casa todas las noches.   *I read my book at home every night.*

DOUBLE-VERB CONSTRUCTION

Look carefully at this construction in Spanish and compare it to English.

Yo deseo estudiar.   *I want to study.*

In both, the first verb has the person–time ending. The second verb is the infinitive: **-ar/-er/-ir** form in Spanish, *to [verb]* in English.

Vocabulario

Verbos que combinan con el infinitivo   *Verbs that combine with the infinitive*

Here are some verbs that may be used as the first verb in this construction:

desear + *infinitive*	*to want to . . .*
necesitar + *infinitive*	*to need to . . .*
esperar + *infinitive*	*to hope to . . .*
odiar + *infinitive*	*to hate to . . .*
deber + *infinitive*	*ought to . . .*

Mi abuela desea mirar un auto nuevo.   *My grandmother wants to look at a new car.*
Necesita comprar un auto barato.   *She needs to buy a cheap car.*

Sometimes a preposition or other word separates the two verbs. Here are some verbs that have a preposition or another word:

aprender a + *infinitive*	*to learn to . . .*
ayudar a + *infinitive*	*to help (to) . . .*
ir a + *infinitive*	*to be going to . . .*
invitar a + *infinitive*	*to invite to . . .*
tratar de + *infinitive*	*to try to . . .*
acabar de + *infinitive*	*to have just . . .*
insistir en + *infinitive*	*to insist on . . .*
tener que + *infinitive*	*to have to . . .*
tener ganas de + *infinitive*	*to feel like . . .*

Voy a estudiar.   *I'm going to study.*
Tengo que estudiar.   *I have to study.*

Esqueleto

(pro)noun + verb + (preposition) + infinitive

Yo voy a visitar a mi abuela mañana.
I am going to visit my grandmother tomorrow.

Ella desea comprar un auto nuevo.
She wants to buy a new car.

7 Complete the sentences with a verb in the infinitive form.

EJEMPLO: Yo odio…   *I hate . . .*
Yo odio limpiar mi cuarto.   *I hate to clean my room.*

a. Yo odio…   e. Yo voy a…
b. Yo necesito…   f. Yo trato de…
c. Yo espero…   g. Yo acabo de…
d. Yo debo…   h. Yo insisto en…

8 Repeat Activity 7 but change it to tell about someone else.

EJEMPLOS: Mi padre acaba de comprar un coche nuevo.   *My father has just bought a new car.*
Angelina trata de aprender a esquiar.   *Angelina tries to learn to ski.*
Tú debes estudiar más.   *You ought to study more.*

REVIEW: OBJECT PRONOUNS

Direct objects tell *who* or *what* receives the action of the verb.
   ¿María? Yo <u>la</u> visito mucho.   *María? I visit <u>her</u> a lot.*

Indirect objects tell *to* or *for* whom something was done.
   Yo <u>le</u> dí un regalo.   *I gave a gift <u>to him</u>* OR *I gave <u>him</u> a gift.*

INDIRECT OBJECT PRONOUNS				DIRECT OBJECT PRONOUNS			
me	*to/for me*	nos	*to/for us*	me	*me*	nos	*us*
te	*to/for you*	os	*to/for you*	te	*you*	os	*you*
le	*to/for you/him/her*	les	*to/for you/them*	lo	*you/him/it*	los	*you/them*
				la	*you/her/it*	las	*you/them*

Remember that these pronouns go:
1. before the verb with the person–time ending [conjugated verb]
2. after and attached to the **-ar/-er/-ir** form of the verb [infinitive]
   Eugenio nos visita.   *Eugenio visits us.*
   Eugenio va a visitarnos.   *Eugenio is going to visit us.*

el pote español

Auténtica cocina española a los precios más razonables en New York

Almuerzo de lunes a viernes de 12-3pm
Cena de lunes a sábado de 5pm a 11pm

718 Segunda Avenida (entre calles 38 y 39)
Para reservas: 889-6680

Willy's Sea Food

El mejor sabor
Un pedazo de Mar en cada plato que servimos

Tel. 840-7060
Ave. Hostos 145
Playa de Ponce
Abierto de 11:00 am.
en adelante

DOUBLE OBJECT PRONOUNS

There may be times when you want to use both an indirect and a direct object pronoun in the same sentence. If you do, put the <u>indirect object pronoun</u> first. If both pronouns begin with **l**, change **le** or **les** to **se**.

María me dio el libro.   *María gave the book to me.*
María <u>me lo</u> dio.   *María gave it to me.*

María te dio la bolsa.   *María gave the purse to you.*
María <u>te la</u> dio.   *María gave it to you.*

María nos dio los libros.   *María gave the books to us.*
María <u>nos los</u> dio.   *María gave them to us.*

María le dio las bolsas.   *María gave the purses to him.*
María <u>se las</u> dio.   *María gave them to him.*

Here are the most common patterns. Practice saying them out loud to get used to them.

me lo	me la	me los	me las
te lo	te la	te los	te las
nos lo	nos la	nos los	nos las
se lo	se la	se los	se las

9 Make a list of several things that were given to you. Then tell who gave each one to you.

EJEMPLOS: un juego de vídeo   *a video game*
Mi madre me lo dio.   *My mother gave it to me.*

una cámara fotográfica   *a camera*
Mi padre me la dio.   *My father gave it to me.*

10 *Sit-Con*   Raquel received many things for her birthday. She left the card with each gift so that she could write thank-you notes. Tell who gave her each gift. Remember to change **le** *(to her)* to **se** because the direct object begins with **l**.

EJEMPLO: un coche deportivo (papá)   Su papá se lo dio.
a sports car (dad)   Her dad gave it to her.

a. un libro de poesía (hermano)
b. un disco compacto (amiga Elena)
c. un reloj (novio)
d. unas pelotas de tenis *[tennis balls]* (entrenador *[coach]*)
e. una cinta de música (profesor de música)
f. unos lápices (amigo Antonio)

11 *Sit-Con*   Several of your friends and acquaintances want to borrow your newest music cassette. Make a list of people you know and tell if you will or will not lend the tape to each of them.

EJEMPLO: A Juan no se la prestaré.   *I will not lend it to Juan.*
A Marta se la prestaré.   *I will lend it to Marta.*

ENCUENTRO PERSONAL

Paulina and some of her friends are trying to decide where to go for something to eat. What kind of restaurant would you like to go to?

¿Comprendes?

1. What kind of food does Paulina like?
2. What is her favorite meal?
3. Where does she want to eat?
4. What kind of food does Salvador like?
5. What is his favorite dish?
6. What difficulty does Eduardo point out? Where does he suggest they go to eat? Why does he suggest this?
7. Do you think Sean really likes Hispanic food? How about you?

¡Te toca!

Pretend your class is going on a field trip to a Hispanic restaurant. Talk with some classmates about your favorite foods and where you want to go to eat.

Leemos y contamos

A. La comida hispana

Adémas de las comidas conocidas *(known)* internacionalmente, como las hamburguesas, la pizza y los perros calientes, cada país tiene sus comidas típicas. En el mundo hispano, cada uno de los veinte países tienen sus comidas típicas.

Por ejemplo, el <u>taco</u> es uno de los platos típicos mexicanos. Menos conocido es el <u>tamal</u>, que se hace con masa *(dough)* y carne de res o de pollo. La masa y la carne se envuelven *(wrap)* en cáscara de mazorcas *(cornhusks)*. Por supuesto, no se come la cáscara.

Muchos norteamericanos conocen la <u>tortilla mexicana</u>, un pan hecho *(made)* con harina *(flour)* de maíz o de trigo. Pero muchos no conocen la <u>tortilla española</u>, un «omelette» de huevos, papas, cebollas y otras especias. (La receta *[recipe]* está en Actividad D.) Otra comida típica de España es la <u>paella</u>, que muchos españoles consideran el plato nacional. La paella se hace con arroz, carne, mariscos, pescado, azafrán *(saffron)* y otras especias. Es un plato muy delicioso.

Los <u>tostones</u> son un ejemplo de comida típica hispanoamericana. Se hacen con plátanos cortados *(cut)* en rebanadas *(slices)*. Las rebanadas se fríen *(are fried)* en aceite bien caliente, se escurren *(are drained)*, se aplastan *(are flattened)* y se refríen *(are fried again)*. Entonces se sacan del aceite y se les echa sal. Salen crujientes *(crispy)* como las papitas fritas. Se comen como merienda, entremés o al lado del plato principal.

Los países de habla española tienen muchos otros platos tradicionales, pero es imposible mencionarlos todos. Debes visitar un país hispano o, por lo menos, ir a un restaurante auténtico para conocer otras comidas hispanas. También puedes preparar algunos platos usando *(using)* las recetas de un libro de cocina *(cookbook)*.

B. Describe the following foods.
1. un taco
2. un tamal
3. una tortilla mexicana
4. una tortilla española
5. la paella
6. los tostones

C. Look for cookbooks that contain recipes from Spanish-speaking countries and describe some of the foods eaten in different areas.

D. You might want to try this recipe for an informal party.

UNA RECETA PARA UNA TORTILLA ESPAÑOLA

1 taza *(cup)* de papas cortadas *(sliced)*
4 cucharadas *(tablespoons)* grandes de aceite de oliva
1 cebolla *(cut onion)*
1 diente de ajo *(clove of garlic)*
4 huevos batidos *(beaten)*

Opcional: salchicha
               vegetales

1. Freír *(Fry)* la cebolla y las papas en aceite.
2. Cuando estén fritas, escurrir *(drain)* la cebolla y las papas. Mezclar con los huevos batidos.
3. Quitar el aceite de la sartén y echar la mezcla *(mixture)* de huevos, cebolla y papas en la sartén.
4. Cocinar unos minutos, luego voltear *(turn over)* y cocinar al gusto *(to taste)*.

¡Así es!

Mealtimes

What do you eat for breakfast, lunch, and dinner? What time do you eat? In most Latin American countries, breakfast is usually very light, consisting of rolls, coffee, and juice. The midday meal is traditionally the largest meal of the day. Typically the whole family will be present. Schools and businesses close down for the siesta, and anyone who wants to go home, may do so. You have seen that the word **comida** has at least three meanings in English. It is related to the verb **comer** *(to eat)* and can mean *food, meal,* or *dinner.* When used in this last sense, it almost always refers to the midday meal. The evening meal is usually served quite late, sometimes as late as nine or ten o'clock, so a late afternoon snack—the **merienda**—is common.

¿Dónde vives? ¿De dónde vienes?
Where do you live?
Where are you coming from?

In this lesson we will learn to describe where you live right now and where you are coming from.

Vocabulario

¿Dónde vives? *Where do you live?*

¿Dónde vives?	*Where do you live?*
Vivo en la ciudad	*I live in the city*
en el campo	*in the country*
en el centro	*downtown*
en las afueras	*in the outskirts, suburbs*
en una granja	*on a farm*
en una casa	*in a house*
en un apartamento	*in an apartment*
en un condominio	*in a condominium*
de un piso	*one story*
de dos pisos	*two stories*
en un barrio…	*in a . . . neighborhood*
tranquilo	*quiet, tranquil*
ruidoso	*noisy*
moderno	*modern*
antiguo	*old*
seguro	*safe*
peligroso	*dangerous*
limpio	*clean*
sucio	*dirty*
a dos cuadras de…	*two blocks from . . .*
a dos millas de…	*two miles from . . .*
a dos kilómetros de…	*two kilometers from . . .*
¿Cuál es tu dirección?	*What is your address?*
Mi dirección es Calle… (número)	*My address is (number). . . Street.*
Paseo…	*. . . Drive.*
Avenida…	*. . . Avenue.*
Camino…	*. . . Road.*

Note: Did you notice that in saying an address, the word order is opposite from English? The word for *street, avenue*, etc., comes first, followed by the name of the street, and the house number comes last.

Mi dirección es Calle Main, número 2345.   *My address is 2345 Main Street.*

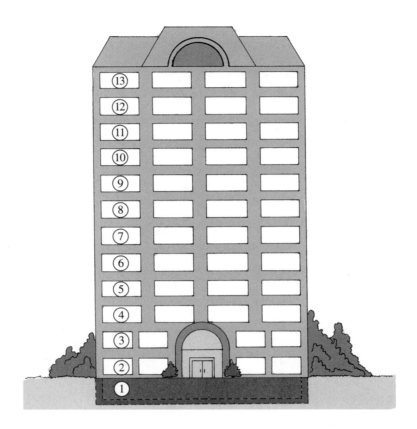

Un rascacielos   *A skyscraper*

 1. el sótano   *the basement*
 2. la planta baja   *the ground floor*
 3. el primer piso*   *the first floor (up)*
 4. el segundo piso   *the second floor*
 5. el tercer piso   *the third floor*
 6.   cuarto   *fourth*
 7.   quinto   *fifth*
 8.   sexto   *sixth*
 9.   séptimo   *seventh*
10.   octavo   *eighth*
11.   noveno   *ninth*
12.   décimo   *tenth*
13. el piso once**   *the eleventh floor*

*Note: Ordinal numbers agree with the gender of the noun: **la primer_a_ casa. Primero** and **tercero** drop the **o** before masculine nouns.

**The ordinal numbers (first, second, etc.) in Spanish are commonly used only to ten. Beyond that, use the regular counting numbers after the noun.

Did you notice in the drawing that the ground floor is called **planta baja** or **piso bajo**? The **primer piso** is what would be called the *second floor* in English.

1 **¿Cuál es tu dirección?** *What is your address?*   Get the addresses of several classmates.

EJEMPLO: ¿Dónde vives?   *Where do you live?*

Vivo en el Paseo Seaside, número 3256.   *I live at 3256 Seaside Drive.*

2 **¿Dónde vives tú?**   Describe where you live.

EJEMPLO: Yo vivo en la ciudad en un edificio de cuatro pisos. Yo vivo en un apartamento
en el cuarto piso. Mi barrio es viejo pero limpio y seguro.
*I live in the city in a four-story building. I live in an apartment
on the fourth floor. My neighborhood is old, but clean and safe.*

PERSON–TIME ENDINGS FOR -IR VERBS
-IR VERB PATTERN

the endings for **-ir** verbs which are in bold print and see if you can find any
differences from the **-er** endings. There aren't many, so look carefully!

	IMPERFECT	PRETERITE	PRESENT	FUTURE
	-ed	-ed	-(s)	will
	was/were -ing	am/is/are -ing		
	used to	did	do/does	
yo	**-ía**	**-í**	**-o**	**-é**
tú	**-ías**	**-iste**	**-es**	**-ás**
Ud./él/ella	**-ía**	**-ió**	**-e**	**-á**
nosotros(as)	**-íamos**	**-imos**	**-imos**	**-emos**
vosotros(as)	**-íais**	**-isteis**	**-ís**	**-éis**
Uds./ellos/ellas	**-ían**	**-ieron**	**-en**	**-án**

Did you find the differences? Only the **nosotros(as)** and **vosotros(as)** forms of the
present are different.

-er verbs		**-ir** verbs	
nosotros(as)	-emos	nosotros(as)	-imos
vosotros(as)	-éis	vosotros(as)	-ís

The verb **vivir** *(to live)* belongs to this third and last category of verbs in Spanish: the **-ir** verbs.

VIVIR *to live*

	IMPERFECT	PRETERITE	PRESENT	FUTURE
	lived	*lived*	*live(s)*	*will live*
	was/were living	*am/is/are living*		
	used to live	*did live*	*do/does live*	
yo	vivía	viví	vivo	viviré
tú	vivías	viviste	vives	vivirás
Ud./él/ella	vivía	vivió	vive	vivirá
nosotros(as)	vivíamos	vivimos	vivimos	viviremos
vosotros(as)	vivíais	vivisteis	vivís	viviréis
Uds./ellos/ellas	vivían	vivieron	viven	vivirán

Antes vivía en la ciudad.   Ahora vivo en las afueras.   En el futuro, viviré en el campo.

3 **¿Dónde vives?** *Where do you live?*   Ask your partner where he or she and people he or she knows used to live/lived/live/will live.

EJEMPLOS: ¿De niños, dónde vivían tus abuelos?
As children, where did your grandparents live?

Mi abuelo vivía en Tejas y mi abuela vivía en Cuba.
My grandfather lived in Texas and my grandmother lived in Cuba.

¿Dónde vivirás a los treinta años?
Where will you live when you are thirty years old?

Viviré en Nueva York.
I will live in New York.

4 **Encuesta: ¿Dónde vives?** *Where do you live?* Ask several of your classmates if they live in a house, an apartment, or a condominium and where it is located.

EJEMPLO: ¿Vives en una casa en el campo?
Do you live in a house in the country?

No, yo vivo en un apartamento del segundo piso en las afueras de la ciudad.
No, I live in a second-floor apartment in the suburbs.

5 **Informes** Make a report about the information you found out in Activity 4 about your classmates.

EJEMPLO: Miguel vive en un apartamento en el centro de la ciudad. Su apartamento está en el cuarto piso. Su dirección es Calle del Mercado, número 1234.
Miguel lives in an apartment downtown. His apartment is on the fourth floor. His address is 1234 Mercado Street.

6 Review the prepositions of location (pages 252–253) and places in the city (pages 258–259) and tell where you live in relation to various landmarks.

EJEMPLO: Vivo a dos cuadras del centro cerca del banco.
I live two blocks from downtown near the bank.

Vivo en la misma calle que Juan pero al otro lado de la calle.
I live on the same street as Juan but on the other side of the street.

Vocabulario

Verbos que terminan en -ir   *Verbs that end in* -ir

1. abrir — *to open*
2. asistir a — *to attend*
3. discutir — *to discuss, to argue*
4. escribir — *to write*

5. insistir (en) — *to insist (on)*
6. recibir — *to receive*
7. subir — *to go up, to get on*
8. sufrir — *to suffer*

7 Ask your partner if he or she used to do/did/does/will do any of the activities above.

EJEMPLO: ¿Discutiste con tu madre? *Did you argue with your mother?*

No, no discutí con mi madre. *No, I did not argue with my mother.*

8 Find out if other people do the activities above.

EJEMPLOS: ¿Escriben los niños cartas a Santa Claus? *Do the children write letters to Santa Claus?*

¿Recibió tu hermano un regalo? *Did your brother receive a gift?*

Now we are going to learn a new verb to help you tell someone where you are coming from.

VENIR *to come*

Look at the forms of **venir** below and compare them to the verb **tener** presented on page 295. Do you see any differences? Hint: remember that **venir** is an **-ir** verb and **tener** is an **-er** verb.

	IMPERFECT *came* *was/were* *coming* *used to come*	PRETERITE *came* *did come*	PRESENT *comes(s)* *am/is/are* *coming* *do/does come*	FUTURE *will come*
yo	venía	**vine**	**vengo**	**vendré**
tú	venías	**viniste**	vienes	**vendrás**
Ud./él/ella	venía	**vino**	viene	**vendrá**
nosotros(as)	veníamos	**vinimos**	venimos	**vendremos**
vosotros(as)	veníais	**vinisteis**	venís	**vendréis**
Uds./ellos/ellas	venían	**vinieron**	vienen	**vendrán**

The only differences between **tener** and **venir** are the stem of the preterite and the **nosotros** and **vosotros** forms of the present tense.

Venir is often followed by **de** (*from*) so don't forget: **de + el = del** .

Yo vengo <u>de</u> Los Ángeles.   *I'm coming from Los Angeles.*
Ellos vinieron <u>del</u> campo.   *They came from the country.*

GALICIA EXPRESS

Salidas

ABRIL
29
SABADO

MAYO
25
JUEVES

ITINERARIO:

Día 1.º MADRID - PONFERRADA - SANTIAGO DE COMPOSTELA
Salida de nuestra TERMINAL, Plaza de Oriente, 8, a las 7.30 horas, hacia Ponferrada, donde se realizará el **almuerzo**, prosiguiendo el viaje, por la tarde, hasta Santiago de Compostela. **Cena y alojamiento.**

Día 2.º SANTIAGO - LA CORUÑA - SANTIAGO
Desayuno, cena y alojamiento en Santiago. Por la mañana, **visita** de la ciudad, uno de los más importantes núcleos monumentales de España, lleno de pintorescos y poéticos rincones. Destaca su famosa Catedral, máxima expresión del románico y barroco, sus colegios universitarios y el encanto de sus rúas. Por la tarde se realizará una **excursión** a La Coruña, para **visitar** panorámicamente esta bella y hospitalaria ciudad, de fuerte sabor marinero.

Día 3.º SANTIAGO - RIAS BAJAS - LA TOJA - VIGO - SANTA TECLA - SANTIAGO
Desayuno, cena y alojamiento en Santiago para realizar un recorrido por la zona más atractiva de las pintorescas Rías Bajas gallegas, para llegar a la isla de La Toja, universalmente conocida por sus baños. Tiempo libre para proseguir el recorrido en dirección a Vigo. (Almuerzo libre.) Continuación hacia el Monte de Santa Tecla, de magníficos panoramas. Finalmente, regreso a Santiago.

9 **Sit-Con** Your family is having a reunion. Tell what cities the various family members are coming from. How many cities on the map can you identify?

EJEMPLO: Mi abuelo viene de San Diego.   *My grandfather is coming from San Diego.*
Mis primos vienen de Chicago.   *My cousins are coming from Chicago.*

DE TODAS PARTES

10 Tell what class you came from and what class you are going to go to when you leave this class.

EJEMPLO: Vine de la clase de álgebra y luego voy a ir a la clase de historia.
I came from algebra class and later I will go to history class.

11 Find out which classes your classmates came from and which classes they will go to next.

EJEMPLO: ¿De qué clase viniste?   *Which class did you come from?*

Vine de la clase de historia.   *I came from history class.*

¿A qué clase irás?   *Which class will you go to?*

Iré a la clase de matemáticas.   *I'll go to math class.*

ENCUENTRO PERSONAL

Paulina's class has a number of students who have moved in from other areas. Listen as they describe where they come from and where they live.

¿Comprendes?

1. Where does María Elena come from?
2. What is the the area like where her family used to live?
3. Where does Salvador come from?
4. What was his family's ranch like?
5. Where did Sean's family use to live?
6. What did they use to do frequently?
7. Where did Paulina use to live?

¡Te toca!

Describe where you live now or where you used to live.

Leemos y contamos

A. Here is a letter from our pen pal, Marisol, who lives in Mexico City.

Queridos amigos,

¿Desean Uds. aprender un poco de donde vivo yo? Bueno, yo vivo en las afueras de la capital, en una región que se llama Ciudad Satélite. Vivimos en el tercer piso de un edificio de apartamentos. Es un barrio nuevo y moderno, pero hay mucha contaminación del aire y está muy ruidoso. En nuestro barrio hay una plaza de toros pequeña. Al sur de la ciudad está la plaza de toros más grande del mundo.

Mi padre trabaja en el centro y para ir al trabajo primero toma el autobús y luego (then) *el metro. Muy cerca del edificio donde trabaja está el Zócalo, la plaza central de la capital.*

Los domingos vamos a la Plaza Garabaldi, al norte del centro, para charlar y escuchar la música de los mariachis. Los días de fiesta vamos frecuentemente al sur de la ciudad, a los jardines flotantes (floating gardens) *de Xochimilco, un parque que todavía es como era durante los días de los Aztecas. Allí damos un paseo* (take a ride) *en una chalupa, que es un tipo de barco. También vamos de compras en las tiendas al aire libre* (outdoor markets). *Hay muchas flores al lado de los canales y todo es muy bonito.*

Al norte de la ciudad en las afueras está la famosa Basílica de Nuestra Señora (Our Lady) de Guadalupe, la santa patrona, no sólo de México, sino de toda América Latina. La leyenda (legend) es que La Virgen María se le apareció (appeared) a un indio pobre en el año 1531 y le dio su imagen en su tilma (Mexican cloak). Esta tilma está en la nueva basílica. A unos 30 kilómetros (18,75 millas) al norte de la capital están las famosas ruinas de Teotihuacán, el antiguo centro de una civilización indígena de 150 a.C. (antes de Cristo) a 750 d.C. Allí hay dos pirámides enormes: la Pirámide de la Luna y la Pirámide del Sol. Ésta es más grande, pero no tan alta como las pirámides de Egipto.

Como pueden ver Uds., aunque hay muchos problemas de una ciudad grande, la región central de México tiene muchos sitios muy interesantes. Ojalá puedan (Hopefully you can) venir a visitarnos en el futuro.

Con cariño,
Su amiga, Marisol

1. Where does Marisol live and what is her neighborhood like?
2. What is there in her neighborhood?
3. Where does her father work and how does he get there?
4. What is near where her father works?
5. Where does her family go on Sundays? And on holidays?
6. What are the "Floating Gardens" like and what do people do there?
7. What does Marisol tell about Our Lady of Guadalupe?
8. What is there to the north of the capital city? Describe the area.

B. Write a description of the area where you live for someone who has never been there but would like to visit you.

¡Así es!

Housing in the Spanish-speaking world

For economic and cultural reasons and because of differences in climate and available building materials, housing in the Spanish-speaking world varies greatly from one area to the next. In Spain, as in the rest of Europe, it is not uncommon to find a family living in a stone or wooden house that is hundreds of years old; but in the larger cities most people rent apartments in modern high-rise buildings.

Throughout Latin America there is a serious housing shortage. Because incomes are lower than in the United States, most families cannot afford to buy a house, and many people rent an apartment. Some build their own dwelling out of discarded materials on unoccupied land, sometimes right next to a prosperous subdivision. Most houses do not have air-conditioning and central heating, and many do not have refrigerators and microwave ovens.

Of course, there are many beautiful houses in Latin America. In the more affluent areas there are expensive houses and apartments, some with swimming pools and large garages. But these are still relatively rare.

In the urban areas the poorer section is usually in the outskirts, what we would call the "suburbs." The people who can afford better housing often prefer to live near the downtown area.

Mi día en la escuela
My day at school

In this lesson we will be talking about school and the classes we are taking.

Vocabulario

En la escuela   *At school*

tomar una clase de…	*to take a . . . class*

Las artes — *Arts*
el arte — *art*
el drama — *drama, acting*
la música — *music*

Las ciencias — *Sciences*
la biología — *biology*
la física — *physics*
la química — *chemistry*

Las ciencias sociales — *Social Sciences*
la geografía — *geography*
la historia — *history*
la sicología — *psychology*

El comercio — *Business*
la informática — *computer science*
la clase de tecleo — *keyboarding*
la taquigrafía — *shorthand*

Las lenguas extranjeras — *Foreign Languages*
el alemán — *German*
el chino — *Chinese*
el español — *Spanish*
el francés — *French*
el italiano — *Italian*
el japonés — *Japanese*
el latín — *Latin*
el ruso — *Russian*

Las matemáticas — *Math*
el álgebra — *algebra*
el cálculo — *calculus*
la geometría — *geometry*
la trigonometría — *trigonometry*

Otras materias — *Other subjects*
la educación física — *physical education*

CURSOS

BELLEZA
(Incluyen videos)
☐ Estheticienne
☐ Peluquería
☐ Masaje

MÚSICA
(Incluyen cassettes)
☐ Guitarra
(Guitarra gratis)
☐ Teclado Electrónico   NUEVO
☐ Solfeo
☐ Acordeón

INFORMÁTICA
☐ Dominio y práctica del PC   NUEVO
(Con disquetes)
☐ Informática de Gestión
☐ Basic

GRADUADO ESCOLAR Y CULTURA
☐ Graduado Escolar
☐ Cultura Gral.
☐ Ortografía
☐ Redacción

IDIOMAS
(Incluyen cassettes)
☐ Inglés
☐ Inglés (Vídeo)
☐ Francés
☐ Alemán
☐ Ruso

MODA Y CORTE
☐ Diseño de Moda
☐ Corte y Confección
(Sitam Italia)
☐ Bordado a Máquina

EMPRESARIALES
☐ Asesor Fiscal
(Diploma CESDE)
☐ Dirección y Gestión Financiera   NUEVO
(Diploma CESDE)
☐ Contabilidad
☐ Análisis de Balances
☐ Marketing
☐ Psicología y Ventas
☐ Secretariado
☐ Mecanografía
☐ Taquigrafía
☐ Auxiliar Administrativo

AGRICULTURA Y GANADERÍA
☐ Agricultura y Ganadería
☐ Cunicultura

Las escuelas y los niveles

Schools and levels

la escuela primaria	*elementary school, grade school*
la escuela secundaria	*secondary school, high school*
la universidad	*college, university*
el colegio	*private high school*
el primer año de secundaria	*freshman*
el segundo año	*sophomore*
el tercer año	*junior*
el cuarto año	*senior*
el primer año de primaria	*first grade*

Lo que hacemos en la escuela   *What we do in school*

1. asistir a las clases	*to attend classes*
2. tomar apuntes	*to take notes*
3. aprender	*to learn*
4. estudiar	*to study*
5. hacer* la tarea	*to do homework*
6. escribir un tema	*to write a paper*
7. teclear	*to input*
8. leer novelas	*to read novels*

lecturas	*readings*
cuentos cortos	*short stories*
poesía	*poetry*

9. escuchar conferencias — *to listen to lectures*
10. memorizar fechas — *to memorize dates*
    hechos — *facts*
11. hacer investigaciones — *to do research*
12. calcular — *to do arithmetic*
    sumar — *to add*
    restar — *to subtract*
    multiplicar — *to multiply*
    dividir — *to divide*
13. tomar un examen — *to take an exam*
    una prueba — *a test/quiz*
14. sacar una *A*, etc. — *to get an A, etc.*
15. aprobar (ue)** un examen — *to pass an exam*
16. suspender un examen — *to fail an exam*

*Note: **hago** = *I do*. **Hacer** is irregular in the preterite and future. See page 431 for the forms.

Note: Change **o to **ue** in the present tense except in the **nosotros** form. (This is a "boot verb" to be explained later in this lesson.)

1 **Mi día en la escuela**   Ask your partner about school.

EJEMPLO: ¿Qué clases tienes?   *What classes do you have?*
¿Qué estudias?   *What do you study?*
¿Cuál es tu materia favorita?   *What is your favorite subject?*
¿Quién es tu profesor(a) de…?   *Who is your . . . teacher?*

2 Find out from your partner what his or her school day was like last year. Use the imperfect to tell what you used to do every day. (Use the preterite to tell what happened once or a stated number of times.)

EJEMPLO: 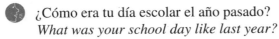 ¿Cómo era tu día escolar el año pasado?
What was your school day like last year?

En la clase de inglés leíamos muchos libros. Leímos *Hamlet* y *Huckleberry Finn*.
In my English class we read a lot of books. We read Hamlet *and* Huckleberry Finn.

3 Find out from your partner what his or her school day was like yesterday. Use the preterite form of the verb.

EJEMPLO: ¿Cómo fue tu día en la escuela ayer?
What was your school day like yesterday?

Ayer llegué tarde a la escuela. Tomé un examen en la clase de matemáticas y lo aprobé.
Yesterday I arrived late to school. I took a test in Math class and I passed it.

4 You have been granted the power to create the ideal school. Plan with your partner what that school will be like. Write a report about it.

EJEMPLO: Estudiaremos solamente las materias donde recibiremos una *A*.
We will study only the subjects in which we will get an A.

Los profesores comerán en la cafetería con nosotros.
The teachers will eat in the cafeteria with us.

"BOOT VERBS" (PRESENT TENSE OF STEM-CHANGING VERBS)

In some Spanish verbs, the vowel preceeding the person–time endings changes in the present tense in all the forms except **nosotros(as)** and **vosotros(as)**. If we draw a line around the forms that have the change, (all except **nosotros** and **vosotros**), the line forms a "boot." We can refer to these verbs as "stem-changing verbs" or "boot verbs."

There are three groups: those that change **e** to **ie**, **e** to **i**, and **o** to **ue**. In dictionaries or vocabulary lists, the change is often indicated after the infinitive.

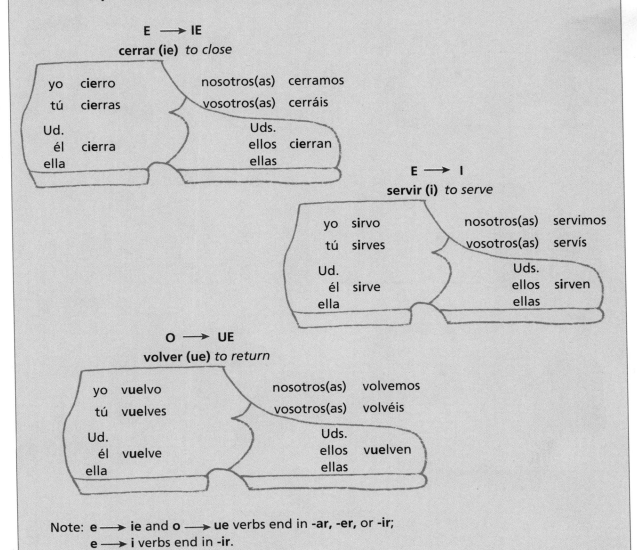

E ⟶ IE
cerrar (ie) *to close*

yo	cierro	nosotros(as)	cerramos
tú	cierras	vosotros(as)	cerráis
Ud. él ella	cierra	Uds. ellos ellas	cierran

E ⟶ I
servir (i) *to serve*

yo	sirvo	nosotros(as)	servimos
tú	sirves	vosotros(as)	servís
Ud. él ella	sirve	Uds. ellos ellas	sirven

O ⟶ UE
volver (ue) *to return*

yo	vuelvo	nosotros(as)	volvemos
tú	vuelves	vosotros(as)	volvéis
Ud. él ella	vuelve	Uds. ellos ellas	vuelven

Note: **e** ⟶ **ie** and **o** ⟶ **ue** verbs end in **-ar, -er,** or **-ir;**
e ⟶ **i** verbs end in **-ir.**

Vocabulario

1

2

3

4

5

6

7

8

9   BUENO   BUENO

10

11

12

13

14   $179.00

15

16

17

18

Verbos que tienen cambios radicales   *Verbs that have stem changes*

Here are some other verbs that have changes in the "boot" forms in the present tense.

E ⟶ IE

1. cerrar   *to close*
2. pensar   *to think*
3. comenzar   *to begin*
4. perder   *to lose*
5. preferir   *to prefer*
6. querer*   *to want, to love*

O ⟶ UE

11. volver   *to return*
12. almorzar   *to eat lunch*
13. recordar   *to remember*
14. costar   *to cost*
15. dormir   *to sleep*
16. morir   *to die*
17. poder*   *to be able, can*

E ⟶ I

7. servir   *to serve*
8. pedir   *to ask for, to request,*
                   to order
9. repetir   *to repeat*
10. seguir**   *to follow, to continue*

U ⟶ UE***

18. jugar   *to play games or sports*

*Querer and **poder** have irregularities in the preterite and future. These will be learned in Lesson 6.

Seguir has an irregular **yo form: **yo sigo** *(I follow).*

***Jugar is the only verb that changes **u ⟶ ue.**

---

5 Use "boot verbs" to tell what you do alone in school and what you do when you are with a friend. Use this pattern:

Yo + "boot verb" + time expression
Mi amigo y yo + "boot verb" + time expression

Remember that there is no change in the **nosotros(as)** form.

EJEMPLO: Yo almuerzo a las doce.   *I eat lunch at twelve o'clock.*
           Nosotros almorzamos a la una.   *We eat lunch at one o'clock.*

---

6 Tell your partner some things you want to do, but can't because you are in class. Use the verbs **querer** and **poder**.

EJEMPLO: Quiero dormir, pero ahora no puedo.   *I want to sleep, but now I can't.*
           Quiero ir al cine, pero ahora no puedo.   *I want to go to the movies, but now I can't.*

---

7 **Encuesta**   Find out from several people how many hours of sleep they get.

EJEMPLO: ¿Cuántas horas duermes?   *How many hours do you sleep?*
           Generalmente duermo ocho horas.   *Generally I sleep eight hours.*

THE MEANINGS OF PENSAR (IE)

The verb **pensar** has several meanings. Here are some of them.

Pensar de + *infinitive/noun = to ask an opinion*

¿Qué piensas de comer en la cafetería?   *What do you think about eating in the cafeteria?*
¿Qué piensas del nuevo profesor?   *What do you think of/about the new teacher?*

Pensar que = *to think (that) [expression of opinion/conclusion]*

Pienso que mi madre es muy simpática.   *I think that my mother is very nice.*

Pensar en + *infinitive/noun = to think of/about (to oneself), to daydream*

Yo pienso mucho en mi novio.   *I think about my boyfriend a lot.*
¿Piensas en viajar?   *Do you think about traveling?*

(Did you notice that Spanish uses an infinitive form (**-ar, -er, -ir**) and English uses an *-ing* form?)

Pensar + *infinitive = to plan to, to intend to*

Pienso estudiar esta noche.   *I plan to study tonight.*

---

8 Ask your partner when he or she plans to do different things.

EJEMPLO: ¿Cuándo piensas ir a México?   *When do you plan to go to Mexico?*

Pienso ir durante el verano.   *I plan to go during the summer.*

9 Ask your partner's opinion about people and activities at your school.

EJEMPLO: ¿Qué piensas del profesor?   *What do you think about the teacher?*

Pienso que es muy interesante.   *I think that he is very interesting.*

10 **Encuesta** Find out what different people think about when they are alone.

EJEMPLO: ¿En qué piensas cuando estás solo(a)?   *What do you think about when you are alone?*

Pienso en mi novio(a).   *I think about my boyfriend/girlfriend.*

Pienso en esquiar en las montañas.   *I think about skiing in the mountains.*

"SLIPPER VERBS" (PRETERITE TENSE OF -IR STEM-CHANGING VERBS)

-Ar and **-er** "boot verbs" have no stem changes in the preterite.

-Ir "boot verbs" change the **e** to **i** and **o** to **u** in the **él** and **ellos** forms of the preterite. If we draw a line around the forms that have a change in the preterite it looks like a slipper.

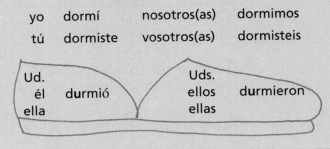

DORMIR (UE,U) *to sleep*

yo	dormí	nosotros(as)	dormimos
tú	dormiste	vosotros(as)	dormisteis
Ud. él ella	durmió	Uds. ellos ellas	durmieron

Here are some **-ir** stem-changing verbs with both stem changes indicated. The first change indicated is for present tense (boot forms). The second change indicated is for the preterite tense (slipper forms).

preferir (ie, i)	*to prefer*
repetir (i, i)	*to repeat*
servir (i, i)	*to serve*
pedir (i, i)	*to ask for, to request, to order*
seguir (i, i)	*to follow, to continue*
dormir (ue, u)	*to sleep*
morir (ue, u)	*to die*

11 Use the **-ir** "boot verbs" to tell some things that people you know do often. (Use the present tense.)

EJEMPLO: Mi hermano duerme ocho horas por noche.
My brother sleeps eight hours a night.

Mi madre siempre sirve una cena deliciosa.
Mi mother always serves a delicious dinner.

12 Use "slipper verbs" to tell if the things done in Activity 11 happened yesterday.

EJEMPLO: Él durmió sólo siete horas anoche.
He only slept seven hours last night.

Ella sirvió una cena deliciosa ayer también.
She served a delicious dinner yesterday also.

USING ADJECTIVES WITHOUT A NOUN—Part I

When referring to something that has already been mentioned in a previous sentence, we use the appropriate article **(el/la/los/las)** with the adjective.

EL/LA
LOS/LAS   + *adjective = the + adjective + one(s)*

¿La chaqueta? Prefiero <u>la</u> azul.   *The jacket? I prefer the blue one.*
¿Los libros? Me gustan <u>los</u> románticos.   *The books? I like the romantic ones.*

---

13 *Sit-Con*   After school you and a friend decided to go shopping for new outfits to wear to the prom. First tell what the salesperson showed you and then tell which you bought.

EJEMPLOS: El dependiente me enseñó un traje azul y un traje pardo. Compré el azul.
The salesperson showed me a blue suit and a brown suit. I bought the blue one.

La dependienta me enseñó una falda larga y una falda corta. Compré la larga.
The salesperson showed me a long skirt and a short skirt. I bought the long one.

14 Tell which you prefer.

EJEMPLO: ejercicios   largos/cortos   *exercises   long/short*
Prefiero los cortos.   *I prefer the short ones.*

a. personas   simpáticas/antipáticas
b. perros   grandes/pequeños
c. clases   fáciles/difíciles
d. coches   baratos/caros
e. muchachos(as)   altos(as)/bajos(as)
f. amigos(as)   sinceros(as)/ricos(as)
g. . . . *[Make up your own.]*

USING ADJECTIVES WITHOUT A NOUN—Part II

When you want to use an adjective to describe something indefinite or vague, use **lo** instead of the article with the masculine form of the adjective.

LO + *adjective [masculine form]* = *the* + *adjective* + *thing/part*

Lo difícil es recordar.   *The hard part is to remember.*
Lo importante es estudiar.   *The important thing is to study.*

15 What advice would you give to a friend who is planning to study Spanish? Tell him or her the following.

a. Lo importante es...
b. Lo difícil es...
c. Lo fácil es...
d. Lo interesante es...
e. Lo aburrido es...
f. Lo necesario es...

16 As you look back on this school year, what are some things you will remember? Tell what was **lo mejor, lo peor, lo más difícil, lo más divertido (fun), lo más triste,** etc.

EJEMPLOS: Lo mejor fue las personas que conocí.
The best thing was the people that I met.

Lo peor fue la semana cuando yo estuve enfermo.
The worst part was the week when I was sick.

Lo último que ha ocurrido en el mundo está en estas páginas.

La obra completa por sólo 3.990 pesetas al mes.

NUEVO DICCIONARIO ENCICLOPÉDICO LAROUSSE

Vocabulario

Palabras neutrales y negativas   *Neutral and negative words*

alguien*	*someone, anyone*	nadie*	*no one, nobody*
algo	*something, anything*	nada	*nothing, not anything*
alguno(a,os,as)**	*some*	ninguno(a,os,as)**	*none, not any, no*
siempre	*always*	nunca	*never, not ever*
también	*also*	tampoco	*neither, not either*
o… o	*either . . . or*	ni… ni	*neither . . . nor*

*Note: Don't forget to use the personal **a** with **alguien** and **nadie** when they are direct objects.

Note: **Alguno and **ninguno** agree in number and gender with the noun they talk about. They drop the **o** before a masculine singular noun:

algún hombre   algunas muchachas
ningún hombre   ninguna muchacha

> Ni mi madre ni mi padre me da ningún dinero.

> ¡Nadie nunca me da nada tampoco!

USING NEGATIVE WORDS

If any part of the sentence is negative, use negative words instead of neutrals in the rest of the sentence. **No** or a negative word must be used before the verb. In English we can have only one negative word in a sentence. In Spanish there is no limit.

Esqueletos

negative word + verb

Yo nunca voy.   *I never go. / I don't ever go.*
Nadie habla.   *Nobody is talking.*

NO + verb + negative word

Yo no voy nunca.   *I never go. / I don't ever go.*
No habla nadie.   *Nobody is talking.*

17 With your partner, take turns being positive and negative about the things that happen to you. First one person says something using positive words, and the other person will contradict by using negative words.

EJEMPLO: La clase siempre sale bien en los exámenes.   *The class always does well on exams.*

Nadie nunca sale bien en los exámenes.   *No one ever does well on exams.*

18 *Sit-Con*   You and your partner are having difficulty understanding the math assignment. You are an optimist about your situation but your partner is a pessimist. Take turns making statements. Every time you make a positive statement, your partner contradicts you with a negative one, and every time he or she makes a negative statement, you contradict him or her.

EJEMPLOS: Alguien nos ayudará.   *Someone will help us.*

Nadie nos ayudará.   *No one will help us.*

El profesor nos ayudará.   *The teacher will help us.*

El profesor no nos ayuda nunca.   *The teacher never helps us.*

19 Ask your partner questions using positive words that he or she will answer using negative words.

EJEMPLOS: ¿Alguien tiene mi lápiz?   *Does someone have my pencil?*

No, nadie tiene tu lápiz.   *No, no one has your pencil.*

¿Tienes algo en la caja?   *Do you have something in the box?*

No, no tengo nada en la caja.   *No, I don't have anything in the box.*

ENCUENTRO PERSONAL

Paulina and Salvador are talking about their classes and how they deal with them. See if you have any of the same problems they have.

¿Comprendes?

1. What is Paulina's favorite class? Why?
2. What is Salvador's favorite class? Why?
3. What problems does Paulina have with her history class?
4. What problems does Salvador have with his biology class?
5. What idea does Paulina have to solve their problems?
6. What is Salvador's reaction to her idea? Do you think it's a good solution?

¡Te toca!

Tell what your favorite class is and why.

Leemos y contamos

A. Marisol, our Mexican pen pal, tells us about schools in her country.

Queridos amigos,

Uds. me preguntaron de nuestro sistema escolar. Bueno, aquí en México estudiamos inglés desde (from) *el sexto grado. Todos queremos aprender inglés para poder comprender las películas y los programas de televisión de los EE. UU. En la escuela secundaria hay la opción de estudiar también el francés y, a veces, el alemán u* (or) *otra lengua extranjera como el italiano.*

Todo el mundo tiene que ir a la escuela hasta (until) *la edad de quince años. Desafortunadamente* (Unfortunately), *en el campo hay muchos muchachos que no van mucho a la escuela porque viven muy lejos. Muchos muchachos en el campo no reciben más de cuatro años de enseñanza* (schooling) *porque no hay bastantes* (enough) *escuelas ni profesores.*

Hay tres niveles de enseñanza: primaria, secundaria y universitaria. La educación es gratis (free) *en las escuelas públicas. En las ciudades, también hay escuelas privadas donde se paga* (one pays). *Muchas de estas escuelas son de la Iglesia Católica.*

Los padres que trabajan pueden llevar a sus niños a la guardería (nursery school). *Ésta es gratis también. En la escuela primaria aprendemos a leer, escribir, calcular y también aprendemos la historia de México para tener orgullo* (pride) *de nuestro país. Vamos a la escuela primaria de los seis a los doce años.*

Después de la primaria, vamos tres años a una escuela pública que se llama «escuela secundaria» o a una escuela privada que se llama «colegio», «liceo» o «instituto».

INSTITUTO PATRIA Y CULTURA
INCORPORADO A LA S.E.P
MAESTROS TITULADOS
PRIMARIA Y JARDIN DE NIÑOS
AMBIENTE FAVORABLE AL NIÑO Y MATERIAS
EXTRACURRICULARES PARA EL MEJOR DESARROLLO DEL CARACTER
Inglés Diariamente - Educación Física
Educación Artística
TEL. 13-84-33
20 DE NOVIEMBRE 4393
C.P. 32340

Hay muchachos y muchachas en las escuelas secundarias pero generalmente en los colegios los muchachos y las muchachas están separados. En los colegios, los estudiantes frecuentemente llevan uniformes.

Si deseamos estudiar en la universidad, tenemos que ir a una escuela preparatoria después de la escuela secundaria. Nuestras escuelas ponen mucho énfasis en las ciencias y en las matemáticas. México no es un país rico; frecuentemente nos faltan (lack) materiales para los laboratorios y las computadoras o calculadoras. Pero estudiamos duro porque no es fácil entrar en una universidad. Aquí hay mucha competencia (competition) para entrar en la universidad y solamente los mejores estudiantes pueden ir. Hay un gran examen al fin de la escuela secundaria para decidir quiénes califican (qualify) para asistir a la universidad. Sólo dos de cada diez estudiantes aprueban esos exámenes.

Muchos hispanos desean estudiar en el extranjero (foreign countries), especialmente en los EE. UU. y en los países europeos, pero también es difícil hacerlo. Primero, cuesta mucho. Segundo, frecuentemente hay cuotas que limitan el número de estudiantes que pueden venir de un país. Y también, hay mucha competencia.

Los que no pueden ir a la universidad a veces van a un politécnico, que es un tipo de escuela donde una persona aprende una carrera (career) práctica como mecánico, secretaria, especialista en computadoras, etc. Creo que Uds. llaman estas escuelas «trade schools» o «technical institutes.»

¿Comprenden Uds. mejor como es el sistema escolar de mi país? ¿Cómo es la enseñanza en su país?

Su amiga,
Marisol

1. When do Mexican students begin studying English?
2. Why do they want to learn English?
3. What other foreign languages are popular?
4. What are the ages for required school attendance?
5. Do all students go to school?
6. Why don't all children go to school the required time?
7. How many levels are there in the educational system?
8. Do parents have to pay for their children's education?
9. What is the difference between public and private schools?
10. Describe the elementary education program.
11. What are public secondary schools called?
12. What are private secondary schools called?
13. Is secondary education coed?
14. Do students wear uniforms?
15. How many years is secondary school?
16. What do students learn in secondary school?
17. What must students do if they wish to go to the university?
18. How is the decision made as to who will go to the university?
19. Why is it difficult for Mexican students to study in other countries?
20. What do students do who cannot go to the university?

B. Answer Marisol's question about American education. Write her a letter telling her about the schools where you live. Use her letter as a guide.

¡Así es!

Grading system

How would you feel if you got a 10 on your next test? You'd be very happy if your teacher was using the Spanish grading system. The grading system varies from country to country, but many schools in Spanish-speaking countries use 0 to 10. Here is a table with the name of the grade in Spanish and its equivalent in English.

BOLETÍN DE CALIFICACIONES		REPORT CARD
9-10	Sobresaliente	*Outstanding*
8	Notable	*Very good*
7	Aprovechado	*Average*
6	Aprobado	*Passing*
0-5	Suspenso	*Failed*

What would your grade in Spanish be?
What would you like it to be?

Un día en mi vida
A day in my life

In this lesson we will talk about ourselves and our daily routine.

REFLEXIVE (-SELF) PRONOUNS

me	myself
te	*yourself [informal]*
se	*yourself [formal]*
	himself/herself/itself/oneself

nos	ourselves
os	*yourselves [informal, used in Spain]*
se	*yourselves/themselves*

A reflexive pronoun shows that the subject is doing something to it<u>self</u>. The action "reflects" back on the subject. The subject and the object are the same.

Yo <u>me</u> miro en el espejo.   *I look at <u>myself</u> in the mirror.*

Reflexive pronouns are similar to the direct and indirect object pronouns. **Me, te, nos,** and **os** are the same as the direct/indirect object forms.

Compare these sentences.
Yo lavo <u>el coche</u>.   *I wash the <u>car</u>. [car is the direct object noun]*
Yo <u>lo</u> lavo.   *I wash <u>it</u>. [it is the direct object pronoun]*
Yo <u>me</u> lavo.   *I wash <u>myself</u>. [myself is the reflexive pronoun]*

POSITION OF REFLEXIVE PRONOUNS

Reflexive pronouns follow the same pattern as direct and indirect object pronouns.

1. Before the verb with the person–time ending
2. Attached to the infinitive if there is one

Yo <u>me</u> comprendo bien.   *I understand myself well.*
Deseo comprender<u>me</u> mejor.   *I want to understand myself better.*

1 *Sit-Con:* **La sala de espejos** *The room of mirrors* You and your friends went to a carnival and looked at yourselves in the funny mirrors. Tell who saw himself or herself and how each appeared in the mirrors. Use preterite/imperfect.

EJEMPLO: Yo me miré en el espejo y yo parecía alta.
I looked at myself in the mirror and I appeared tall.

Nosotros nos miramos en el espejo y parecíamos gordos.
We looked at ourselves in the mirror and we looked fat.

2 **Encuesta** Do you ever talk to yourself? Do a survey of your classmates to find out how often they talk to themselves. Use the following time expressions.

mucho	*a lot*	un poco	*a little*
siempre	*always*	nunca	*never*
raramente	*rarely, seldom*	frecuentemente	*often*

EJEMPLO: ¿Te hablas frecuentemente?
Do you talk to yourself often?

Sí, me hablo mucho. / No, no me hablo nunca.
Yes, I talk to myself a lot. / No, I never talk to myself.

EACH OTHER = NOS AND SE

The plural forms **nos** and **se** sometimes mean *each other.*

Nosotros <u>nos</u> hablamos por teléfono. *We talk to each other on the phone.*
Ellos <u>se</u> saludan con un abrazo. *They greet each other with a hug.*

3 *Sit-Con* Do you and your friends talk to each other a lot? Tell where you talk.

EJEMPLO: Celia y yo nos hablamos en la escuela. *Celia and I talk to each other in school.*

REFLEXIVE VERBS (VERB + -SELF PRONOUN)

Many Spanish verbs use a reflexive pronoun when the action affects the subject, even though it may not be used in English. These verbs are identified by **-se** attached to the end of the infinitive.

Here is a reflexive verb with its forms in the present tense. The other tenses will also have the pronoun in front of the verb.

lavarse *to wash oneself*

yo	<u>me</u>	lavo	*I wash <u>myself</u>*
tú	<u>te</u>	lavas	*you wash <u>yourself</u> [informal]*
Ud.	<u>se</u>	lava	*you wash <u>yourself</u> [formal]*
él	<u>se</u>	lava	*he washes <u>himself</u>*
ella	<u>se</u>	lava	*she washes <u>herself</u>*
nosotros(as)	<u>nos</u>	lavamos	*we wash <u>ourselves</u>*
vosotros(as)	<u>os</u>	laváis	*you wash <u>yourselves</u> [Spain]*
Uds.	<u>se</u>	lavan	*you wash <u>yourselves</u>*
ellos/ellas	<u>se</u>	lavan	*they wash <u>themselves</u>*

Did you notice that once the **-se** is removed from the verb, it is an **-ar** verb and that the endings are regular **-ar** endings? **-Er** and **-ir** verbs will use their own endings.

Vocabulario

La rutina diaria   *Daily routine*

1.	despertarse (ie)	*to wake up*
2.	levantarse	*to get up*
3.	lavarse	*to wash*
4.	bañarse	*to take a bath*
5.	ducharse	*to take a shower*
6.	afeitarse	*to shave*
7.	cepillarse	*to brush*
8.	vestirse (i, i)	*to get dressed*
9.	ponerse*	*to put on (clothing)*
10.	peinarse	*to comb one's hair*
11.	maquillarse	*to put on makeup*
12.	sentarse (ie)	*to sit down*
13.	despedirse (i, i)	*to say good-bye*
14.	irse	*to go away* / to leave
15.	quedarse	*to stay, to remain*
16.	divertirse (ie, i)	*to have fun, to have a good time, to enjoy oneself*
17.	quitarse	*to take off (clothing)*
18.	acostarse (ue)	*to go to bed, to lie down*
19.	dormirse (ue)	*to go to sleep, to fall asleep*

*Note: The **yo** form of **poner** in the present tense is **pongo**. **Poner** is also irregular in the preterite and future. See page 432 for the forms.

Remember to use stem changes in the boot forms (present tense) and slipper forms (preterite **-ir** verbs) for those verbs with stem changes indicated.

Use **el, la, los, las** with clothing or parts of the body, unless it is someone else's. The reflexive pronoun tells us that the clothing item or body part belongs to the subject.

Yo me pongo la chaqueta.   *I put on my jacket.*

Review the calendar and telling time (on pages 101 and 104) for Activities 4 through 11.

4 Describe a typical day for you. Tell at what time you do each activity of your daily routine.

EJEMPLO: Me despierto a la seis y me levanto a las seis y cuarto.
I wake up at six o'clock and I get up at six-fifteen.

5 Ask your partner about his or her daily routine.

EJEMPLO: 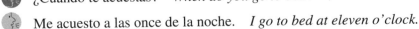 ¿Cuándo te acuestas?   *When do you go to bed?*

Me acuesto a las once de la noche.   *I go to bed at eleven o'clock.*

6 **¿Qué haces durante el verano?** *What do you do during the summer?*   Describe a typical day during the summer. (Use the present tense.)

EJEMPLO: Me despierto a las ocho de la mañana…   *I wake up at eight o'clock in the morning . . .*

7 Find out how your partner wants to spend his or her birthday. Find out when he or she wants to do different routine activities.

EJEMPLO: En tu día de cumpleaños, ¿cuándo quieres despertarte?
On your birthday, when do you want to wake up?

Quiero despertarme a las diez y media de la mañana.
I want to wake up at ten-thirty in the morning.

8 Tell about a special day you had last summer. (Use the preterite tense.)

EJEMPLO: Yo me levanté muy tarde. Me puse los pantalones y una camiseta.
I got up very late. I put on my slacks and a T-shirt.

9 **¿Qué harás este fin de semana que viene?** *What will you do this weekend?*   Tell what your routine will be this weekend. (Use the future tense.)

EJEMPLO: El sábado me despertaré temprano para ir a la playa.
On Saturday I will wake up early to go to the beach.

10 **Encuesta**   Find out if your classmates prefer taking a bath or a shower and then find out if they prefer to do it in the morning or at night.

EJEMPLO: ¿Prefieres bañarte o ducharte?
Do you prefer to take a bath or a shower?

Prefiero ducharme.
I prefer to take a shower.

¿Prefieres ducharte por la mañana o por la noche?
Do you prefer to take a shower in the morning or at night?

Prefiero ducharme por la mañana.
I prefer to take a shower in the morning.

11 Tell about your activities and those of your friends and tell when you did/do/will do them. Be very careful about the endings for your verbs. Use this pattern.

SUBJECT	VERB	WHEN
Yo	me bañé	anoche.
Carlos	se acuesta	a las diez.
Nosotros	nos hablaremos	todos los días.

ADVERBS ENDING IN MENTE

You have been using some words that end in **mente: frecuentemente, raramente,** etc. In English we add *ly* to words that describe nouns (adjectives) when we want to use them to describe actions (adverbs). We can do same thing in Spanish by adding **mente** to adjectives. If the adjective ends in an **o,** change it to **a** before adding **mente.**

feliz   + mente = felizmente   *happily*
triste   + mente = tristemente   *sadly*
correcta   + mente = correctamente *correctly*

12 **¿Cómo hacen la tarea?** *How do they do the homework?*   Tell how some of your classmates do their homework. Here are some adjectives you can change to adverbs.

frecuente   fácil   rápido
cuidadoso   difícil   perfecto

EJEMPLOS: Juan lo hace correctamente.   *Juan does it correctly.*
Carlota lo hace lentamente.   *Carlota does it slowly.*

COMPARING HOW THINGS ARE DONE

We can compare *how* things are done using the same pattern as we used to compare adjectives.

más   +   + que
menos   + *adverb* + que
tan   +   + como

13 **¿Cómo hacen la tarea?** Compare how different people in class do their homework.

EJEMPLO: Marta la hace más rápidamente que Susita.   *Marta does it more quickly than Susita.*

14 Paco and Chato are twins in the same Spanish class. They do everything the same. Tell what Paco and Chato do in class and compare how they do it.

EJEMPLOS: Paco lee tan correctamente como Chato.   *Paco reads as correctly as Chato.*
Paco escribe tan claramente como Chato.   *Paco writes as clearly as Chato.*

ENCUENTRO PERSONAL

Paulina and Salvador are describing what they expect their daily routine will be like during the summer. Listen in and see if yours will be similar.

¿Comprendes?

1. What does Paulina hope to have for the summer?
2. How is she going to dress?
3. What does Salvador feel like doing during the summer?
4. Why does Paulina have to work?
5. What solution does Salvador suggest?
6. What does Paulina propose that they do?
7. Do you think they will have a good summer?

¡Te toca!

Discuss with several friends what you plan to do during summer vacation.

Leemos y contamos

A. Andrés, nuestro amigo por correspondencia, nos escribe otra carta y describe su día típico.

> Imagino que Uds. desean saber cómo es la vida aquí. Por eso les escribo de mi día típico.
>
> Me despierto a las seis en punto cuando suena (rings) el despertador (alarm clock). Casi siempre me levanto bastante temprano porque tenemos solamente un baño y me gusta bañarme antes que mi hermana. Ella se levanta más tarde y se ducha mientras yo me cepillo los dientes, me afeito y me peino en la cocina. Después mi hermano y mi padrastro se levantan, se bañan y se afeitan.
>
> Todos desayunamos juntos y después, si hace fresco y llueve, me pongo una chaqueta o un impermeable y mi hermana y yo nos vamos a pie para la escuela. Mi padrastro se va en auto porque trabaja lejos de la casa. Mi madre se queda en casa para hacer los quehaceres (chores) domésticos. Paso el día en la escuela.
>
> Por la noche, hago mis quehaceres y tareas y después me divierto hablando (talking) por teléfono con amigos o miro la televisión. A veces me quedo en mi alcoba para leer o escuchar música. Me acuesto temprano a menudo (often), pero no me duermo inmediatamente porque me gusta pensar en mi novia.

1. ¿Cómo se despierta Andrés?
2. ¿Por qué se levanta muy temprano?
3. ¿Dónde se cepilla los dientes, se peina y se afeita?
4. ¿Qué se pone si hace fresco o si llueve?
5. ¿Cómo se van para la escuela?
6. ¿Por qué se queda la madre en casa?
7. ¿Cómo se divierte Andrés después de hacer la tarea?
8. ¿En qué piensa antes de dormirse?

B. Describe your typical day to Andrés.

C. Marisol nos escribe de su vida cuando era niña y vivía en un pueblo pequeño.

> *Hace mucho tiempo, cuando yo era niña, no vivíamos en la capital como ahora. Vivíamos en un pueblo pequeño al sur de México, en el estado de Chiapas. Mi padre era electricista y se levantaba muy temprano, se bañaba y se afeitaba y salía para irse al trabajo. No iba en auto porque no teníamos auto.*
>
> *Pero sí teníamos una criada* (housekeeper) *que se llamaba Blanca. Hacía cinco años que Blanca nos ayudaba en la casa, lavando la ropa y preparando la comida. No éramos ricos. Pero tener criada es bastante común en México. No cuesta mucho. Blanca se iba todas las mañanas a la plaza y al mercado al aire libre* (outdoor) *para comprar carne fresca, frutas y legumbres.*
>
> *Todos los días mi hermano y yo nos lavábamos en el baño después de levantarnos. Luego nos vestíamos, desayunábamos con mamá y después de despedirnos de ella nos íbamos a pie para la escuela, que no estaba muy lejos de nuestra casa. Después de la escuela corríamos rápidamente a casa, especialmente los viernes porque nos divertíamos mucho los fines de semana con la familia y los amigos. Siempre nos acostábamos tarde el viernes, pero no nos dormíamos inmediatamente porque a mi hermano y a mí nos gustaba hablar hasta las altas* (late) *horas de la noche en vez de dormirnos.*
> *Para mí era una vida feliz.*

1. ¿Vivía siempre Marisol en la capital?
2. ¿Dónde vivía cuando era más joven?
3. ¿Qué era su padre?
4. ¿Por qué no iba a su trabajo en coche?
5. ¿Quién era Blanca?
6. ¿Era rica la familia?
7. ¿Qué hacía Blanca para la familia?
8. ¿Dónde compraba la comida?
9. ¿Cómo iban Marisol y su hermano a la escuela?
10. ¿Cómo pasaron los fines de semana?

D. Write about your life years ago.

¡Así es!

The Hispanic attitude toward work

Hispanics and Americans place different priorities on some aspects of life. For some Americans, how much money one makes and how much one can accomplish in a busy day is very important. Hispanics often think Americans live a hectic life and cannot take time to enjoy more important things such as family and friends. Hispanics do work hard, but tend to regard work as a necessity rather than an end in itself. So when they can, they like to spend time visiting and conversing with friends or doing other social activities. Social interaction is very important for most Hispanics. People in Hispanic countries celebrate many more holidays than we do in the United States. This gives them an opportunity to relax with family and friends and to enjoy life. Some Americans think it's inefficient and wasteful, but to the Hispanics it is a matter of getting priorities straight. Do you think we have something to learn from the Hispanic attitude toward work?

Salimos de vacaciones
We're leaving on vacation

Can you believe that the school year is nearly over and it's time to be planning for vacation? Let's talk about our plans while we learn some irregular verbs.

Vocabulario

De vacaciones   *On vacation*

Para hacer* un viaje debemos…   ***To make a trip we should . . .***

decidir en la destinación — *decide on the destination*
   ir a una ciudad — *to go to a city*
   ir al campo — *to go to the country*
   ir a la playa — *to go to the beach*
   ir a otro país — *to go to another country*
comprar billetes para el avión — *buy tickets for the airplane*
   el autobús — *the bus*
   el tren — *the train*

hacer* la maleta — *pack the suitcase*
llevar una bolsa — *take along a purse*
   una mochila — *a backpack, book bag*
   una cartera — *a wallet*
   un paraguas — *an umbrella*
traer* dinero — *bring money*
decir* lo que necesitamos — *tell what we need*
decir* adiós a los amigos — *say good-bye to friends*

En un viaje a la ciudad podemos…   ***On a trip to the city we can . . .***

conocer* la ciudad — *become acquainted with the city*
conocer* a la gente — *meet people*
saber* llegar a un lugar — *know how to get to a place*
comer en restaurantes — *eat in restaurants*
visitar museos — *visit museums*
ir de compras — *go shopping*
ir al teatro y a los conciertos — *go to the theater and concerts*
ver* los monumentos — *see the monuments*

PALACIO DE BELLAS ARTES
b BOLETRONICO
ballet folklórico de méxico
PRIMER PISO
PRECIO $250.00
Amalia Hernández
23 de Agt.
21.00 HORAS
Nº 15   FILA "M"

En un viaje al campo podemos...
mirar los animales
alimentar los animales
pasar tiempo al aire fresco
ir a pescar
dar un paseo

On a trip to the country we can . . .
look at the animals
feed the animals
spend time in the fresh air
go fishing
go for a walk

En un viaje a la playa podemos...
oír* las olas en la playa
nadar
recoger** conchas
broncearnos

On a trip to the beach we can . . .
hear the waves on the beach
swim
collect shells
get a suntan

En un viaje a otro país podemos...
viajar por el país
aprender la lengua
comprar recuerdos
sacar fotos
enviar tarjetas postales

On a trip to another country we can . . .
travel through the country
learn the language
buy souvenirs
take pictures
send postcards

Cuando regresamos a casa debemos...
deshacer* las maletas
contar (ue) nuestras aventuras
descansar

When we return home we should . . .
unpack the suitcases
tell about our adventures
rest

*Note: The forms of these irregular verbs are introduced
     later in this lesson.

Recoger has a spelling variation: **g ⟶ j** in the
     yo form.
       Yo recogo *I collect*

La ropa   *Clothing*

When you pack your suitcase, you may want to take these things.

These words pertaining to clothing were presented in Unit I, Lesson 5.

el suéter	*sweater*	los lentes	*eyeglasses*
el sombrero	*hat*	los lentes de contacto	*contact lenses*
el gorro	*cap*	la corbata	*tie*
el abrigo	*coat*	la camisa	*shirt*
el vestido	*dress*	la blusa	*blouse*
el traje	*suit*	la falda	*skirt*
los calcetines	*socks*	la chaqueta	*jacket*
los pantalones	*pants*	las medias	*stockings*
los zapatos	*shoes*		

Here are additional words pertaining to clothing.

1. la camisa…
   de manga larga — *long-sleeved shirt*
2.   de manga corta — *short-sleeved shirt*
3.   deportiva — *sport shirt*
4. la camiseta — *T-shirt*
5. la ropa interior — *underwear*
6. la pijama — *pajamas*
7. las zapatillas — *slippers*
8. las botas — *boots*

9. las sandalias — *sandals*
10. el cinturón — *belt*
11. el traje de baño — *swimsuit*
12. el saco — *sport coat*
13. el impermeable — *raincoat*
14. los zapatos tenis — *tennis shoes*
15. los tacones altos — *high heels*
16. los pantalones vaqueros — *blue jeans*
17. los pantalones cortos — *shorts*

1 **¿Qué llevas hoy?** *What are you wearing today?*   Tell your partner what you are wearing today and what color. (Review **Colores** on page 133.)

EJEMPLO: Hoy llevo unos pantalones vaqueros, un suéter azul y zapatos tenis blancos.
Today I'm wearing jeans, a blue sweater, and white tennis shoes.

2 **¿Qué lleva él/ella?**   Describe the clothing that other people are wearing.

EJEMPLO: Enrique lleva pantalones azules, una camisa roja de mangas cortas y zapatos negros.
Enrique is wearing blue pants, a red shirt with short sleeves, and black shoes.

3 **¿Qué llevaste ayer?** *What did you wear yesterday?*   Tell your partner what you wore yesterday. (Use the preterite tense.)

EJEMPLO: Ayer llevé una falda verde, una camisa amarilla y sandalias blancas.
Yesterday I wore a green skirt, a yellow shirt, and white sandals.

4 **¿Qué llevarás en las vacaciones?** *What will you wear/take on vacation?*   Tell your partner what you will wear or take with you on vacation. Note that **llevar** can mean either *take* or *wear*. (Use the future tense.)

EJEMPLO: Llevaré un traje de baño y sandalias.
I'll take a swimsuit and sandals.

También llevaré mi mochila y mis maletas conmigo.
I'll also take my backpack and my suitcases with me.

5 Describe what the following people are wearing and taking along in the following situations.

EJEMPLO: ¿Qué ropa llevas a la escuela?   *What do you wear at school?*
Llevo los pantalones vaqueros y una camisa de seda.   *I wear jeans and a silk shirt.*

¿Qué cosas llevas a la escuela?   *What do you take to school?*
Llevo mis libros.   *I take my books.*

a. a la escuela

b. a la playa

c. a casa por la noche

d. a la iglesia

e. a una fiesta

f. a un pícnic

g. al cine

h. al restaurante

i. al museo

PRETERITE "COMBO" ENDINGS

The "combo" endings for the preterite are a combination of the endings for **-ar** and **-er/-ir** verbs. Note that accents are not used with the "combo" endings.

-AR ENDINGS	**-ER/-IR** ENDINGS	**"COMBO"** ENDINGS
-é	í	-E
-aste	**iste**	-ISTE
-ó	ió	-0
-amos	**imos**	-IMOS
-asteis	**isteis**	-ISTEIS
-aron	**ieron**	-IERON*

*Note: When the stem ends in **j, i** is dropped from the ending.

dijeron   trajeron   condujeron

We are going to learn some more irregular verbs in this lesson. You have seen that the irregular verbs **tener** and **venir** have some patterns in common. Many other verbs share some of these irregularities. Watch for the following patterns that these new verbs share with **tener** and **venir.**

preterite: irregular stems and "combo" endings
      yo **tuve**, etc.
      yo **vine**, etc.

present: **-go** ending in the **yo** form
      yo ten**go**
      yo ven**go**

future: irregular future stem
      yo **tendre**
      yo **vendré**

Note: In the charts, irregularities will be shown in bold print.

Yo sin *Kleenex* no puedo viajar.

Porque he descubierto que los Pañuelos Desechables Kleenex sirven para todo.

HACER *to do, to make*

	IMPERFECT *did/made* *was/were* *doing/making* *used to* *do/make*	PRETERITE *did/made* *did do/make*	PRESENT *-make(s)* *am/is/are* *doing/making* *do/does do/make*	FUTURE *will do/make*
yo	hacía	**hice**	**hago**	**haré**
tú	hacías	**hiciste**	haces	**harás**
Ud./él/ella	hacía	**hizo**	hace	**hará**
nosotros(as)	hacíamos	**hicimos**	hacemos	**haremos**
vosotros(as)	hacíais	**hicisteis**	hacéis	**haréis**
Uds./ellos/ellas	hacían	**hicieron**	hacen	**harán**

Irregularities:
preterite: irregular stem: **hic-** + "combo" endings (Exception: Ud./él/ella **hizo**)
present: **-go** verb: yo **hago**
future: irregular future stem: **har-**

6 **Encuesta**   Find out if your classmates made a trip last summer and where they went.

EJEMPLO: ¿Hiciste un viaje el verano pasado?
Did you make a trip last summer?

Sí, hice un viaje a Canadá. / No, no hice ningún viaje.
Yes, I made a trip to Canada. / No, I didn't make any trip.

7 Find out if your classmates will do a lot of homework this weekend.

EJEMPLO: ¿Harás mucha tarea este fin de semana?
Will you do a lot of homework this weekend?

Sí, haré la tarea de historia y matemáticas.
Yes, I'll do the homework in history and math.

PONER *to put*

	IMPERFECT	PRETERITE	PRESENT	FUTURE
	put	*put*	*put(s)*	*will put*
	was/were putting		*am/is/are putting*	
	used to put	*did put*	*do/does put*	
yo	ponía	**puse**	**pongo**	**pondré**
tú	ponías	**pusiste**	pones	**pondrás**
Ud./él/ella	ponía	**puso**	pone	**pondrá**
nosotros(as)	poníamos	**pusimos**	ponemos	**pondremos**
vosotros(as)	poníais	**pusisteis**	ponéis	**pondréis**
Uds./ellos/ellas	ponían	**pusieron**	ponen	**pondrán**

Irregularities:

preterite: irregular stem: **pus-** + "combo" endings

present: **-go** verb: yo **pongo**

future: irregular future stem: **pondr-**

---

8 Tell what clothing you will put in your suitcase if you go to different places.

EJEMPLO: Si voy a Hawaii, pondré un traje de baño en mi maleta.
If I go to Hawaii, I will put a swimsuit in my suitcase.

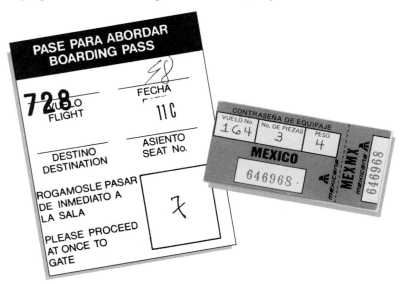

9 When you arrived home from school yesterday, where did you put your books, jacket, and other things?

EJEMPLO: Puse mis libros en mi alcoba.   *I put my books in my bedroom.*

PODER (UE) *to be able, can*

[preterite: succeeded]

	IMPERFECT	PRETERITE	PRESENT	FUTURE
	could	*succeeded*	*can*	*will be able*
	was/were able		*am/is/are*	
	used to be able	*did succeed*	*able*	
yo	podía	**pude**	puedo	**podré**
tú	podías	**pudiste**	puedes	**podrás**
Ud./él/ella	podía	**pudo**	puede	**podrá**
nosotros(as)	podíamos	**pudimos**	podemos	**podremos**
vosotros(as)	podíais	**pudisteis**	podéis	**podréis**
Uds./ellos/ellas	podían	**pudieron**	pueden	**podrán**

Irregularities:
preterite: irregular stem: **pud-** + "combo" endings
present: stem change **o** ⟶ **ue**
future: irregular future stem: **podr-**

---

10 Tell about something you tried to do when you were younger but couldn't. (Use the preterite.) Can you do it now? (Use the present tense.)

EJEMPLO: De niño(a), traté de subir un árbol pero no pude. Pero ahora puedo hacerlo.
As a child, I tried to climb a tree, but I couldn't. But now I can do it.

11 What are some things you will be able to do when you are older?

EJEMPLOS: Podré manejar un coche.   *I will be able to drive a car.*
Podré ir a la universidad.   *I will be able to go to the university.*

QUERER (IE)   *to want, to love*

[preterite: *tried* / preterite negative: *refused*]

	IMPERFECT	PRETERITE	PRESENT	FUTURE
	wanted	*tried*	*want(s)*	*will want*
	was/were wanting		*am/is/are wanting*	
	used to want	*did try*	*do/does want*	
yo	quería	**quise**	quiero	**querré**
tú	querías	**quisiste**	quieres	**querrás**
Ud./él/ella	quería	**quiso**	quiere	**querrá**
nosotros(as)	queríamos	**quisimos**	queremos	**querremos**
vosotros(as)	queríais	**quisisteis**	queréis	**querréis**
Uds./ellos/ellas	querían	**quisieron**	quieren	**querrán**

Irregularities:
preterite: irregular stem: **quis-** + "combo" endings
present: stem change **e ⟶ ie**
future: irregular future stem: **querr-**

12 When you were a child, what did you and your friends want to be? What do you want to be now?

EJEMPLO: De niño, quería ser bombero. Ahora quiero ser programador de computadoras.
As a child, I wanted to be a firefighter. Now I want to be a computer programmer.

13 Who are the people or pets you love, and how long you will love them?

EJEMPLO: Quiero a mi perro. Lo querré siempre.
I love my dog. I will love him forever.

Quiero a mi novia. La querré hasta el fin del tiempo.
I love my girlfriend. I'll love her until the end of time.

DECIR *to say, to tell*

	IMPERFECT
	*said/told
	was/were
	   saying/telling
	used to say/tell*
		PRETERITE
		said/told
		
		did say/tell
			PRESENT
			*say(s)/tell(s)
			am/is/are
			   saying/telling
			do/does say/tell*
				FUTURE
				will say/tell

yo	decía	**dije**	**digo**	**diré**
tú	decías	**dijiste**	dices	**dirás**
Ud./él/ella	decía	**dijo**	dice	**dirá**
nosotros(as)	decíamos	**dijimos**	decimos	**diremos**
vosotros(as)	decíais	**dijisteis**	decís	**diréis**
Uds./ellos/ellas	decían	**dijeron**	dicen	**dirán**

Irregularities:
preterite: irregular stem: **dij-** + "combo" endings, Uds./ellos/ellas = dijeron
present: **-go** verb: **digo, e ⟶ i** stem change in boot forms
future: irregular future stem: **dir-**

14 Where did your friends say they were going for vacation?

EJEMPLO: Miguel dijo que le gustaría ir a México.
Miguel said that he would like to go to Mexico.

Juan y Juanita dijeron que les gustaría ir a Perú.
Juan and Juanita said that they would like to go to Peru.

15 Mario and his girlfriend, Alicia, just broke up. What do his friends say to console him?

EJEMPLO: Carlos dice que hay más muchachas en el mundo.
Carlos says there are more girls in the world.

Yo digo que Alicia no es muy simpática.
I say that Alicia is not very nice.

TRAER *to bring*

		IMPERFECT *brought* *was/were* *bringing* *used to bring*	PRETERITE *brought* *did bring*	PRESENT *bring(s)* *am/is/are* *bringing* *do/does bring*	FUTURE *will bring*
yo		traía	**traje**	**traigo**	traeré
tú		traías	**trajiste**	traes	traerás
Ud./él/ella		traía	**trajo**	trae	traerá
nosotros(as)		traíamos	**trajimos**	traemos	traeremos
vosotros(as)		traíais	**trajisteis**	traéis	traeréis
Uds./ellos/ellas		traían	**trajeron**	traen	traerán

Irregularities:
preterite: irregular stem: **traj-** + "combo" endings, Uds./ellos/ellas = **trajeron**
present: **-go** verb: **traigo**

16 What do you usually bring with you on vacation? Find out what your classmates bring.

EJEMPLO: Traigo mi paraguas. También traigo mucho dinero. ¿Qué traes tú?
I bring my umbrella. I also bring a lot of money. What do you bring?

¡Ay, olvidé mi cepillo de dientes!

17 **Encuesta: ¿Qué trajiste? *What did you bring to school this morning?***   Ask several classmates to name three things that they brought to school this morning.

EJEMPLO: 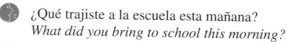 ¿Qué trajiste a la escuela esta mañana?
What did you bring to school this morning?

Yo traje una mochila, una bolsa y un suéter.
I brought a backpack, a purse, and a sweater.

SALIR (DE) *to go out, to leave*

	IMPERFECT *left* *was/were* * leaving* *used to leave*	PRETERITE *left* *did leave*	PRESENT *leave(s)* *am/is/are* * leaving* *do/does leave*	FUTURE *will leave*
yo	salía	salí	**salgo**	**saldré**
tú	salías	saliste	sales	**saldrás**
Ud./él/ella	salía	salió	sale	**saldrá**
nosotros(as)	salíamos	salimos	salimos	**saldremos**
vosotros(as)	salíais	salisteis	salís	**saldréis**
Uds./ellos/ellas	salían	salieron	salen	**saldrán**

Irregularities:
present: -**go** verb: **salgo**
future: irregular future stem: **saldr-**

When you leave from a place, the preposition **de** is used.
  Salgo <u>de</u> mi casa a las siete.   *I leave my house at 7:00.*

---

18 First review the days, months, and dates on pages 101 and 102. Tell when you and your friends will leave on your vacation. If you know where they are going, add that information. Use **para** to tell destination.

EJEMPLO: Saldré para San Juan, Puerto Rico el primero de julio.
I will leave for San Juan, Puerto Rico on July 1.

Miguel saldrá para Dallas el 3 de agosto.
Miguel will leave for Dallas on August 3.

19 Encuesta   Find out what time your classmates leave for school every day. Then find out if they left at that time today.

EJEMPLO: ¿A qué hora sales para la escuela?
At what time do you leave for school?

Salgo de mi casa a las siete menos diez.
I leave my house at ten to seven.

¿A qué hora saliste de la casa esta mañana?
At what time did you leave the house this morning?

Yo salí a las siete y media en punto.
I left at exactly seven-thirty.

OÍR *to hear*

	IMPERFECT	PRETERITE	PRESENT	FUTURE
	heard	*heard*	*hear(s)*	*will hear*
	was/were		*am/is/are*	
	hearing		*hearing*	
	used to hear	*did hear*	*do/does hear*	
yo	oía	oí	**oigo**	oiré
tú	oías	oíste	**oyes**	oirás
Ud./él/ella	oía	**oyó**	**oye**	oirá
nosotros(as)	oíamos	oímos	oímos	oiremos
vosotros(as)	oíais	oísteis	oís	oiréis
Uds./ellos/ellas	oían	**oyeron**	**oyen**	oirán

Irregularities:
preterite: regular but with addition of accent on **i** and **i** ⟶ **y** between vowels
present: **-go** verb: **oigo**, accent on **i** in **oímos**, add **y** between vowels

20 Listen carefully. What are some of the things you hear right now?

EJEMPLO: Oigo los autos afuera.   *I hear the cars outside.*
Oigo a la profesora.   *I hear the teacher.*

21 Find out what your friends heard and tell about it.

EJEMPLO: ¿Qué oíste?   *What did you hear?*

Yo oí la tiza en la pizarra.   *I heard the chalk on the chalkboard.*

22 Make a list of the things you hear from your bedroom when the windows are open.

EJEMPLO: Oigo los pájaros que cantan.
I hear the birds that sing.

Oigo los aviones que vuelan en el cielo.
I hear the planes that are flying in the sky.

VER *to see*

	IMPERFECT *saw* *was/were* *seeing* *used to see*	PRETERITE *saw* *did see*	PRESENT *see(s)* *am/is/are* *seeing* *do/does see*	FUTURE *will see*
yo	**veía**	vi	**veo**	veré
tú	**veías**	viste	ves	verás
Ud./él/ella	**veía**	vio	ve	verá
nosotros(as)	**veíamos**	vimos	vemos	veremos
vosotros(as)	**veíais**	visteis	veis	veréis
Uds./ellos/ellas	**veían**	vieron	ven	verán

Irregularities:
imperfect: stem **ve-**
preterite: regular, but without accents
present: **yo** form **veo**

23 Find out where your friends went for their vacations and what they saw there.

EJEMPLO: ¿Adónde fuiste de vacaciones y que viste?
Where did you go for vacation and what did you see there?

Fui a Nueva York y vi la Estatua de la Libertad.
I went to New York and I saw the Statue of Liberty.

24 **¿Qué veías pero no ves ahora?**   Tell some things that you used to see but don't see anymore.

EJEMPLO: En el pasado, veía a mi tío Joaquín todos los días, pero ahora no lo veo más de
tres veces al año.
*In the past, I used to see my Uncle Joaquín every day, but now I don't see him
more than three times a year.*

SABER *to know (how)*

[preterite: *found out*]

	IMPERFECT *knew* *used to know*	PRETERITE *found out* *did find out*	PRESENT *know(s)* *am/is/are knowing* *do/does know*	FUTURE *will know*
yo	sabía	**supe**	**sé**	**sabré**
tú	sabías	**supiste**	sabes	**sabrás**
Ud./él/ella	sabía	**supo**	sabe	**sabrá**
nosotros(as)	sabíamos	**supimos**	sabemos	**sabremos**
vosotros(as)	sabíais	**supisteis**	sabéis	**sabréis**
Uds./ellos/ellas	sabían	**supieron**	saben	**sabrán**

Irregularities:
preterite: irregular stem: **sup-** + "combo" endings
present: **yo sé**
future: irregular future stem: **sabr-**

Saber can be used

- to say you know *facts* or *information.* It is often followed by **que** *(that),* **si** *(if),* or a question word *(who, where, why,* etc.).

   Tú sabes que Madrid es la capital de España.
   You know that Madrid is the capital of Spain.

   ¿Sabes si España está en Europa?
   Do you know if Spain is in Europe?

   ¿Sabes dónde está Europa?
   Do you know where Europe is?

- to say you know *how* to do something. Then it is followed by the *infinitive* verb form.

   Yo sé leer el mapa.   *I know how to read the map.*
   ¿Sabes manejar un auto?   *Do you know how to drive a car?*

25 Tell some things you found out about various people in your class.

EJEMPLO: Supe que Ramón es jugador de tenis.   *I found out Ramón is a tennis player.*
Supe que estudia contigo.   *I found out he studies with you.*

26 Ask your partner if he or she knows where various places in your city are located.

EJEMPLO:  Sabes dónde está la biblioteca?
Do you know where the library is?

Sí, sé que la biblioteca está en la Calle Evergreen.
Yes, I know the library is on Evergreen Street.

27 Tell some things you will know after a trip to Mexico.

EJEMPLO: Sabré hablar mejor el español.   *I will know how to speak Spanish better.*
Sabré dónde está la capital.   *I will know where the capital is.*
Sabré si la gente es simpática.   *I will know if the people are nice.*

28 Ask your partner if he or she knows how to do five things.

EJEMPLO: ¿Sabes bailar?
Do you know how to dance?

Sí, sé bailar. / No, no sé bailar.
Yes, I know how to dance. / No, I don't know how to dance.

CONOCER *to know a person or place, to be acquainted with*

[preterite = *met a person for the first time*]

Irregularities:
Only the **yo** form of the present is irregular: **conozco.**
All other forms are regular.

Yo sé quien es el presidente de los Estados Unidos, pero no lo conozco personalmente.

29 Tell when you met your current friends.

EJEMPLO: Conocí a Paquita en el octavo grado.   *I met Paquita in the eighth grade.*
Conocí a Francisco hace un año.   *I met Francisco a year ago.*

30 Ask your partner if he or she knows your friends.

EJEMPLO: ¿Conoces a Pablo Núñez?   *Do you know Pablo Núñez?*

Sí, lo conozco. / No, no lo conozco.   *Yes, I know him. / No, I don't know him.*

31 Tell your partner what cities you know (are acquainted with).

EJEMPLO: Conozco Nueva York, Chicago y Los Ángeles.
I am acquainted with New York, Chicago, and Los Angeles.

SUMMARY OF IRREGULAR VERBS

For most students the best way to learn the irregular verbs is by hearing them and saying them out loud. But it also helps to see similarities in the forms. Here is a summary of the patterns of the irregular verbs you have learned in this book. You will need to add the person endings.

IMPERFECT

ir ⟶ IBA   ser ⟶ ERA   ver ⟶ VEÍA

PRETERITE: "COMBO" VERBS

IRREGULAR STEM	"COMBO" ENDINGS
tener ⟶ TUV-	-E
estar ⟶ ESTUV-	-ISTE
poder ⟶ PUD-	-O
poner ⟶ PUS-	-IMOS
saber ⟶ SUP-	-ISTEIS
venir ⟶ VIN-	-IERON*
hacer ⟶ HIC-	
querer ⟶ QUIS-	*Note: No **i** after **j**
decir ⟶ DIJ-	
traer ⟶ TRAJ	

PRESENT: Irregular YO forms

-GO	-OY	OTHER
tener ⟶ TENGO	ser ⟶ SOY	ver ⟶ VEO
venir ⟶ VENGO	estar ⟶ ESTOY	saber ⟶ SÉ
hacer ⟶ HAGO	dar ⟶ DOY	conocer ⟶ CONOZCO
poner ⟶ PONGO	ir ⟶ VOY	
decir ⟶ DIGO		
traer ⟶ TRAIGO		
salir ⟶ SALGO		
oír ⟶ OIGO		

FUTURE: Irregular stems

•drop some letters	•change the last vowel to **d**
hacer ⟶ HAR-	tener ⟶ TENDR-
poder ⟶ PODR-	venir ⟶ VENDR-
decir ⟶ DIR-	poner ⟶ PONDR-
querer ⟶ QUERR-	salir ⟶ SALDR-

Ser and **ir** are irregular in all tenses except the future. (See charts.)

	IMPERFECT	PRETERITE	PRESENT	FUTURE
ser	ERA	FUI	SOY	SERÉ
ir	IBA	FUI	VOY	IRÉ

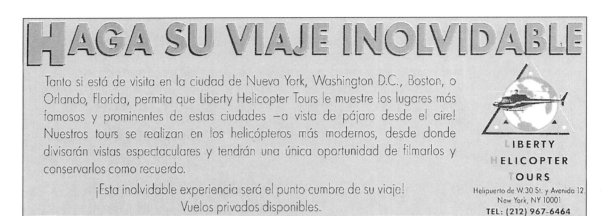

ENCUENTRO PERSONAL

Paulina and her friends in the Spanish Club are making plans for a field trip at the end of school. They have something very special planned. Listen in and see if you would like to go along.

¿Comprendes?

1. What idea does Paulina have for a field trip?
2. How will the students pay for the trip?
3. Who will they meet there?
4. What will they do there?
5. What does Paulina say she will do today?

¡Te toca!

Now it's your turn to plan a field trip with some of your classmates. Suggest some places you can visit and what you want to do there. You might also want to discuss how you would get the money to make the trip. ¡Buen viaje!

Leemos y contamos

A. **De vacaciones en Acapulco** *On vacation in Acapulco*   Paulina just wrote a letter to her friends telling them about her first day of vacation. Let's read the letter and afterward we can write about our own ideal day.

Hola, amigos,

Estoy muy entusiasmada (excited) *hoy. Aunque tengo mucho sueño, no puedo dormir. Tengo que escribirles de mi día hoy. Esta mañana en casa tuve que levantarme muy temprano porque el avión salió del aeropuerto a las seis de la mañana. Nos divertimos mucho en el avión. Yo me senté al lado de la ventana para poder verlo todo.*

Pues, aquí estamos en Acapulco. No puedo creerlo. Hoy conocí a Marisol, mi amiga por correspondencia. Ella es muy simpática y sabe mucho de Acapulco. Cuando llegamos a Acapulco, ¡qué calor hacía! Al llegar al hotel donde nos quedamos, inmediatamente nos pusimos los trajes de baño y fuimos a la playa. Acapulco es un puerto (port) *muy bonito, donde las montañas llegan al mar y hay buenas playas.*

Después de nadar nos duchamos y nos pusimos pantalones cortos y camisetas para salir en barco para La Roqueta, una isla pequeña cerca de la costa, donde hay un restaurante y una tienda para turistas. Allí compramos muchos recuerdos.

Bebimos y comimos felizmente en el restaurante mientras miramos nerviosamente a los jóvenes que zambullían (were diving) *en el océano desde las rocas altas. También vimos unos barcos que se fueron al océano para pescar. Marisol nos dijo que Acapulco es el mejor puerto natural en toda la costa del Océano Pacífico desde Chile hasta Alaska. Sacamos muchas fotos. ¡Qué divertido!* (What fun!)

Regresamos al hotel por la noche y mis amigos y yo nos vestimos elegantemente y nos fuimos para el centro. Conocimos a muchas personas simpáticas en las discotecas y nos divertimos mucho con la música y la conversación. Acabamos de volver al hotel y ya es tarde. Es medianoche pero como ya les dije, no puedo dormirme. Pero, debo despedirme de Uds. porque es hora de acostarnos. ¡Nos vemos pronto!

Su amiga que los recuerda,
Paulina

1. What was the plane ride like?
2. Who did Paulina meet in Acapulco?
3. What was the weather like?
4. What was the first thing they did after arriving?
5. What is the port of Acapulco like?
6. What did they do after swimming?
7. What did they do after returning to the hotel?
8. What time did Paulina finish her letter?

C. **¿Que harás durante las vacaciones de tus sueños?** *What will you do during your dream vacation?* You have been granted the vacation of your dreams with no restrictions of time or money. Tell about the first day in detail. Start with getting up in the morning and end with going to bed at night. Be sure to use a lot of description when telling about your trip.

YATE Hawaiano

RESERVACIONES AL TEL. 2-12-17, 2-07-85 ACAPULCO. GRO. APDO. 494 P.O. BOX

```
        GOCE EL MAR CON NOSOTROS
        11:30 a.m. y 4:30 p.m. diario
    Viaje en el yate más lujoso de Acapulco,
    tres cubiertas para bailar, música disco,
    tropical y romántica.
            LUNADA HAWAIANA
            10:30 p.m. diario
    Diviértase abordo de un verdadero cen-
    tro nocturno flotante con tres pis-
    tas para bailar, con dos variedades:
    Show Sorpresa, Show Hawaiano, concur-
    so de baile abordo y fiesta en la
    playa de la Isla de la Roqueta.
```

¡Así es!

Changing money

RATE OF MONETARY EXCHANGE

COUNTRY	MONEY	EXCHANGE	COUNTRY	MONEY	EXCHANGE
Argentina	peso	.99 = $1	Honduras	lempira	12.8 = $1
Bolivia	boliviano	5.24 = $1	Mexico	nuevo peso	7.9 = $1
Chile	peso	419 = $1	Nicaragua	córdoba	9.2 = $1
Colombia	peso	1059 = $1	Panama	balboa	1 = $1
Costa Rica	colón	227 = $1	Paraguay	guaraní	2149 = $1
Cuba	peso	19 = $1	Peru	nuevo sol	2.7 = $1
Dominican Republic	peso	14 = $1	Spain	peseta	145 = $1
Ecuador	sucre	3817 = $1	Uruguay	peso	9.2 = $1
El Salvador	colón	8.75 = $1	Venezuela	bolívar	478 = $1
Guatemala	quetzal	5 = $1	Puerto Rico	U.S. dollar	

*These exchange rates are for April 1997. Check for current exchange rates in the Monday *Wall Street Journal* or call a major bank.

You will find small money-changing offices in most areas where tourists arrive: airports, railroad and bus stations, and at customs checkpoints. Also, most large hotels, shops and restaurants will take American money, but the rate of exchange at these places will not be as good as at a bank or in a money-changing window on the streets of a big city. The latter are usually identified with a sign **Cambios** *(Exchange)* and have the exchange rate posted on the window. It is best to change a small amount of money, enough for one or two days, while still at home, and then go to a bank after you arrive. Above is a sample of exchange rates and monetary units of various countries published in newspapers. Of course, these rates vary daily, sometimes by a significant amount, so you will have to look up the current information.

Datos útiles

DINERO

La moneda de Estados Unidos es el US DOLAR $. Un dólar equivale a 100 centavos. Los billetes de banco se emiten en denominaciones de $1 dólar, 5, 10, 20, 50 y 100; son todos del mismo color y tamaño por lo que hay que poner atención y cuidado para evitar confusiones. Las monedas se emiten en valores de 1 centavo, 5, 10, 25 y 50; son todas de color plateado excepto el de 1 centavo o penny que es de color bronce.

Vocabulary

≈ Spanish-English ≈

This glossary contains all the vocabulary introduced in Compañeros, **Spanish for Communication, Book 1.** The reference number following each entry indicates the unit and lesson in which each word or expression first appears.

A

a   to, at   I.9
a la derecha de   to the right of   II.2
a la izquierda de   to the left of   III.2
a pie   on foot   III.4
a través de   across   III.3
a veces   sometimes   I.5
la **abeja**   bee   III.6
el/la **abogado(a)**   lawyer   II.5
el **abrazo**   hug   I.1
el **abrigo**   coat   I.5
abril   April   I.9
abrir   to open   IV.3
la **abuela**   grandmother   I.3
el **abuelo**   grandfather   I.3
los **abuelos**   grandparents   I.3
aburrido(a) (estar)   bored   III.1
aburrido(a) (ser)   boring   II.2
acabar de   to have just   IV.2
aceptar   to accept   IV.1
Achís   Achoo   I.4
acostarse (ue)   to go to bed   IV.5
la **actividad**   activity   IV.1
el **actor**   actor   II.5
la **actriz**   actress   II.5
acuático(a)   aquatic   III.6
Adiós   Good-bye   I.1
¿Adónde?   Where (to)?   I.8
afeitarse   to shave   IV.5
las **afueras**   suburbs   III.3
el/la **agente**   agent   II.5
agitado(a)   upset   III.1
agosto   August   I.9
el/la **agricultor(a)**   farmer   II.5
el **agua** *(f.)*   water   I.6
la **ahijada**   goddaughter   II.4
el **ahijado**   godson   II.4
ahora   now   I.3
el **aire**   air   IV.6
el **ajo**   garlic   IV.2
al (a+el)   to the   III.4
al lado de   beside, next to   III.2
al otro lado de   on the other side of   III.2

la **alcoba**   bedroom   I.7
alegre   cheerful, happy   II.2
el **alemán**   German (language)   II.3
Alemania   Germany   II.3
el **alfabeto**   alphabet   I.2
el **álgebra** *(f.)*   algebra   IV.4
algo   something   I.10
alguien   someone   IV.4
algunas veces   sometimes   II.1
alguno(a)   some   IV.4
alimentar   to feed   IV.6
allí   there   I.3
el **almacén**   department store   III.2
la **almeja**   clam   III.6
almorzar (ue)   to eat lunch   IV.2
el **almuerzo**   lunch   I.6
alrededor de   around, surrounding   III.2
alto(a)   high, tall (in height)   I.7
la **altura**   altitude, height   III.3
el **ama de casa** *(f.)*   homemaker   II.5
amable   courteous, kind   II.2
amarillo(a)   yellow   I.7
ambicioso(a)   ambitious   II.2
el/la **americano(a)**   American   II.3
el/la **amigo(a)**   friend   I.2
amistoso(a)   friendly   II.2
anaranjado(a)   orange   I.7
ancho(a)   wide   I.7
el **animal**   animal   I.6
anteayer   day before yesterday   I.9
antés (de)   before   II.1
antiguo(a)   ancient, former   IV.3
antipático(a)   mean, not nice   II.2
añadir   to add   IV.2
el **año**   year, grade in school   I.3
el **año pasado**   last year   II.1
el **apartamento**   apartment   I.7
el **apellido**   last name   I.2
el **apio**   celery   IV.2
aprender   to learn   I.10
aprobar (ue)   to pass (a test, an exam)   IV.4
los **apuntes**   notes (information)   IV.4
aquel(la)   that (far)   III.3
aquello   that *(indefinite)*   III.3

449

aquellos(as)   those   III.3
aquí   here   I.3
la **araña**   spider   I.6
el **arándano**   blueberry   IV.2
el **árbol**   tree   IV.5
el **archivador**   file cabinet   I.8
la **ardilla**   squirrel   I.6
la **arena**   sand   III.5
el **armario**   closet, locker   I.8
el/la **arquitecto(a)**   architect   II.5
el **arroz**   rice   IV.2
el **arte** *(f.)*   art   I.9
el/la **artista**   artist   II.5
así   so, thus   I.1
así, así   so-so   I.1
¡Así es!   That's the way it is!   I.1
asistir (a)   to attend   IV.3
atlético(a)   athletic   II.2
atrás   behind, in back of   III.1
el **aula** *(f.)*   classroom   I.8
aunque   although   IV.3
el **auto**   car   I.8
el **autobús**   bus   I.8
el **automóvil**   automobile   II.2
la **avena**   oats   IV.2
la **avenida**   avenue   IV.3
el **avión**   airplane   I.8
ayer   yesterday   I.9
ayudar (a)   to help   IV.1
el **azúcar** *(f.)*   sugar   IV.2
azul   blue   I.7

B

bailar   to dance   I.10
bajar   to go down   IV.3
bajo(a)   low, short (in height)   I.7
la **ballena**   whale   III.6
el **banco**   bank, bench   III.2
la **bandera**   flag   I.8
el/la **banquero(a)**   banker   II.5
bañarse   to bathe   IV.5
el **baño**   bathroom   I.7
barato(a)   inexpensive   II.6
la **barba**   beard   III.1
el **barco**   boat   III.4
el **barrio**   neighborhood   IV.3
el **básquetbol**   basketball   I.10
bastante   fairly, quite, enough   I.7
la **batata**   sweet potato   IV.2
el **bate**   bat (sports)   III.5
el/la **bebé**   baby   I.2
beber   to drink   I.6
la **bebida**   beverage   IV.2

el **béisbol**   baseball   I.10
el **beso**   kiss   I.1
la **biblioteca**   library   I.8
la **bicicleta**   bicycle   I.8
bien   well   I.1
el **bigote**   mustache   III.1
el **billete**   ticket   IV.6
la **biología**   biology   IV.4
blanco(a)   white   I.7
blando(a)   soft   II.6
el **bloque**   block (of wood)   III.5
la **blusa**   blouse   I.5
la **boca**   mouth   I.4
el **bolígrafo**   ballpoint pen   I.8
la **bolsa**   purse   IV.6
el/la **bombero(a)**   firefighter   II.5
bonito(a)   pretty   II.1
el **borrador**   eraser (chalkboard)   I.8
el **bosque**   forest   III.6
la **bota**   boot   IV.6
el **brazo**   arm   I.4
broncearse   to sunbathe   IV.6
el **buen tiempo**   nice weather   I.5
Buenas noches   Good evening   I.1
Buenas tardes   Good afternoon   I.1
bueno(a)   good   I.1
Bueno   OK   I.9
Buenos días   Good morning   I.1
el **búfalo**   buffalo   III.6
el **burro**   donkey   I.6
buscar   to look for   IV.1

C

el **caballo**   horse   I.6
el **caballo balancín**   rocking horse   III.5
la **cabeza**   head   I.4
la **cabra**   goat   III.6
el **cacahuete**   peanut   IV.2
cada   each   III.4
el **café**   coffee   I.6
la **cafetería**   cafeteria   IV.2
la **caja**   box   IV.2
el **cajón de arena**   sandbox   III.5
los **calcetines**   socks   I.5
la **calculadora**   calculator   I.8
calcular   to do arithmetic   IV.4
el **cálculo**   calculus   IV.4
el **calendario**   calendar   I.9
callado(a)   quiet   II.2
la **calle**   street   IV.3
el **calor**   heat   I.5
calor (tener...)   to be warm/hot   I.5
calvo(a)   bald   II.1

los **camarones**   shrimp   IV.2
el **camello**   camel   III.6
caminar   to walk   I.10
el **camino**   road   IV.3
la **camisa**   shirt   I.5
la **camiseta**   T-shirt   IV.6
el **campo**   countryside   III.3
la **canción**   song   I.10
el **cangrejo**   crab   III.6
el **canguro**   kangaroo   III.6
las **canicas**   marbles   III.5
canoso(a)   gray-haired   II.1
cansado(a)   tired   III.1
cantar   to sing   I.10
la **capital**   capital city   III.3
la **cara**   face   I.4
cariñosamente   affectionately   II.2
la **carne**   meat   IV.2
la **carne molida**   ground meat   IV.2
la **carnicería**   butcher shop   III.2
caro(a)   expensive   II.6
la **carrera**   career   IV.4
la **carreta**   wagon   III.5
el **carro**   car   I.8
la **carta**   letter (mail)   I.8
la **cartera**   briefcase   I.8; wallet   IV.6
la **casa**   house   I.3
la **casa de muñecas**   dollhouse   III.5
casado(a) (estar)   married   III.1
el **casete**   cassette   II.6
el **catarro**   cold (headcold)   I.4
catorce   fourteen   I.3
la **cebolla**   onion   IV.2
la **cebra**   zebra   III.6
celebrar   to celebrate   IV.1
celoso(a)   jealous   III.1
la **cena**   dinner, evening meal   I.6
cenar   to eat dinner   IV.2
el **centro**   center, downtown   III.3
el **centro comercial**   mall   III.2
cepillar(se)   to brush   IV.5
cerca (de)   near   III.2
el **cerdo**   pig   I.6; pork   IV.2
el **cereal**   cereal   IV.2
el **cerebro**   brain   III.1
la **cereza**   cherry   IV.2
cero   zero   I.3
cerrar (ie)   to close   IV.4
la **chaqueta**   jacket   I.5
charlar   to chat   IV.1
¡Chau!   Bye!   I.1
el **chino**   Chinese (language)   IV.4
el **chocolate**   chocolate   I.6
la **chuleta**   chop   IV.2

cien(to)   hundred   I.10
la **ciencia**   science   I.9
el **ciervo**   deer   III.6
cinco   five   I.3
cincuenta   fifty   I.3
el **cine**   movie theater   I.10
la **cinta**   tape   I.8
el **cinturón**   belt   IV.6
el **circo**   circus   IV.2
circular   circular   I.7
la **ciudad**   city   I.5
el/la **ciudadano(a)**   citizen   III.3
claro(a)   clear   I.5; light (in color)   I.7
¡Claro!   Of course!   I.5
la **clase**   class   I.9
la **clase de tecleo**   keyboarding   IV.4
el **coche**   car   I.8
la **cocina**   kitchen   I.7
cocinar   to cook   I.10
el **codo**   elbow   I.4
la **coliflor**   cauliflower   IV.2
el **color**   color   I.7
el **columpio**   swing   III.5
el **comedor**   dining room   I.7
comenzar (ie)   to begin, to start   IV.1
comer   to eat   I.6
el **comercio**   business   IV.4
la **cometa**   kite   III.5
la **comida**   dinner, main meal, food   I.6
como   as, like   I.3
¿Cómo?   How?   I.1
¿Cómo está(n)... ?   How is (are) . . . ?   I.1
¿Cómo está Ud.?   How are you?   I.1
¿Cómo estás?   How are you?   I.1
¿Cómo se dice... ?   How do you say . . . ?   I.1
¿Cómo se escribe... ?   How do you spell . . . ?   I.2
¿Cómo se llama Ud.?   What's your name?   I.2
¿Cómo te llamas?   What's your name?   I.2
el/la **compañero(a)**   friend, classmate   I.2
la **competencia**   competition   IV.4
comprar   to buy   I.10
comprender   to understand   I.1
la **computadora**   computer   I.8
con   with   III.2
Con permiso   Excuse me   I.1
la **concha**   shell   IV.6
el **concierto**   concert   IV.6
los **condimentos**   seasonings   IV.2
el **condominio**   condominium   IV.3
el **conejo**   rabbit   I.6
la **conferencia**   lecture   IV.4
conmigo   with me   III.2

conocer   to know, to be acquainted with   IV.6
el **consultorio**   medical office   III.2
el/la **contador(a)**   accountant   II.5
contar (ue)   to count, to tell a story   IV.6
contento(a)   happy, content   III.1
contigo   with you   III.2
el **corazón**   heart   I.4
la **corbata**   tie   I.5
el **cordero**   lamb   IV.2
correctamente   correctly   IV.5
correcto(a)   correct   IV.5
el **correo**   post office   III.2
correr   to run   I.10
corto(a)   short (in length)   I.7
la **cosa**   thing   I.8
coser   to sew   IV.2
la **costa**   coast   III.3
costar (ue)   to cost   IV.4
creer   to believe   I.8
la **crema**   cream   IV.2
crema   tan (color)   II.6
Creo que...   I think that . . .   II.5
el/la **criado(a)**   servant, housekeeper   II.5
el **cuaderno**   notebook   I.8
la **cuadra**   block (city)   IV.3
cuadrado(a)   square   I.7
el **cuadro**   picture   II.6
¿Cuál?   Which?   I.2
¿Cuándo?   When?   I.5
¿Cuánto?   How much?   II.3
¿Cuántos(as)?   How many?   I.3
¿Cuántos años tienes?   How old are you?   I.3
cuarenta   forty   I.3
cuarto(a)   fourth   IV.3; quarter   I.9
el **cuarto**   room   I.7
cuatro   four   I.3
cuatrocientos   four hundred   I.10
la **cucaracha**   cockroach   III.6
el **cuello**   neck   I.4
el **cuento**   story   IV.4
el **cuerpo**   body   I.4
cuidar   to take care of   I.10
cuidar de los niños   to babysit   I.10
el **cumpleaños**   birthday   I.9
la **cuñada**   sister-in-law   II.4
el **cuñado**   brother-in-law   II.4

D

las **damas**   checkers   III.5
dar   to give   I.10
dar las gracias   to give thanks, to thank   IV.1
dar un paseo   to go for a walk   IV.6

de   from   II.3; of, about   II.4
¿De dónde es... ?   Where is . . . from?   II.3
de hecho   in fact   III.3
De nada   You're welcome   I.1
de niño(a)   as a child   II.1
¿De quién?   Whose?   I.5
de repente   suddenly   II.1
de una vez   all at once   II.1
de vez en cuando   from time to time   II.1
de viejo(a)   as an old person   II.1
debajo (de)   under   III.2
deber   to owe   IV.2
deber + *infinitive*   ought to + *verb*   IV.2
débil   weak   II.1
decidir   to decide   IV.6
décimo(a)   tenth   IV.3
decir   to say, to tell   IV.6
el **dedo (de la mano)**   finger   I.4
el **dedo del pie**   toe   I.4
del (de + el)   of the, from the   I.2
delante de   in front of   III.2
delgado(a)   thin   II.1
el/la **dentista**   dentist   II.5
dentro (de)   inside of   III.2
el/la **dependiente(a)**   salesperson   II.5
el **deporte**   sport   I.10
deportivo(a)   sport   IV.6
la **derecha**   right   III.2
desayunar   to eat breakfast   IV.2
el **desayuno**   breakfast   I.6
descansar   to rest   IV.1
la **descripción**   description   II.1
desde   from (time), since   IV.4
desear   to desire, to want   IV.1
deshacer   to undo   IV.6
el **desierto**   desert   III.3
despacio   slowly   I.1
despedirse (i, i)   to say good-bye   IV.5
el **despertador**   alarm clock   IV.5
despertarse (ie)   to wake up   IV.5
después (de) (que)   after   II.1
la **destinación**   destination   IV.6
el **desván**   attic   I.7
detrás de   behind   III.2
el **día**   day   I.1
dibujar   to draw   I.8
el **diccionario**   dictionary   I.8
diciembre   December   I.9
el **diente**   tooth   I.4
diez   ten   I.3
difícil   difficult   III.1
el **dinero**   money   I.10
la **dirección**   address   IV.3
el **disco compacto**   compact disc, CD   I.8

discutir   to argue, to discuss   IV.3

divertirse (ie, i)   to enjoy oneself, to have a good time, to have fun   IV.5

dividido(a) por   divided by   I.3

dividir   to divide   IV.4

doce   twelve   I.3

doler (ue)   to hurt   I.4

el **dolor**   pain, ache   I. 4, III.1

doméstico(a)   domestic   III.6

domingo   Sunday   I.9

don   title of respect   I.2

doña   title of respect   I.2

¿Dónde?   Where?   I.3

dorado(a)   gold   II.6

dormir (ue, u)   to sleep   I.10

dormirse (ue, u)   to go to sleep   IV.5

dos   two   I.3

dos veces   twice   II.1

doscientos   two hundred   I.10

ducharse   to (take a) shower   IV.5

la **dulcería**   candy store   III.2

los **dulces**   candy   IV.2

duro(a)   hard   II.6

E

e *(before i/hi)*   and   IV.1

la **economía**   economics   I.9

la **edad**   age   I.3

el **edificio**   building   III.2

la **educación física**   physical education   I.9

egoísta   selfish   II.2

el **ejemplo**   example   I.1

el   the   I.2

el (lunes)   on (with days)   I.9

él   he   I.1

El gusto es mío   The pleasure is mine   I.2

eléctrico(a)   electric   III.5

el **elefante**   elephant   I.6

ella   she   I.1

ellas   they *(f.)*   I.2

ellos   they *(m.)*   I.2

el/la **embajador(a)**   ambassador   II.6

en   in, on   I.1

en… meses   in . . . months   II.1

en vez de   instead of   IV.5

enamorado(a)   in love   III.1

encima de   on top of   III.2

el **encuentro**   encounter   I.1

enero   January   I.9

la **enfermedad**   illness   I.4

el/la **enfermero(a)**   nurse   I.4

enfermo(a)   sick   III.1

enfrente (de)   opposite   III.2

enojado(a)   angry   III.1

la **ensalada**   salad   I.6

la **enseñanza**   schooling, teaching   IV.4

entonces   then   II.1

entrar (en)   to enter   IV.4

entre   between   III.2

el **entremés**   appetizer   IV.2

entusiasmado(a)   excited   IV.6

enviar   to send   IV.6

envolver (ue)   to wrap   IV.2

esa   that   I.5

la **escalera**   stairs   I.7

escribir   to write   I.10

escribir a máquina   to type, to input   IV.4

el **escritorio**   desk (of a teacher)   I.8

escuchar   to listen (to)   I.10

la **escuela**   school   I.3

ese   that   I.5

eso   that *(indefinite)*   I.5

esos(as)   those   I.5

la **espalda**   back (of the body)   I.4

España   Spain   II.3

español(a)   Spanish   I.1

el/la **español(a)**   Spaniard   II.3

especial   special   IV.5

especialmente   especially   IV.5

el **espejo**   mirror   IV.5

esperar   to hope to, to wait for   IV.2

la **esposa**   wife   I.3

el **esposo**   husband   I.3

los **esposos**   married couple   I.3

el **esqueleto**   framework, skeleton   II.1

esquiar   to ski   I.10

la **esquina**   corner   III.2

esta   this   I.4

la **estación**   station   III.2

la **estación de gasolina**   gas station   III.2

la **estación**   season   I.5

el **estado**   state   III.3

los **Estados Unidos**   United States   II.3

el/la **estadounidense**   someone of or from the United States, American   II.3

el **estante**   bookshelf   I.8

estar   to be *(condition)*   I.1; to be *(location)*   I.3

este   this   I.4

el **este**   east   III.3

el **estéreo**   stereo   I.8

esto   this *(indefinite)*   I.4

el **estómago**   stomach   I.4

estos(as)   these   I.4

estrecho(a)   narrow   I.7

la **estrella**   star   II.3

el/la **estudiante**   student   II.5

estudiar   to study   I.10
el **examen**   exam   IV.4
la **expresión**   expression   I.1
extranjero(a)   foreign   IV.4

F

fácil   easy   III.3
la **fábrica**   factory   III.2
fácilmente   easily   IV.5
la **falda**   skirt   I.5
faltar   to lack, to need   IV.4
la **familia**   family   I.3
famoso(a)   famous   II.5
fantástico(a)   great   II.2
la **farmacia**   pharmacy   III.2
el/la **farmacista**   pharmacist   II.5
favor de + *infinitive*   please + *verb*   III.6
favorito(a)   favorite   I.5
febrero   February   I.9
la **fecha**   date   I.9
feliz   happy   II.2
felizmente   happily   IV.5
feo(a)   ugly   II.1
feroz   ferocious   III.6
la **fiebre**   fever   I.4
la **fiesta**   party   I.5
la **fila**   row   III.2
el **fin**   end   III.4
finalmente   finally   IV.5
la **física**   physics   IV.4
físico(a)   physical   II.1
el **flan**   custard   IV.2
la **flor**   flower   III.2
la **florería**   flower shop   III.2
la **forma**   shape   I.7
la **foto(grafía)**   photograph   IV.1
la **frambuesa**   raspberry   IV.2
el **francés**   French (language)   II.3
Francia   France   II.3
frecuentemente   often, frequently   II.1
freír (i, i)   to fry   IV.2
el **frente**   front   III.2, I.4
la **frente**   forehead   III.1, I.3
la **fresa**   strawberry   IV.2
fresco(a)   cool   I.5; fresh   IV.6
los **frijoles**   beans   IV.2
el **frío**   cold   I.5
frito(a)   fried   I.6
la **frontera**   border   III.3
la **fruta**   fruit   I.6
fuera de   outside of   III.2
fuerte   strong   II.1
el **fútbol**   soccer, football   I.10

el **fútbol americano**   American football   II.6
el **futuro**   future   II.1

G

la **galleta**   cracker   IV.2
la **galletita dulce**   cookie   IV.2
la **gallina**   hen   I.6
el **gallo**   rooster   I.6
ganar   to earn, to win   I.10
la **garganta**   throat   I.4
gastar   to spend (money)   I.10
el **gato**   cat   I.6
la **gemela**   twin sister   II.4
el **gemelo**   twin brother   II.4
generoso(a)   generous   II.2
la **gente**   people   IV.6
la **geografía**   geography   III.3
la **geometría**   geometry   IV.4
el/la **gerente**   manager   II.5
el **globo**   globe   I.8; balloon   III.5
el **gobierno**   government   III.2
la **goma**   eraser (pencil)   I.8
gordo(a)   fat   II.1
el **gorila**   gorilla   III.6
el **gorro**   cap   I.5
la **grabadora**   tape recorder   I.8
Gracias   Thank you   I.1
las **gracias**   thanks   IV.1
el **grado**   grade (in school)   II.6
grande   big   I.7; large   II.1
la **granja**   farm   III.6
gratis   free (no charge)   IV.4
la **gripe**   flu   I.4
gris   gray   I.7
guapo(a)   good-looking, handsome   II.1
la **guardería**   nursery school   IV.4
los **guisantes**   peas   IV.2
la **guitarra**   guitar   I.10
gustar   to be pleasing, to like   I.6
gustar más/menos   to like more/less   II.6
gustar mucho   to like a lot   II.4

H

había   there was, there were   II.6
el/la **habitante**   inhabitant   III.3
hablador(a)   talkative   II.2
hablar   to speak, to talk   I.10
habrá   there will be   II.6
hace *(+ time)*   ago   II.1
hacer   to do, to make   I.10
hacer (buen) tiempo   to be (nice) weather   I.5
hacer la maleta   to pack a suitcase   IV.6

hacer sol   to be sunny I.5
hallar   to find IV.1
hambre (tener...)   to be hungry III.5
la hamburguesa   hamburger I.6
hasta   to (up to), until IV.4
Hasta la vista   See you later I.1
Hasta mañana   See you tomorrow I.1
hay   there is, there are I.3
el hecho   fact IV.4
la heladería   ice cream store III.2
el helado   ice cream I.6
la hermana   sister I.3
la hermanastra   stepsister I.3
el hermanastro   stepbrother I.3
el hermano   brother I.3
los hermanos   siblings I.3
el hielo   ice III.5
el hígado   liver III.1
la hija   daughter I.3
el hijo   son I.3
los hijos   children I.3
el hipopótamo   hippopotamus III.6
la historia   history I.9
Hola   Hello, Hi I.1
el hombre   man I.2
el hombre de negocios   businessman II.5
el hombro   shoulder III.1
la hora   hour I.9
la hormiga   ant III.6
el hospital   hospital III.2
el hotel   hotel III.2
hoy   today I.9
el huevo   egg I.6
húmedo(a)   humid I.5
¡Huy!   Wow! I.7

I

la iglesia   church I.10
Igualmente   The same here, Likewise I.2
impares (los números ...)   odd numbers I.10
el impermeable   raincoat IV.6
incorrectamente   incorrectly IV.5
incorrecto(a)   incorrect IV.5
la infección   infection III.1
la informática   computer science IV.4
el/la ingeniero(a)   engineer II.5
Inglaterra   England II.3
el inglés   English (language) I.1
inmediatamente   immediately IV.5
el insecto   insect III.6
insistir en   to insist on IV.2
el instrumento   instrument I.10
inteligente   smart II.2

interesante   interesting II.2
las investigaciones   research IV.4
el invierno   winter I.5
la invitación   invitation IV.1
el/la invitado(a)   guest IV.1
invitar   to invite IV.1
ir   to go I.8
ir a + infinitive   to be going to + verb I.10
ir de compras   to go shopping IV.6
irse   to go away IV.5
la isla   island III.3
el italiano   Italian (language) IV.4
la izquierda   left (direction) III.2

J

la jalea   jelly IV.2
el jamón   ham I.6
el japonés   Japanese (language) IV.4
la jirafa   giraffe III.6
joven   young II.1
el/la joven   teenager, young person I.2
la joyería   jewelry store III.2
las judías   string beans IV.2
el juego   game I.10
el juego de damas   checkers game III.5
jueves   Thursday I.9
el/la jugador(a)   player II.5
jugar (ue)   to play (game, sport) I.10
el jugo   juice I.6
el juguete   toy III.5
la juguetería   toy store III.2
julio   July I.9
junio   June I.9
juntos(as)   together III.1

K

el kilómetro   kilometer IV.3

L

la   the I.2; her, you, it I.5
lácteo(a)   relating to dairy IV.2
el lado   side III.2
el lago   lake III.3
la langosta   lobster IV.2
el lápiz   pencil I.8
largo(a)   long I.7
las   the I.2; them I.5
la lástima   pity I.1
el latín   Latin (language) IV.4
lavar   to wash IV.1

lavarse to wash oneself IV.5
le to you, to him, to her I.4
la **lección** lesson I.1
la **leche** milk I.6
la **lechería** dairy store III.2
la **lechuga** lettuce I.6
la **lectura** reading IV.4
leer to read I.10
la **legumbre** vegetable I.6
lejos de far from III.2
la **lengua** language IV.4
lentamente slowly IV.5
los **lentes** eyeglasses I.5
los **lentes de contacto** contact lenses I.5
el **león** lion I.6
el **leopardo** leopard III.6
les to you, to them I.4
la **letra** letter (of alphabet) I.2
levantarse to get up IV.5
la **librería** bookstore III.2
el **libro** book I.8
ligero(a) lightweight II.6
el **limón** lemon IV.2
limpiar to clean IV.1
limpio(a) clean IV.3
listo(a) (estar) ready III.3
listo(a) (ser) clever II.2
llamar to call IV.1
llamarse to be called, to be named I.2
los **llanos** plains III.3
llegar to arrive IV.1
llevar to carry I.10; to bring (people) IV.1
llevar ropa to wear I.5
llover (ue) to rain III.5
llueve it's raining, it rains I.5
lo him, you, it I.5
lo que what I.10
Lo siento I'm sorry I.1
loco(a) crazy III.1
los the I.2; them I.5
luego later, then II.1
el **lugar** place III.2
lunes Monday I.9
la **luz** light (electrical) III.2

M

la **madrastra** stepmother I.3
la **madre** mother I.3
la **madrina** godmother II.4
el **maíz** corn IV.2
mal badly III.1
el **mal tiempo** bad weather I.5
la **maleta** suitcase IV.6

malo(a) (estar) sick I.1
malo(a) (ser) bad III.1
mañana tomorrow I.1
la **mañana** morning I.9
mandar to send IV.1
manejar to drive I.10
la **manga** sleeve IV.6
la **mano** hand I.4
la **mantequilla** butter IV.2
la **manzana** apple IV.2
el **mapa** map I.8
maquillarse to put on makeup IV.5
el **mar** sea III.3
la **mariposa** butterfly III.6
los **mariscos** seafood IV.2
marrón brown (dark) II.6
martes Tuesday I.9
marzo March I.9
más more I.1; and, plus (arithmetic) I.3; most I.7
más… que more . . . than I.7
más de + *number* more than + *number* II.6
más que nada more than anything III.6
la **masa** dough IV.2
las **matemáticas** math I.9
la **materia** subject (class) IV.4
mayo May I.9
mayor older II.4
me me I.4, IV.1, IV.5
me duele(n)… . . . hurt(s) me I.2
Me llamo… My name is . . . I.2
el/la **mecánico(a)** mechanic II.5
mediano(a) medium, average I.7
la **medianoche** midnight I.9
las **medias** stockings I.5
el/la **médico(a)** doctor II.5
medio(a) half I.9
el **medio** middle III.2
el **mediodía** noon I.9
la **mejilla** cheek III.1
mejor better III.1; best II.5
memorizar to memorize IV.4
menor less, minus I.3; least I.7; younger II.4
menos… que less . . . than I.7
el **mentón** chin III.1
la **merienda** snack I.6
el **mes** month I.9
el **mes pasado** last month II.1
la **mesa** table I.8
el/la **mesero(a)** waiter, waitress II.5
el/la **mexicano(a)** Mexican person II.3
México Mexico II.3
mezclado(a) mixed IV.2

la **mezquita** mosque III.2
mi my I.2
mí me *(after prep.)* III.2
miedo (tener...) to be afraid III.5
mientras while II.1
miércoles Wednesday I.9
mil thousand I.10
la **milla** mile IV.3
el **millón** million I.10
mío(a) mine I.5
mirar to look at, to watch I.10
la **mochila** backpack, knapsack I.8
moderno(a) modern IV.3
el **mono** monkey I.6
el **monopatín** skateboard III.5
la **montaña** mountain III.3
el **monumento** monument III.2
morado(a) purple I.7
moreno(a) brunette, dark-haired II.1
morir (ue, u) to die IV.4
la **mosca** fly III.6
el **mosquito** mosquito III.6
la **moto(cicleta)** motorcycle III.4
la **muchacha** girl I.2
el **muchacho** boy I.2
mucho(a) a lot, much I.1
Mucho gusto Pleased to meet you I.2
la **mujer** woman I.2
la **mujer de negocios** businesswoman II.5
multiplicar to multiply IV.4
mundial worldwide III.4
el **mundo** world II.2
la **muñeca** wrist III.1; doll III.5
el **murciélago** bat (animal) III.6
el **museo** museum III.2
la **música** music I.9
el/la **músico(a)** musician II.5
muy very I.1
muy bien fine, very well I.1
muy mal very bad I.1

N

la **nacionalidad** nationality II.3
nada nothing I.1
nadar to swim I.10
nadie no one IV.4
los **naipes** playing cards I.10
las **nalgas** buttocks III.1
la **naranja** orange IV.2
la **nariz** nose I.4
necesitar to need (to) IV.2
los **negocios** business II.5
negro(a) black I.7

nervioso(a) nervous III.1
ni nor II.4
ni... ni neither . . . nor IV.4
la **nieta** granddaughter I.3
el **nieto** grandson I.3
los **nietos** grandchildren I.3
nieva it's snowing, it snows I.5
la **nieve** snow I.10
la **niña** small girl I.2
ninguno(a) none, not any IV.4
el **niño** small boy I.2
no no, not I.1
no muy bien not very well I.1
No sé I don't know I.1
la **noche** evening, night I.1
el **nombre** name I.2
el **norte** north III.3
nos us, to us I.4; each other, ourselves IV.5
nosotros(as) we I.2
la **nota** grade (on tests, etc.) II.4
novecientos nine hundred I.10
la **novela** novel IV.4
noveno(a) ninth IV.3
noventa ninety I.3
la **novia** girlfriend I.2
noviembre November I.9
el **novio** boyfriend I.2
nublado(a) cloudy I.5
la **nuera** daughter-in-law II.4
nuestro(a) our, ours I.5
nueve nine I.3
nuevo(a) new II.6
la **nuez** nut, walnut IV.2
el **número** number I.3
nunca never II.1

O

o or I.6
o... o either . . . or IV.4
el/la **obrero(a)** worker, laborer II.5
el **océano** ocean III.3
ochenta eighty I.3
ocho eight I.3
ochocientos eight hundred I.10
octavo(a) eighth IV.3
octubre October I.9
ocupado(a) busy III.1
odiar to hate (to) IV.2
el **oeste** west III.3
la **oficina** office II.5
oír to hear IV.6
ojalá hopefully IV.3
el **ojo** eye I.4

la **ola**   wave (water) IV.6
once   eleven I.3
la **oreja**   ear I.4
el **orgullo**   pride IV.4
la **orquesta**   band, orchestra I.9
os   you, to you (in Spain) IV.7
oscuro(a)   dark I.7
el **osito de peluche**   teddy bear III.5
el **oso**   bear I.6
la **ostra**   oyster IV.2
el **otoño**   autumn I.5
otra vez   again II.1
otro(a)   other, another I.8
la **oveja**   sheep I.6

P

paciente   patient III.1
el **padrastro**   stepfather I.3
los **padrastros**   stepparents I.3
el **padre**   father I.3
los **padres**   parents I.3
el **padrino**   godfather II.4
pagar   to pay IV.4
el **país**   country II.3
el **pájaro**   bird I.6
la **palabra**   word II.3
las **palomitas de maíz**   popcorn IV.2
el **pan**   bread I.6
el **pan tostado**   toast IV.2
la **panadería**   bakery III.2
el **panecillo**   roll IV.2
los **pantalones**   pants I.5
los **pantalones cortos**   shorts IV.6
los **pantalones vaqueros**   blue jeans IV.6
la **papa**   potato I.6
las **papas fritas**   French fries I.6
el **papel**   paper I.8
la **papelera**   wastepaper basket I.8
la **papelería**   stationery store III.2
las **papitas fritas**   potato chips I.6
para   for, in order to I.6
el **paraguas**   umbrella IV.6
pardo(a)   brown I.7
la **pared**   wall III.2
pares (los números ...)   even numbers I.10
el **parque**   park III.2
la **parte**   part III.2
la **parte de atrás**   back III.2
el **pasado**   past II.1
pasado mañana   day after tomorrow I.9
pasar   to pass III.3
pasar tiempo   to spend time IV.6
el **paseo**   drive IV.3

el **pasillo**   hallway I.7
el **pastel**   pastry III.2
la **pastelería**   pastry shop III.2
la **patata**   potato I.10
los **patines**   skates III.5
los **patines de hielo**   ice skates III.5
los **patines de rueda**   roller skates III.5
el **patio**   inner courtyard, yard I.7
el **pato**   duck I.6
el **pavo**   turkey III.6
los **peces**   fish (live) I.6
el **pecho**   chest III.1
pedir (i, i)   to ask for IV.4
peinarse   to comb IV.5
peligroso(a)   dangerous IV.3
pelirrojo(a)   redhead II.1
el **pelo**   hair I.4
la **pelota**   ball III.5
la **peluquería**   beauty salon, barbershop III.2
pensar (ie)   to think IV.4
pensar (ie) de   to think about (opinion) IV.4
pensar (ie) en   to think about (daydream) IV.4
pensar + *infinitive*   to plan IV.4
el **pepino**   cucumber IV.2
pequeño(a)   small, little I.7
la **pera**   pear IV.2
perder (ie)   to lose IV.4
Perdón   Pardon me I.1
perezoso(a)   lazy II.2
el **perico**   parrot III.6
el/la **periodista**   journalist II.5
el **periquito**   parakeet III.6
Permiso   Excuse me I.1
pero   but I.6
el **perro**   dog I.6
el **perro caliente**   hot dog I.6
la **persona**   person I.2
las **personas**   people I.2
pesado(a)   heavy II.6
el **pescado**   fish (to eat) I.6
pescar   to fish IV.6
el **pez**   fish (live) I.6
el **piano**   piano I.10
el **pie**   foot I.4
la **pierna**   leg I.4
las **pijamas**   pajamas IV.6
el **pimiento**   pepper (vegetable) IV.2
la **pimienta**   pepper (spice) IV.2
la **piña**   pineapple IV.2
el **piso**   floor of a building IV.3
la **pista**   track I.10
la **pizarra**   chalkboard I.8
la **pizza**   pizza III.2
la **pizzería**   pizzeria III.2

planear   to plan   IV.1
plano(a)   flat   I.7
la **planta**   plant   II.6
la **planta baja**   ground floor   I.7
el **plátano**   banana   IV.2
plateado(a)   silver   II.6
el **plato**   plate   IV.1
los **platos**   dishes   IV.2
la **playa**   beach   III.2
la **plaza**   town square   III.2
poco(a)   little, few   II.1
poder (ue)   can, to be able   I.10
poder (*preterite*)   to succeed   IV.6; **no poder** (*preterite*)   to fail   IV.6
la **poesía**   poetry   IV.4
el/la **policía**   police officer   II.5
el **pollo**   chicken   I.6
poner   to put   IV.6
ponerse   to put on   IV.5
popular   popular   II.2
por   by, for, through, times   I.3
por ejemplo   for example   III.2
por eso   therefore   II.2
por favor   please   I.1
por la mañana   in the morning   II.1
por la noche   in the evening   II.1
por la tarde   in the afternoon   II.1
¿Por qué?   Why?   II.3
por supuesto   of course   IV.2
por teléfono   on the phone   I.10
porque   because   I.7
el **postre**   dessert   I.6
practicar   to practice   I.10
preferir (ie, i)   to prefer   IV.4
preguntar   to ask a question   IV.4
preocupado(a)   worried   III.1
la **preparación**   preparation   IV.1
preparar   to prepare   I.10
presentar   to introduce   I.2
el **presente**   present, now   II.1
prestar   to lend   IV.1
primario(a)   elementary   IV.4
la **primavera**   spring   I.5
el **primer año**   freshman year   I.5
el **primer piso**   second floor (one floor up)   I.7
primer(o)(a)   first   I.9
el/la **primo(a)**   cousin   I.3
prisa (tener…)   to be in a hurry   III.5
la **profesión**   occupation   II.5
el/la **profesor(a)**   teacher   II.5
próximo(a)   next (in order)   II.1
la **prueba**   test, quiz   IV.4
el **pueblo**   town   III.3
puedo + *infinitive*   I can + *verb*   I.10

la **puerta**   door   I.8
pues   well, then   II.3
el **pulgar**   thumb   III.1
el **pulmón**   lung   III.1
el **pulpo**   octopus   III.6
el **pupitre**   desk (of a student)   I.8

Q

que   than   I.3; that (*conjunction*)   I.8
¿Qué?   What?   I.1
¿Qué hora es?   What time is it?   I.9
¡Qué lástima!   That's too bad!   I.1
¿Qué pasa?   What's happening?   I.1
¿Qué quiere decir… ?   What does . . . mean?   I.1
¿Qué tal?   How's everything?   I.1
¿Qué tiempo hace?   What's the weather like?   I.5
¿Qué tienes?   What's the matter?   III.1
quedarse   to stay, to remain   IV.5
los **quehaceres**   chores   IV.5
querer (ie)   to want   IV.4
querer (*preterite*)   to try   IV.6; **no querer** (*preterite*)   to refuse   IV.6
querer (ie) a   to love   IV.4
querido(a)   dear   II.2
el **queso**   cheese   IV.2
¿Quién?   Who?   I.2
¿Quiénes?   Who?   II.3
la **química**   chemistry   IV.4
quince   fifteen   I.3
quinientos   five hundred   I.10
quinto(a)   fifth   IV.3
quitar   to remove   IV.2
quitarse   to take off   IV.5

R

el **rábano**   radish   IV.2
el **radio**   radio   I.8
el **ramillete**   bouquet   IV.1
la **rana**   frog   III.6
rápidamente   rapidly   IV.5
rápido(a)   fast   II.6
raramente   rarely   II.1
el **rascacielos**   skyscraper   III.2
la **rata**   rat   III.6
el **ratón**   mouse   I.6
razón (no tener…)   to be wrong   III.5
razón (tener…)   to be right   III.5
la **rebanada**   slice   IV.2
recibir   to receive   I.10

recoger   to collect IV.6
recordar (ue)   to remember IV.4
rectangular   rectangular II.6
el **recuerdo**   memory, souvenir IV.6
redondo(a)   round I.7
el **refresco**   soft drink I.6
los **refrescos**   refreshments, beverages IV.1
el **regalo**   gift, present I.9
la **regla**   ruler II.6
regresar   to return IV.6
regular   normal, OK I.1
la **reina**   queen II.2
el **reloj**   clock I.8
el **reloj (de) pulsera**   wristwatch I.5
la **relojería**   clock store III.2
la **remolacha**   beet IV.2
repente (de...)   suddenly II.1
repetir (i, i)   to repeat IV.4
la **res (carne de...)**   beef IV.2
restar   to subtract IV.4
el **restaurante**   restaurant III.2
el **retroproyector**   overhead projector II.6
rico(a) (estar)   delicious III.1
rico(a) (ser)   rich III.1
el **rincón**   corner III.2
el **rinoceronte**   rhinoceros III.6
el **río**   river III.3
la **rodilla**   knee I.4
rojo(a)   red I.7
el **rompecabezas**   puzzle III.5
romper   to break IV.2
la **ropa**   clothing I.5
la **ropa interior**   underwear IV.6
la **ropería**   clothing store III.2
rosado(a)   pink I.7
el **rosbif**   roast beef I.6
la **rosquilla**   doughnut IV.2
roto(a)   broken III.1
rubio(a)   blond II.1
la **rueda**   wheel III.5
ruidoso(a)   noisy IV.3
el **ruso**   Russian (language) IV.4

S

sábado   Saturday I.9
saber   to know (a fact); IV.1; (how) IV.6
saber (*preterite*)   found out IV.6
el **sacapuntas**   pencil sharpener II.6
sacar   to take out IV.1
sacar fotos   to take pictures IV.1
sacar una A   to get an A IV.4
el **saco**   sport coat IV.6
la **sal**   salt IV.2

la **sala**   living room I.7
la **sala de estar**   family room, den I.7
la **salchicha**   sausage IV.2
salir   to go out, to leave IV.6
la **salsa picante**   hot sauce IV.2
la **salud**   health I.4
¡Salud! (*for a sneeze*)   Bless you! I.4
saludar   to greet IV.1
el **saludo**   greeting I.1
salvaje   wild III.6
las **sandalias**   sandals IV.6
la **sandía**   watermelon IV.2
el **sándwich**   sandwich I.6
el **sapo**   toad III.6
la **sartén**   frying pan IV.2
se   one, you, they (*impersonal*) I.1; each other, yourself, himself, herself, yourselves, themselves IV.5
sé   I know I.1
el/la **secretario(a)**   secretary II.5
secundario(a)   secondary IV.4
sed (tener...)   to be thirsty III.5
seguir (i, i)   to continue, to follow IV.4
segundo(a)   second IV.3
seguro(a) (estar)   sure, certain III.1
seguro(a) (ser)   safe IV.3
seis   six I.3
seiscientos   six hundred I.10
la **selva**   forest, jungle III.3
la **semana**   week II.1
la **semana pasada**   last week II.1
el **señor (Sr.)**   Mr., Sir I.2
la **señora (Sra.)**   Mrs., ma'am I.2
la **señorita (Srta.)**   Miss, Ms. I.2
sentarse (ie)   to sit down IV.5
sentir (ie, i)   to regret, to be sorry IV.4
septiembre   September I.9
séptimo(a)   seventh IV.3
ser   to be (*identity*) I.2; to be (*characteristics*) II.1
la **serpiente**   snake III.6
servir (i, i)   to serve IV.4
sesenta   sixty I.3
setecientos   seven hundred I.10
setenta   seventy I.3
sexto(a)   sixth IV.3
si   if II.3
sí   yes I.1
la **sicología**   psychology IV.4
siempre   always II.1
la **sierra**   mountain range III.3
la **siesta**   nap IV.2
siete   seven I.3
el **siglo**   century III.3

el **silbato**   whistle   III.5
la **silla**   chair   I.8
  silvestre   wild, untamed   II.6
  simpático(a)   nice   II.2
  sin (que)   without   I.2
la **sinagoga**   synagogue   III.2
  sincero(a)   sincere   II.2
  sobre   over   III.2
la **sobrina**   niece   II.4
el **sobrino**   nephew   II.4
  sociable   social   IV.4
el **sol**   sun   I.5
  sol (hacer...)   to be sunny   I.5
  solamente   only   II.3
el **soldado**   soldier   III.5
el **soldado (de juguete)**   (toy) soldier   III.5
el **sombrero**   hat   I.5
  son (=)   equal(s) (=)   I.3
la **sopa**   soup   I.6
el **sótano**   basement   I.7
  su   your, his, her, their   I.3
  subir   to go up   IV.3
  sucio(a)   dirty   IV.3
la **suegra**   mother-in-law   II.4
el **suegro**   father-in-law   II.4
el **suelo**   floor   III.2
  sueño (tener...)   to be sleepy   III.5
  suerte (tener...)   to be lucky   III.5
el **suéter**   sweater   I.5
  suficiente   enough   I.5
  sufrir   to suffer   IV.3
  sumar   to add (arithmetic)   IV.4
el **supermercado**   supermarket   III.2
el **sur**   south   III.3
  suspender   to fail   IV.4
  suyo(a)   yours, his, hers, theirs   I.5

T

el **tablero de anuncios**   bulletin board   II.6
la **tableta de chocolate**   candy bar   IV.2
el **tacón**   heel (of a shoe)   IV.6
el **talón**   heel (of a foot)   III.1
el **tamaño**   size   I.7
  también   also   I.3
el **tambor**   drum   III.5
  tampoco   either, neither   III.6; not at all   IV.5
  tan   as   I.7
  tan... como   as . . . as   I.7
  tanto(a)   as much   I.3
  tantos(as)   as many   I.3
la **taquigrafía**   shorthand   IV.4
  tarde   late   IV.1
la **tarde**   afternoon   I.1

la **tarea**   homework   IV.4
la **tarjeta**   card (greeting)   IV.6
la **tarjeta postal**   postcard   IV.6
el **taxi**   taxi   III.4
la **taza**   cup   III.1
  te   you, to you   I.4: yourself   IV.5
  Te quiero   I love you   II.2
el **té**   tea   I.6
el **teatro**   theater   III.2
el **techo**   ceiling, roof   III.2
  teclear   to input (keyboard)   IV.4
el **teléfono**   telephone   I.8
la **televisión**   television program   I.10
el **televisor**   television set   I.8
el **tema**   theme   IV.4
la **temperatura**   temperature   I.5
el **templo**   temple   III.2
  temprano   early   IV.1
  tener   to have   I.3
  tener... años   to be . . . years old   III.5
  tener calor   to be warm   III.5
  tener cuidado   to be careful   III.5
  tener frío   to be cold   III.5
  tener ganas de + *infinitive*   to feel like + *verb*   IV.2
  tener hambre   to be hungry   III.5
  tener miedo   to be afraid   III.5
  tener prisa   to be in a hurry   III.5
  tener que + *infinitive*   to have to + *verb*   IV.2
  tener razón   to be right;   **no tener razón**   to be wrong   III.5
  tener sed   to be thirsty   III.5
  tener sueño   to be sleepy   III.5
  tener suerte   to be lucky   III.5
el **tenis**   tennis   I.10
  tercer(o)(a)   third   IV.3
  terminar   to end, to finish   III.3
la **ternera**   veal   IV.2
  ti   you *(after prep.)*   III.2
la **tía**   aunt   I.3
el **tiburón**   shark   III.6
el **tiempo**   weather, time   I.5
la **tienda**   store   I.8
el **tigre**   tiger   I.6
las **tijeras**   scissors   II.6
  tímido(a)   shy, timid   II.2
la **tintorería**   dry cleaners   III.2
el **tío**   uncle   I.3
el **tipo**   kind, type   III.6
el **títere**   puppet   III.5
la **tiza**   chalk   I.8
el **tobillo**   ankle   III.1
  tocar   to play (an instrument)   I.10
  toca (te...)   it's your turn   I.1

el **tocino**   bacon   IV.2
todavía   still, yet   II.1
todavía no   not yet   II.1
todo(a)   all, whole   I.9
todos los (días)   every (day)   II.1
tomar   to drink, to take   I.10
tomar apuntes   to take notes   IV.4
el **tomate**   tomato   IV.2
tonto(a)   foolish   II.2
el **toro**   bull   I.6
la **toronja**   grapefruit   IV.2
la **torta**   cake   I.6
la **tortuga**   turtle   III.6
la **tos**   cough   III.1
trabajador(a)   hardworking   II.2
trabajar   to work   I.10
el **trabajo**   job, work   I.3
traer   to bring (things)   IV.6
el **traje**   suit   I.5
el **traje de baño**   swimsuit   IV.6
tranquilo(a)   calm   III.1
tratar de   to try to   IV.2
trece   thirteen   I.3
treinta   thirty   I.3
el **tren**   train   III.4
el **tren eléctrico**   electric train   III.5
tres   three   I.3
trescientos   three hundred   I.10
triangular   triangular   II.6
el **triciclo**   tricycle   III.5
el **trigo**   wheat   IV.2
la **trigonometría**   trigonometry   IV.4
triste   sad   II.2
tristemente   sadly   IV.5
tu   your   I.2
tú   you   I.1
turquesa   turquoise   II.6
tuyo(a)   yours   I.5

U

último(a)   last (in order)   III.3
un(a)   a   I.2
un poco   a little bit   II.1
la **uña**   fingernail   III.1
una vez   once   II.1
la **unidad**   unit   I.1
la **universidad**   university   IV.4
uno(a)   one   I.3
unos(as)   some   I.2
usted (Ud.)   you   I.1
ustedes (Uds.)   you (plural)   I.2
la **uva**   grape   IV.2

V

la **vaca**   cow   I.6
las **vacaciones**   vacation   IV.6
la **vainilla**   vanilla   I.6
la **valle**   valley   III.3
vamos a + infinitive   let's + verb   IV.1
la **vaquera**   cowgirl   II.1
el **vaquero**   cowboy   II.1
el **vecino(a)**   neighbor   IV.1
veinte   twenty   I.3
vender   to sell   IV.2
venir   to come   IV.3
la **ventana**   window   I.8
ver   to see   IV.6
el **verano**   summer   I.5
¿verdad?   right?, true?   II.2
verde (estar)   green (unripe)   III.1
verde (ser)   green (color)   I.7
el **vestido**   dress   I.5
vestirse (i, i)   to dress   IV.5
la **vez (veces)**   time(s), occurrence   II.1
viajar   to travel   I.10
el **viaje**   trip   IV.6
la **vida**   life   IV.5
el **vídeo**   video   III.4
la **videocasetera**   videocassette recorder   II.6
viejo(a)   old   II.1
el **viento**   wind   I.5
viernes   Friday   I.9
violeta   violet   II.6
visitar   to visit   I.10
vivir   to live   I.7
el **vocabulario**   vocabulary   I.1
volver (ue)   to return   IV.4
vosotros(as)   you (plural) (in Spain)   II.6

Y

y   and   I.1
ya   already   II.1
ya no   no longer   II.1
el **yerno**   son-in-law   II.4
yo   I   I.1
el **yogur**   yogurt   IV.2
el **yoyo**   yo-yo   III.5

Z

la **zanahoria**   carrot   IV.2
la **zapatería**   shoe store   III.2
la **zapatilla**   slipper   IV.6
el **zapato**   shoe   I.5
los **zapatos tenis**   tennis shoes   IV.6
el **zorro**   fox   III.6

Vocabulary

≈≈ English-Spanish ≈≈

This glossary contains all the vocabulary introduced in **Compañeros, Spanish for Communication, Book 1.** The reference number following each entry indicates the unit and lesson in which each word or expression first appears.

A

a un(a) I.2
a little un poco II.1
a lot mucho(a) I.1
to be **able** poder (ue) I.10
about de II.4
to **accept** aceptar IV.1
accountant el/la contador(a) II.5
ache el dolor III.1
Achoo Achís I.4
across a través de III.3
activity la actividad IV.1
actor el actor II.5
actress la actriz II.5
to **add** añadir IV.2
to **add (arithmetic)** sumar IV.4
address la dirección IV.3
affectionately cariñosamente II.2
to be **afraid** tener miedo III.5
after después (de) (que) II.1
afternoon la tarde I.1
again otra vez II.1
age la edad I.3
agent el/la agente II.5
ago hace *(+ time)* II.1
air el aire IV.6
airplane el avión I.8
alarm clock el despertador IV.5
algebra el álgebra *(f.)* IV.4
all todo(a) I.9
all at once de una vez II.1
alphabet el alfabeto I.2
already ya II.1
also también I.3
although aunque IV.3
altitude la altura III.3
always siempre II.1
ambassador el/la embajador(a) II.6
ambitious ambicioso(a) II.2
American el/la americano(a), el/la estadounidense II.3
American football el fútbol americano II.6

ancient antiguo(a) IV.3
and y I.1; e *(before i/hi)* IV.1
angry enojado(a) III.1
animal el animal I.6
ankle el tobillo III.1
another otro(a) IV.6
ant la hormiga III.6
apartment el apartamento I.7
appetizer el entremés IV.2
apple la manzana IV.2
April abril I.9
aquatic acuático(a) III.6
architect el/la arquitecto(a) II.5
to **argue** discutir IV.3
arm el brazo I.4
around alrededor de III.2
to **arrive** llegar IV.1
art el arte *(f.)* I.9
artist el/la artista II.5
as como I.3; tan I.7
as . . . as tan… como I.7
as a child de niño(a) II.1
as an old person de viejo(a) II.1
as many tantos(as) I.3
as much tanto(a) I.3
to **ask a question** preguntar IV.4
to **ask for** pedir (i, i) IV.4
at a I.9
athletic atlético(a) II.2
to **attend** asistir (a) IV.3
attic el desván I.7
August agosto I.9
aunt la tía I.3
automobile el automóvil II.2
autumn el otoño I.5
avenue la avenida IV.3
average mediano(a) I.7

B

baby el/la bebé I.2
to **babysit** cuidar de los niños I.10
back la parte de atrás III.2

463

back (in...)   atrás   III.1
back (of the body)   la espalda   I.4
backpack   la mochila   I.8
bacon   el tocino   IV.2
bad   malo(a) (ser)   III.1
bad weather   el mal tiempo   I.5
badly   mal   III.1
bakery   la panadería   III.2
bald   calvo(a)   II.1
ball   la pelota   III.5
balloon   el globo   III.5
ballpoint pen   el bolígrafo   I.8
banana   el plátano   IV.2
band (music)   la orquesta   I.9
bank   el banco   III.2
banker   el/la banquero(a)   II.5
barbershop   la peluquería   III.2
baseball   el béisbol   I.10
basement   el sótano   I.7
basketball   el básquetbol   I.10
bat (animal)   el murciélago   III.6
bat (baseball)   el bate   III.5
to bathe   bañarse   IV.5
bathroom   el baño   I.7
to be (condition)   estar   I.1
to be (location)   estar   I.3
to be (characteristics)   ser   II.1
to be (identity)   ser   I.2
beach   la playa   III.2
beans   los frijoles   IV.2
bear   el oso   I.6
beard   la barba   III.1
beauty salon   la peluquería   III.2
because   porque   I.7
bedroom   la alcoba   I.7
bee   la abeja   III.6
beef   la carne de res   IV.2
beet   la remolacha   IV.2
before   antes (de)   II.1
to begin   comenzar (ie)   IV.1
behind   atrás   III.1; detrás de   III.2
to believe   creer   I.8
belt   el cinturón   IV.6
bench   el banco   III.2
beside   al lado de   III.2
best   el/la mejor   II.2
better   mejor   III.1
between   entre   III.2
beverage   la bebida   IV.2
bicycle   la bicicleta   I.8
big   grande   I.7
biology   la biología   IV.4
bird   el pájaro   I.6
birthday   el cumpleaños   I.9

black   negro(a)   I.7
Bless you! (for a sneeze)   ¡Salud!   I.4
block (city)   la cuadra   IV.3
block (of wood)   el bloque   III.5
blond   rubio(a)   II.1
blouse   la blusa   I.5
blue   azul   I.7
blue jeans   los pantalones vaqueros   IV.6
blueberry   el arándano   IV.2
boat   el barco   III.4
body   el cuerpo   I.4
book   el libro   I.8
bookshelf   el estante   I.8
bookstore   la librería   III.2
boot   la bota   IV.6
border   la frontera   III.3
bored   aburrido(a) (estar)   III.1
boring   aburrido(a) (ser)   II.2
bouquet   el ramillete   IV.1
box   la caja   IV.2
boy   el muchacho   I.2
boyfriend   el novio   I.2
brain   el cerebro   III.1
bread   el pan   I.6
to break   romper   IV.2
breakfast   el desayuno   I.6
briefcase   la cartera   I.8
to bring (people)   llevar   IV.1
to bring (things)   traer   IV.6
broken   roto(a)   III.1
brother   el hermano   I.3
brother-in-law   el cuñado   II.4
brown   pardo(a)   I.7
brown (dark)   marrón   II.6
brunette   moreno(a)   II.1
to brush   cepillarse   IV.5
buffalo   el búfalo   III.6
building   el edificio   III.2
bull   el toro   I.6
bulletin board   el tablero de anuncios   II.6
bus   el autobús   I.8
business   el comercio   IV.4
business   los negocios   II.5
businessman   el hombre de negocios   II.5
businesswoman   la mujer de negocios   II.5
busy   ocupado(a)   III.1
but   pero   I.6
butcher shop   la carnicería   III.2
butter   la mantequilla   IV.2
butterfly   la mariposa   III.6
buttocks   las nalgas   III.1
to buy   comprar   I.10
by   por   I.3
Bye!   ¡Chau!   I.1

C

cafeteria   la cafetería   IV.2
cake   la torta   I.6
calculator   la calculadora   I.8
calculus   el cálculo   IV.4
calendar   el calendario   I.9
to call   llamar   IV.1
to be called   llamarse   I.2
calm   tranquilo(a)   III.1
camel   el camello   III.6
can   poder (ue)   I.10
candy   los dulces   IV.2
candy bar   la tableta de chocolate   IV.2
candy store   la dulcería   III.2
cap   el gorro   I.5
capital city   la capital   III.3
car   el auto, el carro, el coche   I.8
card (greeting)   la tarjeta   IV.6
cards (playing)   los naipes   I.10
career   la carrera   IV.4
to be careful   tener cuidado   III.5
carrot   la zanahoria   IV.2
to carry   llevar   I.10
cassette   el casete   II.6
cat   el gato   I.6
cauliflower   la coliflor   IV.2
ceiling   el techo   III.2
to celebrate   celebrar   IV.1
celery   el apio   IV.2
center   el centro   III.3
century   el siglo   III.3
cereal   el cereal   IV.2
chair   la silla   I.8
chalk   la tiza   I.8
chalkboard   la pizarra   I.8
to chat   charlar   IV.1
checkers game   el juego de damas   III.5
cheek   la mejilla   III.1
cheerful   alegre   II.2
cheese   el queso   IV.2
chemistry   la química   IV.4
cherry   la cereza   IV.2
chest   el pecho   III.1
chicken   el pollo   I.6
children   los hijos   I.3
chin   el mentón   III.1
Chinese (language)   el chino   IV.4
chocolate   el chocolate   I.6
chop   la chuleta   IV.2
chores   los quehaceres   IV.5
church   la iglesia   I.10
circular   circular   I.7
circus   el circo   IV.2

citizen   el/la ciudadano(a)   III.3
city   la ciudad   I.5
clam   la almeja   III.6
class   la clase   I.9
classmate   el/la compañero   I.2
classroom   el aula (f.)   I.8
clean   limpio(a)   IV.3
to clean   limpiar   IV.1
clear   claro(a)   I.5
clever   listo(a) (ser)   II.2
clock   el reloj   I.8
clock store   la relojería   III.2
to close   cerrar (ie)   IV.4
closet   el armario   I.8
clothing   la ropa   I.5
clothing store   la ropería   III.2
cloudy   nublado(a)   I.5
coast   la costa   III.3
coat   el abrigo   I.5
cockroach   la cucaracha   III.6
coffee   el café   I.6
cold   el frío   I.5
to be cold   tener frío   III.4
cold (headcold)   el catarro   I.4
to collect   recoger   IV.6
color   el color   I.7
to comb   peinarse   IV.5
to come   venir   IV.3
comfortable   cómodo(a)   IV.5
comfortably   cómodamente   IV.5
compact disc   el disco compacto   I.8
competition   la competencia   IV.4
computer   la computadora   I.8
computer science   la computación   IV.4
concert   el concierto   IV.6
condominium   el condominio   IV.3
contact lenses   los lentes de contacto   I.5
content   contento(a)   III.1
to continue   seguir (i, i)   IV.4
to cook   cocinar   I.10
cookie   la galletita dulce   IV.2
cool   fresco(a)   I.5
corn   el maíz   IV.2
corner   la esquina, el rincón   III.2
correct   correcto(a)   IV.5
correctly   correctamente   IV.5
to cost   costar (ue)   IV.4
cough   la tos   III.1
to count   contar (ue)   IV.6
country   el país   II.3
countryside   el campo   III.3
courteous   amable   II.2
cousin   el/la primo(a)   I.3
cow   la vaca   I.6

cowboy   el vaquero   II.1
cowgirl   la vaquera   II.1
crab   el cangrejo   III.6
cracker   la galleta   IV.2
crazy   loco(a)   III.1
cream   la crema   IV.2
cucumber   el pepino   IV.2
cup   la taza   III.1
custard   el flan   IV.2

D

dairy (of or relating to)   lácteo(a)   IV.2
dairy store   la lechería   III.2
to **dance**   bailar   I.10
dangerous   peligroso(a)   IV.3
dark   oscuro(a)   I.7
dark-haired   moreno(a)   II.1
date   la fecha   I.9
daughter   la hija   I.3
daughter-in-law   la nuera   II.4
day   el día   I.1
day after tomorrow   pasado mañana   I.9
day before yesterday   anteayer   I.9
dear   querido(a)   II.2
December   diciembre   I.9
to **decide**   decidir   IV.6
deer   el ciervo   III.6
delicious   rico(a) (estar)   III.1
den   la sala de estar   I.7
dentist   el/la dentista   II.5
department store   el almacén   III.2
description   la descripción   II.1
desert   el desierto   III.3
to **desire**   desear   IV.1
desk (of a student)   el pupitre   I.8
desk (of a teacher)   el escritorio   I.8
dessert   el postre   I.6
destination   la destinación   IV.6
dictionary   el diccionario   I.8
to **die**   morir (ue, u)   IV.4
difficult   difícil   III.1
dining room   comedor   I.7
dinner   la cena   I.6
dirty   sucio(a)   IV.3
to **discuss**   discutir   IV.3
dishes   los platos   IV.2
to **divide**   dividir   IV.4
divided by   dividido(a) por   I.3
to **do**   hacer   I.10
to **do arithmetic**   calcular   IV.4
doctor   el/la médico   II.5
dog   el perro   I.6

doll   la muñeca   III.5
dollhouse   la casa de muñecas   III.5
domestic   doméstico(a)   III.6
donkey   el burro   I.6
door   la puerta   I.8
dough   la masa   IV.2
doughnut   la rosquilla   IV.2
downtown   el centro   III.3
to **draw**   dibujar   I.8
dress   el vestido   I.5
to **dress**   vestirse (i, i)   IV.5
to **drink**   beber   I.6; tomar   I.10
drive   el paseo   IV.3
to **drive**   manejar   I.10
drum   el tambor   III.5
dry cleaners   la tintorería   III.2
duck   el pato   I.6

E

each   cada   III.4
each other   nos, se   IV.5
ear   la oreja   I.4
early   temprano   IV.1
to **earn**   ganar   I.10
easily   fácilmente   IV.5
east   el este   III.3
easy   fácil   III.3
to **eat**   comer   I.6
to **eat breakfast**   desayunar   IV.2
to **eat dinner**   cenar   IV.2
to **eat lunch**   almorzar (ue)   IV.2
economics   la economía   I.9
egg   el huevo   I.6
eight   ocho   I.3
eight hundred   ochocientos   I.10
eighth   octavo(a)   IV.3
eighty   ochenta   I.3
either   tampoco   III.6
either . . . or   o... o   IV.4
elbow   el codo   I.4
electric (train)   (el tren) eléctrico(a)   III.5
elementary   primario(a)   IV.4
elephant   el elefante   I.6
eleven   once   I.3
encounter   el encuentro   I.1
end   el fin   III.4
to **end**   terminar   III.3
engineer   el/la ingeniero(a)   II.5
England   Inglaterra   II.3
English (language)   el inglés   I.1
to **enjoy oneself**   divertirse (ie, i)   IV.5
enough   suficiente, bastante   I.5

to **enter**   entrar (en)   IV.4
equal(s) (=)   son (=)   I.3
eraser (chalkboard)   el borrador   I.8
eraser (pencil)   la goma   I.8
especially   especialmente   IV.5
even numbers   los números pares   I.10
evening   la noche   I.1
evening meal   la cena   I.6
every (day)   todos(as) (los días)   II.1
exam   el examen   IV.4
example   el ejemplo   I.1
excited   entusiasmado(a)   IV.6
Excuse me   Con permiso, Perdón   I.1
expensive   caro(a)   II.6
expression   la expresión   I.1
eye   el ojo   I.4
eyeglasses   los lentes   I.5

F

face   la cara   I.4
fact   el hecho   IV.4
factory   la fábrica   III.2
to **fail**   suspender   IV.4; no poder *(preterite)*   IV.6
fairly, quite   bastante   I.7
family   la familia   I.3
family room   la sala de estar   I.7
famous   famoso(a)   II.5
far from   lejos de   III.2
farm   la granja   III.6
farmer   el/la agricultor(a)   II.5
fast   rápido(a)   II.6
fat   gordo(a)   II.1
father   el padre   I.3
father-in-law   el suegro   II.4
favorite   favorito(a)   I.5
February   febrero   I.9
to **feed**   alimentar   IV.6
to **feel like + *verb***   tener ganas de + *infinitive*   IV.2
ferocious   feroz   III.6
fever   la fiebre   I.4
few   poco(a)   II.1
fifteen   quince   I.3
fifth   quinto(a)   IV.3
fifty   cincuenta   I.3
file cabinet   el archivador   I.8
finally   finalmente   IV.5
to **find**   hallar   IV.1
fine   muy bien   I.1
finger   dedo (de la mano)   I.4
fingernail   la uña   III.1
to **finish**   terminar   III.3

firefighter   el/la bombero(a)   II.5
first   primer(o)(a)   I.9
fish (live)   el pez   I.6
fish (to eat)   el pescado   I.6
to **fish**   pescar   IV.6
five   cinco   I.3
five hundred   quinientos   I.10
flag   la bandera   I.8
flat   plano(a)   I.7
floor   el suelo   III.2
floor (of a building)   el piso   IV.3
flower   la flor   III.2
flower shop   la florería   III.2
flu   la gripe   I.4
fly   la mosca   III.6
to **follow**   seguir (i, i)   IV.4
food   la comida   I.6
foolish   tonto(a)   II.2
foot   el pie   I.4
for   por   I.3; para   I.6
for example   por ejemplo   III.2
forehead   la frente   III.1
foreign   extranjero(a)   IV.4
forest   la selva   III.3; el bosque   III.6
former   antiguo(a)   IV.3
forty   cuarenta   I.3
found out   saber *(preterite)*   IV.6
four   cuatro   I.3
four hundred   cuatrocientos   I.10
fourteen   catorce   I.3
fourth   cuarto(a)   IV.3
fox   el zorro   III.6
framework   el esqueleto   II.1
France   Francia   II.3
free (no charge)   gratis   IV.4
French (language)   el francés   II.3
French fries   las papas fritas   I.6
fresh   fresco(a)   IV.6
freshman year   el primer año   I.5
Friday   viernes   I.9
fried   frito(a)   I.6
friend   el/la amigo(a), el/la compañero(a)   I.2
friendly   amistoso(a)   II.2
frog   la rana   III.6
from   de   II.3
from (time)   desde   IV.4
from the   del (de + el)   I.2
from time to time   de vez en cuando   II.1
front   el frente   III.2
fruit   la fruta   I.6
to **fry**   freír (i, i)   IV.2
frying pan   la sartén   IV.2
future   el futuro   II.1

G

game   juego   I.10
garlic   ajo   IV.2
gas station   la estación de gasolina   III.2
generous   generoso(a)   II.2
geography   la geografía   III.3
geometry   la geometría   IV.4
German (language)   el alemán   II.3
Germany   Alemania   II.3
to **get an A**   sacar una A   IV.4
to **get up**   levantarse   IV.5
gift   el regalo   I.9
giraffe   la jirafa   III.6
girl   la muchacha   I.2
girlfriend   la novia   I.2
to **give**   dar   I.10
to **give thanks**   dar las gracias   IV.1
globe   el globo   I.8
to **go**   ir   I.8
go ahead   adelante   I.2
to **go away**   irse   IV.5
to **go down**   bajar   IV.3
to **go out**   salir   IV.6
to **go shopping**   ir de compras   IV.6
to **go to bed**   acostarse (ue)   IV.5
to **go to sleep**   dormirse (ue)   IV.5
to **go up**   subir   IV.3
goat   la cabra   III.6
goddaughter   la ahijada   II.4
godfather   el padrino   II.4
godmother   la madrina   II.4
godson   el ahijado   II.4
to be **going to + verb**   ir a + *infinitive*   I.10
gold   dorado(a)   II.6
good   bueno(a)   I.1
Good afternoon   Buenas tardes   I.1
Good evening   Buenas noches   I.1
Good morning   Buenos días   I.1
Good-bye   Adiós   I.1
good-looking   guapo(a)   II.1
gorilla   el gorila   III.6
government   el gobierno   III.2
grade (on tests, etc.)   la nota   II.4
grade (school year)   el año   I.3;
   el grado   II.6
grandchildren   los nietos   I.3
granddaughter   la nieta   I.3
grandfather   el abuelo   I.3
grandmother   la abuela   I.3
grandparents   los abuelos   I.3
grandson   el nieto   I.3
grape   la uva   IV.2
grapefruit   la toronja   IV.2

gray   gris   I.7
gray-haired   canoso(a)   II.1
great   fantástico(a)   II.2
green (color)   verde (ser)   I.7
green (unripe)   verde (estar)   III.1
to **greet**   saludar   IV.1
greeting   el saludo   I.1
ground floor   la planta baja   I.7
ground meat   la carne molida   IV.2
guest   el/la invitado(a)   IV.1
guitar   la guitarra   I.10

H

hair   el pelo   I.4
half   medio(a)   I.9
hallway   el pasillo   I.7
ham   el jamón   I.6
hamburger   la hamburguesa   I.6
hand   la mano   I.4
handsome   guapo(a)   II.1
happily   felizmente   IV.5
happy   feliz   II.2; contento(a)   III.1
hard   duro(a)   II.6
hardworking   trabajador(a)   II.2
hat   el sombrero   I.5
to **hate (to)**   odiar   IV.2
to **have**   tener   I.3
to **have a good time**   divertirse (ie, i)   IV.5
to **have fun**   divertirse (ie, i)   IV.5
to **have just**   acabar de   IV.2
to **have to + verb**   tener que + *infinitive*   IV.2
he   él   I.1
head   la cabeza   I.4
health   la salud   I.4
to **hear**   oír   IV.6
heart   el corazón   I.4
heat   el calor   I.5
heavy   pesado(a)   II.6
heel (of a foot)   el talón   III.1
heel (of a shoe)   el tacón   IV.6
height   la altura   III.3
Hello   Hola   I.1
to **help**   ayudar (a)   IV.1
hen   la gallina   I.6
her   su   I.3; la   I.5
here   aquí   I.3
hers   suyo(a)   I.5
herself   se   IV.5
Hi   Hola   I.1
high   alto(a)   I.7
him   le   I.4; lo   I.5
himself   se   IV.5
his   su   I.3; suyo(a)   I.5

hippopotamus   el hipopótamo   III.6
history   la historia   I.9
homemaker   el ama de casa *(f.)*   II.5
homework   la tarea   IV.4
to hope to   esperar   IV.2
hopefully   ojalá   IV.3
horse   el caballo   I.6
hospital   el hospital   III.2
hot dog   el perro caliente   I.6
hot sauce   la salsa picante   IV.2
hotel   el hotel   III.2
hour   la hora   I.9
house   la casa   I.3
housekeeper   el/la criado(a)   II.5
How?   ¿Cómo?   I.1
How are you?   ¿Cómo estás?, ¿Cómo está Ud.?   I.1
How do you say . . . ?   ¿Cómo se dice… ?   I.1
How do you spell . . . ?   ¿Cómo se escribe… ?   I.2
How is . . . ?   ¿Cómo está… ?   I.1
How many?   ¿Cuántos(as)?   I.3
How much?   ¿Cuánto(a)?   II.3
How old are you?   ¿Cuántos años tienes?   I.3
How's everything?   ¿Qué tal?   I.1
hug   el abrazo   I.1
humid   húmedo(a)   I.5
hundred   cien(to)   I.10
to be hungry   tener hambre   III.5
to hurt   doler (ue)   I.4
hurt(s) me   me duele(n)   I.2
husband   el esposo   I.3

I

I   yo   I.1
I am   soy   I.1
I can + *verb*   puedo + *infinitive*   I.10
I (don't) know   (No) sé   I.1
I love you   Te quiero   II.2
I think that . . .   Yo creo que…   II.5
I'm sorry   Lo siento   I.1
ice   el hielo   III.5
ice cream   el helado   I.6
ice cream store   la heladería   III.2
ice skates   los patines de hielo   III.5
if   si   II.3
illness   la enfermedad   I.4
immediately   inmediatamente   IV.5
in   en   I.1
in . . . (months)   en… (meses)   II.1
to be in a hurry   tener prisa   III.5

in fact   de hecho   III.3
in front of   delante de   III.2
in love   enamorado(a)   III.1
in order to   para   I.6
in the afternoon   por la tarde   II.1
in the evening   por la noche   II.1
in the front of   en el frente de   III.2
in the morning   por la mañana   II.1
incorrect   incorrecto(a)   IV.5
incorrectly   incorrectamente   IV.5
inexpensive   barato(a)   II.6
infection   la infección   III.1
inhabitant   el/la habitante   III.3
inner courtyard   el patio   I.7
to input (keyboard)   teclear   IV.4
insect   el insecto   III.6
inside of   dentro (de)   III.2
to insist on   insistir en   IV.2
instead of   en vez de   IV.5
instrument   el instrumento   I.10
interesting   interesante   II.2
to introduce   presentar   I.2
invitation   la invitación   IV.1
to invite   invitar   IV.1
island   la isla   III.3
it   lo, la   I.5
Italian (language)   el italiano   IV.4

J

jacket   la chaqueta   I.5
January   enero   I.9
Japanese (language)   el japonés   IV.4
jealous   celoso(a)   III.1
jelly   la jalea   IV.2
jewelry store   la joyería   III.2
job   el trabajo   I.3
journalist   el/la periodista   II.5
juice   el jugo   I.6
July   julio   I.9
June   junio   I.9
jungle   la selva   III.3

K

kangaroo   el canguro   III.6
keyboarding (class)   la clase de tecleo   IV.4
kilometer   el kilómetro   IV.3
kind   el tipo   III.6
kind, courteous   amable   II.2
kiss   el beso   I.1
kitchen   la cocina   I.7
kite   la cometa   III.5
knapsack   la mochila   I.8

knee   la rodilla   I.4
to **know (be acquainted with)**   conocer   IV.6
to **know (a fact)**   saber   I.1;   **(how)**   IV.6

L

laborer   el/la obrero(a)   II.5
to **lack**   faltar   IV.4
lake   el lago   III.3
lamb   el cordero   IV.2
language   la lengua   IV.4
large   grande   II.1
last (in order)   último(a)   III.3
last month   el mes pasado   II.1
last name   el apellido   I.2
last week   la semana pasada   II.1
last year   el año pasado   II.1
late   tarde   IV.1
later, then   luego   II.1
Latin (language)   el latín   IV.4
lawyer   el/la abogado(a)   II.5
lazy   perezoso(a)   II.2
to **learn**   aprender   I.10
least (the . . .)   el/la menos   I.7
to **leave**   salir   IV.6
lecture   la conferencia   IV.4
left (direction)   la izquierda   III.2
left of (to the . . .)   a la izquierda de   III.2
leg   la pierna   I.4
lemon   el limón   IV.2
to **lend**   prestar   IV.1
leopard   el leopardo   III.6
less   menos   I.3
less . . . than   menos… que   I.7
lesson   la lección   I.1
let's   vamos a + *infinitive*   IV.1
letter (mail)   la carta   I.8
letter (of alphabet)   la letra   I.2
lettuce   la lechuga   I.6
library   la biblioteca   I.8
life   la vida   IV.5
light (electrical)   la luz   III.2
light (in color)   claro(a)   I.7
light (in weight)   ligero(a)   II.6
like   como   I.3
to **like a lot**   gustar mucho   II.4
to **like more/less**   gustar más/menos   II.6
Likewise   Igualmente   I.2
lion   el león   I.6
to **listen (to)**   escuchar   I.10
little   pequeño(a)   I.7
little bit   un poco   II.1
to **live**   vivir   I.7
liver   el hígado   III.1

living room   la sala   I.7
lobster   la langosta   IV.2
locker   el armario   I.8
long   largo(a)   I.7
to **look at**   mirar   I.10
to **look for**   buscar   IV.1
to **lose**   perder (ie)   IV.4
loud   alto(a)   I.1
to **love**   querer (ie) a   IV.4
low   bajo(a)   I.7
to be **lucky**   tener suerte   III.5
lunch   el almuerzo   I.6
lung   el pulmón   III.1

M

ma'am   señora   I.2
main meal   la comida   I.6
to **make**   hacer   I.10
mall   el centro comercial   III.2
man   el hombre   I.2
manager   el/la gerente   II.5
map   el mapa   I.8
marbles   las canicas   III.5
March   marzo   I.9
married   casado(a) (estar)   III.1
married couple   los esposos   I.3
math   las matemáticas   I.9
May   mayo   I.9
me   me   I.4, IV.1
me (to/for ...)   mí   III.2
meal   la comida   I.6
mean (not nice)   antipático(a)   II.2
meat   la carne   IV.2
mechanic   el/la mecánico(a)   II.5
medical office   el consultorio   III.2
medium   mediano(a)   I.7
to **memorize**   memorizar   IV.4
memory   el recuerdo   IV.6
Mexican   el/la mexicano(a)   II.3
Mexico   México   II.3
middle   el medio   III.2
midnight   la medianoche   I.9
mile   la milla   IV.3
milk   la leche   I.6
million   el millón   I.10
mine   mío(a)   I.5
minus   menos   I.3
mirror   el espejo   IV.5
Miss, Ms.   la señorita (Srta.)   I.2
mixed   mezclado(a)   IV.2
modern   moderno(a)   IV.3
Monday   lunes   I.9
money   el dinero   I.10

monkey   el mono   I.6
month   el mes   I.9
monument   el monument   III.2
more   más   I.1
more than anything   más que nada   III.6
more . . . than   más… que   I.7
more than + *number*   más de + *number*
   II.6
morning   la mañana   I.9
mosque   la mezquita   III.2
mosquito   el mosquito   III.6
most (the . . .)   el más…   I.7
mother   la madre   I.3
mother-in-law   la suegra   II.4
motorcycle   la moto(cicleta)   III.4
mountain   la montaña   III.3
mountain range   la sierra   III.3
mouse   el ratón   I.6
mouth   la boca   I.4
movie theater   el cine   I.10
Mr.   el señor (Sr.)   I.2
Mrs.   la señora (Sra.)   I.2
much   mucho(a)   I.5
to **multiply**   multiplicar   IV.4
museum   el museo   III.2
music   la música   I.9
musician   el/la músico(a)   II.5
mustache   el bigote   III.1
my   mi   I.2
My name is . . .   Me llamo…   I.2
myself   me   IV.5

N

nail (finger)   la uña   III.1
name   el nombre   I.2
to be **named**   llamarse   I.2
nap   la siesta   IV.2
narrow   estrecho(a)   I.7
nationality   la nacionalidad   II.3
near   cerca (de)   III.2
neck   el cuello   I.4
to **need**   faltar   IV.4
to **need (to)**   necesitar   IV.2
neighbor   el/la vecino(a)   IV.1
neighborhood   el barrio   IV.3
neither   ni   III.6
neither . . . nor   ni… ni   IV.4
nephew   el sobrino   II.4
nervous   nervioso(a)   III.1
never   nunca   II.1
new   nuevo(a) (ser)   II.6
next (in order)   próximo(a)   II.1
next to   al lado de   III.2

nice   simpático(a)   II.2
nice weather   el buen tiempo   I.5
to be **(nice) weather**   hacer (buen) tiempo   I.5
niece   la sobrina   II.4
night   la noche   I.1
nine   nueve   I.3
nine hundred   novecientos   I.10
ninety   noventa   I.3
ninth   noveno(a)   IV.3
no   no   I.1
no longer   ya no   II.1
no one   nadie   IV.4
noisy   ruidoso(a)   IV.3
none   ninguno(a)   IV.4
noon   el mediodía   I.9
nor   ni   II.4
normal   regular   I.1
north   el norte   III.3
nose   la nariz   I.4
not any   ninguno(a)   IV.4
not   no   I.1
not at all   tampoco   IV.5
not well   no muy bien   I.1
not yet   todavía no   II.1
notebook   el cuaderno   I.8
notes (information)   los apuntes   IV.4
nothing   nada   I.1
novel   la novela   IV.4
November   noviembre   I.9
now   ahora   I.3
number   el número   I.3
nurse   el/la enfermero(a)   I.4
nursery school   la guardería   IV.4
nut   la nuez   IV.2

O

oats   la avena   IV.2
occupation   la profesión   II.5
ocean   el océano   III.3
October   octubre   I.9
octopus   el pulpo   III.6
odd numbers   los números impares   I.10
of   de   II.4
of course   claro   I.10; por supuesto   IV.2
of the   del (de + el)   I.2
office   la oficina   II.5
office (medical)   el consultorio   III.2
often   frecuentemente   II.1
OK   regular   I.1; Bueno   I.9
old   viejo(a)   II.1
older   mayor   II.4
on   en   I.1
on (with days)   el (lunes)   I.9

on foot   a pie   III.4
on the phone   por teléfono   I.10
once   una vez   II.1
one   uno   I.3
one *(impersonal)*   se   I.1
onion   la cebolla   IV.2
only   solamente   II.3
to **open**   abrir   IV.3
or   o   I.6
orange (color)   anaranjado(a)   I.7
orange (fruit)   la naranja   IV.2
orchestra   la orquesta   I.9
other   otro(a)   I.8
ought to + *infinitive*   deber + *infinitive*   IV.2
our, ours   nuestro(a)   I.5
ourselves   nos   IV.5
outside of   fuera de   III.2
over   sobre   III.2
overhead projector   el retroproyector   II.6
to **owe**   deber   IV.2
oyster   la ostra   IV.2

P

to **pack a suitcase**   hacer la maleta   IV.6
pain   el dolor   I.4
pajamas   las pijamas   IV.6
pants   los pantalones   I.5
paper   el papel   I.8
parakeet   el periquito   III.6
Pardon   Perdón   I.1
parents   los padres   I.3
park   el parque   III.2
parrot   el perico   III.6
party   la fiesta   I.5
to **pass**   pasar   III.3
to **pass (a test, quiz, etc.)**   aprobar (ue)   IV.4
past   el pasado   II.1
pastry   el pastel   III.2
pastry shop   la pastelería   III.2
patient   paciente   III.1
to **pay**   pagar   IV.4
peanut   el cacahuete   IV.2
pear   la pera   IV.2
peas   los guisantes   IV.2
pencil   el lápiz   I.8
pencil sharpener   el sacapuntas   II.6
people   las personas   I.2; la gente   IV.6
pepper (vegetable)   el pimiento   IV.2
pepper (spice)   la pimienta   IV.2
person   la persona   I.2
pharmacist   el/la farmacista   II.5
pharmacy   la farmacia   III.2
photograph   la foto(grafía)   IV.1

physical   físico(a)   II.1
physical education   la educación física   I.9
physics   la física   IV.4
piano   el piano   I.10
picture   el cuadro   II.6
pie   el pastel   IV.2
pig   el cerdo   I.6
pineapple   la piña   IV.2
pink   rosado(a)   I.7
pity   la lástima   I.1
pizza   la pizza   III.2
pizzeria   la pizzería   III.2
place   el lugar   III.2
plains   los llanos   III.3
to **plan**   planear   IV.1; pensar + *infinitive* IV.4
plant   la planta   II.6
plate   el plato   IV.1
to **play (a game)**   jugar (ue)   I.10
to **play (an instrument)**   tocar   I.10
player   el/la jugador(a)   II.5
please   por favor   I.1
please + *verb*   favor de + *infinitive*   III.6
Pleased to meet you   Mucho gusto   I.2
Pleasure is mine (The . . .)   El gusto es mío   I.2
to be **pleasing**   gustar   I.6
plus   y, más   I.3
poetry   la poesía   IV.4
police officer   el/la policía   II.5
popcorn   las palomitas de maíz   IV.2
popular   popular   II.2
pork   el cerdo   IV.2
postcard   la tarjeta postal   IV.6
post office   el correo   III.2
potato   la papa   I.6; la patata   I.10
potato chips   las papitas fritas   I.6
to **practice**   practicar   I.10
to **prefer**   preferir (ie, i)   IV.4
preparation   la preparación   IV.1
to **prepare**   preparar   I.10
present (gift)   el regalo   IV.1
present (time)   el presente   II.1
pretty   bonito(a)   II.1
pride   el orgullo   IV.4
psychology   la sicología   IV.4
puppet   el títere   III.5
purple   morado(a)   I.7
purse   la bolsa   IV.6
to **put**   poner   IV.6
to **put on**   ponerse   IV.5
to **put on makeup**   maquillarse   IV.5
puzzle   el rompecabezas   III.5

Q

quarter cuarto(a) I.9
queen la reina II.2
quiet callado(a) II.2
quite bastante I.7
quiz la prueba IV.4

R

rabbit el conejo I.6
radio el radio I.8
radish el rábano IV.2
to **rain** llover (ue) III.5
raincoat el impermeable IV.6
rains, it's raining llueve I.5
rapidly rápidamente IV.5
rarely raramente II.1
raspberry la frambuesa IV.2
rat la rata III.6
to **read** leer I.10
reading la lectura IV.4
ready listo(a) (estar) III.3
to **receive** recibir I.10
rectangular rectangular II.6
red rojo(a) I.7
redhead pelirrojo(a) II.1
refreshments los refrescos IV.1
to **refuse** no querer (*preterite*) IV.6
to **regret** sentir (ie, i) IV.4
to **remain** quedarse IV.5
to **remember** recordar (ue) IV.4
to **remove** quitar IV.2
to **repeat** repetir (i, i) IV.4
research las investigaciones IV.4
to **rest** descansar IV.1
restaurant el restaurante III.2
to **return** volver (ue) IV.4; regresar IV.6
rhinoceros el rinoceronte III.6
rice el arroz IV.2
rich rico(a) (ser) III.1
right la derecha III.2
right of (to the . . .) a la derecha de III.2
to be **right** tener razón III.5
right?, true? ¿verdad?, ¿no? II.2
river el río III.3
road el camino IV.3
roast beef el rosbif I.6
rocking horse el caballo balancín III.5
roll el panecillo IV.2
roller skates los patines de rueda III.5
roof el techo III.2
room el cuarto I.7
rooster el gallo I.6

round redondo(a) I.7
row la fila III.2
ruler la regla II.6
to **run** correr I.10
Russian (language) el ruso IV.4

S

sad triste II.2
sadly tristemente IV.5
safe seguro(a) (ser) IV.3
salad la ensalada I.6
salesperson el/la dependiente(a) II.5
salt la sal IV.2
Same here Igualmente I.2
sand la arena III.5
sandals las sandalias IV.6
sandbox el cajón de arena III.5
sandwich el sándwich I.6
Saturday sábado I.9
sausage la salchicha IV.2
to **say** decir IV.6
to **say good-bye** despedirse (i, i) IV.5
school la escuela I.3
schooling la enseñanza IV.4
science la ciencia I.9
scissors las tijeras II.6
sea el mar III.3
seafood los mariscos IV.2
season la estación I.5
seasoning los condimentos IV.2
second segundo(a) IV.3
second floor (one floor up) el primer piso I.7
secondary secundario(a) IV.4
secretary el/la secretario(a) II.5
to **see** ver IV.6
See you later Hasta la vista I.1
See you tomorrow Hasta mañana I.1
selfish egoísta II.2
to **sell** vender IV.2
to **send** mandar IV.1; enviar IV.6
September septiembre I.9
servant el/la criado(a) II.5
to **serve** servir (i, i) IV.4
seven siete I.3
seven hundred setecientos I.10
seventh séptimo(a) IV.3
seventy setenta I.3
to **sew** coser IV.2
shape la forma I.7
shark el tiburón III.6
to **shave** afeitarse IV.5
she ella I.1

sheep   la oveja   I.6
shell   la concha   IV.6
shirt   la camisa   I.5
shoe   el zapato   I.5
shoe store   la zapatería   III.2
short (in height)   bajo(a)   I.7
short (in length)   corto(a)   I.7
shorthand   la taquigrafía   IV.4
shorts   los pantalones cortos   IV.6
should   deber + *infinitive*   IV.2
shoulder   el hombro   III.1
to **shower**   ducharse   IV.5
shrimp   los camarones   IV.2
shy   tímido(a)   II.2
siblings   los hermanos   I.3
sick   enfermo(a)   III.1
to be **sick**   estar malo(a)   I.1
side   el lado   III.2
silver   plateado(a)   II.6
since   desde   IV.4
sincere   sincero(a)   II.2
to **sing**   cantar   I.10
sir   el señor   I.2
sister   la hermana   I.3
sister-in-law   la cuñada   II.4
to **sit down**   sentarse (ie)   IV.5
six   seis   I.3
six hundred   seiscientos   I.10
sixth   sexto(a)   IV.3
sixty   sesenta   I.3
size   el tamaño   I.7
skateboard   el monopatín   III.5
skates   los patines   III.5
skeleton   el esqueleto   II.1
to **ski**   esquiar   I.10
skirt   la falda   I.5
skyscraper   el rascacielos   III.2
to **sleep**   dormir (ue, u)   I.10
to be **sleepy**   tener sueño   III.5
sleeve   la manga   IV.6
slice   la rebanada   IV.2
slipper   la zapatilla   IV.6
slowly   despacio   I.1; lentamente   IV.5
small   pequeño(a)   I.7
small boy   el niño   I.2
small girl   la niña   I.2
smart   inteligente   II.2
snack   la merienda   I.6
snake   la serpiente   III.6
snow   la nieve   I.10
snows, it's snowing   nieva   I.5
so   así   I.1
soccer, football   el fútbol   I.10
sociable   sociable   IV.4

socks   los calcetines   I.5
soft   blando(a)   II.6
soft drink   el refresco   I.6
soldier (toy)   el soldado (de juguete)   III.5
some   unos(as)   I.2; alguno(a)   IV.4
someone   alguien   IV.4
something   algo   I.10
sometimes   a veces   I.5; algunas veces   II.1
son   el hijo   I.3
son-in-law   el yerno   II.4
song   la canción   I.10
to be **sorry**   sentir (ie, i)   IV.4
soup   la sopa   I.6
south   el sur   III.3
souvenir   el recuerdo   IV.6
Spain   España   II.3
Spaniard   el/la español(a)   II.3
Spanish   español(a)   I.1
to **speak**   hablar   I.10
special   especial   IV.5
to **spend (money)**   gastar   I.10
to **spend time**   pasar tiempo   IV.6
spider   la araña   I.6
sport   el deporte   I.10
sport   deportivo(a)   IV.6
sport coat   el saco   IV.6
spring   la primavera   I.5
square   cuadrado(a)   I.7
squirrel   la ardilla   I.6
stairs   la escalera   I.7
star   la estrella   II.3
to **start**   comenzar (ie)   IV.1
state   el estado   III.3
station   la estación   III.2
stationery store   la papelería   III.2
to **stay**   quedarse   IV.5
stepbrother   el hermanastro   I.3
stepfather   el padrastro   I.3
stepmother   la madrastra   I.3
stepparents   los padrastros   I.3
stepsister   la hermanastra   I.3
stereo   el estéreo   I.8
still   todavía   II.1
stockings   las medias   I.5
stomach   el estómago   I.4
store   la tienda   I.8
story   el cuento   IV.4
strawberry   la fresa   IV.2
street   la calle   IV.3
string beans   las judías   IV.2
strong   fuerte   II.1
student   el/la estudiante   II.5
to **study**   estudiar   I.10
subject (class)   la materia   IV.4

to **subtract**   restar   IV.4
suburbs   las afueras   III.3
to **succeed**   poder *(preterite)*   IV.6
suddenly   de repente   II.1
to **suffer**   sufrir   IV.3
sugar   el azúcar *(f.)*   IV.2
suit   el traje   I.5
suitcase   la maleta   IV.6
summer   el verano   I.5
sun   el sol   I.5
to **sunbathe**   broncearse   IV.6
Sunday   domingo   I.9
to be **sunny**   hacer sol   I.5
supermarket   el supermercado   III.2
sure, certain   seguro (estar)   III.1
surrounding   alrededor de   III.2
sweater   el suéter   I.5
sweet potato   la batata   IV.2
to **swim**   nadar   I.10
swimsuit   el traje de baño   IV.6
swing   el columpio   III.5
synagogue   la sinagoga   III.2

T

table   mesa   I.8
to **take**   tomar   I.10
to **take care of**   cuidar   I.10
to **take notes**   tomar apuntes   IV.4
to **take off**   quitarse   IV.5
to **take out**   sacar   IV.1
to **take pictures**   sacar fotos   IV.1
to **talk**   hablar   I.10
talkative   hablador(a)   II.2
tall   alto(a)   I.7
tan (color)   la crema   II.6
tape   la cinta   I.8
tape recorder   la grabadora   I.8
taxi   el taxi   III.4
tea   el té   I.6
teacher   el/la profesor(a)   II.5
teaching   la enseñanza   IV.4
teddy bear   el osito de peluche   III.5
T-shirt   la camiseta   IV.6
teenager   el/la joven   I.2
telephone   el teléfono   I.8
television program   la televisión   I.10
television set   el televisor   I.8
to **tell**   decir   IV.6
to **tell a story**   contar (ue)   IV.6
temperature   la temperatura   I.5
temple   el templo   III.2
ten   diez   I.3
tennis   el tenis   I.10

tennis shoes   los zapatos tenis   IV.6
tenth   décimo(a)   IV.3
test   la prueba   IV.4
than   que   I.3
Thank you   Gracias   I.1
thanks   las gracias   IV.1
that   ese(a)   I.5
that *(conjunction)*   que   I.8
that (far away)   aquel(la)   III.3
that *(indefinite)*   eso   I.5; aquello   III.3
That's the way it is!   ¡Así es!   I.1
That's too bad!   ¡Qué lástima!   I.1
the   el, la, los, las   I.2
their   su   I.3
theirs   suyo(a)   I.5
therefore   por eso   II.2
they *(impersonal)*   se   I.1
theater   el teatro   III.2
them   los, las   I.5
themselves   se   IV.5
theme   el tema   IV.4
then   entonces, luego   II.1
there   allí   I.3
therefore   por eso   II.2
there is, there are   hay   I.3
there was, there were   había   II.6
there will be   habrá   II.6
these   estos(as)   I.4
they   ellos, ellas   I.2
thin   delgado(a)   II.1
thing   la cosa   I.8
to **think**   pensar (ie)   IV.4
to **think about (daydream)**   pensar (ie) en   IV.4
to **think about (opinion)**   pensar (ie) de   IV.4
third   tercer(o)(a)   IV.3
to be **thirsty**   tener sed   III.5
thirteen   trece   I.3
thirty   treinta   I.3
this   este(a)   I.4
this *(indefinite)*   esto   I.4
those   esos(as)   I.5; aquellos(as)   III.3
thousand   mil   I.10
three   tres   I.3
three hundred   trescientos   I.10
throat   la garganta   I.4
through   por   I.3
thumb   el pulgar   III.1
Thursday   jueves   I.9
ticket   el billete   IV.6
tie   la corbata   I.5
tiger   el tigre   I.6
time   el tiempo   I.5
time(s) (occurrence)   la vez (veces)   II.1
times (x)   por   I.3

timid   tímido(a)   II.2
tired   cansado(a)   III.1
title of respect   don, doña   I.2
to   a   I.9
to (up to)   hasta   IV.4
to her   le   I.4
to him   le   I.4
to the   al (a + el)   III.4
to them   les   I.4
to us   nos   I.4
to you   le, les   I.4
toad   el sapo   III.6
toast   el pan tostado   IV.2
today   hoy   I.9
toe   el dedo del pie   I.4
together   juntos(as)   III.1
tomato   el tomate   IV.2
tomorrow   mañana   I.1
tooth   el diente   I.4
top (on . . . of)   encima de   III.2
town   el pueblo   III.3
town square   la plaza   III.2
toy   el juguete   III.5
toy store   la juguetería   III.2
track   la pista   I.10
train   el tren   III.4
to **travel**   viajar   I.10
tree   el árbol   IV.5
triangular   triangular   II.6
tricycle   el triciclo   III.5
trigonometry   la trigonometría   IV.4
trip   el viaje   IV.6
to **try**   querer *(preterite)*   IV.6
to **try to**   tratar de   IV.2
Tuesday   martes   I.9
turkey   el pavo   III.6
turn (It's your . . .)   Te toca   I.1
turquoise   turquesa   II.6
turtle   la tortuga   III.6
twelve   doce   I.3
twenty   veinte   I.3
twice   dos veces   II.1
twin brother   el gemelo   II.4
twin sister   la gemela   II.4
two   dos   I.3
two hundred   doscientos   I.10
to **type**   escribir a máquina   IV.4
type   el tipo   III.6

U

ugly   feo(a)   II.1
umbrella   el paraguas   IV.6
uncle   el tío   I.3

under   debajo (de)   III.2
to **understand**   comprender   I.1
underwear   la ropa interior   IV.6
to **undo**   deshacer   IV.6
unit   la unidad   I.1
United States   los Estados Unidos   II.3
university   la universidad   IV.4
untamed   silvestre   II.6
until   hasta   IV.4
upset   agitado(a)   III.1
us   nos   I.4

V

vacation   las vacaciones   IV.6
valley   la valle   III.3
vanilla   la vainilla   I.6
veal   la ternera   IV.2
vegetable   la legumbre   I.6
very   muy   I.1
very bad   muy mal   I.1
very well   muy bien   I.1
video   el vídeo   III.4
videocassette recorder   la videocasetera
     II.6
violet   violeta   II.6
to **visit**   visitar   I.10
vocabulary   el vocabulario   I.1

W

wagon   la carreta   III.5
to **wait for**   esperar   IV.2
waiter   el mesero   II.5
waitress   la mesera   II.5
to **wake up**   despertarse (ie)   IV.5
to **walk**   caminar   I.10
to **walk (to go for a . . .)**   dar un paseo   IV.6
wall   la pared   III.2
wallet   la cartera   IV.6
walnut   la nuez   IV.2
to **want**   desear   IV.1; querer (ie)   IV.4
to be **warm**   tener calor   III.5
to **wash**   lavar   IV.1
to **wash (oneself)**   lavarse   IV.5
wastepaper basket   la papelera   I.8
to **watch**   mirar   I.10
water   el agua *(f.)*   I.6
watermelon   la sandía   IV.2
wave (water)   la ola   IV.6
we   nosotros(as)   I.2
weak   débil   II.1
to **wear**   llevar   I.5

weather   el tiempo   I.5
Wednesday   miércoles   I.9
week   la semana   II.1
well   bien   I.1
well, then   pues   II.3
west   el oeste   III.3
whale   la ballena   III.6
what   lo que   I.10, II.5
What?   ¿Qué?   I.1
What does . . . mean?   ¿Qué quiere decir… ?
   I.1
What time is it?   ¿Qué hora es?   I.9
What's happening?   ¿Qué pasa?   I.1
What's the matter?   ¿Qué tienes?   III.1
What's the weather like?   ¿Qué tiempo
   hace?   I.5
What's your name?   ¿Cómo te llamas?,
   ¿Cómo se llama Ud.?   I.2
wheat   el trigo   IV.2
wheel   la rueda   III.5
When?   ¿Cuándo?   I.5
Where?   ¿Dónde?   I.3
Where (to)?   ¿Adónde?   I.8
Where is . . . from?   ¿De dónde es… ?   II.3
Which?   ¿Cuál?   I.2
while   mientras   II.1
whistle   el silbato   III.5
white   blanco(a)   I.7
Who?   ¿Quién?   I.2; ¿Quiénes?   II.3
whole (the . . . day)   todo(a) (el día)   I.9
Whose?   ¿De quién?   I.5
Why?   ¿Por qué?   II.3
wide   ancho(a)   I.7
wife   la esposa   I.3
wild   salvaje   III.6
to **win**   ganar   I.10
wind   el viento   I.5
window   la ventana   I.8
winter   el invierno   I.5
with   con   III.2
with me   conmigo   III.2
with you   contigo   III.2
without   sin (que)   I.2
woman   la mujer   I.2

word   la palabra   II.3
work   el trabajo   I.3
to **work**   trabajar   I.10
worker   el/la obrero(a)   II.5
world   el mundo   II.2
worldwide   mundial   III.4
worried   preocupado(a)   III.1
Wow!   ¡Huy!   I.7
to **wrap**   envolver (ue)   IV.2
wrist   la muñeca   III.1
wristwatch   el reloj (de) pulsera   I.5
to **write**   escribir   I.10
to be **wrong**   no tener razón   III.5

Y

yard   el patio   I.7
year   el año   I.3
to be . . . **years old**   tener… años   III.5
yellow   amarillo(a)   I.7
yes   sí   I.1
yesterday   ayer   I.9
yet   todavía   II.1
yogurt   el yogur   IV.2
you   tú, usted (Ud.)   I.1; ustedes (Uds.)   I.2
you *(after prep.)*   ti   III.2
you *(impersonal)*   se   I.1
you (in Spain)   vosotros(as)   II.6
you, to you   te   I.4
you, to you (in Spain)   os   IV.7
You're welcome   De nada   I.1
young   joven   II.1
young person   el/la joven   I.2
younger   menor   II.4
your   tu   I.2; su   I.3
yours   tuyo(a), suyo(a)   I.5
yourself, yourselves   te, se   IV.5
yo-yo   el yoyo   III.5

Z

zebra   la cebra   III.6
zero   cero   I.3

Index

⇻ Structure ⇺

⋙Pronunciation⋙

⋙Vocabulary⋙

This book was
first used by
Noadira Hamilton
        A.K.A
    Princess

⊰Culture⊱